European Business Organization Review – EBOR

G000153449

Copyright Information

For Authors

As soon as an article is accepted for publication, authors will be requested to assign copyright of the article (or to grant exclusive publication and dissemination rights) to the publisher (respective the owner if other than Asser Press/Springer Nature). This will ensure the widest possible protection and dissemination of information under copyright laws.

More information about copyright regulations for this journal is available at www.springer.com/40804

For Readers

While the advice and information in this journal is believed to be true and accurate at the date of its publication, neither the authors, the editors, nor the publisher can accept any legal responsibility for any errors or omissions that may have been made. The publisher makes no warranty, express or implied, with respect to the material contained herein.

All articles published in this journal are protected by copyright, which covers the exclusive rights to reproduce and distribute the article (e.g., as offprints), as well as all translation rights. No material published in this journal may be reproduced photographically or stored on microfilm, in electronic data bases, on video disks, etc., without first obtaining written permission from the publisher (respective the copyright owner if other than Asser Press/Springer Nature). The use of general descriptive names, trade names, trademarks, etc., in this publication, even if not specifically identified, does not imply that these names are not protected by the relevant laws and regulations.

Springer Nature has partnered with Copyright Clearance Center's RightsLink service to offer a variety of options for reusing Springer Nature content. For permission to reuse our content please locate the material that you wish to use on link.springer.com or on springerimages.com and click on the permissions link or go to copyright.com and enter the title of the publication that you wish to use. For assistance in placing a permission request, Copyright Clearance Center can be contacted directly via phone: +1-855-239-3415, fax: +1-978-646-8600, or e-mail: info@copyright.com.

Ownership and Copyright

Journal Website

www.springer.com/40804

For the actual version of record please always check the online version of the publication.

Subscription Information

European Business Organization Law Review is published quarterly. Volume 23 (4 issues) will be published in 2022

ISSN: 1566-7529 print
ISSN: 1741-6205 electronic

For information on subscription rates please contact Springer Nature Customer Service Center: customerservice@springernature.com

The Americas (North, South, Central America and the Caribbean)
Springer Nature Journal Fulfillment
Harborside Plaza II, 200 Hudson Street,
Jersey City, NJ 07302, USA
Tel.: 800-SPRINGER (777-4643); 212-460-1500
(outside North America)

Outside the Americas
Springer Nature Customer Service Center GmbH
Tiergartenstr. 15, 69121 Heidelberg, Germany
Tel.: +49-6221-345-4303

Advertisements

E-mail contact: anzeigen@springer.com

Disclaimer

Asser Press/Springer Nature publishes advertisements in this journal in reliance upon the responsibility of the advertiser to comply with all legal requirements relating to the marketing and sale of products or services advertised. Asser Press/ Springer Nature and theeditors are not responsible for claims made in the advertisements published in the journal. The appearance of advertisements in Springer Nature publicationsdoes not constitute endorsement, implied or intended, of the product advertised or the claims made for it by the advertiser.

Office of Publication

Springer International Publishing AG,
Gewerbestrasse 11, CH-6330 Cham (ZG), Switzerland

European Business Organization Law Review – EBOR

Aims and Scope

The *European Business Organization Law Review* aims to promote a scholarly debate which critically analyses the whole range of organizations chosen by companies, groups of companies, and state-owned enterprises to pursue their business activities and offer goods and services all over the European Union. At issue are the enactment of corporate laws, the theory of firm, the theory of capital markets and related legal topics.

Editorial Policy

The European Business Organization Law Review is a peer-reviewed publication. The journal encourages submissions from lawyers, both academic and practitioners, and economists.

Contributions of authors from other disciplines, such as political and social scientists, are welcome. Occasionally, policy makers and business people will be invited to express their opinion within their fields of expertise. Theoretical and applied works are equally considered.

Manuscripts should range between 3,000 and 10,000 words and be preceded by an abstract of no longer than 200 words and a maximum of six keywords. They are to be submitted accompanied by an assurance that the article has not been published or accepted elsewhere. However, exceptional contributions originally written in other languages may be considered for publication in proximity to their publication in that other language. The articles should be comprehensible to readers outside the specific field of expertise.

Editorial Office

European Business Organization Law Review
T.M.C. ASSER INSTITUUT
P.O. Box 30461, 2500 GL The Hague,
The Netherlands
Tel.: +31(70)3420300,
Fax: +31(70)3420359
E-mail: EBOR@asser.nl
http://www.asser.nl/ebor

Published in cooperation with the T.M.C. Asser Instituut, The Hague, The Netherlands

European Business Organization Law Review (2022) 23:1–7
https://doi.org/10.1007/s40804-021-00230-2

EDITORIAL

Law and Regulation for Sustainable Finance

Iris H-Y Chiu[1,2] · Lin Lin[3] · David Rouch[4,5]

Published online: 17 February 2022
© T.M.C. Asser Press 2022

There is a marked global trend of investment assets moving into 'ESG' (environmental, social and governance) or 'sustainable' investing strategies. It is reported in the US,[1] at the end of 2020, that 33% of assets under management were allocated to ESG strategies, in other words, approaches that in some way seek to take specific account of environmental, social or governance factors, instead of being agnostic towards them. Indeed, ESG funds have apparently continued to attract significant inflows, even as investment sentiments suffered during the COVID-19 pandemic and many conventional investment funds experienced outflows.[2]

Yet, for all this, sustainable finance and investing suffers from an identity crisis. Is it finance that will be profitable in the long term and hence be itself sustainable? Is it finance that is justifiable to society? Is it finance that can help solve sustainability challenges and, if so, which ones, and to what extent can or should it seek to do that? Further, is sustainable investing the same as responsible investing, ESG investing or ethical investing? We have not yet defined 'responsible investing' in relation to responsibility to whom and for what. Does sustainable investing take account of all or just some ESG factors and in what ways and for what reasons? Ethical investing is also unclear in terms of which ethical basis, and are there forms of investing that are therefore 'neutral' or 'unethical'?

---

[1] '"Sustainable investing" is surging, accounting for 33% of total U.S. assets under management', CNBC News, 21 Dec 2020. https://www.cnbc.com/2020/12/21/sustainable-investing-accounts-for-33percent-of-total-us-assets-under-management.html (accessed 29 October 2021).

[2] 'ESG funds defy havoc to ratchet huge inflows', Financial Times, 6 February 2021. https://www.ft.com/content/8e9f8204-83bf-4217-bc9e-d89396279c5b (accessed 29 October 2021).

✉ Iris H-Y Chiu
hse-yu.chiu@ucl.ac.uk

[1] Professor of Corporate Law and Financial Regulation, University College London, London, UK

[2] Visiting Professor (February to April 2021), Centre for Banking and Financial Law, National University of Singapore, Singapore, Singapore

[3] Associate Professor of Law, Faculty of Law, National University of Singapore, Singapore, Singapore

[4] Partner, Freshfields Bruckhaus Deringer LLP, London, UK

[5] Keynote speaker at the Sustainable Finance and Capital Markets Conference, Centre for Banking and Financial Law, National University of Singapore, Singapore, Singapore

The issue is essentially one of purpose of investment. Is sustainable finance about making money by realising opportunities presented by sustainability challenges and preserving financial value by addressing the risks? Or is it about tackling sustainability challenges as goals in themselves? Is it about financial value or pursuing wider outcomes that align with core social values?[3] In reality, a good deal of sustainable finance appears to be about both, but aspirations to solve sustainability problems are often hiding in the shadows, uncertain whether they are allowed to show their face.

At one level, investors' and financiers' interest in the ESG performance of their investments clearly results from an increased recognition of the financial risk of ESG failures, sharpened considerably in some cases by policy initiatives such as those surrounding the Taskforce on Climate-related Financial Disclosure. We could think of this as 'instrumental sustainable finance', pursued with the goal of preserving or enhancing financial value. Drivers of financial risk include obsolete business strategies, stranded assets,[4] and reputational risk from ESG failures that could galvanise negative stakeholder and social opinion. Although not incontrovertibly resolved,[5] there is increasingly less question regarding the alignment between investment performance and positive ESG attainment in business and economic activities.[6] Yet growing attention to sustainability in investment processes is arguably also due to the concurrent concern regarding the non-financial impact of private investment activity, which can engage wider social aspirations. We could think of sustainable finance motivated by 'core valued goals', although, in practice, human motivation cannot be easily compartmentalised so that altruistic motivations may often be indistinguishable from instrumental sustainable finance.

Against this backdrop there is a range of new legal and regulatory initiatives to support and reinforce a trend policy-makers view as healthy. In particular, EU reforms, including the Sustainability Disclosure and Taxonomy Regulations, offer the possibility of regulatory competition towards more rigorous regulatory underpinning for sustainable finance. They move towards a universal baseline for sustainability risk integration by all regulated firms, and establish standards for the design and labelling of environmentally sustainable investment products. These are only the beginning of the EU sustainable reform agenda. More work is envisaged, for example, on the regulation of financial intermediaries and a social taxonomy for socially labelled investment products.[7] The EU reforms seek to move sustainable finance beyond current ESG investing practice, which is sometimes criticised as being opaque and not susceptible to meaningful comparison or evaluation.[8] In particular,

[3] Carney (2021)

[4] Buhr (2017); Fang et al. (2019).

[5] Ielasi et al. (2018); Boulatoff and Boyer (2017); de Haan et al. (2012).

[6] Schröder (2014); Dorfleitner et al. (2018).

[7] European Commission, Communication from the Commission to the European Parliament, the Council, the European Economic and Social Committee and the Committee of the Regions, EU Taxonomy, Corporate Sustainability Reporting, Sustainability Preferences and Fiduciary Duties: Directing finance towards the European Green Deal (21 April 2021). https://eur-lex.europa.eu/legal-content/EN/TXT/?uri=CELEX:52021DC0188 (accessed 30 April 2021).

[8] Arribas et al. (2019).

the sustainable label may help move the market for ESG investment products from strategies of exclusion[9] towards more innovative strategies that evaluate the influence of investment activity on sustainability factors. These EU reforms are likely to provoke policy thinking and development in many other jurisdictions, as the markets for ESG, green and sustainable investment products continue to grow globally and investors seek a more meaningful understanding and governance of products such as green bonds, sustainable investment funds and development finance.

However, hitherto, much policy activity has operated within an instrumental sustainable finance framework, even if such framework references the contribution of finance to wider sustainability goals. We are now at a juncture of legal and regulatory developments where policy choices need to address how finance should connect with the wider public interest and social good in sustainability outcomes—what is the role of 'core valued goals' in sustainable finance? Since the goals, and assumed goals, of an activity have a profound impact on decisions on how to regulate sustainable finance and the resulting behaviour on the part of investors, this moment of re-evaluation is extremely important.

In this light, the editors of this Special Volume curated the Centre for Banking and Financial Law Conference on Sustainable Finance, National University of Singapore, on 16 April 2021. We are thankful to the Centre for its sponsorship and support of the Conference. As a result, we have assembled a collection of articles offering a broad perspective on the connection between finance and the public and social good of sustainability outcomes, as well as discussions on the recent legal and regulatory developments in key sustainable finance markets, i.e., the EU and the Asia-Pacific, particularly China.

In his keynote speech at the Conference, David Rouch of Freshfields, also leading the firm's project for the UNEP FI on investing for sustainability impact, focused on the need for policy-makers interested in achieving sustainability goals to draw both on financial incentives and on wider social aspirations in seeking to move finance further towards supporting sustainable outcomes. Since many sustainability challenges are systemic, the two may often coincide: financial markets depend on sustainable economies, which in turn depend on sustainable social and environmental systems. Critically, this systemic dimension also means that responses ultimately need to galvanise whole systems. Solutions do not lie in the hands of markets or policy-makers alone. Both need to be engaged, but there is also a need to stimulate wider social coordination to maximise policy impact.[10] In finance specifically, wider sustainability aspirations based on core social values need to be recognised and affirmed, and existing competition paradigms need to be supplemented with a cooperation paradigm, since common goods require some degree of common action. These themes of purpose and motivation are strong in the articles in this collection, as is the balance between private action and public intervention.

---

[9] Which remain a dominant strategy, surveyed by EFAMA at end 2020. https://www.efama.org/Pages/Submitted%20after%202018-03-12T16%2022%2007/EFAMA-publishes-report-on-level-and-nature-of-sustainable-investment-by-the-European-asset-management-industry.aspx (accessed 29 October 2021).
[10] Rouch (2020).

The first article in this collection is MacNeil and Esser's contribution entitled 'From a Financial to an Entity Model of ESG'. It provides the broad background-setting and ideological thinking for sustainable finance, charting the development of sustainable finance from the era of 'corporate social responsibility' to 'ESG' investing, which focuses on the impact of material environmental, social and governance factors on portfolio risk. The article persuades us to view the increasing legitimacy of ESG integration into conventional portfolio risk management as being wedded to the dominant ideology and practice of shareholder primacy and financial primacy in investment management. This is in no small part attributed to academics', policy-makers' and industry's aligned efforts in framing the fiduciary duty for investment management in its modernised version as integrating material ESG. The article rightly challenges that the development of the financial sector's internalisation of material ESG may ironically result in a marginalisation in corporate activities of what the public or stakeholders conceive of as wider public or social good. It advocates that reform work inevitably must connect with regulating corporate decision-making and operations, and not merely reporting.

Policy intervention in primary corporate and wider economic activity is undoubtedly needed. Particularly in view of the systemic nature of the challenges, it is not realistic to expect financial markets to deliver solutions on their own. Yet, the fact that the challenges are systemic also means that financial markets have a role, and here some key questions are: whether finance needs to go beyond integration of sustainability factors from a financial risk perspective to orientating towards tackling the sources of risk themselves; whether financial incentives alone are a sufficient motivation or whether it is possible to draw on aspirations related to broader socially valued goals; and the extent to which policy action should involve direct regulatory intervention and how far it should rely on market initiatives.

There has clearly been an acceleration in the use of financial market-based policy initiatives to tackle sustainability challenges, especially concerning investors' influence upon portfolio companies' economic activities. There is certainly a logic to this micro-level, frequently financial incentive-based approach. Equally, there is always the risk that it could leave finance activity too narrowly focused on short-term financial considerations and fail to generate real behaviour change. To what extent can policy-making that depends on leveraging financial incentives steer markets towards sustainable outcomes the ultimate value of which is not purely financial? Can market-based interventions also draw on common aspirations for those sustainability outcomes to be achieved? Clearly, the policy rhetoric underlying the soft law of stewardship has begun to set normative expectations in terms of the roles of asset managers to achieve financial provision and wider social good in the long term. Further, private wealth and family offices often marry sustainable and development causes with financial interests in their investment mandates.

In this context, a number of articles in our collection examine the role of regulatory policy and design in steering and incentivising financial activity to achieve an integrated good that meets private financial interests while achieving long-term sustainability goods. The recent EU sustainable finance reforms are a highlight of this volume, and we also compare these with policy activity in China, concerning the market for green bonds.

In relation to the EU, Zetzsche and Anker-Sørensen provide a comprehensive overview of the policy rationales and the legislative matrix of recent reforms. The EU's programme is ambitious, comprising many amendments to existing investment firm and fund regulation, as well as new legislative initiatives. The article cautions policy-makers to observe and take stock of the implementation of the reforms for at least 5 years, in order to piece together crucial data relating to sustainability objectives and their effects upon corporate profit and investment performance. The paper warns that regulators will be regulating in the dark if more substantive initiatives are added before data gaps are addressed. Experimental forms of regulation may be more appropriate for EU policy-makers to observe the results of their pioneering initiatives.

Chiu's article also addresses the EU's reforms but argues that there is perhaps one further area for more regulatory development, despite the already ambitious programme. The EU's reforms are distinguished by the quest for 'double materiality' in investment fund management, i.e., the achievement of sustainable goods, for the purposes of public and social interest, alongside the private objectives of investment performance. The article argues that more policy governance is needed for implementing 'double materiality'. In particular, further development and governance are needed for metrics that would form the backbone for evaluating double materiality.[11] Evaluating the success of the EU's reforms crucially depends on the development and governance of the metrics that relate to double materiality, and the extent to which they are able to show the difference double materiality makes, compared to the financialised trend in single materiality highlighted in MacNeil and Esser's opening article. However, metrics governance is inevitably intertwined with market preferences, and in general, market-based governance for public goods still needs to be critically appraised, as argued in Tan's reflective paper discussed below. Both articles examining the EU's reforms agree that there are promises but also a continuing need for policy reflection.

Further, the success of sustainable finance reforms undoubtedly partly depends on credible and standardised corporate transparency to inform investment management and intermediary evaluation. Hence, Miglionico's paper concerns how technological advances such as algorithmic and machine learning processes for data collection and processing may help with sustainable information transparency and corporate decision-making in the corporate sector. The article focuses on climate risk information management for a start and provides insight into developing standardised and granular processes for managing corporations' climate risk information and data.

Turning to the Chinese policy experience, Lin and Hong's article discusses explicit policy steers in China to build a credible market for green bonds. This involves government leadership in facilitating issues of green bonds, as well as incentivising the demand side of the market. Although these policy steers have resulted in massive growth in bond issuances and investment, allowing China to grow phenomenally in its green bonds market, the article cautions against an excessively state-led approach because of the dangers of misallocation and other

---

[11] See further Hilf and Rouch (2021).

rent-seeking externalities. The article however shows that lessons can be learnt from the policy fostering of a credible market through law reforms and regulatory changes supporting the growth of a sophisticated investment sector.

We observe strong policy steers of the sort described above in relation to the EU and China, but these need to be accompanied by a growth in market-based initiatives. Private investors must ultimately develop the capacity and confidence to evaluate and participate in sustainable investment opportunities and tackling sustainability challenges that have a bearing on them. Turning to the issue of investors' incentives and motivations, this collection compares and contrasts two groups of investors. Lin's paper looks at how venture capitalists, dedicated to seeking out sustainable and profitable investment opportunities, can make a determined difference to nurturing greener and more sustainable innovations and also make market successes of them. However, there are clear needs in the legal and regulatory frameworks supporting venture capital finance which need to be met in order to mobilise and develop the sustainable venture capital market. On the other hand, the main group of private sector investors that must make a difference are institutional investors. Micheler's paper takes stock of large and small portfolio institutions and their incentives and motivations, showing that many are finely balanced between altruistic and financial considerations. The paper argues that many institutions would likely need more proactive motivating policy to allocate more towards sustainable causes, suggesting that government tax incentives can play a role.

The broader issue of how policy-makers can engage private finance to contribute to public and social good remains an ongoing experiment with mixed results so far. Despite a belief that policy can strengthen the integration of sustainability risks and opportunities in financial practice, and hence affect allocational decisions and influence the shape of corporate sector activity, deliberate involvement of private finance in securing public and social goods also carries risks. Realisation of public goods such as sustainability needs to take account of a broad range of political, social, ecological and justice issues, principally expressed and resolved through political and social structures. Market activity can help to sustain these. However, there is a balance beyond which it can also undermine them through marketisation and financialisation. Among other things, this could weaken the key role of states and public finance, ideologically and practically, for example in the important areas of governance and distribution. Worse, over-reliance on private sector finance can be hazardous for states in managing their sovereign debt exposures and volatile foreign capital flows. Tan's paper critically teases out the increased governance roles of private financial actors and how these roles interact with the need for public goods and the roles of public sector actors. It critically questions whether we are closer to or further away from achieving the real outcomes socially desired in the UN Sustainable Development Goals.

Finally, the Special Issue rounds off where we ideologically started—which is to raise the question whether financial market-reliant interventions in current law and regulation can ultimately do much in achieving the public interest goals of sustainability. Sheehy's paper provides the ideological 'last word' in this collection to remind us that sustainability goals concern issues of intergenerational justice and may need more than incentive-based regulatory frameworks. Although law and regulation may be able to restrain excessive corporate damage to the environment, there is still a need for corporate law reforms to compel corporations to internalise socially and justice-oriented behaviour in their economic activities. Sheehy's paper, in some ways not dissimilar to MacNeil and Esser's opening article, posits corporate law reforms in terms of board reorganisation for decision-making that integrates socially-facing sustainability concerns and the introduction of 'stakeholder' organs in corporations. These ideological concepts are radical and would champion a move away from existing corporate governance structures in most jurisdictions.

The discussions in this volume ultimately offer a topical examination and critique of recent policy action focused on mobilising institutional investors in shaping broader corporate sector activities towards avoiding sustainable harm and achieving sustainable goods. The critique is however intended to enhance the capacity of the financial sector while pointing out the gaps in areas of policy reform that need to be addressed. All contributors in this volume are committed to advancing this continuing discourse as further reforms and market-based initiatives emerge. We thank the Centre for Banking and Financial Law, NUS, our contributors and participants at the Conference and Rainer Kulms, Editor of the European Business Organization Law Review, for giving us the opportunity to bring together this collection of articles as a whole.

References

Arribas I, Espinós-Vañó MD, García F, Morales-Bañuelos PB (2019) The inclusion of socially irresponsible companies in sustainable stock indices. Sustainability 11:2047

Boulatoff C, Boyer CM (2017) What is the impact of private and public R&D on clean technology firms' performance? An international perspective. J Sustain Finance Invest 7:147–168

Buhr B (2017) Assessing the sources of stranded asset risk: a proposed framework. J Sustain Finance Invest 7:37–53

Carney M (2021) Value(s): building a better world for all. William Collins, London

de Haan M, Dam L, Scholtens B (2012) The drivers of the relationship between corporate environmental performance and stock market returns. J Sustain Finance Invest 2:338–375

Dorfleitner G, Utz S, Wimmer M (2018) Patience pays off – corporate social responsibility and long-term stock returns. J Sustain Finance Invest 8:132–157

Fang M, Tan KS, Wirjanto TS (2019) Sustainable portfolio management under climate change. J Sustain Finance Invest 9:45–67

Hilf J, Rouch D (2021) A legal framework for impact. Freshfields Bruckhaus Deringer, London

Ielasi F, Rossolini M, Limberti S (2018) Sustainability-themed mutual funds: an empirical examination of risk and performance. J Risk Finance 19:247–261

Rouch D (2020) The social licence for financial markets: reaching for the end and why it counts. Palgrave, London

Schröder M (2014) Financial effects of corporate social responsibility: a literature review. J Sustain Finance Invest 4:337–350

Publisher's Note Springer Nature remains neutral with regard to jurisdictional claims in published maps and institutional affiliations.

European Business Organization Law Review (2022) 23:9–45
https://doi.org/10.1007/s40804-021-00234-y

ARTICLE

From a Financial to an Entity Model of ESG

Iain MacNeil[1] · Irene-marié Esser[2,3]

Accepted: 13 December 2021 / Published online: 10 January 2022
© The Author(s) 2022

Abstract

ESG investing evolved over time from the earlier concept of CSR. The process of evolution moved the focus from the external impact of corporate activities to the risk and return implications for financial investors of failing to address ESG issues in their portfolio selection and corporate engagement. The bridge between the two approaches was the framing of sustainability in the early part of the millennium as an overarching concept that could be mapped onto the supply of capital and the techniques employed by institutional investors. The financial model of ESG investing is now the standard approach around the world and is reflected in ESG ratings, codes, guidance and regulatory rules. It focuses on the role of capital and investors in driving change in sustainability practices and pays much less attention to the role of board decision-making and directors' fiduciary duties. In this research, we trace the origins and trajectory of this change in emphasis from CSR to ESG and attempt to explain why it occurred. We identify shortcomings in the financial model of ESG investing and propose an alternative 'entity' model, which we argue would more effectively promote sustainability in the corporate sector around the world.

Keywords ESG · CSR · Sustainability · Fiduciary duty · Stakeholders · Due diligence

✉ Iain MacNeil
Iain.Macneil@glasgow.ac.uk

✉ Irene-marié Esser
Irene-marie.Esser@glasgow.ac.uk

[1] Alexander Stone Chair of Commercial Law, University of Glasgow, Glasgow, UK

[2] Professor of Corporate Law and Governance, University of Glasgow, Glasgow, UK

[3] Extraordinary Professor, Stellenbosch University, Stellenbosch, South Africa

🍂 Springer 🌀 ASSER PRESS

1 Introduction

Sustainability is now a key theme in corporate and financial law. It has many strands but one of the key overarching themes is a focus on how corporate governance and financial regulation might contribute to resolving or mitigating externalities. That debate is nested within the broader question of whether corporate governance and financial regulation are the most appropriate techniques for addressing these issues. It is often argued that (Pigouvian) taxes or further regulation would be better solutions in the sense that they would address (at least some) externalities more directly and consistently.[1] While we see a role for both taxes and further regulation, we start from the viewpoint that corporate governance and financial regulation have a role to play in the transition to a sustainable economic model, especially in a global context in which political agreement on taxes and further regulation seems unlikely. Moreover, since the institutional frameworks surrounding corporate governance and financial regulation have already demonstrated some capability to mobilise voluntary action in connection with sustainability,[2] we believe that further movement in that direction is possible.

While corporate social responsibility (CSR) had been the dominant paradigm through which the social responsibility of business was framed for much of the latter part of the twentieth century, the pattern changed with the approach of the millennium. Sustainability emerged as a key concern and with it the proposition that investors should incorporate ESG factors into portfolio construction so as to mitigate environmental (especially climate change), social (especially human rights) and governance risks that would potentially harm investment performance over the long term. The financial model of ESG investing is now the standard approach around the world and is reflected in ESG metrics, ratings, guidance and regulatory rules. It focuses on the role of capital and investors in driving change in sustainability practices and pays less attention to the role of board decision-making and directors' fiduciary duties. In recent years, sustainability, CSR and ESG have co-existed and have often been treated as equivalents by practitioners, standard setters and academics alike. In our view, however, the apparent similarities conceal some fundamental differences.

Viewed in terms of their fundamentals, the three approaches are quite different. In line with other commentators,[3] we see sustainability as the overarching concept, with CSR and ESG as sub-sets that operate within the corporate and financial domains respectively. Sustainability is focused most explicitly on externalities and, from a corporate governance perspective, on how the de facto norm of shareholder primacy has limited the internalisation of externalities through a focus on

---

[1] See generally Leicester (2013). For an overview of carbon taxes see https://www.unpri.org/pri-blogs/costing-jobs-or-cutting-emissions-what-is-the-real-impact-of-europes-carbon-taxes/6712.article (accessed 15 May 2021).

[2] See further Sect. 2.1 below.

[3] See, for example, https://www.measurabl.com/esg-vs-sustainability-whats-the-difference/ (accessed 15 May 2021).

shareholder interests.[4] The ethical foundation of CSR means in principle that the focus is on doing the right thing in the context of the operational setting of the business. In that sense the ethical choice is not framed as an instrument for improving financial performance, albeit that the expectation might be that observance of ethical standards would, in the long term, have that effect. ESG is focused on financial risk and return and therefore integration of ESG factors into the investment process has the primary purpose of improving returns over the long term by mitigating the risks associated with those ESG factors.

There is undoubtedly overlap between the different approaches, especially at the level of implementation, where techniques such as metrics or key performance indicators (KPIs) may address concerns that are common across all three approaches. Nevertheless, we believe that the fundamental difference in the objectives of each approach means that they cannot be fully reconciled. Their co-existence must therefore inevitably lead to tensions that cannot be resolved. Those tensions may lie below the surface when one approach dominates the others—and that is how we perceive the current situation, with ESG as the dominant paradigm (see Fig. 1).[5]

Put another way, it could be said that the three approaches represent a trilemma, in the sense that there could not be simultaneously a full implementation of all three. Sustainability, as the overarching concept, could be effectively combined with either CSR or ESG but not simultaneously with both. We aim to demonstrate this in three stages. In Sect. 2 we outline the evolution of ESG and key attributes of CSR and ESG respectively so as to differentiate them. In Sect. 3 we explain, by reference to fiduciary duty, why the financialised model of ESG superseded CSR as the

Fig. 1 Sustainability, ESG and CSR—a trilemma

---

[4] See e.g., Sjåfjell and Taylor (2015). The 'externality' framing really just confirms that ESG is not co-extensive with sustainability. The G in ESG certainly could not be framed as a classic externality as the cost will be borne most directly by shareholders (even if there is some effect on the broader corporate system). See also Agudelo et al. (2019), p 18, linking the sustainable agenda with CSR.

[5] See generally Deutsche Bank Group (2012). They show, based on extensive studies, that CSR has essentially evolved into ESG. Not many commentators focus on the transition from CSR to ESG, but note Schanzenbach and Sitkoff (2020), p 388, referring to SRI as having been 'rebranded' as ESG in the late 1990s and early 2000s by adding the 'G'. See for a good summary of the differences between ESG investing and sustainable investing https://lib.standardlife.com/library/uk/invp77.pdf (accessed 15 May 2021).

Fig. 2 Timeline

dominant paradigm. We seek to explain the emergence of the financial channel not by reference to explicit choices made by the participants but by reference to underlying legal influences which provided incentives to make the choices that were made.[6] In Sect. 4 we argue that reverting to an entity model with a stronger CSR focus would be more effective and we sketch out how this might be done.

2 The Origins and Development of ESG Investing

We begin by tracing the origins of ESG investing back to earlier developments, in particular CSR and sustainability, and then develop a comparison framework to illustrate the key dimensions in which ESG represented a move away from the foundations of CSR. We focus in particular on the move from CSR to ESG as we see sustainability both as a broader overarching concept (as above) and as a bridge that facilitated the process of financialisation that is represented by ESG. Thus, viewing the trilemma above more as a timeline, it can be represented as follows (see Fig. 2).

2.1 From CSR to ESG via Sustainability

Elements of the substantive concerns addressed by CSR—such as the welfare of employees and a broader role of business in terms of social solidarity—can be traced back quite far in history.[7] However, it was in the 1930s that CSR in its modern sense began to evolve as ownership diffusion broke the link between ownership and management and focused attention more closely on the purpose for which companies should be managed.[8] In the 1940s, broader discussions started to develop about the social responsibilities of companies, as they began to be seen as institutions thinking beyond mere profits, considering the consequences of their actions.[9] However, it was only in the 1950s that CSR started to take full shape. An influential definition from that time framed CSR (or SR as it was then termed) as follows:

---

[6] Academic discourse around the evolution of ESG would suggest that there was no choice to be made, but we dispute that framing of history, which emerged mainly through the lens of financial economics and without dissent in legal scholarship.

[7] Carroll (2008), p 21.

[8] Ibid., p 23. This debate can be traced back to Berle and Dodd. See Stout (2002), p 1198, for a discussion of the debate.

[9] Agudelo et al. (2019), p 3, referring to Heald (1970). See also Carroll (2008), p 24.

It (SR) refers to the obligations of businessmen to pursue those policies, to make those decisions, or to follow those lines of action which are desirable in terms of the objectives and values of our society.[10]

A later definition of CSR integrated a key insight on the economic foundation of CSR:

The social responsibility of business encompasses the economic, legal, ethical, and discretionary expectations that society has of organisations at a given point in time.[11]

From that perspective, economic viability is something business does for society as well as for itself, by perpetuating the business system. Others then linked CSR more explicitly with ethics and proposed that CSR relates primarily to achieving outcomes from organisational decisions regarding specific issues which have benefits rather than adverse effects for stakeholders.[12]

The 1980s saw a clearer focus on sustainable development and its links to institutional and legal change.[13] The focus on externalities also linked sustainability more explicitly to mainstream economic thinking than had been the case with CSR, which struggled to gain traction against influential notions of the nature and purpose of the corporate entity.[14] At this time the role of stakeholders came more clearly to the fore in research[15] and policy as a mechanism for addressing and resolving externalities associated with sustainable development. The publication of the Brundtland Report in 1987 was a landmark event as it developed guiding principles for sustainable development as it is generally understood today.[16] It can be linked directly to the emergence of the concept of the 'triple bottom line approach' as a sustainability framework that balances the company's environmental, social and economic impacts (the people, profit and planet dimensions).[17] This approach became popular in the 1990s as a practical approach to sustainability, linking the ethical dimension of the UN SDGs[18] more explicitly to the operation of the real economy. Despite the

---

[10] Bowen (1953), p 6. See also Hazen (2020), p 5, stating that 'CSR reflects the general principle that companies should be mindful of the public good and not simply be motivated by profit maximization'.

[11] Carroll (1979), p 500.

[12] E.g., Epstein (1987), p 104. See also Carroll (2008), p 36, referring to this.

[13] See Jones (1980), characterising CSR as a decision-making process that influences corporate behaviour. See further Agudelo et al. (2019), p 7.

[14] See further Ferrarini (2020), at Part II: the evolution of corporate purpose in economics and finance.

[15] See, e.g., Freeman's influential 1984 book 'Strategic management: a stakeholder approach'.

[16] The World Commission on Environment and Development (WCED), set up in 1983, published its report entitled 'Our common future'. See https://www.are.admin.ch/are/en/home/sustainable-development/international-cooperation/2030agenda/un-_-milestones-in-sustainable-development/1987--brundtland-report.html (accessed 15 May 2021).

[17] First coined by Elkington in 1994. See Elkington (1994), pp 90-100, and Elkington (1999).

[18] See Antoncic et al. (2020), p 3: 'SDGs are much broader than the ESGs and focus on good health and well-being, the elimination of poverty, zero hunger, quality education, clean water and sanitation, reduced inequity, as well as the environment and other issues encapsulated in ESGs. Most importantly, the SDGs call for leaving no one behind.'

underlying tensions noted above, that approach also resonated in CSR discourse,[19] demonstrating the overlap and potential for conflation of the differing concepts in practice.

The 1990s saw the emergence of ESG as a portfolio risk management concept linked to financial performance.[20] ESG investing is based on the presumption that its constituent factors are material for the risk and return profile of financial investments.[21] In the equity market, ESG investing is closely aligned with so-called 'responsible investment',[22] which can extend across the entire spectrum of 'sustainable investment'.[23] The definition of sustainable investment can vary considerably between stakeholders,[24] but generally entails applying one of the following strategies:[25]

- Screening of potential investments to enable exclusion of investment in specific sectors, or companies or projects that show poor ESG performance relative to industry peers (negative/exclusionary screening) or companies or projects that do not comply with international norms and standards (norms-based screening);
- ESG integration, whereby ultimate investors may require systematic and explicit inclusion, by investment managers, of environmental, social and governance factors into investment appraisal;[26]

---

[19] See Agudelo et al. (2019), p 9. ESG references elements of CSR with the 'E' focusing on environmental issues and sustainability, the 'S' on diversity and inclusion, fair wages and health issues, and the 'G' on governance issues like independent directors, etc. See on this Hazen (2020), p 5. There is also an argument that CSR had never really encompassed the 'social' dimension in the sense developed by critical legal scholars starting with Polanyi. See on this Moncrieff (2015), pp 434–459.

[20] See generally Boffo and Patalano (2020), pp 37–40, for a literature review on CSR, SRI and ESG investing.

[21] See Amel-Zadeh and Serafeim (2017), addressing the question of what motivates investors to use ESG data. The clear majority of respondents (82%) suggest that they use ESG information because it is financially material to investment performance. Overall, they found evidence that the use of ESG information has primarily financial rather than ethical motives. (Note large sample of mainstream investors).

[22] See https://www.cfainstitute.org/en/research/esg-investing (accessed 15 May 2021) for differences between ESG and SRI. 'ESG investing grew out of investment philosophies such as Socially Responsible Investing (SRI), but there are key differences. Earlier models typically use value judgments and negative screening to decide which companies to invest in. ESG investing and analysis, on the other hand, looks at finding value in companies—not just at supporting a set of values.'

[23] For the spectrum of sustainable investment see https://ec.europa.eu/environment/enveco/sustainable_finance/pdf/studies/Defining%20Green%20in%20green%20finance%20-%20final%20report%20published%20on%20eu%20website.pdf (accessed 15 May 2021).

[24] See, e.g., https://lib.standardlife.com/library/uk/invp77.pdf (accessed 15 May 2021) for a stylised summary of the differences between ESG investing and sustainable investing, the former linked to risk and the latter to values.

[25] See generally Global Sustainable Investment Alliance Report 2016 at http://www.gsi-alliance.org/wp-content/uploads/2017/03/GSIR_Review2016.F.pdf (accessed 15 May 2021).

[26] Integration techniques concern the weighing and altering of portfolio components based on ESG information, without banning securities from the start through fundamental, quantitative, smart beta and passive strategies. The UNPRI drafted a practical guide to ESG integration: https://www.unpri.org/listed-equity/a-practical-guide-to-esg-integration-for-equity-investing/10.article (accessed 15 May 2021).

- Shareholder engagement and activism (in some instances promoted by soft law measures such as the Stewardship Code in the UK);[27]
- Sustainability themed investing;
- Impact investing, focusing on measurable positive social or environmental outcomes alongside financial returns.[28]

The move to ESG marked a clear shift away from the earlier model of CSR, where the focus was at the entity level and on the impact of corporate activities on the real world. There was also an increased focus on stakeholder activism, proxy voting and corporate disclosure of ESG policies. Third-party ESG ratings also became available to meet demand. By the turn of the century it was noted that

> the criteria of CSR—now referred to here as contemporary CSR—expanded to formally encompass ESG, corporate citizenship and economic responsibility.[29]

At a global level the early 2000s were marked by voluntary CSR initiatives[30] such as the launch of the United Nations Global Compact. The term ESG featured prominently in 2005 in the 'Who Cares Wins'[31] document, issued by the Global Compact. This study provided recommendations to better integrate environmental, social and governance issues in financial analysis, asset management and securities brokerage. As ESG did not replace CSR,[32] companies would still report on CSR issues and disclose how they fulfilled certain social obligations and how they balanced these values with profit maximisation, whereas ESG reporting or disclosure became more metrics driven.[33] The move from CSR to ESG was described as driven by the 'business case' for CSR,[34] framed in terms of sustainability. This marks a shift from social obligations (underpinned by moral obligation) in CSR to a risk management perspective (e.g., litigation and regulatory risk) in ESG.

---

[27] This is dealt with in detail in Sect.3.2 below where we link the rise of the financial model of ESG investment to the emergence of stewardship as a global force in equity investment.

[28] See further https://www.bridgesfundmanagement.com/wp-content/uploads/2017/08/Bridges-Spect rum-of-Capital-screen.pdf (accessed 15 May 2021), p 3, for a mapping of ESG onto sustainable investing and impact investing respectively. The model breaks ESG down further into mitigation of ESG risk to protect value and progressive ESG policies to enhance value.

[29] Deutsche Bank Group (2012), p 24.

[30] See Agudelo et al. (2019), p 9.

[31] See https://www.ifc.org/wps/wcm/connect/topics_ext_content/ifc_external_corporate_site/sustainabi lity-at-ifc/publications/publications_report_whocareswins__wci__1319579355342 (accessed 15 May 2021) for the document. This seems to be one of the first attempts to operationalise general principles (SDGs, PRI) at the level of investment practice. Endorsing institutions were convinced that a better consideration of environmental, social and governance factors would ultimately contribute to stronger and more resilient investment markets, as well as to the sustainable development of societies.

[32] Hazen (2020), p 5.

[33] CSR reporting seems to be largely superseded by 'sustainability reporting' based on the GRI, see https://www.icas.com/landing/sustainability/practical-tools-and-links/sustainability-reporting (accessed 15 May 2021). It is thus not entirely clear if reporting can help to clarify the distinction between CSR and ESG.

[34] See Pollman (2019), p 5.

Following the Global Financial Crisis (GFC) 2008, the focus on reforming financial regulation provided further momentum both to sustainability as an objective and to ESG as a transmission mechanism. The Task Force on Climate-related Financial Disclosures (TCFD)[35] Report, issued in 2016, proposed a framework for more effective climate-related disclosures that could promote more informed investment, credit, and insurance underwriting decisions and, in turn, enable stakeholders to understand better the concentrations of carbon-related assets in the financial sector and the financial system's exposures to climate-related risks. The Green Bond Principles (a voluntary set of guidelines for issuing green bonds) were launched in 2018 to promote integrity in the green bond market through guidelines that recommend transparency, disclosure and reporting.[36]

2.2 Key Attributes of CSR and ESG

Having outlined the evolution of ESG and its links to CSR, we now identify in Table 1 the key attributes of both approaches to focus more clearly on how they differ. This provides a foundation for the analysis that follows in Sect. 3, which focuses on the manner in which fiduciary duty influenced their development and interaction.

CSR evolved with a clear *focus* on ethical responsibility and accountability, albeit that the 'business case' for CSR shifted the focus to 'doing well by doing good' as the potential for CSR to improve performance became clearer over time. In contrast, ESG was motivated by concerns over the risk and return implications for investors arising from its three constituents. That difference in approach is fundamental even if ESG and CSR are often assimilated in academic discourse and can overlap in their objectives.

The *transmission channel* for CSR and ESG differs. CSR developed on the basis that corporate entities and their boards would lead on the framing and implementation of CSR policies. ESG, in contrast, was based on the premise that the supply of finance would be the primary driver of behavioural change and that investors would be the agents of change. Engagement with the board is an important element of ESG, but it is framed in a context that prioritises shareholder interests and marginalises stakeholders.

In the case of CSR, the prioritisation of the board as the transmission channel means that *implementation* is linked more directly with operations than in the case of ESG, which focuses on the supply of capital. This provides a more detailed and contextual understanding of the operational environment as directors will generally be better informed on those issues than shareholders and better able to integrate and balance CSR issues with other elements of board oversight. Implementation in the

---

[35] See https://www.fsb-tcfd.org/ (accessed 15 May 2021).

[36] https://www.icmagroup.org/assets/documents/Regulatory/Green-Bonds/Green-Bonds-Principles-June-2018-270520.pdf (accessed 15 May 2021), p 3: 'Green Bonds are any type of bond instrument where the proceeds will be exclusively applied to finance or re-finance, in part or in full, new and/or existing eligible Green Projects (see section 1 Use of Proceeds) and which are aligned with the four core components of the GBP.'

Table 1 CSR and ESG comparison

	CSR	ESG
Focus	Ethical responsibility and accountability	Portfolio risk and return, linked to metrics, benchmarks and indices
Channel	Corporate entities	Institutional investors and the investment chain
Implementation	Board decision-making	Integration into portfolio selection and engagement
Metrics	None	Multiple, with different custodians, scope and legal effect. Limited verification. Ratings add another layer of complexity
Reporting	Mainly non-financial reporting (NFR)	Mainly through 5 sustainability frameworks (CDP, CDSB, GRI, IIRC, SASB)[a]

[a]The CDP (Disclosure Insight Action), the Climate Disclosure Standards Board (CDSB), the Global Reporting Initiative (GRI), the International Integrated Reporting Council (IIRC) and the Sustainability Accounting Standards Board (SASB) have co-published a shared vision of the elements necessary for more comprehensive corporate reporting and a joint statement of intent to drive towards this goal. See https://www.cdp.net/en/articles/media/comprehensive-corporate-reporting (accessed May 2021).

case of ESG is through the investment process, with the launch of the Principles for Responsible Investment (PRI) in 2006 representing a catalyst in the movement towards ESG.[37]

While there is sometimes reference to the 'measurement of CSR' or to *metrics* relevant to CSR,[38] it is far less common compared to ESG. Metrics are usually aimed at ESG factors and relevant to investors when making portfolio choices. To date, the lack of an objective standard[39] for evaluating the sustainability characteristics of investment projects, products and portfolios has been a major problem and has led to allegations of so-called 'greenwashing'. Recent initiatives such as the EU Taxonomy aim to resolve that issue.[40]

The development of *reporting* frameworks linked to ESG was a key factor in the movement from CSR to ESG. In the EU, the Non-Financial Reporting Directive (NFRD)[41] of 2014 focused on corporate disclosure, although it could be viewed as neutral as between CSR and ESG as transmission mechanisms. More broadly, the development of reporting frameworks encompassed a variety of different techniques that combined reliance on private initiatives with public endorsement through regulatory frameworks.[42]

---

[37] See https://www.forbes.com/sites/georgkell/2018/07/11/the-remarkable-rise-of-esg/?sh=7c9612a016 95#575351571695 (accessed 15 May 2021). It is clear that the UN has been a key player at the global level through the Global Compact, the SDGs and support for the establishment and development of the PRI. The Global Compact is much broader in its focus and membership. But, as demonstrated by the 'Who Cares Wins' Report, referred to earlier, ESG was already in the ascendancy in Global Compact discourse and action by 2005.

[38] See, for example, https://walterschindler.com/key-csr-metrics-for-sustainability-advisors/ and https://www.csrtraininginstitute.com/2018/06/19/csr-metrics-measure-and-manage-the-meaningful/(accessed 15 May 2021). The ISO 26000 standards can also be linked to CSR, see https://www.iso.org/iso-26000-social-responsibility.html (accessed 15 May 2021). The ISO is an independent, non-governmental international organisation with a membership of 165 national standards bodies. The seven key underlying principles of social responsibility are: accountability, transparency, ethical behaviour, respect for stakeholder interests, the rule of law, international norms of behaviour and human rights.

[39] Lack of objective standards has led to a proliferation of metrics. In a survey conducted in 2019 it was found that the top 10 ESG metrics sought by private equity investors are: ESG policy, assignment of ESG responsibility, the presence of a formal code of ethics, whether there is any litigation ongoing, diversity among employees, board members and management and the net employee composition, the presence of an environmental policy, estimation of the CO2 footprint, data management processes in place to reduce cybersecurity incidents, as well as health and safety of employees, contractors and the wider value chain. See https://www.finextra.com/blogposting/16750/the-top-10-esg-metrics-private-equity-funds-should-collect (accessed 15 May 2021).

[40] See further n 125 below.

[41] Directive 2014/95/EU, amending Directive 2013/34/EU as regards disclosure of non-financial and diversity information by certain large undertakings and groups, [2014] OJ L330/1. See also Esser et al. (2018), pp 729–772, and Esser et al. (2020), pp 209-242. On 21 April 2021 the Commission adopted a proposal for a Corporate Sustainability Reporting Directive (CSRD), which would amend the existing reporting requirements of the NFRD. See https://ec.europa.eu/info/publications/210421-susta inable-finance-communication_en#csrd (accessed 15 May 2021). For example, it extends the scope to all large companies and all companies listed on regulated markets. It also introduces more detailed reporting requirements, and a requirement to report according to mandatory EU sustainability reporting standards.

[42] See Harper Ho and Park (2020) for a survey of global trends in ESG-related reporting, focusing in particular on a systematic characterisation of the different modes of interaction between private standards and public regulation across seven key jurisdictions.

Developments at the global (e.g., GRI, TCFD)[43] and sectoral levels (e.g., Green Bond Principles) were more clearly aligned with ESG as the dominant paradigm. The EU's 2018 sustainability strategy[44] set out a clear pathway for developing the financial model of ESG. This was followed through with the 2019 Regulation requiring disclosure from financial firms to inform investors about the sustainability characteristics of their products and portfolios.[45] The more recent Taxonomy Regulation[46] has established a framework to evaluate the sustainability characteristics of portfolio companies.

3 The Financialisation of ESG

We noted in Sect. 2 that ESG emerged from CSR, which had focused more on corporate responsibility and the role of the board of directors. We will now outline and rationalise the key influences through which ESG became 'financialised'. We start from the high-level observation that the financial model of ESG enabled investors to exert greater control over 'non-financial' issues linked to sustainability as their political salience gathered momentum. It provided an overarching technique for empowering shareholders through various mechanisms linked to the supply of finance. That approach avoided the more direct confrontation between investors and directors that would likely have resulted from pursuing the ESG agenda through an entity model focused more directly on board decision-making. As outlined in Sect. 2, we see the move from CSR to ESG as a transformation in the CSR agenda driven by shareholder interest. That approach brought elements of CSR into the mainstream of shareholder-focused corporate governance and provided a financial logic that linked shareholder influence with fiduciary duties owed to underlying investors. In that sense, the transition from CSR to ESG empowered investors relative to other stakeholders, who were marginalised by comparison with the more traditional CSR approach.

Nevertheless, that observation prompts the question why it was necessary for investors to take control of the ESG agenda rather than leaving CSR implementation to happen at board level, driven by the fiduciary duty owed by directors and subject to the established patterns of accountability. We argue that investors could not rely on corporate fiduciary duty to deliver an appropriate and consistent model of CSR as a result of legal uncertainty and the (increasing) role of other stakeholders in the process of board decision-making. While ESG outcomes (developed through

---

[43] Since 2000 the Global Reporting Initiative provides the world's most widely used standards for sustainability reporting—the GRI Standards. The GRI and the GSSB [they have sole responsibility to set the GRI standards on sustainability reporting, see https://www.globalreporting.org/standards/global-sustainability-standards-board/ (accessed 15 May 2021)] do not check the accuracy or content of the material and its claim, see https://www.globalreporting.org/reportregistration/verifiedreports (accessed 15 May 2021).

[44] See https://ec.europa.eu/environment/sustainable-development/strategy/index_en.htm (accessed 15 May 2021).

[45] See further n 125 below.

[46] Ibid.

the financial channel) might well deliver benefits for stakeholders, they would be indirect in two senses: first, that ESG frames stakeholder protection as a second-order effect, with priority given to portfolio risk and return; and second, that the real-world effects of ESG might or might not be realised[47] and would in any case not generally be subject to verification. As we discuss below, shifting the focus from CSR to a financial model of ESG would mitigate those challenges and would in principle move the focus of fiduciary compliance more explicitly into a paradigm focused on financial risk and return. It also represents a preference for ex ante over ex post control mechanisms that was already evident in the soft law evolution of the governance dimension of ESG that started with the Cadbury Code in the UK in 1992.[48]

3.1 Fiduciary Duty As an Enabler of ESG Investing

We now focus on how fiduciary duty has been deployed to facilitate the development of a 'financialised' model of ESG investing. We focus first on how fiduciary duty operates differently in the investment chain ('intermediary fiduciary duty') and in the context of board decision-making ('corporate fiduciary duty') and evaluate the consequences of that asymmetry. We then focus on the role of legal uncertainty in the context of both forms of fiduciary duty and its implications for the implementation of a CSR or ESG agenda.

3.1.1 Asymmetry in Fiduciary Duties

Two forms of fiduciary duty operate to control the extent to which corporate strategy and operations could focus on CSR or ESG-related outcomes. The first is the duty owed by directors to the company (and in some instances to shareholders). The second is the duty owed by institutional investors to their underlying investors.[49] It might well be argued that in an ideal world, both forms of fiduciary duty would be aligned so as to reflect the underlying logic that they serve the same purpose. But that perspective conflates the interests of the company and the shareholders in a manner that is inconsistent with the (increasing) role of stakeholders in many systems around the world. Thus, if stakeholders are to have a meaningful role in corporate governance, it seems inevitable that corporate fiduciary duty would have to adjust to accommodate that role.[50] On the other hand, that adjustment would not carry direct implications for fiduciary duty in the investment chain since that duty

---

[47] On the link between ESG portfolio investment techniques and real-world effects see, e.g., Harnett et al. (2020).

[48] MacNeil and Esser (2021).

[49] That duty is itself a variety of different duties linked to the model of investment. See further MacNeil (2012), chapter 5, for the different models in the UK. For the US see Schanzenbach and Sitkoff (2020). For the purposes of exposition we focus here on the trust model that applies to pension fund trustees.

[50] That process was evident in the process of reforming company law in the UK in the early 2000s. See, e.g., s172 of the Companies Act 2006 in the UK, introducing a so-called 'enlightened shareholder value' approach. For discussion of the linkage of this model with shareholder value see Ferrarini (2020), p 24.

is focused primarily on financial risk and return and the relationship between institutional investors and their underlying clients. Thus, the different focus of the two forms of fiduciary duty means they have different objectives and represent different interests. Even if they share an overarching objective of promoting the success of the company, their respective framing of the role of shareholders and stakeholders is quite different and so they are unlikely to operate in unison.

In the light of this asymmetry, it was inevitable that, as the momentum of public policy moved towards sustainability, a choice would have to be made as to which form of fiduciary duty would be prioritised in pursuit of those goals. While elements of each approach (financial or entity) were present under the old CSR model and would likely persist whatever option was selected, it is implicit in the trilemma we present above that a choice of approach would be necessary for a coherent system to evolve. The development of ESG suggests that there was little or no explicit debate around this choice,[51] but that does not in principle exclude the possibility of choice. In hindsight it seems that the absence of debate is itself evidence of the 'financialised' version of ESG having been in the ascendancy from an early stage and having effectively precluded debate around the 'entity' option. It would also tend to suggest that the public policy 'push' towards the financialised version represented by initiatives such as the SDGs and the endorsement of the PRI paid more attention to the 'what' (sustainability) rather than the 'how' (which would likely have led to a more explicit focus on policy choices). And while the GFC might have been expected to generate some pushback against the financialised model,[52] reflecting the more general pattern of reaction to the global financial crisis, the trend was already well established by then and so less amenable to change. On the contrary, the boost to 'stewardship' provided by the GFC, driven by the perception that it exposed weaknesses in corporate governance,[53] likely solidified the financialised model by opening up a clearer process for investor activism and engagement and by linking it to 'intermediary' fiduciary duty.[54]

3.1.2 Legal Uncertainty

Legal uncertainty is endemic and there are a range of mitigation and risk transfer techniques that attempt to limit its impact in the commercial world.[55] One of the main concerns is to identify ex ante techniques that can limit the extent to which transactions or decisions would be open to ex post challenge. In the context of ESG, the risk would be that ESG actions, whether strategic or operational decisions taken by a board or portfolio investment decisions taken by an institutional investor, would

---

[51] See, e.g., the Freshfields Report 2005 [A legal framework for the integration of environmental, social and governance issues into institutional investment, https://www.unepfi.org/fileadmin/documents/fresh fields_legal_resp_20051123.pdf (accessed 15 May 2021)], which considers only intermediary fiduciary duty.

[52] See further Palley (2007).

[53] See further MacNeil (2010b), pp 518–520.

[54] This led eventually to the development of the first Stewardship Code in the UK in 2010.

[55] See generally MacNeil (2009).

be open to challenge by either shareholders or underlying investors (respectively) on the basis that the action was in breach of fiduciary duty. In this Section we outline the parameters of this paradigm and evaluate its likely impact on the development of ESG. We focus on legal uncertainty *within* national jurisdictions as it is in that context that the legal framework (including fiduciary duty) for institutional investment generally operates, albeit that the major asset management firms operate and set investment policy at a global and regional level.[56]

Legal uncertainty would likely affect both corporate and intermediary fiduciary duty. So the presence of such uncertainty might suggest that neither would be better placed than the other, from the perspective of legal risk, as a conduit for developing ESG. However, three factors suggest otherwise.

- *Individual vs collective action* In widely dispersed ownership systems, such as the UK and US, which were the main drivers of ESG, individual investors could not effectively influence boards to undertake ESG actions without collaboration. Even if that were legally possible (and it might not always be[57]) it would be more costly and less effective than ESG portfolio techniques undertaken unilaterally 'in house' through the techniques identified in Sect. 2.1 above. The portfolio approach would in principle distribute ESG effects more broadly across (listed) companies and would gain traction as points two and three below started to ramp up.
- *Mitigation of legal uncertainty through opinions and standards* While some academic opinion supported an interpretation of fiduciary duty that would enable boards to implement an 'entity' model of ESG, they tended to be minority views and were not backed by influential legal opinions or powerful NGOs. The opposite was the case for the financialised model and intermediary fiduciary duty, which were supported at an early stage by an influential legal opinion (the Freshfields Report[58]) and standards (the PRI) endorsed by the UNEP FI.[59]
- *Data* The accumulation of evidence on the financial performance of ESG strategies[60] lent credibility to the financial model of ESG, whereas there was no comparable data to support operational activities undertaken by companies through 'CSR' initiatives. In that sense the available 'evidence' supported the financialised model.

Thus, in terms of the context in which ESG operates, we take the view that legal uncertainty posed less risk to a financial model of ESG than it did to an entity

---

[56] The MiFID framework in the EU and the federal system of securities regulation in the US could be viewed as exceptions to the extent that they impose quasi-fiduciary obligations extending beyond state boundaries.

[57] See MacNeil (2010a), p 428.

[58] See n 51 above. It was issued by the UNEP Finance Initiative in 2005. For background see https://www.unepfi.org/about/background/ (accessed 15 May 2021).

[59] For background on both the PRI and UNEP FI see https://www.unpri.org/pri/about-the-pri (accessed 15 May 2021).

[60] See ICGN Guidance on Investor Fiduciary Duties (2018): http://icgn.flpbks.com/icgn-fiduciary_duties/ (accessed 15 May 2021), p 16, for a concise summary of some key academic studies.

model. Viewed in those terms, investors were better placed to develop the financial model than directors were to develop an entity model of ESG that might have more closely resembled the model of CSR from which ESG emerged. But that high-level perspective glosses over the nature and extent of legal uncertainty in the respective domains and it is to that issue that we now turn.

3.1.3 Corporate Fiduciary Duty

Corporate fiduciary duty has attracted relatively more attention from the perspective of corporate purpose and the role of stakeholder interests (the traditional focus of CSR) by comparison with ESG where these issues are relevant but subordinated to the more explicit focus on portfolio risk and return. The key issues have been whether corporate purpose encompasses objectives other than profit maximisation and whether, and if so how, interests other than those of shareholders can legitimately be considered in board decision-making.[61] Both issues are instrumental in determining the extent to which directors could adopt a sustainable or stakeholder-focused strategy. We therefore turn now to consider whether corporate fiduciary duty would permit directors to adopt such an approach and how legal uncertainty might influence their stance and that of investors. We focus on the UK and the US as the two key jurisdictions in which these issues have been debated.

Turning first to the issue of corporate purpose, we note that in both the US and the UK purpose tends not to be defined explicitly in either statutory corporate law or constitutional documents.[62] Thus, the default position in both jurisdictions is that it falls to the board of directors to determine corporate purpose in accordance with the standard process of majority decision-making. While in principle that would open up considerable scope for directors to pursue CSR activities, it has been observed that the emergence of a de facto norm of shareholder value maximisation constrained any inclination on the part of boards to act in that way.[63] While that pattern is evident in both the UK and the US, different influences seem to have been at work and may explain the common outcome in two systems that can be differentiated by reference to the distribution of powers between shareholders and directors, with the US typically characterised as an example of director primacy and the UK as an example of shareholder primacy.[64]

In the UK, it has been argued that this development can be linked to the reforms introduced by the Companies Act 1948, which strengthened the powers of shareholders with regard to the dismissal of directors and facilitated the emergence of

---

[61] These two issues are sometimes treated in a manner whereby one subsumes the other. While there might often be overlap in their implementation, we prefer to view them separately as they are not co-extensive.

[62] But for proposals to change that approach see British Academy (2019). Contra that approach see Rock (2020).

[63] See Sjåfjell and Taylor (2019), p 47 (note that they use 'shareholder value' to denote a legal norm and 'shareholder primacy' to denote a social norm).

[64] Cabrelli and Esser (2018). Differences in the distribution of powers between shareholders and directors would likely influence the extent to which shareholders could control the evolution and implementation of corporate purpose at the operational level.

hostile takeovers.[65] Both developments strengthened the role of shareholders and can credibly be viewed as supporting the emergence of a de facto norm of shareholder value maximisation. Another relevant development in the UK was the move to a so-called 'enlightened shareholder value' model of board decision-making as part of the reforms introduced by the Companies Act 2006 (CA 2006). While that reform was widely regarded as a codification of the model of corporate purpose that was already in place, in the sense that shareholders' interests remained in the ascendancy (within the so-called enlightened shareholder value model),[66] the alternative view of s172 CA 2006 as narrowing the (CA 1985) open-ended formulation of 'the interests of the company' is also credible and supports a view of the CA 2006 as narrowing the discretion of directors with regard to CSR activities.[67]

In the US, the emergence of a de facto norm of shareholder value maximisation has also been noted.[68] That approach was supported by the Business Roundtable Statement of 1997, which explicitly subordinated the interests of other stakeholders to those of shareholders.[69] It also attracted support in judicial opinions of the Delaware court and has been argued, in the US context, to be 'the best description of the characteristics of the corporate form in traditional jurisdictions', even in the absence of an explicit statutory rule of shareholder primacy.[70] There were dissenting views within the academic community,[71] but they remained a minority view even in that context. However, there is now considerable support for the view that corporate law does not mandate profit maximisation. The Business Roundtable Statement on the Purpose of a Corporation (August 2019) attracted considerable attention as a reversal of its earlier position and followed other high-profile statements supporting the proposition that corporate purpose should be reframed so as to encompass broader stakeholder interests.[72] Some judicial support for that approach was evident earlier[73] and has continued in more recent Delaware case law.[74]

---

[65] Johnston (2017). The relevant provision was s184 of the Companies Act 1948. Prior to the change in the law, directors could be dismissed only by a special or extraordinary resolution, both of which required a 75% majority of shareholders voting on the resolution.

[66] See, e.g., Keay (2010).

[67] See Johnston (2017); and Rühmkorf (2015), pp 43-44.

[68] See, e.g., Johnson and Millon (2015), pp 14–15, for a concise history of the evolution of this norm and its link to influential economic theories about the nature and operation of companies.

[69] See Rock (2020).

[70] Ibid., p 9. 'Traditional' jurisdictions in this context refers to states without 'constituency statutes', which expressly permit priority to be given to stakeholder interests in some instances. See further Bebchuk and Tallarita (2020), presenting empirical evidence that directors have generally not used those powers to protect stakeholder interests (in takeover situations).

[71] See, e.g., Stout (2012). For a concise summary of the book by the author see https://scholarship.law.cornell.edu/cgi/viewcontent.cgi?article=2311&context=facpub (accessed 15 May 2021).

[72] Rock (2020), pp 3–5.

[73] As one commentator observed in respect of the 2015 Supreme Court decision in the *Hobby Lobby* case: 'In Hobby Lobby, the Supreme Court did not describe state law as unsettled or uncertain on the issue of corporate purpose; instead, it had no difficulty concluding that state corporate law simply does not require profit maximization.' *Burwell v. Hobby Lobby Stores, Inc.*, 134 S. Ct. 2751 (2014). See Johnson and Millon (2015).

[74] See further Fisch and Davidoff Solomon (2021), p 22: '[…] recent Delaware *Caremark* decisions suggest that insufficient attention to stakeholder interests may itself be legally actionable […] In the wake of *Marchand*, Delaware courts have seen an uptick in *Caremark* claims, and corporations have increased their focus on risk assessment and compliance.'

3.1.4 'Intermediary' Fiduciary Duty

It follows from the general principle that the content of fiduciary duty can be adjusted by contract that investment mandates can modify the default model of fiduciary duty owed by asset managers to underlying investors.[75] The growth of SRI and ethical funds had already foreshadowed this development, as the explicit identification of such objectives in the fund agreements clearly adjusted fiduciary duties so that those objectives could be achieved, even if the outcome might be to forego other more lucrative investment opportunities.

However, implementation of an ESG focus more broadly across mainstream funds managed by a fiduciary asset manager presents a different issue as in those circumstances what is proposed is a change from past practice in terms of portfolio selection and engagement without any explicit change to fiduciary duty. To the extent that the change in practice aligns with fiduciary duty, there would be no problem. However, if the change in practice conflicted with fiduciary duty, a general move towards ESG would be more problematic. Thus, a key issue in the evolution of ESG, and which retains at least some salience currently, is whether a general move towards ESG on the part of asset managers corresponds with fiduciary duty. We trace that debate from its early origins in the Freshfields Report through to more recent developments and evaluate their significance.

In the investment chain, in both the UK and the US, fiduciary duty was conventionally understood as focused on financial return.[76] While there are differences in the context in which common law fiduciary duty is applied by reference to different types of fund and specific statutory provisions, the core of the duty can be split into two elements: a duty of care which relates to the professional standards applicable to portfolio strategy and investment selection; and a duty of loyalty which relates to the protection of the interests of the beneficiaries of the fund.[77] The conventional interpretation emphasises the overarching priority of financial return in the context of the duty of care and close attention to the interests of the beneficiaries in the duty of loyalty. Thus, it could be said that, within those parameters, the conventional position already permitted reference to ESG factors, albeit that in the early stage of the development of ESG investment there was less evidence of past investment performance and less clear calibration of future risks than would be the case later. We refer below to this model of fiduciary duty as the permissive model and contrast it with the emerging 'mandatory' model, which posits that it would be a breach of

---

[75] See generally MacNeil (2012), p 445, discussing relevant case law in the context of UK financial markets.

[76] See ICGN Guidance on Investor Fiduciary Duties (2018), http://icgn.flpbks.com/icgn-fiduciary_duties/ (accessed 15 May 2021), p 16: 'Historically, concepts of fiduciary duty have focused on maximising investment returns without due consideration of environmental, social and governance (ESG) factors.'

[77] See further with respect to the UK, MacNeil (2012), chapter 5 'Institutional Investment'; and with regard to the US, Schanzenbach and Sitkoff (2020).

fiduciary duty to ignore ESG factors in investment practice regardless of their financial materiality.[78]

There is relatively little case law in the UK on intermediary fiduciary duty and
it has in any event not kept pace with developments in investment practice such as
ESG.[79] While that situation inevitably cast some doubt over the precise contours of
the duty, contractual solutions in the form of investment mandates adopting a variety
of ESG strategies provided a partial solution. So too did the growing evidence of
ESG outperformance,[80] which over time limited the legal risk associated with ESG
integration, especially for pension funds where the time horizon is generally longer.
More recently the growth of so-called 'impact investing' has extended the spectrum
of investment to include investments made with the intention to generate positive,
measurable social and environmental impact alongside a financial return. The priority given to impact in this model distinguishes it from ESG integration and raises
related issues for fiduciary investors that have to date been less clearly addressed.[81]

The conventional approach was challenged by the Freshfields Report in 2005.[82]
Its conclusion was essentially that it was permissible for a fiduciary to incorporate
ESG factors into investment decision-making in both the US and the UK, albeit
that financial return would normally remain the overriding objective (unless modified by the investment mandate or the clear preference of the beneficiaries).[83] It was
observed also that it was

> arguable that ESG considerations must be integrated into an investment deci-
> sion where a consensus (express or in certain circumstances implied) amongst
> the beneficiaries mandates a particular investment strategy.[84]

That approach underpinned the development of the PRI in 2006 and supported the
subsequent expansion of ESG investing. By 2015, and with the benefit of increasing
evidence of the financial outperformance of ESG investing, the PRI had adopted a

---

[78] It is probably true to observe that the distinction may be less significant in practice than in theory, as
fiduciary duty focuses more on process and less on outcomes (meaning that due consideration and no
more might be given to ESG factors), but it nevertheless serves a useful purpose to demarcate the two
opposing views which have influenced the development of hard and soft law.

[79] See further Law Commission Consultation on Fiduciary Duties of Investment Intermediaries (2014),
https://www.lawcom.gov.uk/project/fiduciary-duties-of-investment-intermediaries/ (accessed 15 May
2021).

[80] See, e.g., Boffo and Patalano (2020); Antoncic et al. (2020).

[81] But see in this regard the Impact Investing Institute (October 2020). This legal opinion crafts a
nuanced case for impact investing for fiduciary investors.

[82] See the Freshfields Report (n 51 above), p 6, where the key question to be addressed by the Report
reflects the dominance of financial factors in prevailing investment practice: 'Is the integration of environmental, social and governance issues into investment policy (including asset allocation, portfolio construction and stock-picking or bond-picking) voluntarily permitted, legally required or hampered by law
and regulation; primarily as regards public and private pension funds, secondarily as regards insurance
company reserves and mutual funds?'

[83] Ibid., p 12. The Report was less categorical with regard to the position of other jurisdictions that were
included in the survey of relevant laws.

[84] Ibid., p 13.

more robust position, arguing that fiduciary investors were required to consider ESG factors and that policymakers and regulators should act to clarify the position.[85]

While the progressive Freshfields stance gained traction in the soft law space in which guidance such as the PRI operates, it was less influential for the interpretation of hard law. In its 2014 consultation the Law Commission adopted a more conventional formulation of intermediary fiduciary duty:

> The report concludes that trustees should take into account factors which are financially material to the performance of an investment. Where trustees think ethical or environmental, social or governance (ESG) issues are financially material they should take them into account.[86]

That approach seems to align with the permissive view of ESG factors in investment practice but stopped short of the mandatory view espoused by the PRI. A similar position was adopted by the influential International Corporate Governance Network (ICGN), whose guidance on model terms stated:

> The term ESG is used here to mean material and relevant investment risks and opportunities for asset owners with long-term horizons.[87]

Similarly, Principle 7 of the UK Stewardship Code[88] focuses on integration of *material* ESG factors. Thus, while the progressive view has been influential, it is by no means the dominant view, especially within the regulatory and investment community, where alignment with the more conventional view formulated by the Law Commission seems to be to the fore.

Turning now to the US, it was noted in the Freshfields Report in 2005 that EU asset managers were ahead of US counterparts in adopting ESG integration strategies. Legal uncertainty likely remained a more prominent issue in the US, as evidenced by a 2019 study commenting on the use of ESG information by investors.[89] That observation nevertheless masks progress towards recognition of ESG as consistent with fiduciary duty in the US.[90] While that shift falls short of the more

---

[85] See PRI, Fiduciary duty in the twenty-first century, https://perma.cc/JK62-72VZ (accessed 15 May 2021), pp 9 and 10.

[86] Law Commission Consultation on Fiduciary Duties of Investment Intermediaries (2014), https://www.lawcom.gov.uk/project/fiduciary-duties-of-investment-intermediaries/ (accessed 15 May 2021).

[87] ICGN Model Mandate Initiative. Model contract terms between asset owners and their fund managers, https://d3n8a8pro7vhmx.cloudfront.net/intentionalendowments/pages/27/attachments/original/1420777456/ICGN_Model_Mandate_Initiative.pdf?1420777456 (accessed 15 May 2021). The ICGN Global Stewardship Principles refer to ESG factors as 'core components of fiduciary duty' but it seems clear from the model terms that ICGN adopts a financial materiality threshold for consideration of ESG factors.

[88] See further https://www.frc.org.uk/investors/uk-stewardship-code (accessed 15 May 2021). The custodian of the Stewardship Code is the Financial Reporting Council, which exercises oversight of financial reporting and audit in the UK.

[89] See Amel-Zadeh and Serafeim (2017), p 87: 'We find a higher proportion of US compared to European investors (22% vs 4%) thinking that the information is not material for investment purposes and that using the information would violate their fiduciary duty (22% vs 8%).'

[90] Schanzenbach and Sitkoff (2020), commenting at p 382: '[…] ESG investing is permissible under American trust fiduciary law if two conditions are satisfied: (1) the trustee reasonably concludes that

assertive stance of the PRI that ESG investing is and ought to be mandatory, the prospects for the PRI's position has recently been strengthened by the stance of the Regenerative Crisis Response Committee, which recommends more explicit recognition of ESG standards by relevant US regulators as a means for the US to 'leapfrog' the measures adopted in other global markets such as the UK.[91] Nevertheless, as evidenced by the 2019 initiative of UNEP FI and the PRI to clarify the legal framework,[92] there can be little doubt that there remains some uncertainty in the US and globally over the extent to which ESG factors can be integrated into investment decision-making.

3.1.5 Fiduciary Duty As a Driver of the Financial Model of ESG

Having identified and evaluated the key elements of fiduciary duty that facilitated the emergence of the financial model, we now integrate them into a more concise statement of our position and attempt to place them in the broader context of the evolution from CSR to ESG.

Fiduciary duty is the key driver of the development of ESG but to date the significance of two aspects of fiduciary duty has been largely ignored. The first is the asymmetry between fiduciary duty in the investment chain and in corporate decision-making respectively. We argue that this asymmetry led to an implicit choice between the financial and corporate (entity) models of ESG because the two forms of fiduciary duty operate in ways that are inconsistent. An important aspect of that choice was the effect of legal uncertainty surrounding the operation of fiduciary duty in each model. We argue that legal uncertainty posed greater risks for the entity model by comparison with the financial model. Furthermore, we observe that while legal uncertainty was clearly present in both models over the timeline of development of ESG, mitigating actions supported the financial model and thereby strengthened its relative attractiveness.

From a broader perspective, several other influences supported the choice of the financial model. In the first instance, the financial model provided a global conduit for investors to influence board decision-making indirectly through the supply of finance, irrespective of the relative distribution of power between the shareholders and the board. That model could likely be mobilised more rapidly and effectively

---

Footnote 90 (continued)

ESG investing will benefit the beneficiary directly by improving risk-adjusted return; and (2) the trustee's exclusive motive for ESG investing is to obtain this direct benefit.'

[91] See Regenerative Crisis Response Committee, Fact Sheet: Modernizing Fiduciary Duty, https://regen erativecrisisresponsecommittee.org/recentwork/factsheet-fiduciaryduty (accessed 15 May 2021). See also the news release from the US Dept. of Labour of 10 March 2021 (https://www.dol.gov/newsroom/relea ses/ebsa/ebsa20210310 (accessed 15 May 2021)) indicating that it would not enforce recently published final rules on 'Financial Factors in Selecting Plan Investments' and 'Fiduciary Duties Regarding Proxy Voting and Shareholder Rights'. The rationale was that these rules created disproportionate risks for ESG investing by pension funds by requiring investment based solely on 'pecuniary factors'.

[92] See UNEP, PRI and Generation Foundation, 'A legal framework for impact', https://www.unepfi.org/ wordpress/wp-content/uploads/2019/02/Legal-Framework-for-Impact_UNEPFI_PRI_Generation.pdf (accessed 15 May 2021).

at a global level than one which had to pay greater attention to substantial differences in national legal regimes in terms of the respective powers of shareholders and directors.[93] Secondly, the financial channel provided exclusive access for shareholders to corporate decision-making, with stakeholders being marginalised, even if they were indirectly the beneficiaries of ESG actions. Thirdly, the entity model would have run counter to the prevailing ethos in the public and private initiatives through which the transformation of CSR into ESG was underway. That ethos focused on the global aspects of sustainability, stressed the common challenges that were faced and the shared responsibility for developing solutions. Finally, innovation in the supply of ESG-themed funds tapped into increased awareness of and demand for 'green' investments without the need to resolve the legal uncertainty issues discussed above. Against that background, an emerging global asset management industry was well placed to align sustainability with its own globalised financial ambitions by taking control of ESG in a way that was quite different from the way it had largely distanced itself from CSR in the past. Proponents of the financial model of ESG could rightly claim that it facilitated the survival and evolution of elements of CSR into a proposition better aligned with global capital markets, but such 'alchemy' as was achieved was only partial and omitted key elements of the older tradition.

3.2 Stewardship As an Accelerator of ESG

We link the rise of the financial model of ESG investment to the emergence of stewardship as a global force in equity investment. In its modern form, supported by self-regulatory codes, stewardship emerged after the turn of the millennium and was linked to evolution in the investment ownership chain driven by the move to institutional ownership and centralisation and digitalisation in the custody arrangements for investments. These influences distanced institutional investors from their clients and raised concern over the extent to which intermediation might compromise compliance with intermediary fiduciary duty.[94] It was against that background that stewardship codes emerged around the world[95] and, as we argue below, provided a conduit for the financial model of ESG investment to consolidate its dominance.

In its early phase of development, the stewardship movement was driven by concerns over short-termism in the practice of investment management and divergence in the interests of managers from those of underlying investors.[96] The perception was that liquid markets often made the 'exit' option relatively easy compared with 'voice', which might well offer better returns over the longer term. Alongside those concerns, the rapid growth in low-cost 'passive' investment strategies suggested that

---

[93] See further Cabrelli and Esser (2018).

[94] See further The Myners Review of Institutional Investment for HM Treasury (2000), https://silo.tips/download/the-myners-review-of-institutional-investment (accessed 15 May 2021).

[95] See generally Katelouzou and Siems (2020).

[96] See the Myners Review, n 94 above; and 'A review of corporate governance in UK banks and other financial industry entities', July 2009, aka 'The Walker Review', https://webarchive.nationalarchives.gov.uk/+/http:/www.hm-treasury.gov.uk/d/walker_review_261109.pdf (accessed 15 May 2021).

the relatively high cost of engagement with portfolio companies and the potential for 'free-riding' might well limit its attraction as a proposition for enhancing returns. Against that background, there was considerable potential for sustainability to gain traction through its focus on the long term and its reconfiguration (in terms of ESG) as a technique for financial risk mitigation.

A key factor enabling stewardship to act as an accelerator for the financial model of ESG was alignment with the shareholder primacy model of corporate governance. As already noted, the transition from CSR to ESG had largely marginalised stakeholder interests and this trend was continued by the rise in stewardship codes.[97] In the UK Stewardship Code, for example, sustainable benefits are framed as the outcome of a stewardship process that creates long-term value for investors.[98] Thus, the role of sustainability is subordinated to shareholder value and its relationship with ESG is surprisingly not clarified, despite the rapid growth of ESG assets under management among signatories ahead of the 2020 revision of the Code.

Stewardship codes have also supported the financial model of ESG investing by linking stewardship obligations to ESG and intermediary fiduciary duty. That link is more evident in general references to ESG factors than it is to explicit recognition of ESG factors as part of institutional investors' fiduciary responsibilities. For example, a survey of 25 codes found that 21 refer at least once to ESG factors.[99] Despite being the originator of the stewardship movement, the UK Code is relatively weak in its linkage of stewardship with fiduciary duty. The UK Stewardship Code does not link engagement with fiduciary duty—indeed the 2020 Code makes no mention of fiduciary duty. Thus, although engagement is one of the main ESG strategies, the Code avoids framing even a soft law requirement for engagement.[100] Thus, the inference seems to be that the UK has a weaker causal link running between fiduciary duty, ESG and stewardship than some other countries. But at the global level, and perhaps most importantly in jurisdictions where shareholder rights are weaker than in the UK,[101] stewardship codes likely did provide some impetus to shareholder

---

[97] The inevitability of that outcome is noted by Chiu and Katelouzou (2018), p 73, who go on to argue that the marginalisation of public interest in the UK system of shareholder-centric stewardship suggests that more regulation is required of the intermediary role in in the investment chain.

[98] Principle 1 of the 2020 Code. See also Chiu and Katelouzou (2018), p 85, commenting on the evolution of the UK Stewardship Code from its previous incarnation: 'The Code [the superseded Institutional Shareholders' Code] has been rebranded into a "Stewardship" code, framing shareholder engagement into an exercise of responsible ownership which connects the private interests of institutions to their perceived socially important role.'

[99] See Katelouzou and Klettner (2020). The strongest stance is in South Africa (Code for Responsible Investing 2011 in SA) building on the PRI, followed by Australia. The survey also found frequent references to fiduciary duty in stewardship codes, prompting reference to the capacity of stewardship codes to 'interpret and extend' hard law, albeit that '[...] from the nineteen codes that explicitly link stewardship practices to the fulfilment of investors' legal duties, only four codes (i.e. Brazil 2016, ICGN 2016, Kenya 2017 and Thailand 2017) clearly regard the consideration of ESG factors as part of institutional investors' fiduciary responsibility' (Katelouzou and Klettner (2020), p 25).

[100] In contrast, the 2010 version of the Code had recognised that activism is a strategy that should be considered by institutional investors in order to discharge their fiduciary obligations to end-beneficiaries. See MacNeil (2010a), p 425.

[101] See MacNeil (2010b), pp 421–423, for a concise summary of UK shareholder rights in this context.

engagement and activism, especially as global investment strategies became more common from the turn of the millennium. In the EU, the Shareholder Rights Directive (SRD) II supported that trend by requiring disclosure by asset managers to clients and public reporting by the client on the use of ESG factors, or not, according to the 'comply or explain' model.[102]

4 An Entity Model of ESG Investing

We now turn to sketching out the contours of an entity model of ESG investing. We frame it within the contours of the standard company form while recognising at the same time that entity design and selection present an alternative approach, especially with recent developments in entity design with a social and stakeholder focus.[103] Although we specify the model by reference to ESG, what we really have in mind is closer to a CSR model, in terms of the criteria referenced in Section 2 and Table 1 above. An entity model of ESG would be a step in that direction. It would alter not just the transmission channel for ESG but also the substance and operation of ESG principles.

The underlying premise of the financial model is that there is no clear or consistent obligation to implement sustainability at the entity/operational level. Once that constraint is overcome, it is no longer necessary to use the financial channel to drive ESG as all funding can only be channelled to entities that comply with such an obligation. Thus, the financial model in its current form is an interim market-driven solution, which responds to legal risk and is a precursor to a more systematic approach at the entity level. This approach would also mitigate greenwashing as it would remain a risk mainly at the corporate level and not have two potential layers as per the financial model (i.e., greenwashing by companies and financial firms respectively) (see Table 2).

Our model combines law reform with a residual role for soft law (especially governance and stewardship codes) and voluntary action (such as purpose provisions in articles and 'say on purpose'). Framing the latter two in a residual role (with priority given to law reform) mitigates the shareholder primacy model embedded in many systems of corporate law, which would stand in the way of voluntary action in some instances, as shareholders would be able to block change. In other words, voluntary change within the current system should not be ignored as the rise of the financial model of ESG has shown that it is feasible. We sketch the contours of the model in the same terms we employed to trace the transition from CSR to ESG in Table 1 above so as to extend the trajectory of evolution in a consistent manner to the next stage.

---

[102] For a concise summary of these ESG-related aspects of SRD II see https://www.lexology.com/library/detail.aspx?g=6dd6ed8f-7c90-49a4-bf87-27e229560325&utm_source=Lexology+Daily+Newsfeed&utm_medium=HTML+email+-+Body+-+General+section&utm_campaign=Lexology+subscriber+daily+feed&utm_content=Lexology+Daily+Newsfeed+2020-11-18&utm_term= (accessed 15 May 2021).

[103] See Brakman Reiser (2012–2013).

4.1 Focus

Following our approach in distinguishing CSR from ESG in Sect. 2.2 above, we use the term 'focus' here to refer to the overarching objectives and key beneficiaries that are embedded in the respective models of ESG. Our proposed entity model would shift the focus of ESG investing to stakeholders. That would occur primarily through the introduction of a duty of due diligence, supported by a stakeholder board committee. We discuss both issues in more detail in the following Section. We view the focus on stakeholder empowerment primarily as a mechanism to drive internalisation of externalities. While regulation (e.g., in the form of carbon taxes or import duties) might also drive that process, we see a role for stakeholder empowerment to contribute in terms of capturing the organisational and operational aspects of a business in more detail than would typically be possible through regulation.

The focus of the financial model on the investment chain as the primary driver of ESG subordinates the accountability of the board of directors of companies for the operational aspects of ESG. Boards are less likely to lead on ESG development in a situation where they lack discretion because of the mandate that is transmitted through the investment chain or where there is no direct consequence because of inaction. That in turn is likely to limit their capacity and inclination to drive internalisation of externalities at the operating level to achieve real-world change. In contrast, the entity model locates accountability more clearly with the board alongside other forms of strategic decision-making. Furthermore, it offers potential to integrate ESG more effectively with remuneration and incentives. Currently, remuneration plans do not necessarily promote sustainable value creation for companies. Various proposals have been made to rectify that situation and ESG-linked remuneration seems likely to feature in the legislative proposal to be brought forward by the European Commission in summer 2021.[104]

4.2 Channel

Shifting to an entity model of ESG would align with a prominent role for a duty of due diligence. Such a duty can be framed as a business process (a procedural requirement) or a standard of conduct (where the focus is on discharging obligations that go beyond internal process) or some combination of both.[105] This provides a more focused and precise alternative to adjustment of directors' duties to encompass sustainability, which might well be frustrated by pressures such as the established norm

---

[104] See the EY Study on directors' duties and sustainable corporate governance, final report (July 2020), https://op.europa.eu/en/publication-detail/-/publication/e47928a2-d20b-11ea-adf7-01aa75ed71a1/language-en (accessed 15 May 2021). It proposes both soft and hard law forms of linkage. For a hard law model linking a specified percentage of remuneration to ESG see Johnston et al. (2019).

[105] Bonnitcha and McCorquodale (2017). Their focus is on human rights, but it is equally applicable in the context of sustainability more generally. See further Martin-Ortega (2013), p 56: 'Therefore, human rights due diligence [...] switches the focus from the risk to the corporation to that posed by those affected by its activities. It goes beyond the corporate governance standard of risk management to include a whole range of purposes: to identify, prevent, mitigate and account for human rights impact.'

Table 2 From a financial to an entity model of ESG

	Financial	Adjustment mechanism	Entity
Focus	Portfolio risk and return, linked to metrics, benchmarks and indices.	Regulatory intervention focused on corporate responsibility, stakeholder integration and remuneration.	Internalise externalities via stakeholder integration. Link ESG to remuneration and sustainability strategy.
Channel	Institutional investors and the investment chain.	*Law reform* duty of due diligence, stakeholder committee. *Soft law* CG Codes. *Voluntarism*: purpose provision in articles and 'say on purpose'.	Corporate entities via board decision-making.
Implementation	Integration into portfolio selection and engagement.	Broader scope (beyond capital markets) and focus on systemic risks. Residual role for 'stewardship'.	Operational focus in ESG implementation linked to 'real-world' effects.
Metrics	Multiple, with different custodians, scope, and legal effect. Limited verification. Ratings add another layer of complexity.	Standardise and integrate with NFR and the sustainability strategy linked to the duty of due diligence.	Metrics become more focused on operational decision-making. Financial market indices and benchmarks transmit the entity model.
Reporting	Two levels of disclosure: corporate and financial channels. Mainly through 5 sustainability frameworks (see Table 1).	Less reliance on reporting/disclosure as the transmission mechanism for ESG.	Align ESG reporting obligations with NFR. Financial channel disclosure then focuses on narrower principal-agent issues in the investment chain.

of shareholder primacy.[106] France has introduced substantive due diligence obligations (going further than mere reporting) with a law known as the duty of vigilance ('*le devoir de vigilance*') where corporations are required to take reasonable care in identifying and preventing risks to human rights, fundamental freedoms, health and safety, and the environment.[107] The EU's recent study on sustainable corporate governance proposed a due diligence obligation and it seems likely that this will be included in a legislative proposal by mid-2021.[108] While the focus has been primarily on due diligence with respect to human rights and environmental obligations (building on models already in place at the global and EU levels), the European Parliament's proposal also includes governance[109] within its remit and covers within its scope all undertakings governed by the law of a Member State or established within the EU.

A duty of due diligence would give more prominence to the role of board decision-making in ensuring sustainable outcomes. We see this as having several advantages over the prevailing financial model of ESG. First, by placing the process closer to the operations of the company there is likely to be better contextual understanding of how they can adapt to a more sustainable model.[110] Second, a mandatory duty provides a mechanism whereby any tendency to prioritise shareholder interest over sustainability can be overcome. Third, a more prominent role for board decision-making opens the potential for more effective stakeholder integration into the process by comparison with the financialised model of ESG. Our earlier suggestion of a

---

[106] See, e.g., https://corpgov.law.harvard.edu/2020/01/07/corporate-governance-for-sustainability-statement/ (accessed 15 May 2021). Examples of this approach can be seen in recent developments in France, the Netherlands and Switzerland, which have all introduced versions of such a duty. See p 104 ff of the EY study (n 104 above) for more details.

[107] See http://www.bhrinlaw.org/frenchcorporatedutylaw_articles.pdf (accessed 15 May 2021). The duty comprises three obligations: establishing a vigilance plan with measures to identify risks; implementation of the plan; and reporting on the effective implementation of the plan. Civil liability for breach of the plan is based on the general principles of tort.

[108] See further the EY Study (n 104 above). On 29 April 2020, the European Commissioner for Justice, Didier Reynders, announced that the Commission committed to introducing rules for mandatory corporate environmental and human rights due diligence, as part of a Sustainable Corporate Governance initiative. The announcement was made during a high-level online event hosted by the European Parliament's Responsible Business Conduct Working Group, during which the Commissioner presented the findings of the Commission study on options for regulating due diligence requirements: see https://www.business-humanrights.org/en/latest-news/eu-commissioner-for-justice-commits-to-legislation-on-mandatory-due-diligence-for-companies/ (accessed 15 May 2021). More recently, the European Parliament's Legal Affairs Committee has supported this initiative: see https://www.europarl.europa.eu/news/en/press-room/20210122IPR96215/meps-hold-companies-accountable-for-harm-caused-to-people-and-planet (accessed 15 May 2021).

[109] We note in principle that the inclusion of governance carries implications for the operation of 'comply or explain' codes of corporate governance in the EU, as a duty of due diligence would represent a form of migration from soft to hard law in this context. See generally MacNeil and Esser (2021).

[110] Compliance with the duty of due diligence would potentially also provide a degree of legal certainty to the board in the context of legal challenges against states and companies linked to sustainability: see, e.g., https://www.jus.uio.no/english/research/areas/companies/blog/companies-markets-and-sustainability/2021/mandatory-sustainability-due-diligence--sjafjell-mahonen.html (accessed 15 May 2021).

stakeholder board committee might well play a role here to fulfil an oversight function or even be required to sign off on the due diligence.[111]

However, we are conscious that challenges remain regarding setting a basis for
liability and enforcement of such a duty, especially if it is to be framed to encompass
standards as well as a procedural dimension. Over time, the use of metrics and targets might provide a basis for liability for breach of standards, but even so, private
enforcement (for example, via the derivative action in the UK) would likely remain
problematic and so an element of public enforcement would be worth considering.[112] However, for the immediate future we would favour a model for the UK that
adopted a procedural approach linked to reporting. We see the key element of due
diligence as being the integration of stakeholder interests and perspectives in board
decision-making. In line with the European Parliament's proposal, a stakeholder
board committee seems a sensible approach and could be linked in the UK context with a requirement to include the operation of the committee in the s172 statements that listed companies are required to produce.[113] Thus, unlike the European
proposal, our model would not make substantive adjustments to directors' duties nor
change the pattern of enforcement to provide legal remedies to stakeholders against
directors, albeit that we do see merit in the grievance procedure in the European proposal (which could be based on a collective or sectoral model) for resolving disputes
between stakeholders and companies.[114]

Voluntary action could also play a role in moving towards an entity model. An
important strand in the current debate is the role of corporate purpose.[115] This has

---

[111] See Esser and MacNeil (2019), p 218, and MacNeil and Esser (2020), p 12. The South African
social and ethics committee (see s 72(4) of the South African Companies Act 2008 and Regulation 43)
is, in principle, a good initiative to give effect to the interests of stakeholders. The role of directors is to
develop and implement a sustainable business model for the company that provides a competitive return
to shareholders. When doing this, they need to have regard to the interests of various stakeholders. By
having a committee that addresses the board on issues that are relevant when making business decisions,
directors should be in a better position to make the best decision for the company. However, there are
various shortcomings and uncertainties with this committee. Its terms of reference are not clear enough.
There is uncertainty as to whether this is a board committee or a company committee and this has various implications. The tension that can be created between the board and the shareholders is also problematic based on the fact that the committee should report back to the shareholders. Despite this, the
aims and functions of the social and ethics committee should at least sensitise the board in respect of
the interests and importance of other stakeholders. See generally on this committee Esser and MacNeil
(2019) and Esser and Delport (2017a) and (2017b).
[112] See generally the EY study, at n 104 above, for a discussion of enforcement options. It is also recommended in the Corporate Governance for Sustainability Statement—https://corpgov.law.harvard.edu/
2020/01/07/corporate-governance-for-sustainability-statement/ (accessed 15 May 2021)—that a national
regulatory body should be empowered to bring proceedings against the executive directors where the
proposed sustainability strategy was not implemented and that resulted in harm to third parties.
[113] See further Chalaczkiewicz-Ladna et al. (2021).
[114] For more trenchant resistance to the EU model see the ICGN response to the EU sustainable corporate governance consultation at https://www.icgn.org/sites/default/files/3.%20ICGN%20response%
20to%20Sustainable%20Governance%20EU%20Consultation%202021.pdf (accessed 15 May 2021). Our
model differs in two key dimensions: viewing stakeholder integration into board-decision making as a
fundamental element of sustainability; and viewing 'comply or explain' governance codes as an inadequate basis for the integration of fundamental elements of governance structure and process.
[115] See generally Ferrarini (2020).

been approached in different ways but a common thread is that companies should define their purpose so as to integrate more explicitly the public interest in their activities and thereby to move beyond a model that prioritises shareholder interests.[116] Voting by shareholders on corporate policy has been suggested as a way to facilitate a broader concept of 'shareholder welfare' that captures the long-term benefits from integrating stakeholder interests.[117] Another, more direct, possibility is to deal with stakeholder issues and sustainability through a purpose provision by embedding it into the governance structure either explicitly[118] or implicitly.[119] It has been suggested that a purpose statement, as being part of the articles of association, can include and refer to the pursuit of social goals, frame directors' duties and liabilities (although this is often already codified in the relevant company law legislation), clarify which matters the board views as material to the corporation and allow the board to pursue long-term strategies.[120] This is already in line with corporate governance codes in some jurisdictions,[121] as well as with rules and recommendations (in hard law and soft law) concerning non-financial reporting (NFR).[122]

---

[116] See, e.g., the British Academy Project on the 'Future of the Corporation' (led by Colin Mayer) at https://www.thebritishacademy.ac.uk/documents/223/future-of-the-corporation-principles-purposeful-business-executive-summary.pdf (accessed 15 May 2021). The research suggests a need to develop a new framework for the corporation around a new definition of corporate purpose. This is their definition: 'Profitably solving the problems of people and planet, and not profiting from creating problems for people and planet'. They produced a set of new principles of purposeful business, focused on: law, regulation, ownership, governance, measurement, performance, finance and investment. Their framework for twenty-first century business is based on corporate purposes; commitments to trustworthiness; and ethical corporate cultures.

[117] Hart and Zingales (2017), p 24.

[118] See in this regard the Roundtable discussion 'Corporate Governance for a Changing World' (2016), p 23, https://papers.ssrn.com/sol3/papers.cfm?abstract_id=2805497 (accessed 15 May 2021). Purpose can be embedded in the governance structure through governance documents and share structure. A potential change to the 'objects clause' of the company could be linked to shareholder voting, i.e., a majority can agree to a change reflecting a broader purpose (see p 24, n 87): 'In UK Company Law, s31(1) CA 2006 allows companies to have an objects clause. Making the purpose explicit in an objects clause has the effect that directors are then under a duty to comply—and the objects clause can be entrenched s22(1) CA 2006 so as to create a hurdle for future changes.'

[119] See here also the reform proposals of the SMART project, proposing that '[b]usiness must shift to sustainable business models and be encouraged to innovate sustainably. To achieve this, the purpose of business needs to be redefined towards sustainability, to protect the decision-makers in business against the pressure to maximise financial returns.' See generally Sjåfjell et al. (2020).

[120] Roundtable discussion 'Corporate Governance for a Changing World' (n 118 above), p 24.

[121] See, for example, the Netherlands and South Africa in this regard (n 118 above); Principle A on board leadership and company purpose in the 2018 UK Corporate Governance Code (2018 UKCGC) where reference is made to 'wider society'; and the blog post by Martin Lipton et al., https://corpgov.law.harvard.edu/2019/10/28/the-new-paradigm/ (accessed 15 May 2021), drawing attention to the alignment of the 2018 UKCGC and 2020 Stewardship Code with the World Economic Forum's 'The New Paradigm: A Roadmap for an Implicit Corporate Governance Partnership Between Corporations and Investors to Achieve Sustainable Long-Term Investment and Growth'.

[122] See further Sect. 4.5 below. We see the use of purpose provisions in this context as an 'add-on' to our proposed model. Purpose provisions, in the UK for example, can be broadly drafted to state that directors should act in a sustainable manner. This approach would be aligned with s172 CA 2006 but require more than mere subjective consideration of stakeholder issues.

Another example of a voluntary (or soft law) mechanism is provided by the new Provision 5 in the UKCGC on workforce engagement mechanisms. It takes the stakeholder agenda a step forward by requiring listed companies to adopt one of three options (i.e., a designated non-executive director ('NED'), a formal employee advisory council, or a director from the workforce) for workforce engagement. Unlike much of the history of the Code, in which the soft law provisions of the Code have generally run ahead of hard law, there is a clear link between the workforce engagement provision and the stakeholder focus on NFR, which has been implemented in hard law. We view this development as a key stage in the evolution of the UKCGC in terms of integrating stakeholder interests into board decision-making.[123]

4.3 Implementation

Implementation of our proposed entity model would have multiple effects. We address here the key impacts that we envisage for the scope of ESG investing, the portfolio effects for asset managers, the 'real-world' impact of ESG investing, and the role of 'stewardship'.

The entity model of ESG would broaden the scope of ESG as in principle all companies and all types of external finance would be covered. And while it is likely that, in line with the NFRD, only larger companies would initially be covered, the scope of regulation could be extended over time.[124] In contrast, the legislative framework in the EU has to date been narrower in scope as it follows the financial model of ESG by focusing on various forms of asset management.[125] While this approach is in principle open-ended and limited only by the type of assets held by

---

[123] At a high level, the key statutory provision providing for integration of stakeholder interests (s172 CA 2006) is focused on outcome: it specifies that the board should consider the relevant stakeholder interests but provides no process for engagement with stakeholders or integration of their interests. The move to Provision 5 indicates a move towards some verification on what is required under s172 (i.e., the consideration of stakeholder interests), thus making provision for a more explicit process for the integration of a (limited set) of stakeholder interests. The shift towards specifying process also represents a move away from the reliance on disclosure as the primary regulatory technique that has been evident in the development of stakeholder interests through non-financial reporting. See further Chalaczkiewicz-Ladna et al. (2021).

[124] The proposed UK model of TCFD-based climate-related disclosure provides a model that is more extensive in scope than that of the EU, albeit limited to the 'E' of ESG, see further https://www.gov.uk/government/publications/uk-joint-regulator-and-government-tcfd-taskforce-interim-report-and-roadmap (accessed 15 May 2021). The EU Regulations referenced in n 125 below generally fall outside the 'onshoring' mechanism applicable to EU legislation taking effect before the end of the Brexit transitional period (under section 3 of the European Union (Withdrawal) Act 2018).

[125] See the EU Disclosure Regulation (Regulation 2019/2088 on sustainability-related disclosures in the financial services sector [2019] OJ L317/1) and the EU Taxonomy Regulation (Regulation 2020/852 on the establishment of a framework to facilitate sustainable investment, and amending Regulation (EU) 2019/2088, [2020] OJ L198/13). A key pair of definitions for both Regulations is 'financial market participant' and 'financial product': working in tandem, they drive the disclosure obligations in the 2019 Regulation and the scope of the taxonomy provisions in the 2020 Regulation. See for 'financial market participant' Article 2(1) of the Disclosure Regulation and for 'financial product' Article 2(12) of that Regulation. The two definitions are functionally aligned so as to capture the products offered by the relevant participants.

the relevant market participants, there are some key financial products that are likely to be either omitted or under-represented. The most obvious and substantial omission is bank loans, which represent a substantial element of EU and UK corporate funding, especially in the case of SMEs.[126] Private equity and hedge fund managers are included as forms of 'alternative investment managers', but that still leaves a substantial gap in the coverage of unlisted companies, especially those that are either family or closely held businesses.[127]

The impact of our proposed entity model can be considered from two perspectives: the impact on a portfolio with some form of ESG strategy; and the impact on the 'real-world' effects of ESG investing. While ESG strategies may mitigate portfolio risk,[128] they may not represent a viable long-term solution in the case of universal investors (such as pension funds). Those investors cannot diversify away from systemic risks such as climate change, inequality and pandemics, and can only mitigate whole-system threats by effecting change in the real economy.[129] Moreover, the focus on portfolio risk/return in the financial model means that there is at best only an indirect focus on the 'real-world' effects (impact) of ESG investing. Thus, it has been found that holding green assets is not a sufficient strategy for generating green outcomes. Taking the perspective of ESG as a 'green' transmission mechanism operating across different asset classes, higher impact is observed in fixed income and private equity, less so in listed equity, despite the latter attracting most attention in the ESG-focused literature.[130] That outcome may be linked to the propensity of

---

[126] See, generally, 'ECB pushes for EU capital markets integration and development', March 2020, https://www.ecb.europa.eu/press/pr/date/2020/html/ecb.pr200303~5eaf4c119d.en.html (accessed 15 May 2021), showing the continued dominance of non-marketable financial instruments in the mix of corporate finance for EU companies, especially in the case of non-financial companies. We note the alignment with the Collective Commitment to Climate Action (CCCA) sponsored by the UNEP FI on the part of some global banks, but it represents less than 10% of global banking assets. See https://www.unepfi.org/banking/bankingprinciples/collective-commitment/ (accessed 15 May 2021). Moreover, since much of corporate lending is a on a 'general corporate purposes' basis, linkage of bank assets with real-world ESG effects is inherently problematic.

[127] Even among listed companies, there appears to be a bias in favour of larger capitalisation companies among ESG rating agencies: see Boffo and Patalano (2020).

[128] Boffo and Patalano (2020), p 10: 'The analysis also found that asset concentration associated with tilting portfolios toward high scoring ESG issuers can, depending on the conditions, affect volatility, risk-adjusted returns and drawdown risk. Various combinations of constructed portfolios based on tilts that provide greater exposure to higher-scoring issuers often performed at or below traditional indices for periods of time. The results are consistent with portfolio theory in that, greater concentration of exposures in a given portfolio can increase volatility, all else equal. On the contrary, the analysis of maximum drawdown risk showed that ESG portfolios have a lower drawdown risk when compared to non-ESG portfolios.'

[129] See Quigley (2020), p 2: 'A positive investment approach, then, eschews stock-picking in the public markets in favour of a focus on primary market asset allocation—flows of new capital to the companies they own—and forceful stewardship within the secondary market. In essence, (S)RI and ESG aim to protect individual portfolios from systemic risks; universal owners aim to mitigate systemic risks in the real world, which has the effect of internalising externalities and protecting the long-term health of the system as a whole.'

[130] See Harnett et al. (2020), see n 47 above.

different asset classes to finance new as opposed to established activities, with listed equity balanced more towards the old.

Compared with ESG techniques focused on the supply of capital (such as the financial model) the integration of ESG into board decision-making would in principle increase the monitoring and intervention role of investors ('stewardship'). This would be the natural consequence of freeing the supply of capital from ESG conditionality (i.e., moving ESG decision-making to the board), with the result that investor influence would in principle have to be channelled through stewardship. Thus, collaboration would be likely to increase, as would collective action by passive and long-term investors to focus on systemic risks (such as climate change). In overall terms, these changes would re-focus ESG on corporate governance at the entity and operational level, a process which has to date been subordinated to the focus on the role of the capital market in the financial model.[131] Importantly, however, the relative power of stewardship as a driver for corporate decision-making would decline if stakeholders were empowered in the manner we envisage.

4.4 Metrics

As already indicated, there is no distinct set of metrics associated with CSR. Most of the metrics are framed in terms of ESG and are aimed at investors. The integration of ESG is often undertaken by reference to ESG ratings from agencies but the consistency and reliability of such ratings is a matter of widespread concern.[132] We do however see a role for metrics in the context of CSR and our entity model of ESG. In particular, the initiative of the World Economic Forum on stakeholder capitalism metrics could provide a standardised set of criteria that map onto our entity model.[133] Although there have been a variety of different initiatives on ESG reporting in recent years, it is notable that Deloitte, EY, KPMG and PwC have collaborated with the Forum in identifying

> a set of universal, material ESG metrics and recommended disclosures that could be reflected in the mainstream annual reports of companies on a consistent basis across industry sectors and countries.[134]

---

[131] But see the (forthcoming) ICGN 2020 CG Principles for a rare example of reference to ESG in the context of CG Principles to be applied by operating companies. UKCG 2018 refers to sustainability but not ESG.

[132] See, e.g., Boffo and Patalano (2020), p 10: '[…] ESG ratings can vary greatly from one ESG provider to another. The different methodologies used to translate raw data into a more sophisticated rating suffer some level of criticism because of the wide variance in the results. This implies that if investors are using and relying on different service providers, the score inputs that shape securities selection and weighting could be driven by choice of rating provider.'

[133] In 2020 the WEF white paper, https://www.weforum.org/reports/measuring-stakeholder-capitalism-towards-common-metrics-and-consistent-reporting-of-sustainable-value-creation (accessed 15 May 2021), set out 21 core metrics and 34 expanded metrics, covering environmental, social and governance (ESG) issues ranging from emissions to social factors such as pay and gender ratios and governance targets. See also Barby et al. (2021).

[134] The WEF framework is the preferred model of the influential Institute and Faculty of Actuaries (IFoA). See IFoA 'The best ESG reporting framework for your business', https://www.rio.ai/hubfs/ESG%

Such metrics would also support the entity model by providing a clearer framework for directors' decision-making as well as the due diligence standard, discussed above.

4.5 Reporting

At the global level, the focus on sustainability led to the development of 'double materiality' as a concept that captured both financial materiality and the company's own social and environmental impacts.[135] In principle that approach is neutral, as between the financial and entity models,[136] but its development in the EU, as the global leader on ESG, demonstrates a clear bias towards the financial model. The financial model of ESG investing prioritises disclosure as the key mechanism for driving the transition to a sustainable economy, based on the premise that the supply of capital would be the principal driver.

Taking the EU regulatory model as an example, this approach led to the development of two forms of disclosure: 'reporting', such as financial or non-financial reporting to shareholders and stakeholders; and transaction or product-related disclosure in the context of financial markets.[137] The earlier approach of the EU, in the form of the NFR Directive,[138] was closer in its design to our proposed entity model in that it focused on the first form of reporting and implicitly recognised the role of stakeholders in driving corporate decision-making towards a sustainable model. Later developments in the EU framework reflect concern that

> non-financial reporting requirements have proven insufficient to overcome pressures to focus on short-term financial performance and to influence companies and their investors to prioritise sustainability'.[139]

That led to some adjustments to NFR introduced by the Taxonomy Regulation so as to align it more closely with the more systematic and rigorous approach to

---

Footnote 134 (continued)

20Reporting%20Frameworks%20Guide.pdf (accessed 15 May 2021), p 28: '[…] we like the WEF framework because it incorporates the most important aspects of a number of other frameworks (CDP, CDSB, GRI, IIRC and SASB) and ties in closely with the SDGs.'

[135] See https://29kjwb3armds2g3gi4lq2sx1-wpengine.netdna-ssl.com/wp-content/uploads/Statement-of-Intent-to-Work-Together-Towards-Comprehensive-Corporate-Reporting.pdf (accessed 15 May 2021) (see Fig. 1, p 5, Dynamic materiality).

[136] See, e.g., ICGN 2020 CG Principles (forthcoming), referencing 'double materiality' as an element of ESG reporting, encompassing the company's own social and environmental impacts as well as how ESG factors may impact the company's own financial performance. This is focused on corporate reporting (entity model).

[137] These two forms of disclosure are embedded in the EU Disclosure and Taxonomy Regulations respectively, see n 125 above.

[138] See n 41 above.

[139] See the EY Study for the European Commission (n 104 above), p 39. See also Hess (2018), p 10: '[…] to the extent that policy makers rely on general transparency initiatives to improve companies' human rights performance and exclude consideration of alternative policy interventions (including other transparency-based regulatory options), they are creating a "transparency trap" that does not further their stated goals.'

sustainability in the latter.[140] But it remains the case that NFR and the later taxonomy/disclosure regimes are not aligned[141] and differ in their respective focus on the entity and financial channels as transmission mechanisms for ESG.[142]

Less reliance on disclosure, and with a procedural version of a duty of due diligence as outlined at 4.2 above, would be an important element in moving from a financial to an entity model of ESG.[143] As a regulatory technique, disclosure has many attractions but also some shortcomings. For example, it is often difficult to report on performance outcomes and easier to rather report on policies and procedures. A company can report on what policies they have in place, but they cannot accurately report on the effectiveness of such policies. Thus, we found in earlier research that the main reason for disclosing non-financial information is purely compliance, while genuine interest in ESG matters is at the bottom of the list.[144] Companies often use the reports as a tool to manage the public's impression of the company (so-called 'greenwashing') rather than to make meaningful changes to respect human rights, for example.[145] Our proposal to expand s172 reporting to include the operation of a stakeholder board committee would not of itself overcome those shortcomings but it would at least facilitate more effective stakeholder integration into board decision-making.

5 Conclusions

As outlined in Sect. 2, we observe that the evolution of ESG over time reveals fundamental differences between CSR, sustainability and ESG. The early development of CSR was marked by a focus on ethics and accountability, sustainability then focused on externalities and stakeholders, while the advent of ESG focused attention on adjusting the supply of capital to reflect risks to portfolio returns. The three strands overlapped to

---

[140] Note in this regard the linkage between the NFR Directive (2014/95) and the Taxonomy Regulation (2020/852). The latter (Article 8) extends NFR disclosure to include the proportions of turnover and capital expenditure linked to activities classified as environmentally sustainable under Articles 3 and 9 of the Taxonomy Regulation.

[141] See recital 25 of the EU Disclosure Regulation, n 125 above.

[142] But the more recent focus on developing an EU sustainability reporting standard to be implemented in tandem with the revised version of the NFR Directive signals the potential for clearer alignment—see EFRAG proposals for a relevant and dynamic EU sustainability reporting standard-setting (February 2021), https://ec.europa.eu/info/files/210305-report-efrag-sustainability-reporting-standard-setting_en (accessed 15 May 2021).

[143] This does not imply that transaction or product-related disclosure of ESG information in the investment chain has no value. It does, but its role should be focused on principal-agent issues in that context (as per Stewardship Codes) and not, more ambitiously, on changing corporate governance to resolve sustainability issues.

[144] These conclusions are based on interviews where qualitative information was gathered from stakeholders on how they perceive and use the strategic report. The interviews concerned two research questions. First, whether compliance with the statutory strategic report requirements provides stakeholders with adequate information to facilitate understanding of how companies integrate ESG issues into decision-making; and second, whether strategic reporting forms a basis for stakeholder engagement. See Esser et al. (2020).

[145] Hess (2018).

a considerable extent in form and function but there remained underlying tensions that made them difficult to reconcile. We argue that sustainability (as the overarching concept) could not easily be combined with both CSR and ESG as techniques for implementation. That led to a struggle for supremacy in which ESG emerged as the clear winner.

We link that outcome to the instrumental role of fiduciary duty in setting the legal framework underpinning CSR and ESG respectively. We highlight first the role of asymmetry in the two forms of fiduciary duty: corporate fiduciary duty in the case of CSR and 'intermediary fiduciary duty' in the case of ESG. The presence of asymmetry necessitated a choice between two different approaches. We argue that greater legal uncertainty in the case of corporate fiduciary duty was a key factor that limited the potential for development of CSR by comparison with ESG. In that sense, CSR posed greater legal risk for directors than ESG did for fiduciary investment managers.

We conclude by sketching the contours of an entity model of ESG investing, which is inspired by the earlier CSR tradition. It includes some key legal reforms, in particular a duty of due diligence, which has already been implemented in some countries, with the EU likely to follow soon. The model includes a role for soft law and voluntary action in recognition of the important steps that have already been taken in that direction by investors. But ultimately, we believe that more meaningful and enduring action requires hard law intervention in connection with a duty of due diligence. Our proposal, framed in the context of the UK system, would avoid the changes to directors' duties and enforcement implicit in the proposed EU model, but could nevertheless drive significant change through more effective integration of stakeholders in corporate decision-making.

Acknowledgements This article is based on our understanding of law and regulation as of 15 May 2021. We are grateful for comments from participants at the National University of Singapore conference 'Sustainable Finance and Capital Markets' on 16 April 2021 and the LSE-UCL Law and Finance Seminar Series webinar on 4 May 2021.

References

Agudelo MAL, Jóhannsdóttir L, Davídsdóttir B (2019) A literature review of the history and evolution of corporate social responsibility. Int J Corp Soc Responsib. https://doi.org/10.1186/s40991-018-0039-y

Amel-Zadeh A, Serafeim G (2017) Why and how investors use ESG information: evidence from a global survey. https://hbswk.hbs.edu/item/why-and-how-investors-use-esg-information-evidence-from-a-global-survey. Accessed 15 May 2021

Antoncic M, Bekaert G, Rothenberg R, Noguer M (2020) Sustainable investment—exploring the linkage between alpha, ESG, and SDG's. https://papers.ssrn.com/sol3/papers.cfm?abstract_id=36234
59. Accessed 15 May 2021

Barby C et al. (2021) Measuring purpose: an integrated framework. https://ssrn.com/abstract=3771892.
Accessed 15 May 2021

Bebchuk LA, Tallarita R (2020) The illusory promise of stakeholder governance. Cornell Law Review
106:91-178. Harvard Law School John M. Olin Center Discussion Paper No. 1052. Harvard Law
School Program on Corporate Governance Working Paper 2020-1. https://ssrn.com/abstract=35449
78. Accessed 15 May 2021

Boffo R, Patalano R (2020) ESG investing: practices, progress and challenges. OECD, Paris. https://
www.oecd.org/finance/ESG-Investing-Practices-Progress-and-Challenges.pdf. Accessed 15 May
2021

Bonnitcha J, McCorquodale R (2017) The concept of 'due diligence' in the UN Guiding Principles on
Business and Human Rights. Eur J Int Law 28(3):899–919

Bowen HR (1953) Social responsibilities of the businessman. Harper, New York

Brakman Reiser D (2012-2013) Theorising forms for social enterprise. Emory L J 62:681

British Academy (2019) The future of the corporation: principles for purposeful business. https://www.
thebritishacademy.ac.uk/publications/future-of-the-corporation-principles-for-purposeful-business.
Accessed 15 May 2021

Cabrelli D, Esser I-M (2018) A rule-based comparison and analysis of the case studies. In: Siems M,
Cabrelli D (eds) Comparative company law: a case-based approach (2nd edn). Hart Publishing,
Oxford

Carroll AB (1979) A three-dimensional conceptual model of corporate performance. Acad Manag Rev
4(4):497–505

Carroll AB (2008) A history of corporate social responsibility: concepts and practices. In: Crane A,
McWilliams A, Matten D, Moon J, Siegel D (eds) The Oxford handbook of corporate social responsibility. Oxford University Press

Chalaczkiewicz-Ladna K, Esser I, MacNeil I (2021) Workforce engagement and the UK Corporate Governance Code. https://papers.ssrn.com/sol3/papers.cfm?abstract_id=3834387. Accessed 15 May
2021

Chiu IHY, Katelouzou D (2018) Making a case for regulating institutional shareholders' corporate governance roles. J Bus Law 1:67–99

Deutsche Bank Group (2012) Sustainable investing establishing long-term value and performance,
https://www.researchgate.net/publication/256048484_Sustainable_Investing_Establishing_Long-
Term_Value_and_Performance. Accessed 15 May 2021

Elkington J (1994) Towards the sustainable corporation: win-win-win business strategies for sustainable
development. Calif Manag Rev 36(2):90–100

Elkington J (1999) Cannibals with forks: triple bottom line of 21st century business. Capstone Publishing, Oxford

Epstein EM (1987) The corporate social policy process: beyond business ethics, corporate social responsibility, and corporate social responsiveness. Calif Manag Rev 29:99–114. https://doi.org/10.2307/
41165254. Accessed 15 May 2021

Esser I-M (2019) Regulating ESG issues: a comparison of South Africa and the United Kingdom. In:
Coetzee H, Fritz C (eds) De serie legenda: developments in commercial law: entrepreneurial law,
vol III. LexisNexis South Africa, Durban

Esser I-M, Delport PA (2017a) The protection of stakeholders: the South African social and ethics
committee and the United Kingdom's enlightened shareholder value approach: part 1. De Jure
50(1):97–110

Esser I-M, Delport PA (2017b) The protection of stakeholders: the South African social and ethics
committee and the United Kingdom's enlightened shareholder value approach: part 2. De Jure
50(2):221–240

Esser I-M, MacNeil I (2019) Disclosure and engagement: stakeholder participation mechanisms. Eur Bus
Law Rev 30(2):201–222

Esser I-M, MacNeil I, Chalaczkiewicz-Ladna K (2018) Engaging stakeholders in corporate decision-
making through strategic reporting: an empirical study of FTSE 100 companies. Eur Bus Law Rev
29(5):729–772

Esser I-M, MacNeil I, Chalaczkiewicz-Ladna K (2020) Engaging stakeholders in corporate decision-making through strategic reporting: an empirical study of FTSE 100 companies (part 2). Eur Bus Law Rev 31(2):209–242

Ferrarini G (2020) Corporate purpose and sustainability. European Corporate Governance Institute – Law Working Paper #559/2020. https://ssrn.com/abstract=3753594. Accessed 15 May 2021

Fisch JE, Davidoff Solomon S (2021) Should corporations have a purpose? Texas Law Review, forthcoming. U of Penn, Inst for Law & Econ Research Paper No. 20-22. European Corporate Governance Institute—Law Working Paper No. 510/2020. https://ssrn.com/abstract=3561164. Accessed 15 May 2021

Freeman RE (1984) Strategic management: a stakeholder approach. Pitman

Harnett E, Caldecott B, Clark A, Koskelo K (2020) Sustainable finance and transmission mechanisms to the real economy. http://ccsi.columbia.edu/2020/09/09/grasfi2020/. Accessed 15 May 2021

Harper Ho VE, Park S (2020) ESG disclosure in comparative perspective: optimizing private ordering in public reporting. Univ Pa J Int Law 41(2), 2019. https://ssrn.com/abstract=3470991. Accessed 15 May 2021

Hart O, Zingales L (2017) Companies should maximize shareholder welfare not market value. J Law Finance Account 2:247–274

Hazen TL (2020) Social issues in the spotlight: the increasing need to improve publicly held companies' CSR and ESG disclosures. U Pa J Bus L 23:740-796. https://ssrn.com/abstract=3615327 or https://doi.org/10.2139/ssrn.3615327. Accessed 15 May 2021

Heald M (1970) The social responsibilities of business: company and community 1900–1960. Press of Case Western Reserve University

Hess D (2018) The transparency trap: non-financial disclosure and the responsibility of business to respect human rights. Am Bus Law J 56(1):5–53. https://doi.org/10.13140/RG.2.2.10315.85283. Accessed 15 May 2021

Impact Investing Institute (2020) Impact investing by pension funds, fiduciary duty—the legal context. https://www.impactinvest.org.uk/wp-content/uploads/2020/11/Impact-investing-by-pension-funds-Fiduciary-duty-%E2%80%93-the-legal-context.pdf. Accessed 15 May 2021

Johnson LPQ, Millon DK (2015) Corporate law after Hobby Lobby. Bus Law 70(1), 2015

Johnston A (2017) The shrinking scope of CSR in UK corporate law. Wash. & Lee L. Rev. 74 1001 (2017). https://scholarlycommons.law.wlu.edu/wlulr/vol74/iss2/16. Accessed 15 May 2021

Johnston A et al. (2019) Corporate governance for sustainability. https://ssrn.com/abstract=3502101. Accessed 15 May 2021

Jones TM (1980) Corporate social responsibility revisited, redefined. Calif Manag Rev 22(3):59–67. https://doi.org/10.2307/41164877. Accessed 15 May 2021

Katelouzou D, Klettner A (2020) Sustainable finance and stewardship: unlocking stewardship's sustainability potential. (An edited version of the paper will be published as a chapter in Katelouzou D, Puchniak DW (eds) Global shareholder stewardship: complexities, challenges and possibilities. Cambridge University Press (forthcoming)). European Corporate Governance Institute—Law Working Paper No. 521/2020. https://ssrn.com/abstract=3578447. Accessed 15 May 2021

Katelouzou D, Siems M (2020) The global diffusion of stewardship codes. (An edited version of the paper will be published as a chapter in Katelouzou D, Puchniak DW (eds) Global shareholder stewardship: complexities, challenges and possibilities. Cambridge University Press (forthcoming)). European Corporate Governance Institute—Law Working Paper No. 526/2020. King's College London Dickson Poon School of Law Legal Studies Research Paper Series: Paper No. 2020-41. LawFin Working Paper No. 10. https://ssrn.com/abstract=3616798. Accessed 15 May 2021

Keay A (2010) The duty to promote the success of the company: is it fit for purpose? Univ. of Leeds Sch. of Law, Ctr. for Bus. Law & Practice Working Paper. https://papers.ssrn.com/sol3/papers.cfm?abstractid=1662411. Accessed 15 May 2021

Leicester A (2013) Environmental taxes; economic principles and the UK experience. https://www.ifs.org.uk/docs/chapter_leicester_uk2.pdf. Accessed 15 May 2021

MacNeil I (2009) Uncertainty in commercial law. Edinb Law Rev 13(1):68–99

MacNeil I (2010a) Activism and collaboration among shareholders in UK listed companies. Cap Mark Law J 5(4):419–438

MacNeil I (2010b) The trajectory of regulatory reform in the UK in the wake of the financial crisis. Eur Bus Org Law Rev 11(4):483–526

MacNeil I (2012) An introduction to the law on financial investment, 2nd edn. Hart Publishing, Oxford

MacNeil I, Esser I-M (2020) The pandemic response in the UK in the context of corporate and financial law—within and without law. https://ssrn.com/abstract=3636292. Accessed 15 May 2021

MacNeil I, Esser I-M (2021) The emergence of 'comply or explain' as a global model for corporate governance codes. European Business Law Review (forthcoming, 2022). https://ssrn.com/abstract=3775736. Accessed 15 May 2021

Martin-Ortega O (2013) Human rights due diligence for corporations: from voluntary standards to hard law at last? Neth Q Hum Rights 32(1):44–74

Moncrieff L (2015) Karl Polanyi and the problem of corporate social responsibility. J Law Soc 42(3):434–459

Palley TI (2007) Financialization, what it is and why it matters. Working Paper No 525, The Levy Economics Institute and Economics for Democratic and Open Societies Washington, D.C. http://www.levyinstitute.org/pubs/wp_525.pdf. Accessed 15 May 2021

Pollman E (2019) Corporate social responsibility, ESG and compliance. In: Sokol DD, van Rooij B (eds) Cambridge handbook of compliance. Cambridge University Press

Quigley E (2020) Universal ownership in practice: a practical positive investment framework for asset owners. https://papers.ssrn.com/sol3/papers.cfm?abstract_id=3638217. Accessed 15 May 2021

Rock EB (2020) For whom is the corporation managed in 2020?: the debate over corporate purpose. European Corporate Governance Institute—Law Working Paper No. 515/2020. NYU School of Law, Public Law Research Paper No. 20-16. NYU Law and Economics Research Paper. https://ssrn.com/abstract=3589951. Accessed 15 May 2021

Rühmkorf A (2015) Corporate social responsibility, private law and global supply chains. Edward Elgar Publishing

Schanzenbach MM, Sitkoff RH (2020) Reconciling fiduciary duty and social conscience: the law and economics of ESG investing by a trustee. Stanf Law Rev 74:381–454

Sjåfjell B, Taylor MB (2015) Planetary boundaries and company law: towards a regulatory ecology of corporate sustainability. University of Oslo Faculty of Law Research Paper No. 2015-11. https://ssrn.com/abstract=2610583. Accessed 15 May 2021

Sjåfjell B, Taylor MB (2019) Clash of norms: shareholder primacy vs. sustainable corporate purpose. Int Comp Corp Law J 13(3):40–66

Sjåfjell B, Mähönen JT, Novitz TA, Gammage C, Ahlström H (2020) Securing the future of European business: SMART reform proposals. University of Oslo Faculty of Law Research Paper No. 2020-11. Nordic & European Company Law Working Paper No. 20-08. https://ssrn.com/abstract=3595048. Accessed 15 May 2021

Stout L (2002) Bad and not-so-bad arguments for shareholder primacy. South Calif Law Rev 75(5):1189–1210

Stout L (2012) The shareholder value myth. Berrett-Koehler Publishers Inc, San Francisco

Publisher's Note Springer Nature remains neutral with regard to jurisdictional claims in published maps and institutional affiliations.

European Business Organization Law Review (2022) 23:47–85
https://doi.org/10.1007/s40804-021-00237-9

ARTICLE

Regulating Sustainable Finance in the Dark

Dirk A. Zetzsche[1] · Linn Anker-Sørensen[2]

Accepted: 13 December 2021 / Published online: 24 January 2022
© The Author(s) 2022

Abstract

Analyzing the revised EU Sustainable Finance Strategy disclosed in two steps in April and July 2021, we identify as core issues of any sustainability-oriented financial regulation a lack of data on profitability of sustainable investments, a lack of broadly acknowledged theoretical insights (typically laid down in standard models) into the co-relation and causation of sustainability factors with financial data, and a lack of a consistent application of recently adopted rules and standards. The three factors together are now hindering a rational, calculated approach to allocating funds with a view to sustainability which we usually associate with 'finance'. These deficiencies will be addressed once (1) the EU's sustainability taxonomy is implemented by most issuers of financial products, (2) several years of taxonomy-based reporting by issuers and originators of financial products is made available, and (3) these data have been used for validating emerging new sustainable finance benchmarks and models for investment and risk management. Until that day (which we expect to be at least 5 years from now), relying on Roberta Romano's famous adage, regulators seeking to further sustainability by legal means, effectively 'regulate in the dark.'

In order to avoid undesirable and unforeseeable effects of regulation, we argue against any regulation addressing capital requirements, mandating sustainability risk modelling or the inclusion of sustainability factors in investment or remuneration policies. Adopting such rules in the current premature state risks that Europe will not be able to rely on the capital markets to finance the sustainability transformation as planned. Instead, regulators should focus on enhancing expertise on the side of intermediaries and supervisors alike. In particular, regulators should introduce smart regulation tools, such as sandboxes, innovation hubs, and waiver programmes benefiting early adopters of sustainable finance modelling/models, utilizing approaches developed in other fields of experimental financial regulation (in particular Fintech and RegTech).

Keywords Sustainable finance · Financial regulation · Data · EU Sustainable Finance Strategy 2021 · EU Green Deal

✉ Dirk A. Zetzsche
dirk.zetzsche@uni.lu

Extended author information available on the last page of the article

🍃 Springer ⬤ ASSER PRESS

1 Introduction

Furthering the transformation of the EU economy into a sustainable one is high on the political agenda. As the latest political commitments underline, the European Commission appointed in late 2019 has promised to implement a Green Deal Action Plan[1] and adopted a Strategy for financing the transition into a sustainable economy in two steps on 21 April 2021 and 6 July 2021 (hereafter Sustainable Finance Strategy),[2] with a view to accelerating the efforts which the previous European Commission had proposed as the Sustainable Finance Action Plan in March 2018 (hereafter SFAP 2018).[3]

This paper analyses what type of financial regulation should be adopted under the EU Green Deal and the Sustainable Finance Strategy 2021. We find that the main issue in regulating financial intermediaries with a view to furthering sustainable finance by legal means concerns in some respects the lack of data on profitability of sustainable investments, in other respects a lack of broadly acknowledged theoretical insights (typically laid down in standard models) into the co-relation and causation of sustainability factors with financial data, and in a third respect an inconsistent and partly incomplete application of sustainability-oriented financial regulation. In addition, we may add as transition risk the unknown impact of rules yet to be adopted and often yet to be written. All of this supports the provocative thesis that regulators, aiming at securing the sustainable transformation of the EU economy, effectively regulate in the dark.

Regulators are (and should be) concerned with how asymmetric information creates moral hazard and adverse selection and how this potentially leads to the mis-allocation of resources and excessive risk-taking that can undermine investor protection and financial stability. For that purpose, regulators must have an in-depth understanding of how sustainability-oriented financial legislation affects the functioning of financial intermediation and investment streams; regulators cannot achieve their mission if they regulate continuously in the dark. This is all the more true if sustainability-oriented financial regulation will eventually guide capital flows into sustainable assets, as a contribution to the transformation of the EU economy into a sustainable economy.

As such, we encourage regulators to focus on shedding light on the darkness. Regulators should focus on the proper implementation of the EU Sustainability Taxonomy, the disclosure rules adopted throughout the SFAP 2018, and focus on where disclosures are non-standardized and patchy at best, such as in the field of the EU Non-Financial Disclosure Directive. Given the lack of a factual basis for regulation,

---

[1] See European Commission, The European Green Deal (11 December 2019), COM/2019/640 final. https://eur-lex.europa.eu/legal-content/EN/TXT/?uri=COM%3A2019%3A640%3AFIN. Accessed 28 Oct 2021.

[2] For a detailed discussion of the European Commission's work programme announced per 21 April 2021 and 6 July 2021, see *infra* Section 3.

[3] See European Commission, Action Plan: Financing Sustainable Growth (3 March 2018), COM/2018/097 final. https://eur-lex.europa.eu/legal-content/EN/TXT/?uri=CELEX:52018DC0097. Accessed 28 Oct 2021.

we argue against any heavy-handed approach meddling with the organization, operations or governance of financial intermediaries *for now*. Any regulation addressing capital requirements, mandatory risk modelling, and inclusion of sustainability factors in investment models or remuneration schemes is premature.

We further propose regulatory steps aimed at enhancing expertise, including (1) the development of proportionate training strategies for intermediaries *and* regulators, (2) where the available data warrant the efforts, the development (as opposed to mandatory application) of and experimentation with investment and risk models, and (3) smart regulation tools utilized in the FinTech domain, such as sandboxes, innovation hubs, and waiver programmes.

The paper is structured as follows. Section 2 summarizes the policy measures taken under the SFAP 2018, which took a careful approach reflecting the uncertain definition as well as the lack of insights about the profitability of sustainable investment strategies. This stance can be understood as a 'nudging' approach—pressing financial intermediaries to deal with sustainable investments through streamlined definitions, enhanced disclosure rules and the notion of unsustainable investments as risk, but refraining from forcing intermediaries to invest sustainably.

Section 3 then analyses what the EU Green Deal and the revised Sustainable Finance Strategy promise to bring for EU financial intermediaries. The consultation on the renewed SF strategy and the AIFMD II review as well as the Sustainable Finance Strategy 2021 hints in the direction of a *mandatory* sustainability-tailored modification to basic financial law principles such as the best investor interest, suitability definitions, portfolio composition, risk management and prudential requirements.

Section 4 lays out that any facts-based approach to regulation suffers from data shortages on the link between sustainability factors and financial performance as well as a lack of theoretical insights (typically laid down in models) into the co-relation and causation of sustainability factors with established financial data. Further, for now the recently adopted rules are inconsistently applied, and will remain so for the next few years to come, until consistent, uniform sustainability-oriented reporting standards have been adopted across all financial sectors; thus, any data-based analysis or testing of new models for the time being will lack a reliable database of at least grossly comparable data.

Section 5 asks what regulators *should* focus on, given what we already know about sustainable finance and financial regulation. It analyses which rules are most suitable to achieve progress in the field of sustainable finance while avoiding unwanted effects when regulators regulate in the dark. Section 6 concludes.

2 The SFAP 2018: A Nudging Approach

The SFAP 2018 aims at a sustainability transformation of the European economy, through essentially the following measures: initial state funding shall be leveraged through financial markets, and this leverage shall be facilitated by measures of law, partly nudging and partly forcing EU financial intermediaries to undertake steps that

could further the transformation.[4] This paper focuses on the legal elements of the SFAP's strategy.

2.1 Six Building Blocks

With regard to legal measures, the SFAP 2018 comprises six building blocks.

At the heart stands Taxonomy Regulation (EU) 2020/852,[5] introducing a joint terminology and standardized approach to 'environmental sustainability'. The taxonomy is cross-sectoral, in that it calls for obedience in all parts of the financial services value chain but also covers issuers of corporate bonds as well as large stock corporations and limited liability companies.[6]

There are also four legislative measures which all aim at enhanced, harmonized and comparable disclosures relating to sustainability.

These measures comprise the following:

- The cross-sectoral Sustainable Finance Disclosure Regulation (EU) 2019/2088,[7] introducing mandatory disclosure for financial market participants and financial advisers on sustainability factors defined by the Taxonomy Regulation (hereafter SFDR) in all EU financial law legislation;
- The revised Benchmark Regulation (EU) 2019/2089,[8] adding provisions on sustainability benchmarks to the EU rules on benchmark providers;
- The proposed revisions to EU product distribution rules (in IDD II, MiFID II), demanding that sustainability factors are considered when the suitability of a product for clients is assessed by insurance distributors and investment firms;[9]
- The proposed revision of Directive 2014/95/EU on non-financial reporting (NFRD).[10]

---

[4] See SFAP 2018, *supra* n. 3, Sect. 2.3.

[5] Regulation (EU) 2020/852 of the European Parliament and of the Council of 18 June 2020 on the establishment of a framework to facilitate sustainable investment, and amending Regulation (EU) 2019/2088 [2020] OJ L 198/13-43.

[6] See Art. 1(2) Taxonomy Regulation (EU) 2020/852.

[7] Regulation (EU) 2019/2088 of the European Parliament and of the Council of 27 November 2019 on sustainability-related disclosures in the financial services sector [2019] OJ L 317/1-16.

[8] Regulation (EU) 2019/2089 of the European Parliament and of the Council of 27 November 2019 amending Regulation (EU) 2016/1011 as regards EU Climate Transition Benchmarks, EU Paris-aligned Benchmarks and sustainability-related disclosures for benchmarks [2019] OJ L 317/17-27.

[9] See SFAP 2018, *supra* n. 3, section 2.5. The SFAP 2018 resulted in two legislative proposals, yet the proposals were not adopted by the old European Commission, leaving this work strand for the new European Commission appointed in late 2019.

[10] See SFAP 2018, *supra* n. 3, section 4.1. A consultation preparing the revision was then performed under the new European Commission appointed in late 2019; see also proposed amendments to the NFRD: Proposal for a Directive of the European Parliament and of the Council amending Directive 2013/34/EU, Directive 2004/109/EC, Directive 2006/43/EC and Regulation (EU) No. 537/2014, as regards corporate sustainability reporting, COM/2021/189 final.

Finally, under the SFAP 2018 the European Commission considers legislative measures on the set-up and operational conditions of financial intermediaries, with a view to embedding sustainability risks into financial intermediaries' risk management[11] and combatting undue short-termism.[12]

Methodically speaking, the Taxonomy Regulation aims at answering the question 'what is sustainability?', while the disclosure obligations shall help identify 'who acts sustainably' or 'which product is sustainable' respectively. Finally, the review of the set-up and business conduct rules shall ensure that financial intermediaries act sustainably, yet the previous European Commission did not present (draft) legislation on this matter.

2.2 Defining Sustainability

While details will not be laid out in this paper,[13] the definition of sustainability provided in Article 3 of the Taxonomy Regulation rests on a positive criterion, a negative criterion, compliance with a set of minimum legal safeguards and compliance with delegated acts which provide for technical screening criteria.

The positive criterion is that a financial product described as being sustainable needs to substantially contribute to one of six environmental objectives defined in Article 9 of the Taxonomy Regulation and in the modes prescribed by Articles 10–16 of the Taxonomy Regulation. This objective could include, for instance, climate change mitigation (e.g., furthering carbon neutrality in energy production), climate change adaptation, or the protection or restoration of biodiversity and ecosystems.

If such a substantial contribution is made, calling a financial product sustainable further requires that the same conduct does not create significant harm ('the DNSH rule') to one of the other environmental objectives in line with Articles 9 and 17 of the Taxonomy Regulation. For instance, if the furthering of carbon neutrality comes at the expense of biodiversity it will not qualify as sustainable under the Taxonomy Regulation.

The third set of criteria is inherently legal. Under Article 18 of the Taxonomy Regulation, conduct must not be called sustainable if it comes with a violation of the OECD Guidelines for Multinational Enterprises (addressing, for instance, supply

---

[11] See SFAP 2018, *supra* n. 3, section 3. The Juncker European Commission collected feedback in consultations. The implementation was left to the new Commission. See, for instance, ESMA's technical advice to the European Commission on integrating sustainability risks and factors in MiFID II. https://www.esma.europa.eu/sites/default/files/library/esma35-43-1737_final_report_on_integrating_sustainability_risks_and_factors_in_the_mifid_ii.pdf. Accessed 28 Oct 2021; ESMA's technical advice to the European Commission on integrating sustainability risks and factors in the UCITS Directive and AIFMD. https://www.esma.europa.eu/sites/default/files/library/esma34-45-688_final_report_on_integrating_sustainability_risks_and_factors_in_the_ucits_directive_and_the_aifmd.pdf. Accessed 28 Oct 2021.

[12] See SFAP 2018, *supra* n. 3, section 4.2.

[13] For a detailed analysis, see Technical Expert Group, Taxonomy: Final Report of the Technical Expert Group on Sustainable Finance (March 2020). https://ec.europa.eu/info/sites/info/files/business_economy_euro/banking_and_finance/documents/200309-sustainable-finance-teg-final-report-taxonomy_en.pdf. Accessed 28 Oct 2021.

chain issues),[14] the UN Guiding Principles on Business and Human Rights[15] the Declaration of the International Labour Organization on Fundamental Principles and Rights at Work, and the International Bill of Human Rights providing minimum standards for labour, work safety and social insurance.[16]

Finally, pursuant to Article 18 of the Taxonomy Regulation, issuers must comply with technical screening criteria issued as so-called Level 2 legislation by the European Commission. These screening criteria fill the broad terms used throughout the Taxonomy Regulation with details; they will apply from 1 January 2022 for climate-related objectives[17] and from 1 January 2023 for the other environmental objectives. For that reason, the European Commission's Technical Expert Group has provided sample tables for economic activities aiming at the furthering of climate change mitigation and climate change adaptation, based on the EU's NACE (*Nomenclature des activités économiques dans la Communauté européenne*) industry classification system,[18] as well as a number of other industry classification systems. This is a precondition for the second step of the SFAP 2018 concept, namely disclosure of three basic figures for each of these economic activities: turnover, capital expenditure (CapEx)[19] and operating expenditures (OpEx).[20] CapEx figures help to analyse in which assets a company has invested and will invest in the future (i.e., in the environmental context, they give an indication of a company's strategy), while OpEx indicates the company's current activities. Turnover is then used as a primary way of aggregating from an economic activity to a company level. The result of that process should be some %-figure indicating the taxonomy compliance of any given issuer.

While starting with climate-related objectives, the four elements of the definition make it clear that a mere focus on climate change is insufficient to lead to the qualification of a product as sustainable. The sustainability definition requires a broader view considering all environmental, social and governance (ESG) factors. This broad approach brings the EU sustainability definition closer to the UN Principles for Sustainable Development which also go far beyond mere environmental concerns. However, it also comes with a challenge: where everything is connected with everything and eventually with financial output, drafting theoretical models

---

[14] OECD Guidelines for multinational enterprises. https://www.oecd.org/corporate/mne/. Accessed 28 Oct 2021.

[15] UN Human Rights, Guiding Principles on Business and Human Rights. https://www.ohchr.org/documents/publications/guidingprinciplesbusinesshr_en.pdf. Accessed 28 Oct 2021.

[16] ILO Declaration on Fundamental Principles and Rights at Work. https://www.ilo.org/declaration/lang--en/index.htm. Accessed 28 Oct 2021.

[17] See Commission Delegated Regulation (EU) __/__ supplementing Regulation (EU) 2020/852 of the European Parliament and of the Council by establishing the technical screening criteria for determining the conditions under which an economic activity qualifies as contributing substantially to climate change mitigation or climate change adaptation and for determining whether that economic activity causes no significant harm to any of the other environmental objectives, published 21 April 2021.

[18] See Technical Expert Group, *supra* n. 13, pp 56-63.

[19] Under IAS 16, a capital expenditure (capex) is a payment for goods or services recorded, or capitalized, on the balance sheet instead of expensed on the income statement.

[20] Operating expenses (OpEx) are shorter-term expenses required to meet the ongoing operational costs of running a business. See Technical Expert Group, *supra* n. 13, p 28.

describing causation and connection between multiple factors becomes an extremely complex and difficult task; further, data shortages in merely one of the many sectors covered by the sustainability definition challenge the validation of the overall model. We will get back to that issue *infra*, at Section 4.

Notwithstanding the former, the Taxonomy Regulation is an ambitious project pursuing a clear vision: if (a) all issuers were to fully disclose data in line with the Taxonomy Regulation, and (b) all intermediaries process these data using models that integrate financial and sustainability data, while (c) their clients (investors or beneficiaries) prefer taxonomy-compliant financial products over non-compliant products, the Taxonomy Regulation would steer capital flows into environmentally sustainable economic activities, as defined by the Taxonomy Regulation.

2.3 SFAP: Unveiling Unsustainable Conduct

While an empirical assessment of the SFAP is not yet available given the early stage of its implementation, we can already identify that the SFAP's main objective is to make sustainable investment 'the new normal':[21] given that from 2031 to 2050, annual average investments between €1.2 to 1.5 trillion will be necessary to meet the '80% greenhouse gas (GHG) reduction scenarios' contained in the European Commission's long-term vision 'A Clean Planet for All'[22] (aiming at a carbon-neutral economy), nothing less will do to achieve these ambitious goals than turning sustainable investments from something niche into the new mainstream. This requires putting EU financial markets in a position where investors have a good understanding of the market's depth and liquidity with regard to products defined as sustainable investments.

To come closer to that objective, the SFAP's core mission is the clarification of terminology so as to ensure that investors can compare sustainable investments and measure their success—by comparing these investments with non-sustainable investments. This addresses one of the main deficiencies in any sustainable finance assessment: the fact that few understand what, exactly, a sustainable investment was,[23] and in turn how profitable truly sustainable investments

---

[21] The European Commission uses the term 'mainstream investment'. For the term used in this paper, see BakerMcKenzie, Sustainable Finance: From Niche to New Normal, 2019.

[22] See European Commission, In-Depth Analysis in Support of the Commission Communication, COM(2018) 773. https://ec.europa.eu/clima/sites/clima/files/docs/pages/com_2018_733_analysis_in_support_en_0.pdf. Accessed 28 Oct 2021.

[23] On the divergence of sustainability ratings, see, e.g., Doni and Johannsdottir (2019), p 440 (arguing on the differences in 'scope, coverage and methodology' among different ESG rating providers); Berg et al. (2020) (on the importance of considering original or rewritten data of ESG rating providers: the same providers may change methodology over the years which can significantly change ESG firms ratings impacting empirical research and investment decisions); Dorfleitner et al. (2015), p 465 (comparing three of the most used ESG rating approaches, the authors find a clear lack of convergence in ESG measurement); Berg et al. (2020) (comparing six of the most relevant ESG rating providers, the authors find evident divergences in 'scope of categories, different measurement of categories, and different weights of categories').

could be.[24] The legal definition of the term sustainability is a crucial step towards comparability, yet not necessarily accuracy. For the purpose of *comparability* of financial products, whether the definition is 100% accurate, and whether the definition leads to truly sustainable investments, is a lesser concern—more important is that the definition is consistently applied throughout the EU financial sector—and potentially beyond.

A second focus point of the SFAP 2018, particularly through the Sustainable Finance Disclosure Regulation (SFDR), is enhancing disclosure. For sure, the SFDR is not lightweight and severely impacts financial market participants and financial advisers which need to review, among others, their risk and remuneration policies as well as amend all product-related disclosures (prospectuses, etc.).

As laid out in Table 1 below, financial market participants (which cover all financial intermediaries issuing financial products) need to reveal whether and how they integrate sustainability risks in their investment decisions and remuneration policies, but also whether and how they consider the impact of their decisions on sustainability factors. Further disclosure items relate to the methodologies used for assessing the sustainability risks and the impact of their decisions on sustainability factors, as well as to reliance on indices and the factual basis for relying on terms such as sustainability and carbon reduction throughout the development, investment and marketing of a given financial product.

If sustainability factors are disclosed in a harmonized, comparable way by the product originators (that is, financial market participants), regulators can then mandate that these disclosures are read, assessed and used in the remaining parts of the financial services value chain. In line with this, intermediaries involved in the distribution of financial products through investment advice and the provision of life insurance products should disclose certain sustainability information to end investors.[25] The SFDR implements this requirement with the same catch-all disclosure approach it foresees for financial market participants (see Table 2).

The SFDR certainly comes at a cost for financial intermediaries given disclosure is never without its financial drawbacks and many questions need to be answered to ensure a consistent application.[26] And regardless of whether the definition applied

---

[24] Regarding divergent results of studies on profitability of sustainable investments (independent of the asset class), see, e.g., Cunha et al. (2019), pp 688–689 (the authors analyze 'the performance of sustainable investments in developed and emerging stock markets from 2013 to 2018' by using 'global, regional and country-level sustainability indices as benchmarks' and comparing them with 'respective market portfolios', and conclude that given the discordant results, conclusions cannot be drawn yet; however, there is increasing hope for investors to obtain higher risk-adjusted returns if engaging in sustainable investments in certain geographies); Friede et al. (2015) (arguing that 90% of the studies surveyed show a nonnegative correlation between ESG and corporate financial performance); but see also Fiskerstrand et al. (2019) (showing no significant relation between ESG and stock returns in the Norwegian stock market); on sustainable investing and higher financial returns, see, e.g., Filbeck et al. (2016) (analyzing socially responsible investing hedge funds compared to conventional hedge funds); on sustainable investing and lower financial performance in mutual funds, see, e.g., El Ghoul and Karoui (2017); Riedl and Smeets (2017).

[25] See SFAP 2018, *supra* n. 3, section 2.5.

[26] For further details, see Busch (2020); Hooghiemstra (2020).

Table 1 SFDR rules for financial market participants

Topic and Article SFDR	What to disclose	Mode
Investment (Arts. 3(1), 6(1)(a))	Policies on the integration of sustainability risks in the investment decision-making process	Website, precontractual disclosure (prospectus, Key Investor Information Document (KID))
Investment (Art. 4(1))	Where principal adverse impacts of investment decisions on sustainability factors are expected, a statement on due diligence policies with respect to those impacts, taking due account of their size, the nature and scale of their activities and the types of financial products they make available (as well as the reasons for doing so if they do not consider such adverse impacts)	Website
Remuneration (Art. 5(1))	How remuneration policies are consistent with the integration of sustainability risks	Website
Financial product (Arts. 6(1)(b), 7)	The results of the assessment of the likely impacts of sustainability risks on the returns of the financial products they make available (and reasons explaining why they deem such risks not relevant if applicable) as well as details on the information gathering and assessment process	Pre-contractual disclosure
Financial product (Art. 8(1))	If a financial product promotes ESG characteristics, information on how those characteristics are met, and if an index has been designated as a reference benchmark, information on whether and how this index is consistent with those characteristics	Pre-contractual disclosure
Financial product (Arts. 9(1), (2), (3), 10, 11)	If a financial product has sustainable investment or carbon reduction as its objective, how that objective is to be attained (including methodology), and if an index has been designated as a reference benchmark, information on how the designated index is aligned with that objective and an explanation as to why and how the designated index aligned with that objective differs from a broad market index	Website, pre-contractual disclosure, periodic reports
Marketing (Art. 13)	Ensure consistency with mandatory disclosures of the SFDR	

Table 2 SFDR rules for financial advisers

Topic and Article SFDR	What to disclose	Mode
Advice (Arts. 3(2), 6(2)(a))	Policies on the integration of sustainability risks in their investment advice or insurance advice	Website, precontractual disclosure (KID, prospectus)
Advice (Art. 4(5))	Information as to whether they consider in their investment advice or insurance advice the principal adverse impacts on sustainability factors (as well as the reasons, if applicable, for not considering such adverse impacts)	Website
Remuneration (Art. 5(1))	How remuneration policies are consistent with the integration of sustainability risks	Website
Financial product (Art. 6(2)(b))	The result of the assessment of the likely impacts of sustainability risks on the returns of the financial products they advise on (and the reasons explaining why they deem such risks not relevant if applicable).	Pre-contractual disclosure
Marketing (Art. 13)	Ensure consistency with mandatory disclosures of the SFDR	

under the SFDR furthers truly sustainable investments, the enhanced disclosure with regard to sustainability factors and methodologies applied by financial intermediaries serves a purpose in itself. These disclosures are 'nudging'[27] intermediaries to deal with sustainability as a topic, as well as investors to consider sustainability to a greater extent than previously—whether a product is sustainable or not will thus be an issue confronting the prospective investor. In turn, they can review whether the product is profitable *and* sustainable, and have all the means to determine their investment preference with regard to those products.

Beyond additional disclosures, the SFAP 2018 refrains from a 'going-all-in' approach. Even if implementing legislation under the SFDR were to ask for a quantification of sustainability risks for disclosure purposes, financial intermediaries would not be required to integrate the quantification of sustainability risks in their risk models. Moreover, the SFAP 2018 refrains from sanctions in the case of an intermediary tailoring its portfolio in entire disregard of sustainability concerns as long as the intermediary explains why it is doing so. Further, its implementation lacks details: in a financial world each risk requires careful considerations on how to manage it, and unsustainable conduct could create risks; yet regulators do not review whether the risk assessment is in fact correct (from their point of view). So far, each intermediary's own view matters—which will most likely result in a huge variety of risk assessments regarding sustainability factors. When it comes to details, the SFAP 2018 remains silent on what conclusions financial intermediaries could or should draw from *particular* sustainability assessments in terms of risk modelling, investment decisions, capitalization, and remuneration.

We do not understand this self-limitation aspect of the SFAP 2018 as a deficiency, but rather as part of its merits: the 'nudging' approach stands in contrast to any approach 'mandating' sustainability—understood as the forcing of investors to invest in sustainable products.[28] As we will lay out below, refraining from mandating sustainability is almost cogent given the current state of ignorance prior to the market-wide adoption of, application of, as well as reporting of data defined by the Taxonomy Regulation.

3 The Sustainable Finance Strategy 2021—What is to Come?

3.1 Green Deal—What Is in it for SF?

Building on the SFAP 2018, the new European Commission appointed in late 2019 committed to an even more ambitious Green Deal in December 2019.[29] Along with

---

[27] See Thaler and Sunstein (2008). See also Enriques and Gilotta (2015) (discussing the function of market disclosure as a 'soft-form substitute of more substantive regulations', dubbed 'stealth substantive regulation'). But see also Gentzoglanis (2019) (arguing that firms preferring a non-regulated or less regulated state of operations will comply with a set of disclosure requirements in order to avoid 'substantive' regulation).

[28] See, e.g., Mancini (2020).

[29] European Commission, Green Deal, *supra* n. 1.

it came an even more ambitious plan to utilize private investments, concluding that efforts must be stepped up and an even more comprehensive and ambitious strategy is necessary.

The EU's Green Deal promises to:

- activate (even) more capital to transform the EU economy, with an EU Green Bond Standard (GBS) at the core;[30]
- utilize public-private partnerships to leverage public investments into sustainable transformation;
- set up additional EU programmes aiming at financing the transformation.

The EU Green Deal expresses the move from a high importance topic to a super-high importance topic on the political agenda. Along with this super-high priority came the need to enhance speed and deliver faster results with regard to the sustainability transformation.

3.2 Revised Sustainable Finance Strategy

The EU Green Deal agenda started with two consultations: the first was a consultation on the proposed review of the Non-Financial Disclosure Directive which focused on enhancing disclosures and rendering disclosures of listed companies on sustainability issues more comparable by implementing the EU Sustainability Taxonomy.[31] While the former is in line with the SFAP 2018's nudging approach through enhanced disclosure across all sectors of the economy, the European Commission initiated a new consultation on the Renewed Sustainable Finance Strategy[32] in March 2020 to identify how to accelerate the sustainability transformation. The renewed strategy shall focus on three items:[33]

1. Strengthening the foundations for sustainable investment by creating an *enabling* framework, with appropriate tools and structures. Many financial and non-financial companies still focus excessively on short-term financial performance instead of their long-term development and sustainability-related challenges and opportunities.

---

[30] See European Commission, Sustainable Europe Investment Plan, European Green Deal Investment Plan, COM(2021) 21 final, p 10.

[31] See European Commission, Consultation strategy for the revision of the Non-Financial Reporting Directive (Feb. 2020); European Commission, Summary Report of the Public Consultation on the Review of the Non-Financial Reporting Directive, 20 February 2020–11 June 2020, Ref. Ares(2020)3997889–29/07/2020.

[32] European Commission, Consultation Document on the Renewed Sustainable Finance Strategy (March 2020). https://ec.europa.eu/info/sites/info/files/business_economy_euro/banking_and_finance/docum ents/2020-sustainable-finance-strategy-consultation-document_en.pdf. Accessed 28 Oct 2021.

[33] Ibid., p 2.

2. Increased opportunities to have a positive impact on sustainability for citizens, financial institutions and corporates. This second pillar aims at maximizing the impact of the frameworks and tools in our arsenal in order to 'finance green'.
3. Climate and environmental risks will need to be fully managed and integrated into financial institutions and the financial system as a whole, while ensuring social risks are duly taken into account where relevant.

The related discussion document raises a number of issues including:

- How to further green funds?[34]
- Should retail investors be asked about sustainability preferences?[35]
- How to enhance consumers' sustainable finance literacy?[36]
- What should be done to counter short-termism?[37]
- Which role does passive index investing play in the context of sustainable finance?[38]
- How to adapt rules on the asset managers' fiduciary duties, the best interests of investors, the prudent person rule guiding investment decisions of financial intermediaries, risk management and internal structures and processes in sectorial rules to directly require financial intermediaries to consider and integrate adverse impacts of investment decisions on sustainability factors (negative externalities).[39]

In particular, the last set of items tests the water for a fundamental policy change. While the SFAP 2018 relied on the idea of nudging, the revised strategy consultation document examines whether a much stricter strategy is feasible: a mandatory push towards sustainability primarily through the means of increased disclosure.

The consultation resulted in a new Sustainable Finance Strategy disseminated in two steps on 21 April 2021 and 6 July 2021.[40]

The four key components announced on 21 April 2021, meant to 'help drive a greener, fairer, and more sustainable Europe and support the implementation of the Sustainable Development Goals', include:

- Enhancing EU taxonomy while allowing for certain investments that assist in achieving environmental objectives that do not qualify under the strict terms of the taxonomy's 'do no significant harm' (DNSH) principle;

---

[34] Ibid., p 15.
[35] Ibid., pp 20, 35.
[36] Ibid., p 21.
[37] Ibid., p 17.
[38] Ibid., p 19.
[39] Ibid., p 33.
[40] European Commission, EU Taxonomy, Corporate Sustainability Reporting, Sustainability Preferences and Fiduciary Duties: Directing finance towards the European Green Deal, COM/2021/188 final (21 April 2021); European Commission, Strategy for Financing the Transition to a Sustainable Economy, COM/2021/180 final (6 July 2021).

- Expanding sustainability-related disclosures by introducing a Corporate Sustainability Reporting Directive (CSRD) and revising the Non-Financial Reporting Directive, so that approximately 50,000 companies will be subject to reporting, compared to 11,000 firms previously;
- Ensuring reflection on sustainability preferences in insurance and investment advice through amendments to MiFID II's and the Insurance Distribution Directive's distribution rules, as a top up to the financial risk-oriented suitability assessment;
- Adding sustainability considerations in product governance as well as financial intermediaries' fiduciary duties. In particular, asset managers, insurance and reinsurance undertakings, and investment firms will need to consider sustainability risks such as the impact of climate change and environmental degradation on the value of investments in their investment decisions.

In this context, the European Commission proposed six Delegated Acts[41] which, if adopted, require sustainability risks to be included in all financial intermediaries' activities and, where required under Article 4 SFDR, to take into account principal adverse impacts on sustainability factors when complying with the due diligence requirements set out in the sectoral legislation. Even more detailed, the Delegated Acts require sustainability risks to be considered as part of the intermediaries' investment processes, their conflicts of interest policy as well as their risk management.[42] These items together are understood by the European Commission as a collective description of the intermediaries' fiduciary duties, broadly understood.[43] In light of these proposals, asset owners and asset managers will have no choice but to include sustainability risks, and when they are larger organizations subject to Article 4(3) and (4) SFDR, sustainability factors as well, into their overall activities.

---

[41] European Commission, Proposal for a Commission Delegated Directive amending 1) Directive 2010/43/EU as regards the sustainability risks and sustainability factors to be taken into account for Undertakings for Collective Investment in Transferable Securities (UCITS); 2) Delegated Regulation (EU) No. 231/2013 as regards the sustainability risks and sustainability factors to be taken into account by Alternative Investment Fund Managers; 3) Delegated Regulations (EU) 2017/2358 and (EU) 2017/2359 as regards the integration of sustainability factors, risks and preferences into the product oversight and governance requirements for insurance undertakings and insurance distributors and into the rules on conduct of business and investment advice for insurance-based investment products; 4) Delegated Directive (EU) 2017/593 as regards the integration of sustainability factors into the product governance obligations; 5) Delegated Regulation (EU) 2015/35 as regards the integration of sustainability risks in the governance of insurance and reinsurance undertakings; 6) Delegated Regulation (EU) 2017/565 as regards the integration of sustainability factors, risks and preferences into certain organizational requirements and operating conditions for investment firms (all proposals as of 21 April 2021).

[42] See Commission Delegated Regulation (EU) __/__ supplementing Regulation (EU) 2020/852 of the European Parliament and of the Council by establishing the technical screening criteria for determining the conditions under which an economic activity qualifies as contributing substantially to climate change mitigation or climate change adaptation and for determining whether that economic activity causes no significant harm to any of the other environmental objectives, C/2021/2800 final.

[43] European Commission, EU Taxonomy, Corporate Sustainability Reporting, Sustainability Preferences and Fiduciary Duties: Directing finance towards the European Green Deal, COM/2021/188 final (21 April 2021), p 13.

The Sustainable Finance Strategy announced on 6 July 2021 integrates the measures announced on 21 April 2021 and complements these measures by focusing on the links between financial intermediation and the real economy. With regard to financial regulation, the following additional measures are noteworthy:

- Improving the taxonomy framework and furthering the financing of intermediary steps towards sustainability, by acknowledging investments crucial for transition and expanding EU regulation on labelling and indices to include new sectors and financial products (Action item 1);
- Enhancing the inclusiveness of sustainable finance by streamlining definitions and supporting the issuance of green loans and mortgages as well as continuing the work on a social taxonomy (Action item 2);
- Focusing on sustainability risk to further economic and financial resilience, by promoting work on financial reporting standards, including sustainability risks in credit ratings, modifying capital requirements for credit institutions and insurance undertakings, and complementing the risk management environment for sustainability risks with macro-prudential and environmental tools (Action item 3);
- Enhancing financial supervision and cooperation among all relevant public authorities to monitor greenwashing and capital flows, furthering knowledge exchange between researchers and the financial industry, and supporting and promoting international sustainable finance initiatives and standards (Action items 5 and 6).

3.3 AIFMD II Review

The consultation document on the review of the Directive on Alternative Investment Fund Managers 2011/61/EU (AIFMD II), which was initiated in October 2020,[44] indicates what including sustainability risks and factors could mean, in practice. The AIFMD II consultation document contains an entire section on ESG investing and sustainability, with reporting to regulators, investment decision and quantitative risk management being the key concerns.[45]

3.3.1 Sustainability Reporting

As to the AIFMR supervisory reporting template, the consultation inquires whether a more detailed form of portfolio reporting, in particular on sustainability-related information, should become mandatory.[46] This could include risk exposures, the impact of sustainability risk on returns, or vice versa. Examples of enhanced

---

[44] European Commission, Consultation document: Public consultation on the review of the alternative investment fund managers directive (AIFMD), 22 October 2020. https://ec.europa.eu/info/files/2020-aifmd-review-consultation-document_en. Accessed 28 Oct 2021.

[45] See AIFMD II, *supra* n. 44, pp 77 et seq.

[46] Ibid., p 49.

reporting obligations include those on sustainability-related data, in particular on exposure to climate and environmental risks, and physical and transition risks (e.g., shares of assets for which sustainability risks are assessed; types and magnitudes of risks; forward-looking, scenario-based data, etc.).

3.3.2 Investment Decisions

Several questions deal with adding sustainability as mandatory criterion to guide investment decisions.[47] These questions lead us to ask, for instance, whether

- regulation should require integrating into the investment decision processes of any AIFM the assessment of non-financial materiality, i.e., potential principal adverse sustainability impacts? (Q91)
- AIFMs, when considering investment decisions, should be required to take account of sustainability-related impacts beyond what is currently required by EU law (such as environmental pollution and degradation, climate change, social impacts, human rights violations) alongside the interests and preferences of investors? (Q93)
- the EU Taxonomy Regulation should play a role when AIFMs are making investment decisions, and in particular those regarding sustainability factors? (Q94)
- other sustainability-related requirements or international principles beyond those laid down in Regulation (EU) 2020/852 should be considered by AIFMs when making investment decisions? (Q95)

3.3.3 Quantitative Risk Management

As a third set of questions, the AIFMD II review asks whether the adverse impacts on sustainability factors should be integrated in the quantification of sustainability risks (Q92).

3.4 From Nudging to Mandatory?

The Sustainable Finance Strategy 2021 and the AIFMD II review bear the same signature: while the SFAP 2018 with the SFDR and EU Taxonomy Regulation as key measures was characterized by enhanced disclosure and 'nudging', the Sustainable Finance Strategy 2021 and AIFMD II—with some details yet to be determined—are harbingers of a heavy-handed mandatory push towards sustainable investment.

For instance, if the best interest of investors is defined from a sustainability, rather than risk-to-profitability, point of view, or at least a combination of the two, we may expect a fundamental change in the discretion exercised by asset managers in investment policies; given that asset management requires procedural guidelines for asset allocation and risk management, intermediaries will need to apply models in which

---

[47] Ibid., pp 77 et seq.

one or the other dimension is prioritized if in conflict. In a similar way, if sustainability risks need not only to be assessed from a qualitative perspective, but these risks must be quantified and the quantification must be embedded into risk models, the investment decision may be influenced as much by sustainability aspects as it is by profitability factors.

Such a step may be justified if incentivizing market actors through nudging has not resulted in a satisfactory sustainability orientation of market actors and financial products. Yet, one wonders on which basis this insight has been created, given that the SFAP measures had not even been fully implemented by the time the Sustainable Finance Strategy 2021 was released? In the next section we will thus examine whether the time is ripe for such a shift from nudging to mandating sustainable finance. We are inspired to ask that question by the joint letter of the three European Supervisory Authorities (ESAs) to the European Commission on the consultation on the revised strategy, issued on 15 July 2020.[48] First, the ESAs proposed to establish a publicly accessible, single EU data platform covering both financial and ESG information in order to grant market participants equal and timely access to publicly reported information. Second, the ESAs demanded the development of a robust and proportionate regulatory framework to promote efficient risk management and a long-term perspective in financial decision making. Third, regulation should aim to ensure that investors and consumers can buy and use sustainable financial products in a safe and transparent way. Finally, the ESAs stressed the need to align EU policy action with that of other regulators and policy bodies active on a global scale, such as IOSCO, BCBS, IAIS and others, to prevent potential negative spillovers from policy fragmentation and limiting arbitrage opportunities.

The difference between the strict approach in the European Commission's Sustainable Finance Strategy 2021 and the four ESA priorities is obvious: the ESAs do not stress the need for including sustainability factors and sustainability risks in all of the intermediaries' activities, nor demand defining fiduciary duties in that light. So, why do regulators with insights from implementing the SFAP 2018 take this cautious approach?

4 The State of Ignorance

To assess the ambitions of the Sustainable Finance Strategy 2021, it is crucial to put the proposed policy steps into the context of sustainable finance research, which is what we know and what we do not know about sustainable finance.

A closer look reveals that the core issue of any sustainability-oriented regulation comprises in some respect the lack of data on the profitability of sustainable investments, and in other respects a lack of broadly acknowledged theoretical insights (typically laid down in standard models) into the co-relation and causation of

---

[48] ESAs, Letter to the European Commission, Public consultation on a Renewed Sustainable Finance Strategy (15 July 2020). https://www.esma.europa.eu/sites/default/files/library/2020_07_15_esas_letter_to_evp_dombrovskis_re_sustainable_finance_consultation.pdf. Accessed 28 Oct 2021.

sustainability factors with financial data. Both together are now hindering a rational, calculated approach to allocating funds with a view to sustainability which we usually associate with 'finance': with regard to the nexus of financial and sustainability factors, a rational, data-driven approach to investing is at its infancy.

Three main factors contribute to this state of ignorance: in some respects the lack of consensus among experts, in other respects the lack of data, and, finally, the lack of a consistent, skilful application of existing tools.

4.1 Lack of Expert Consensus

Research results on some of the most important matters of sustainable finance are inconclusive, probably for two reasons.

First, we often find sustainability experts with little or no finance expertise actively promoting certain sustainable *finance* ratings and portfolio reviews. These non-financial experts are of little help in achieving the consensus necessary for practical applications of *finance* knowledge.

Second, there is a mismatch between the very detailed climate data and the highly stylized damage functions economists write about so as to speculate about how climate change and other sustainability factors alter macroeconomic and growth opportunities,[49] ending up with an enormous variety of results.

The uncertainty extends to the very basics of finance, and thus investment. So, questions unanswered equivocally so far include:

(1) How in detail sustainability and which sustainability factors in particular impact on firm and macroeconomic profitability and in which way;[50] the uncertainty even relates to smaller questions such as whether warm weather impacts on firms' productivity;[51]

---

[49] Cf. Barnett et al. (2020) (assessing models to integrate both climate and emissions impacts, as well as uncertainty in the broadest sense, in social decision-making).

[50] See, e.g., Friede (2020), pp 1276-1278; OECD (2020); further, see *supra* n. 24 on results of studies regarding sustainability and financial performance. Some of the more recent studies include Balachandran and Nguyen (2018) (suggesting a causal influence of carbon risk on firm dividend policy); Balvers et al. (2017) (stating that financial market information can provide an objective assessment of losses anticipated from temperature changes if the model considers temperature shocks as a systematic risk factor); Colacito et al. (2019) (finding that seasonal temperature rises have significant and systematic effects on the U.S. economy).

[51] Choi et al. (2020) (finding that stocks of carbon-intensive firms underperform firms with low carbon emissions in abnormally warm weather, since retail investors tend to sell that stock, indicating a premium for low-carbon firms in that environment) *versus* Addoum et al. (2020) (not finding evidence that temperature exposures significantly affect establishment-level sales or productivity, including among industries traditionally classified as 'heat sensitive').

(2) How investors respond to sustainability risks, i.e., whether there is something like a greenium for sustainable conduct;[52]
(3) Whether investors 'are willing to pay' for sustainable investments, that is, when they forego profits when investing in ESG products;[53]
(4) How investment decisions impact on sustainability factors,[54] i.e., whether investor preferences actually make a difference with regard to de-browning or greening the planet.

The deficiencies addressed by the Sustainable Finance Action Plan so far—the remarkable variation with regard to sustainability ratings,[55] and the lack of conformity of ESG, and that sustainability indices are far from uniform und unambiguous—[56] complete the picture. In line with these academic insights, the ESAs air general concerns about the lack of 'clear and appropriate taxonomy and labels'[57] on ESG terms.

---

[52] See, on the one hand, Larcker and Watts (2020) (finding that in real market settings investors appear entirely unwilling to forgo wealth to invest in environmentally sustainable projects. When risk and payoffs are held constant and are known to investors ex ante, investors view green and non-green securities by the same issuer as almost exact substitutes. Thus, the greenium is essentially zero); Murfin and Spiegel (2020) (finding limited price effects of rising sea levels); Baldauf et al. (2020) (stating that house prices reflect heterogeneity in beliefs about long-run climate change risks rather than the severity of the risk itself). Against Eichholtz et al. (2019) (arguing in favor of a premium for corporate environmental (ESG) performance based on commercial real estate investments); Krueger et al. (2020) (arguing that institutional investors believe climate risks have financial implications for their portfolio firms); Alok et al. (2020) (finding that managers within a major disaster region underweight disaster zone stocks to a much greater degree than distant managers, indicating a bias); Painter (2020) (finding that counties more likely to be affected by climate change pay more in underwriting fees and initial yields to issue long-term municipal bonds compared to counties unlikely to be affected by climate change); Bernstein et al. (2019) (finding that homes exposed to sea level rise (SLR) sell for approximately 7% less than observably equivalent unexposed properties equidistant from the beach); Huynh and Xia (2020) (finding that investors are willing to pay a premium for better environmental performance); Hartzmark and Sussman (2019) (presenting 'causal evidence' from fund inflows that investors market-wide value sustainability).

[53] Riedl and Smeets (2017) (finding that investors are willing to forgo financial performance in order to invest in accordance with their social preferences); Joliet and Titova (2018) (arguing that SRI funds add some SRI factors to make investment decisions, and thus more than financial fundamentals matter); Rossi et al. (2019) (analyzing retail demand for socially responsible products and finding that social investors are willing to pay a price to be socially responsible while individuals who consider themselves financially literate are less interested in SR products than others); Gutsche and Ziegler (2019) (arguing that a left/green political orientation correlates with the willingness to pay for certified sustainable investments).

[54] See, e.g., Busch et al. (2016), p 311 (arguing that the long-term impact of investment strategies may depend on multiple factors and that the consequences of the ESG integration strategies are still uncertain on several aspects). Against Pedersen et al. (2020) (seeking to model the impact of ESG preferences, trying to define the 'ESG-efficient frontier' and showing the costs and benefits of responsible investing); Bender et al. (2019) (analyzing metrics for capturing climate-related investment considerations).

[55] See the references *supra* n. 23.

[56] See, e.g., Jebe (2019), p 685 (arguing on the necessity of merging and harmonizing ESG and financial information disclosure).

[57] See ESAs, July Letter, *supra* n. 48.

At the core of this inconclusiveness lies a lack of broadly acknowledged theoretical insights (typically laid down in generally accepted standard models) into the co-relation and causation of sustainability factors with financial data.

For sure, finance researchers and investment professionals are different constituencies. Nevertheless, the fact that the top finance journals, beyond corporate social responsibility (as too broad a topic to discuss here),[58] so far have published few sustainability-related articles is supporting our claim that a lack of expert consensus slows down the sustainability transformation. As the editors of the prominent Review of Financial Studies stated in 2020:

> Even though questions such as pricing and hedging of [climate-related] risks, the formation of expectations, and financial innovations are natural ones for financial economists to tackle, little research has been published to date in our top finance journals.[59]

A reason for this sorry state may be the long review and acceptance periods in those journals.

In effect, top-rated research often deals with datasets where the latest series is at least 5 years old.

Assuming that at least three years of sustainability disclosures need to be assessed leads us to conclude that the first research on the measures adopted under the SFAP 2018 (with the SDFR, benchmark reforms and the Taxonomy Regulation only adopted in 2019 and 2020, and coming into force January 2022 and 2023) will be available in 2030—which coincides with the year when politics has promised to deliver results. We conclude that at least until 2030, the SFAP measures will lack support by standard models and empirical testing. This means the following: until 2030 regulators will lack a scientific basis for drafting rules and standards; while this is often the case, in principle, with regard to minor legislative steps, the extraordinary risk as regards sustainable finance follows from the fact that regulators seek to transform the financial intermediation function of the whole financial services values chain. The task is enormous, and so are the risks of getting it wrong entirely.[60]

4.2 Lack of Data Linking Sustainability and Finance

For achieving consensus among finance experts, the availability of data is an important factor as this allows for the empirical validation of theoretical models.

---

[58] In the years 2016 to 2020, we identified 39 articles on corporate social responsibility in the top 10 finance journals.

[59] Hong et al. (2020).

[60] The Global Financial Crisis of 2007–2009 was evidence of the large impact of unwanted effects stemming from rules relating to interest rates, mortgage credit criteria, derivatives, securitization techniques and accounting rules on society. Compared to the SFAP and Sustainable Finance Strategy 2021, the rules that may have collectively contributed to the Global Financial Crisis were relatively minor in scope. By that comparison, if the Sustainable Finance Strategy 2021 gets it wrong, we expect value destruction of an enormous size.

A closer look reveals that, while data on some sustainability factors such as climate data are abundant, we often miss data that help explain the crucial link between these sustainability factors and financial fundamentals.[61] This assessment, based on research and the state of the law, is confirmed by the July 2020 letter of the three ESAs:

> The current shortage of high-quality data renders it challenging for both firms and investors to identify, assess and measure sustainability risks and opportunities, therefore, to take measures accordingly. … Moreover, the comparability and reliability of ESG data will only improve if clear and sufficiently granular taxonomies for 'green', 'brown' and 'social' activities are developed and consistently implemented by the financial sector, together with common and uniformly enforced ESG-related disclosure standards for companies ….[62]

We identify four reasons for this data shortage. The first reason is that many entities have not yet reported both types of data in a consistent and periodically reliable fashion. This is partly due to the discretion corporations and financial intermediaries have been granted under the previous non-disclosure regime. Research suggests there is insufficient disclosure as to sustainability factors on the side of intermediaries. For instance, a Frankfurt School UCITS study of 2020[63] showed that 28 out of 101 'green' UCITS did not disclose sufficient data to assess whether they are compliant with the upcoming taxonomy requirements; currently, disclosures on cash flows of the remainder often cannot uniformly be classified by the taxonomy standards. Where important sustainable financial intermediaries do not disclose data, data processing does not result in solid results. In such an environment, we do not even need to think about disclosures by traditional financial intermediaries, such as non-green UCITS, AIFs and investment firms acting as portfolio managers. The ESAs' proposal to set up a single EU Data Platform[64] covering both financial and ESG information, while reducing the costs of sustainability research, will not provide a fundamental change in the short term given that only data *which are reported by issuers and intermediaries* can be made available via that Platform, and only if that happens in a more or less standardized manner will such data be useful for data-driven analysis.[65]

Note that the Frankfurt School UCITS study describes the status quo on the eve of the coming into force of the revised Benchmark Regulation as well as the SFDR

---

[61] See, e.g., Bender et al. (2019), pp 191–213 (reviewing data characteristics for metrics such as carbon intensity, green revenue, and fossil fuel reserves, highlighting their coverage and distributional characteristics; even though the data can illuminate risk factors to be included in a corporate or investment strategy, we lack a financial adaptation strategy building on such data).

[62] ESAs, July Letter, *supra* n. 48.

[63] See Hessenius et al. (2020). 1

[64] See ESAs, July Letter, *supra* n. 48.

[65] This basic insight is supported by research on corporate carbon disclosures. See, for instance, Liesen et al. (2017) (arguing that financial markets were inefficient in pricing publicly available information on carbon disclosure and performance; mandatory and standardized information on carbon performance would consequently not only increase market efficiency but result in better allocation of capital within the real economy).

in 2021, requiring enhanced disclosures by institutional investors and asset managers on how they integrate sustainability risks in the investment decision or advisory process (see Section 2.3). The situation will indeed improve over time; yet this will take time, and improvement will not be noticeable generally and in all respects. For instance, under the SFDR, consistent with the SFAP's nudging approach, even products non-compliant with the EU Taxonomy may be marketed as sustainable—if only the intermediary explains how it got to this conclusion.[66]

The second reason for inadequate data so far is that any study up to the adoption of the revised Benchmark Regulation and the Taxonomy Regulation lacked authority as to the indices and terms used.[67] That is: where data on the past *are* available, they often do not provide the basis of an expert consensus for lack of a harmonized legal framework in place when these were reported. This technical deficiency will vanish over time, yet what we expressed in the context of modelling applies: it will take years before data are generated and reported in the way prescribed by the SFAP measures.

The third reason may be that the SFAP 2018 measures, from a finance perspective, lack additional factors necessary to establish the link between sustainability factors and financial fundamentals. For instance, if the investor type has some influence on the social benefit to be expected, as some research suggests,[68] calculating the impact of sustainable investment faces limitations given that data on investors in and their exposures to a given asset are often not transparent. The EU shareholder disclosure rules on listed companies only provide transparency as to larger institutional investors (depending on implementation in the Member States between 0.5 and 5%). Meanwhile, the Shareholder Rights Directive (SRD) II has increased transparency with regard to the ESG orientation of asset owners and asset managers. Again, the SRD II just came into force in 2019—so sufficient data for empirical testing of models will not be available until 2024—and shareholder data are only made available to the issuer (in contrast to the public). Not even adding the fact that alternative ways to generate exposure to an asset—from bonds, via joint ventures, to certain derivatives—often evade existing shareholder disclosure rules.[69]

---

[66] Arts. 9 and 10 SFDR do not limit 'sustainable' investments and products to products in line with the sustainability definition of the Taxonomy Regulation. While Article 25 of the Taxonomy Regulation inserts some references to the Taxonomy Regulation (in particular the DNSH principle), financial market participants can still include another explanation on how the sustainability objective is to be attained by other means, as long as this information is accurate, fair, clear, not misleading, simple and concise.

[67] See references *supra* nn. 23 and 56.

[68] Chowdhry et al. (2018) (studying joint financing between profit-motivated and socially motivated investors); Barber et al. 2021 (finding that losses due to social commitments vary with investor types, with investors subject to legal restrictions (e.g., the Employee Retirement Income Security Act) exhibiting lower losses than publicly and NGO-sponsored vehicles).

[69] Other lack of data may relate to factors taking place in the future. This pertains, for instance, to political risk such as future rule making. For instance, climate policy uncertainty in some countries (like in the US under former President Trump) makes it difficult for investors to quantify the impact of future climate regulation. See Ilhan et al. (2021) (arguing that climate policy uncertainty makes it difficult for investors to quantify the impact of future climate regulation).

The fourth and final reason is that European politics started to implement its SFAP at the back end of the financial services value chain, while information flows need to start at the front end, that is, the real economy: (1) the SFDR, adopted first in 2019, covers the financial intermediation chain, while (2) Article 1(2) of the Taxonomy Regulation adopted in June 2020 (hence, after the SFDR) covers, beyond financial market participants subject to the SFDR, listed companies that issue 'sustainable' (usually green) bonds as well as large undertakings which are public-interest entities with more than 500 employees during the financial year. Yet, the Taxonomy Regulation will not come fully into force until 2023. In turn, reliable data from the real economy will not be available until 2025 or later. But even then, we should not expect miracles. In the beginning, many issuers will have only partial information at hand, given that the NACE methodology has so far not been the basis of intra-corporate reporting and, further, some data may be impossible to get if part of a group's activities are outside the EU where different laws apply. Under these circumstances we should not expect 'complete' reporting, that is, truly good disclosures within the next decade. At least until the disclosures triggered by the Taxonomy Regulation have reached the required quality, and been tested and adopted in models, the incomplete disclosures of financial intermediaries at the back end of the financial services chain and deficient information intermediation by benchmark providers will render any market-based transformation of the EU economy a major challenge as markets need decent information.

In addition, smaller companies and other important contributors to the 'real economy' such as larger unlisted companies (including firms held by families, private equity investors and sovereign wealth funds) are not covered by the Taxonomy Regulation. While this treatment may be justified politically if these firms in fact 'pollute less' than large firms,[70] from a data perspective the privilege of 'less polluting firms' would result in an adverse selection bias, and as such trigger a potential over-engineering of economy-wide SFAP measures based on these biased data. Furthermore, smaller firms can be indirectly covered due to the fact that eventually all financial intermediaries directly or indirectly invest in such entities and are required to disclose their sustainability weighted portfolio. Hence, an argument for an ongoing nudging approach to those entities not covered by the Taxonomy Regulation still applies if they want to be considered as interesting investment objects in particular for institutional investors.

In this context, it is crucial to speed up the review and expansion of the Non-Financial Disclosure Directive (NFDD) as promised in the Sustainable Finance Strategy 2021. Again, after the review, firms will need time to implement and adjust their disclosures, so the full impact of taxonomy-based information on markets will not be observed, analysed or *understood* until some years later, possibly in the 2030s.

---

[70] See Shive and Forster (2020) (finding that private firms pollute less than public firms).

4.3 Lack of Consistent Application

Regulators have started thinking about how to accelerate data gathering and transmission. For instance, the ESAs have proposed a number of legislative steps all aimed at enhanced, better and standardized disclosures, for instance, through (1) legally binding minimum requirements of what ESG ratings measure and on the related methodologies, (2) EU-level supervision of ESG rating providers, (3) ratings to focus on assessing creditworthiness, (4) developing methodologically robust and reliable ESG benchmarks, (5) specific labels for retail sustainable financial products, and (6) standardization and labelling for green bonds and green securitization.[71]

In light of the data shortage, the ESAs' demand for supervisory convergence is more important than it seems at first sight because the more streamlined sustainability reporting takes place worldwide, and the more third country regulators ask for the same disclosures, the more datafication of information processing is likely to occur and the better this information can be used across the EU/EEA. Yet, regardless of which steps are being taken, each of them will take time and not deliver results until several years from now.

Both aspects together hint at a third deficiency: the lack of consistent application of existing and newly adopted reporting standards. The inconsistent application is to a lesser extent a result of the unfitness or unwillingness of the financial intermediaries, issuers and services providers subject to the new legislation. Instead, the inconsistent application is evidence of the enormous size of the challenge. Consistent application and reporting under the standards just mentioned requires nothing less than:

(1) the adoption of entirely new scoring and reporting frameworks under both the revised Benchmark Regulation (leading to indices aiming at 'de-browning' in pursuit of the Paris Accord) and the entirely new Taxonomy Regulation (identifying 'green' investment expenditures);

(2) the integration of these standards in generally accepted reporting tools and standards (such as IFRS) and other legal measures to narrow down discretion in sustainability reporting to the extent possible;

(3) on the side of reporting entities, the necessity:

- to build expertise and to make decisions accordingly, prior to useful disclosures (for instance, management must allocate different parts of the firm to different NACE codes);
- to have software tools in place that collect, aggregate and report the data requested under the new frameworks (for instance, accounting systems must be adapted for sustainability purposes) in a granular manner;

---

[71] We are aware of other data-gathering exercises by regulators worldwide. For instance, the Bank of England undertakes a large data gathering since 2015. See https://www.bankofengland.co.uk/climate-change (accessed 28 Oct 2021) for an overview of the various initiatives all aiming at adding data-driven insights on sustainability risk.

(4) on the side of information intermediaries (including benchmark providers), the necessity:

- to build expertise prior to the development and implementation of a useful scoring methodology (including the development and testing for consistency of new scoring models);
- to have software tools for data aggregation and analysis in place;

(5) on the side of financial intermediaries (including asset managers), the necessity:

- to build expertise prior to the integration of the scores into investment decisions and risk management (including the development and testing for consistency of new portfolio and risk management models);
- to have software tools for data aggregation, analysis and application in place;

(6) on the side of supervisors of reporting entities, information and financial intermediaries, the necessity:

to build expertise prior to issuing supervisory guidelines;
to develop and implement data-driven supervisory tools; and
to have sufficiently qualified and skilled staff for rigid enforcement.

With regard to all of these steps and all the participants listed *supra* from (1) to (6), the implementing projects have just begun.

In turn, a consistent application of measures just adopted is in fact years away—and equally long will the state of ignorance most likely persist in the absence of uniform sustainability-oriented reporting. Any data-driven analysis or testing of new models for the years to come will lack a reliable database of at least grossly comparable data.

4.4 Regulatory Risks in the Dark

Financial regulation aims, in principle, at ensuring investor protection, securing transparency, market efficiency and market integrity, as well as systemic risk prevention,[72] all with a view to avoiding externalities. With the SFAP as well as the Sustainable Finance Strategy 2021, the EU seeks to make use of financial regulation to factor environmental and partially social externalities into the investment decisions of financial intermediaries. This is not the place to discuss the general difficulties in widening the objectives of financial regulation; suffice here to say that these externalities were, for long, the domain of (other) fields of public law, in particular environmental, tort and tax laws. We stress this aspect to emphasize our main argument that regulators have little experience with sustainability-oriented financial regulation, meaning an increased risk of getting it wrong.

In light of the issues just raised, we see challenges for all three dimensions of financial regulation: sustainability-conscious retail investors could get hurt following

---

[72] See Moloney et al. (2015).

marketing of apparently sustainable products with an uncertain risk and profitability profile to them. Sustainability indices, ratings and other metrics may come to inconsistent results,[73] leading institutional investors towards less standardized and thus less comparable and potentially less reliable approaches. Risks and uncertainties for both retail and institutional investors may undermine societal support for the sustainability transformation. Market efficiency may suffer if, due to insufficient data, untested models and inconsistent application of the law, capital flows to less productive uses. Large-scale capital misallocation based on unreliable models may also destabilize the financial system, for instance, if the pension portfolios of the future are characterized by large-scale, under-performing asset classes due to the unknown financial effects of sustainability-oriented investments. Depending on how large the issues become, they may delay the aspired transformation towards a sustainable economy or even bring it to a halt altogether.

This is all the more so since there is a potential domino effect on the horizon. In other words, more and more legislation and disclosure rules build now on the EU Taxonomy Regulation: the International Financial Reporting Standards (IFRS), the Non-Financial Reporting Standards which the European Financial Reporting Advisory Group is asked to develop, as well as disclosure and accounting frameworks from accounting firms, law firms and other consultants will draw on the taxonomy. If the EU taxonomy turns out to trigger disastrous effects on some parts of the European economy, this could put the whole sustainability transformation project into doubt.

4.5 Factoring in Transition Risk

Beyond the externalities that 'unmastered' financial regulation can create, further externalities that should keep regulators on their toes could stem from the transition towards the new sustainable financial order: managing the transition in the new world of sustainable finance poses a formidable challenge in itself.

Firstly, understanding and implementing the Taxonomy Regulation as well as the Benchmark Regulation and integrating them into disclosures and operating processes, such as investment and risk management models, takes time and money. In particular, small and medium-sized financial intermediaries may well wait until software vendors come up with standard approaches on which to rely—requiring them to first develop, program and market such approaches.

To make the size of the challenge easier to assess, currently only three out of 101 'green' UCITS studied by the Frankfurt School qualify as green under the Taxonomy Regulation. In turn, 98 other 'green' UCITS need to make adjustments. These adjustments are not limited to their disclosures, but rather a huge portfolio reallocation is required. At the moment, given that we have no reliable data on the profitability of sustainable products under the Taxonomy Regulation and we may experience, at least in the beginning, a shortage of assets compliant with the Taxonomy

---

[73] See on governance of metrics Chiu (2021).

Regulation, this portfolio reallocation could potentially result in huge losses for investors. While, of course, this very shortage could also be the reason to adapt to the Taxonomy Regulation faster, this swift transformation may reach its factual limits given the data shortage (see above), in which case the shortage of TR-compliant assets may create opportunities for mis-selling and fraud.

Secondly, the transformation requires the use of new models, many of which have not been tested with abundant data (as most financial models today) simply due to data shortages (see above). To test these models, we need to create data pools sufficient for a 5-years modelling span. Even if we apply some backward testing (hoping these data are available), it becomes apparent that regulators face two alternatives: either they ask for the use of models utterly insufficiently tested when put to use (meaning model risk from bad specifications, programming or technical errors, or data or calibration errors, resulting in the potentially large-scale reallocation of funds into the 'wrong' assets from an economic perspective), or they need to accept that the transformation to reliable models will take 5 years *after the disclosure starts*; the latter meaning operational adjustments.

Thirdly, the EU's taxonomy is in itself untested. Some glitches, such as the notion that weapon production could qualify as sustainable business under the taxonomy, became apparent—and were remedied—during the legislative process leading to the adoption of the Level 2 (L2) Delegated Acts. However, in a piece of legislation as complex as the Taxonomy Regulation other deficiencies will certainly become more apparent over time. The fact that any regulatory command has limits, downsides and deficiencies is nothing new to lawyers. Hence, the larger the scope of a piece of regulation, the greater the need for thorough debate and analysis ahead of its adoption. In light of this, given that the EU Taxonomy and Sustainable Finance Strategy 2021 covers the whole economic sector while the legislative process was short, particular caution is warranted. In turn, regulators should assume that they know less about the unwanted effects of the regulation than what is seen on the surface. Similar to the facts on which the SFAP is grounded, the potentially unwanted effects of the taxonomy lie in the dark. This is also why the taxonomy in itself can best be described as a dynamic disclosure regime where input from regulated entities will support the assessment of the extent to which the goals of the Paris Agreement can be met under the current suggested labels for 'green' and 'brown' activities. When more data are gathered and compared, the measurements in the taxonomy will be adjusted accordingly.[74] Hence, the taxonomy will function as a reciprocal tool that will balance the data received from regulated entities with the overarching goal of securing and not transgressing further planetary boundaries.[75]

The transition risks underline the data shortage pointed out above: no data can yet include all the physical, legal or transition risks that come about as a consequence of the new sustainable financial order because these risks are yet to crystalize. Whether

---

[74] See Art. 20 Taxonomy Regulation, providing a mandate for a permanent expert group: the Platform on Sustainable Finance.

[75] On the objective of adhering to planetary boundaries, see Rockström et al. (2009); Steffen et al. (2015).

the taxonomy will function as the correct tool or restrain the necessary adjustments or the development of the methodology for ongoing adjustments, as the case may be, remains to be seen.

5 Regulating in the Dark

All in all, as an intermediate result, regulators regulate, and enforce the regulations, to a large extent in the dark. Yet the alternative is not refraining from any sustainability-oriented financial regulation altogether; the legislative train has left the station at high speed and any call for a halt is unrealistic and potentially undesirable, given the factual pressure created by climate change and other indicators of a sustainability crisis.[76]

Yet, in light of the darkness surrounding them, we ask regulators to carefully choose which policy steps to prioritize and in which order. How regulators should prioritize and where they spend their scarce resources is the topic of this section.

5.1 Three Principles for Financial Regulation in the Dark

If regulators regulate in the dark, the best advice for them is to aim at avoiding any harm to the sustainability transformation project by unexpected, if not undesirable and unwanted effects of the newly adopted financial regulation and move forward with care, caution and readiness to adjust adopted regulation quickly instead. While responding to uncertain facts with sunset clauses, as suggested by Roberta Romano,[77] has remained a mere theoretical option, the regular 5-year reviews of EU financial law at least enable revisions of undesirable rules when their downsides become apparent; in a similar vein, we welcome the regulators' and market participants' close scrutiny of the new sustainable finance order.

Beyond caution, regulating in the dark requires, from the outset, a focus on illuminating the darkness rather than quack legislation through incorporating experimentation and case-by-case assessments.[78] Further, cost-style comply-or-explain approaches, proportionality clauses and principles in contrast to rules are the preferred style of regulation when regulating in the dark.

We argue that the following three elements of a regulatory policy are suitable to further the cause.

First and foremost, regulators should support all efforts that assist in *creating expertise* on all sides of the sustainable finance value chain, including intermediaries and supervisors alike.

Second, regulators should focus on the *consistent application of existing rules* rather than expanding into new, untested fields. In the context of the SFAP 2018, regulators should focus on supporting consensus and creating comparable datasets

---

[76] Ibid.

[77] See Romano (2014), pp 38–56.

[78] Ibid., p 28.

through disclosure. Any meddling with the set-up and the operating business before sufficient data and models are available risks unwanted effects of regulation.

Third, regulators must ensure they *retain the openness of the regulatory framework to innovation*, given that much of what is known on sustainable finance may turn out, with hindsight, to be a myth, while some myth may turn out to be the truth.

5.2 Principles vs. Proposals

The three principles face repercussions as to whether it is desirable to regulate the organization, operations and prudential rules relating to financial intermediaries.

5.2.1 Sustainable Intermediary Set-up

5.2.1.1 Fitness and Properness For now, financial supervisory authorities assess key executives of a financial intermediary in two ways: whether they are experienced in running a financial intermediary (fitness) and whether they are law-abiding, trustworthy people (properness).

What fitness implies depends on the intermediary—asset management is different from banking and insurance. Financial supervisory authorities will appreciate any executive that has detailed expertise regarding the type of intermediary they are going to work for.

The question is what the sustainability transformation does to the fitness test. At least for now, few executives will be sustainability experts. Yet, over time this question will disappear because if sustainable investment is the new normal, then leading any intermediary will come with sustainability matters on a day-to-day basis. The question then is how to accelerate the transformation.

Should the law require the executives to be trained in sustainability matters or the firm to have a certain number of sustainability experts (similar to accounting experts of today) or should the law, like the UK Senior Managers Regime, require the board to appoint a sustainability officer? The answer is twofold. On the one hand, financial regulation already requires the training of board members.[79] No doubt, these provisions apply to any new development of relevance to the firm. For instance, for intermediaries where technology is important (as is more or less the case for all intermediaries) special care should be taken when training board members and appointing

---

[79] See Title IV of the Joint ESMA and EBA Guidelines on the assessment of the suitability of members of the management body and key function holders under Directive 2013/36/EU and Directive 2014/65/EU (CRD IV and MiFID II), at para. 41 ('Institutions need to provide sufficient resources for induction and training of members of the management body. Receiving induction should make new members familiar with the specificities of the institution's structure, how the institution is embedded in its group structure (where relevant), and business and risk strategy. Ongoing training should aim to improve and keep up to date the qualifications of members of the management body so that at all times the management body collectively meets or exceeds the level that is expected. Ongoing training is a necessity to ensure sufficient knowledge of changes in the relevant legal and regulatory requirements, markets and products, and the institution's structure, business model and risk profile.'). Similar provisions requiring induction and training of the governing body can be found in all EU regulations, see for instance Art. 21(d) AIFMD Implementing Regulation (L2).

a chief technology officer.[80] The same principle applied to sustainability would then result in sustainability-trained boards and the appointing of a sustainability officer.

The risk of quack governance, however, is real. We see other issues of social or economic importance that would also warrant attention. For instance, we could envision a gender officer, a globalization officer, and so on. If we followed through with this approach, the executive suite would comprise a lot of special functions, each with separate agendas. This stands in contrast to the principle that—before and after the sustainability transformation—the board and the executive suite as a whole should have the expertise necessary to deal with important matters of the firm.[81] This is particularly true if sustainable investment is the new mainstream. In other words, the chief operating, investment, risk and technology officers all must understand the implications of sustainability for their business model—*in addition to having solid finance skills*. In creating this expertise, small and large firms face entirely different constraints.

Thus, we propose to encourage creating sustainability expertise on the board as much as the executive level by asking the intermediaries to draft *firm-specific* sustainability development strategies (which may or may not include training and coaching)—yet beyond that, to refrain from details.

5.2.1.2 Governance For several years, an expected or perceived short-termism of financial intermediaries guided EU policymakers' rulemaking. Most notably, short-termism due to conflicts of interests in the asset management services chain was the reason rules on financial intermediaries by way of SRD II were imposed.[82] The same argument now comes back in the context of the sustainability transformation. For instance, the ESAs are of the opinion that,

> [t]o ensure a more forward-looking perspective, robust corporate governance arrangements that support a sound risk management and risk culture at all levels as well as an effective strategy setting and oversight by management bodies are key.

Governance concerns were guiding regulators already prior to the SFAP. Governance rules have been implemented into all pieces of EU financial legislation, starting with CRD IV,[83] but not stopping there. This prompts the question: what more could be done?

This is not to say that a system once adopted cannot be improved. Yet, any regulatory reform in the financial sector should be based on facts rather than politically driven assumptions. In the absence of clear-cut governance failures in the regulated

---

[80] See Buckley et al. (2020a, b).

[81] See Enriques and Zetzsche (2014).

[82] See Ch. Ib of Directive (EU) 2017/828 of the European Parliament and of the Council of 17 May 2017 amending Directive 2007/36/EC as regards the encouragement of long-term shareholder engagement [2017] OJ L 132/1-25.

[83] See Enriques and Zetzsche (2014), p 217.

sector[84] showing deficiency of the fairly new EU governance rules, we encourage the situation to be first assessed prudently *with a focus on understanding the interaction between governance and sustainability factors* prior to regulating in the dark; again, given the fairly recent coming into force of SRD II (2019) any assessment prior to 2024 would be a mere political façade.

With regard to sustainability, a further difficulty appears: the link to environmental and supply chain rules,[85] all of which are currently under revision by EU institutions. Taking the combination of the various rules—company law, financial law, environmental and other ESG rules—into account, the verdict of 'short-termism' cannot be issued without a very careful assessment which cannot start before the facts on how legislation just adopted impacts on markets have been gathered and analysed.

5.2.1.3 Remuneration

Disclosures on the impact of sustainability factors on remuneration policies are required already by the SFDR (see Section 2.3). In fact, EU financial regulation has a history of tampering with executive pay,[86] following the logic that management will follow financial incentives.

However, that logic runs the risk of getting it wrong. Already in the absence of sustainability concerns, drafting sound remuneration schemes is a (legal) challenge. This challenge does not become easier with sustainability due to a lack of historical data, experience and expertise on all sides concerned, including the board of directors, executives and remuneration consultants.

For instance, if management is granted a bonus for a larger stake in sustainable products, we would expect management to shift investments around. Now factor in the uncertainty as to whether sustainable products are profitable and the lack of data which render professional, quantitative investment and risk management a challenge. In extreme cases, if we get it wrong, this could mean unhedged risks and huge losses which, if we are unlucky, could lead to the failure of the financial institution.

These factors together make any cross-sectoral mandatory remuneration requirements regarding sustainability a game too risky to play. After all, financial intermediaries are thinly capitalized, hence the costs of failure will fall on clients, investors and society at large. And in the world of asset management, any management decision directly impacts on the value of the investors' portfolio.

However, we acknowledge one exemption: if an intermediary *organization* (in contrast to a financial product which is already regulated by Articles 8 and 9 of the SFDR) frames itself as being sustainable (e.g., by claiming it is zero carbon) to attract clients, such an organization should penalize managers if in fact the

---

[84] Note that the Wirecard scandal is not evidence to the contrary. Wirecard, under German law, was not regulated at the top level. Further, many important subsidiaries were not regulated. See Langenbucher et al. (2020).

[85] Of course, one could think to rewrite the limited liability rule, a basic principle of company law (or adopt similar radical proposals). Cf. on limited liability in the context of environmental laws, Akey and Appel (2021). But the argument against quack legislation aired herein is all the truer for tampering with basic governance features.

[86] See CRD IV, Arts. 92–96.

organization does not meet the sustainability factors it has publicly usurped for itself (for instance, if it is *de facto* not carbon neutral). Such a penalty would align clients' expectations with managerial incentives.

While the ESAs' letter from July 2020 seems to go further, a closer look reveals that this is not the case: while demanding a robust regulatory framework (which every regulator must insist upon) the ESAs state that

> the work that the ESAs are conducting based on the mandates attributed to them in the area of sustainable finance *may inform further potential legislative changes*. In this context, we note the importance of assessing the impact of newly implemented legislation before taking additional legislative steps.

In simple terms, the ESAs ask for a break to assess what the SFAP 2018 has achieved, to test and to learn in the existing environment. We second that.

5.2.2 Sustainable Operating Business?

A sustainability-oriented regulation of the operating business must be handled with even greater care because of the potential impact on the intermediary's operational results, that is profit and cash flow, and the financial stability issues associated with getting it wrong.

Sustainability-oriented investment and risk models are in their infancy, with multiple questions awaiting answers.[87]

In light of the foregoing analysis, investment and risk management is a field where data shortage and a lack of established models come together. With a reliable data trail missing, backward testing is out of the question. Yet, since supervisors who themselves lack data do not know which model is right or wrong, they can hardly impose or assess details of investment portfolio and risk modelling. This renders any demand for a robust sustainability risk assessment and mandatory consideration of these risks[88] less convincing.

At the same time, keeping the status quo does not seem a sensible approach.

We hold that a prudent approach would ask financial intermediaries to

- consider the risks from unsustainable conduct in their risk management policies *where robust data support the assumption that certain risks could be material*; and
- develop risk models for these cases *for experimental purposes* for the time being, *to model* the impact of sustainability factors on virtual portfolios.

---

[87] See Engle et al. (2020) (researching a model to hedge climate risk, and discussing multiple directions for future research on financial approaches to managing climate risk); Fernando et al. (2017) (distinguishing between environmental risk and 'greening' a firm, and arguing that institutional investors shun stocks with high environmental risk exposure, which we show have lower valuations, as predicted by risk management theory. These findings suggest that corporate environmental policies that mitigate environmental risk exposure create shareholder value, while 'greening' as such does not).

[88] See ESAs, July Letter, *supra* n. 48.

These two steps would improve sustainability risk management expertise in the financial sector proportionate to the improvement of the data quality, yet avoid the risk that enhanced risk management requirements enhance model risk in a world where regulators and intermediaries alike know that the data pools are deficient.

Any mandatory requirement, such as the embedding of a sustainability factor into investment strategies and risk models, must thus be restricted to cases where the data situation *justifies* such a requirement. For the rest, which at the beginning may form the vast majority, a 'test-and-learn' approach is of the essence. That does not mean we are not in favor of furthering sustainability, as a policy objective, and encouraging the link between sustainability factors and finance to be further examined, yet the tools should be such of experimentation and learning rather than mandatory law.

5.2.3 Sustainable Prudential Requirements?

A crucial part for regulating the operational business concerns the prudential requirements, in particular minimum capital requirements, limitations on financial intermediaries' investment portfolio, liquidity or loan portfolio diversification standards, mandatory insurance for certain risk types, as well as other restrictions intended to limit the type of risks a financial intermediary may undertake.

The complexity of building sophisticated sector-wide prudential rules is well known from the several generations of creating and (re-)shaping the Basel rules (in the EU: the Capital Requirements Regulation as well as, in a lighter form, the Investment Firms Directive). These various editions came with several financial crises in between, so caution when amending capital requirements with a sustainability angle is certainly justified. Consider that these experiences have been gathered in light of near-to-complete financial datasets. The same efforts for sustainability factors where we lack these datasets add up to an insurmountable risk. This is particularly true in light of Mark Carney's concept titled 'Tragedy of the Horizon' whereby financial institutions bear the costs of implementation today while benefits accrue to future generations of clients. Allocating costs and setting incentives in such an environment does not come easy.

How to tackle the challenge? (1) Against the learned and well-reasoned opinion of influential commentators,[89] we encourage regulators to refrain from any detailed sector-wide CRR-style rule tied to model results for any type of financial services for now. (2) At the same time, regulators should ask financial intermediaries to develop their own models to the extent that the data quality on certain sectors allows it, and capitalize risks on a case-by-case basis. Such model development should be both supported and scrutinized by standard setters and financial services authorities, so that the limits of these models as well as how one model outcome compares to another is well understood. For instance, an insurance company covering storm risks should slowly but surely increase risk provisioning; a bank engaging with clients whose main business relates to oil should take into account the effects of

---

[89] See the discussion in Alexander and Fisher (2019), pp 15–20 (arguing that sustainability risks, collectively, are of systemic dimensions); see also Alexander (2014), pp 16–17.

environmental legislation and taxation on their clients' business; and an asset manager investing in real estate in the Maldives should consider the rising sea level. All this factoring in of sustainability risk is necessary and sound, and already provided for in Article 3 SFDR as well as sectoral risk management rules. In particular, banks should consider sustainability risks in their Own Risk Assessments as part of the Internal Capital Adequacy Assessment Process (ICAAP), while regulators are encouraged to enforce these rules on a case-by-case basis, utilizing institution-specific reviews and, where necessary, capital surcharges based on CRR Pillars 2 and 3 to cover additional sustainability risks. Regulators seeking to avoid the large-scale impact of sustainability risks on financial institutions[90] have already quite a strong position utilizing existing risk management rules.[91]

Beyond that, regulators should refrain from tying mandatory capital surcharges to unsustainable products and services for the time being; this is not a sign of disrespect of the importance of sustainability, but rather—in line with a market-based transformation—markets first need time to figure out how to combine sustainability and profitability. As was pointed out above (Sect. 4.1) it will take some years to understand that nexus properly; drafting rules prior to understanding this nexus represents regulatory hazard. In a world where for the most part pension funds and other intermediaries serving retail beneficiaries provide the funding, only a *profitable* market-based sustainability strategy is truly sustainable.

Again, we encourage regulators to wait until we have insights as to where this learning curve leads to, and focus on disclosure and facilitating experimentation instead.

5.3 Enhancing 'Test-and-Learn' Through Smart Regulation

The common conclusion of our view on the three fields—intermediary set-up, operations and prudential rules—is that regulators should, first, implement the taxonomy across sectors, second, ensure reporting based on that taxonomy, third, collect data (and ensure data platforms, comparability, etc.), fourth, assess data with some representative time series, and *finally*, draft rules and standards on the organization, operations and prudential requirements of intermediaries.

However, until that date, regulators should not sit idle, but are best advised to further a 'test-and-learn' approach across the financial industry with regard to all aspects of sustainability risks and impacts of finance on sustainability factors.

With regard to furthering experimentation, regulating sustainability innovation is not entirely different from regulating other innovations, such as financial and regulatory technologies (FinTech and RegTech), for which the need for smart regulation where regulators retain flexibility and openness to innovation while keeping risks

---

[90] See Alexander and Fisher (2019), pp 7–34 (arguing that sustainability risks, collectively, are of systemic dimensions).

[91] See Kivisaari (2021), pp 88–91, 98–100. See also Alexander (2014).

under control, is recognized.[92] This is particularly true given that the level of uncertainty and the dynamics of change/progress are similarly pronounced in the area of sustainable investing and FinTech. In turn, the regulatory challenges seem, to some extent, quite comparable. Waiver programmes, sustainability innovation hubs, regulatory sandboxes and partnerships between financial intermediaries (as experts in finance) and sustainability research centres could work particularly well for certain sustainability matters where regulators and intermediaries lack experience, including risk models, remuneration schemes and portfolio composition.

Such tools could be implemented to benefit early adopters of sustainable finance modelling, under the condition that the elements underlying the models are made available to the public to incentivize the experts' discussion. In a similar vein, regulators could grant some leeway for various modes of portfolio compositions in terms of investment limits or the provision of new types of sustainability data (previously undisclosed), and even grant prudential benefits for firms that come up with innovative, theoretically grounded models of sustainability risk, as long as these models are being made available to the public to ensure sound discussion among experts.

While many of these approaches will not stand the test of time, the more experts discuss approaches and the more data are being reported which may be included in modelling, the faster we expect the data gap to be closed, risk, governance and remuneration models to be developed, and the consensus to be established that is necessary to make sustainable finance the new mainstream.

6 Conclusion

Sustainable investments are of paramount importance to ensure the sustainability transformation of the European economy. Yet, at the moment we lack, in some respects, data, in other respects, broadly acknowledged theoretical insights (typically laid down in standard models) on the co-relation and causation of sustainability factors with financial data, and, in a third respect, a consistent application of recently adopted sustainability disclosure rules. The three together are now hindering a rational, calculated approach to allocating funds with a view to sustainability which we usually associate with 'finance'. With regard to the nexus of financial and sustainability factors a rational, data-driven approach to investing is at its infancy.

While the Taxonomy Regulation's definition of sustainable investments creates legal certainty and can lead to comparability of sustainability-related disclosures, the implementation of the taxonomy resulting in valuable datasets necessary for empirical assessment and financial modelling will require years. Prior to the availability of these datasets, financial market participants, regulators and investors are subject to transition risk at an enormous scale, given that much of the sustainability agenda within the EU financial markets stands on hollow ground, meaning its

---

[92] Cf. Brummer and Yadav (2019), pp 248–249 (arguing that innovation poses a challenge for regulators since regulators are expected to warrant financial innovation, simple rules and market integrity at the same time, with limited resources); Zetzsche et al. (2017); Buckley et al. (2020a, b); Zetzsche et al. (2020); Enriques and Ringe (2020).

regulatory premises are not data-driven, but rather policy-driven. We thus welcome that the first step of the EU's sustainability agenda focuses on defining sustainable investments, enhancing comparability and sustainability-related disclosures, as these measures all address the core issue in sustainable finance: the lack of data. We also applaud that the SFAP 2018 does not go beyond 'nudging', that is encouraging sustainable investments, without forcing investors towards sustainability in circumstances where the profitability of sustainable investments and the link between sustainability factors and financial factors is not sufficiently understood. A large-scale, long-term *unprofitable* sustainable investment is in itself unsustainable.

Important for the future regulatory strategy is the insight that the effects of the SFAP 2018 have not yet been absorbed. Important building blocks such as the Taxonomy Regulation have just been adopted and in many cases are not yet in force. Despite major investments on all sides, regulators and financial intermediaries are at the early stage of understanding and applying the taxonomy. Even in the best of all possible scenarios, the full absorption of the taxonomy in data creation, financial modelling, testing and transposition in lending and investment strategies will take years.

Yet, the same data shortage that has hindered investors to assess and identify sustainable *and* profitable products also prevents financial supervisory authorities from applying a prudent *mandatory* regulatory strategy: if a regulator cannot identify a conduct as 'right', that is where regulators effectively fly in the dark, and it is unwise to prohibit certain other conduct by naming it 'wrong', as the latter would reduce the options for diversification and increase the risk of unwanted effects.

In turn, sustainable regulation of sustainable finance must aim at generating data and expertise on sustainability factors and sustainable products on the side of both regulators and financial intermediaries, in an effort to prepare the ground for a mature and profitable sustainable investment market. For this purpose, we encourage learning from regulating financial technologies (FinTech), where the same issue is prevalent and a number of pro-innovative 'smart regulation' tools have been adopted, such as waiver programmes, regulatory sandboxes, innovation hubs, and restricted licenses. Besides efforts aiming at generating expertise and data, regulators must refrain from meddling with the organization and operating business of intermediaries for now. Fields particularly vulnerable to quack regulation include the following: (a) remuneration models, (b) investment strategies, and (c) prudential rules, including politically driven capital surcharges for unsustainable investments.

Acknowledgements The authors thank Kern Alexander, Michael Halling, Michael Hanke, Andreas Hoepner, Robert Palantano, Maria Lucia Passador, Beate Sjåfjell, Jukka Tapio Mähönen and participants of conferences at the Universities of Geneva, Luxembourg, Oslo and Zürich for comments and remarks on earlier drafts. The authors are grateful for diligent research assistance provided by Roberta Consiglio.

References

Addoum JM, Ng DT, Ortiz-Bobea A (2020) Temperature shocks and establishment sales. Rev Fin St 33:1331–1366. https://doi.org/10.1093/rfs/hhz126. Accessed 28 Oct 2021

Akey P, Appel I (2021) The limits of limited liability: evidence from industrial pollution. J Fin 76:5–55. https://doi.org/10.1111/jofi.12978. Accessed 28 Oct 2021

Alexander K (2014) Stability and sustainability in banking reform: are environmental risks missing in Basel III? UNEP, Cambridge

Alexander K, Fisher P (2019) Banking regulation and sustainability. In: van den Boezem F-JB, Jansen C, Schuijling B (eds) Sustainability and financial markets. Wolters Kluwer, Deventer, pp 7–34

Alok S, Kumar N, Wermers R (2020) Do fund managers misestimate climatic disaster risk. Rev Fin St 33:1146–1183. https://doi.org/10.1093/rfs/hhz143. Accessed 28 Oct 2021

Balachandran B, Nguyen JH (2018) Does carbon risk matter in firm dividend policy? Evidence from a quasi-natural experiment in an imputation environment. J Bank Fin 96:249–267. https://doi.org/10.1016/j.jbankfin.2018.09.015

Baldauf M, Garlappi L, Yannelis C (2020) Does climate change affect real estate prices? Only if you believe in it. Rev Fin St 33:1256–1295. https://doi.org/10.1093/rfs/hhz073

Balvers R, Du D, Xiaobing Z (2017) Temperature shocks and the cost of equity capital: implications for climate change perceptions. J Bank Fin 77:18–34. https://doi.org/10.1016/j.jbankfin.2016.12.013. Accessed 28 Oct 2021

Barber BM, Morse A, Yasuda A (2021) Impact investing. J Fin Econ 139:162–185. https://doi.org/10.1016/j.jfineco.2020.07.008. Accessed 28 Oct 2021

Barnett M, Brock W, Hansen LP (2020) Pricing uncertainty induced by climate change. Rev Fin St 33:1024–1066. https://doi.org/10.1093/rfs/hhz144. Accessed 28 Oct 2021

Bender J, Bridges TA, Shah K (2019) Reinventing climate investing: building equity portfolios for climate risk mitigation and adaptation. J Sustain Fin Invest 9(3):191–213

Berg F, Koelbel JF, Rigobon R (2020) Aggregate confusion: the divergence of ESG ratings. MIT Sloan School, Working Paper 5822-19. https://papers.ssrn.com/sol3/papers.cfm?abstract_id=3438533

Berg F et al. (2020) Rewriting history II: the (un)predictable past of ESG ratings. ECGI Finance Working Paper 708/2020. http://ssrn.com/abstract_id=3722087. Accessed 28 Oct 2021

Bernstein A, Gustafson MT, Lewis R (2019) Disaster on the horizon: the price effect of sea level rise. J Fin Econ 134:253–272. https://doi.org/10.1016/j.jfineco.2019.03.013. Accessed 28 Oct 2021

Brummer C, Yadav Y (2019) Fintech and the innovation trilemma. Geo LJ 107:235–307

Buckley RP, Arner DW, Veidt R, Zetzsche DA (2020a) Building FinTech ecosystems: regulatory sandboxes, innovation hubs and beyond. Wash U J Law & Pol'y 61:55–98

Buckley RP, Arner DW, Zetzsche DA, Selga E (2020b) Techrisk. Sing JLS, pp 35–62

Busch T et al. (2016) Sustainable development and financial markets: old paths and new avenues. Bus Soc 5:303–329. https://doi.org/10.1177/0007650315570701

Busch D (2020) Sustainability disclosure in the EU financial sector. European Banking Institute Working Paper Series 70/2020. https://ssrn.com/abstract=3650407. Accessed 28 Oct 2021

Chiu IHY (2021) The EU sustainable finance agenda—developing governance for double materiality in sustainability metrics. Eur Bus Organ Law Rev (this volume)

Choi D, Gao Z, Jiang W (2020) Attention to global warming. Rev Fin St 33:1112–1145. https://doi.org/10.1093/rfs/hhz086. Accessed 28 Oct 2021

Chowdhry B, Davies SW, Waters B (2018) Investing for impact. Rev Fin St 32:864–904. https://doi.org/10.1093/rfs/hhy068. Accessed 28 Oct 2021

Colacito R, Hoffmann B, Phan T (2019) Temperature and growth: a panel analysis of the United States. J Money Credit Bank 51:313–368. https://doi.org/10.1111/jmcb.12574. Accessed 28 Oct 2021

Cunha FAFDS et al. (2019) Can sustainable investments outperform traditional benchmarks? Evidence from global stock markets. Bus Strategy Environ 29:682–697

Doni F, Johannsdottir L (2019) Environmental social and governance (ESG) ratings. In: Filho WL, Azul AM, Brandli L, Özuyar PG, Tony W (eds) Climate action. Encyclopedia of the UN Sustainable Development Goals. Springer, Cham, pp 435–449. https://doi.org/10.1007/978-3-319-95885-9_36. Accessed 28 Oct 2021

Dorfleitner G, Halbritter G, Nguyen M (2015) Measuring the level and risk of corporate responsibility—an empirical comparison of different ESG rating approaches. J Asset Manag 16:450–466. https://doi.org/10.1057/jam.2015.31

Eichholtz P, Holtermans R, Kok N, Yönder E (2019) Environmental performance and the cost of debt: evidence from commercial mortgages and REIT bonds. J Bank Fin 102:19–32. https://doi.org/10.1016/j.jbankfin.2019.02.015. Accessed 28 Oct 2021

El Ghoul S, Karoui A (2017) Does corporate social responsibility affect mutual fund performance and flows? J Bank Fin 77:53–63

Engle RF et al. (2020) Hedging climate change news. Rev Fin St 33:1184–1216. https://doi.org/10.1093/rfs/hhz072. Accessed 28 Oct 2021

Enriques L, Gilotta S (2015) Disclosures and market regulation. In: Moloney N, Ferran E, Payne J (eds) The Oxford handbook of financial regulation. OUP, pp 511–537

Enriques L, Ringe W-G (2020) Bank–fintech partnerships, outsourcing arrangements and the case for a mentorship regime. Cap Markets Law J 15:374–397

Enriques L, Zetzsche D (2014) Quack corporate governance, round III? Bank board regulation under the new European Capital Requirement Directive. Theor Inquiries Law 16(1):211–244

Fernando CS, Sharfman MP, Uysal VB (2017) Corporate environmental policy and shareholder value: following the smart money. J Fin Quant 52:2023–2051. https://doi.org/10.1017/S0022109017000680. Accessed 28 Oct 2021

Filbeck G, Krause TA, Reis L (2016) Socially responsible investing in hedge funds. J Asset Manage 17:408–421

Fiskerstrand SR et al. (2019) Sustainable investments in the Norwegian stock market. J Sustain Fin Invest 10:294–310

Friede G (2020) Why don't we see more action? A metasynthesis of the investor impediments to integrate environmental, social, and governance factors. Bus Strategy Environ 28:1260–1282. https://doi.org/10.1002/bse.2346. Accessed 28 Oct 2021

Friede G, Busch T, Bassen A (2015) ESG and financial performance: aggregated evidence from more than 2000 empirical studies. J Sustain Fin Invest 5:210–233

Gentzoglanis A (2019) Corporate social responsibility and financial networks as a surrogate for regulation. J Sustain Fin Invest 9(3):214–225

Gutsche G, Ziegler A (2019) Which private investors are willing to pay for sustainable investments? Empirical evidence from stated choice experiments. J Bank Fin 102:193–214. https://doi.org/10.1016/j.jbankfin.2019.03.007. Accessed 28 Oct 2021

Hartzmark SM, Sussman AB (2019) Do investors value sustainability? A natural experiment examining ranking and fund flows. J Fin 74:2789–2837. https://doi.org/10.1111/jofi.12841. Accessed 28 Oct 2021

Hessenius M et al. (2020) European commission, testing draft EU ecolabel criteria on UCITS equity funds (June 2020), Climate Company and Frankfurt School of Finance & Management. https://op.europa.eu/en/publication-detail/-/publication/91cc2c0b-ba78-11ea-811c-01aa75ed71a1/language-en/format-PDF/source-137198287. Accessed 28 Oct 2021

Hong H, Karolyi GA, Scheinkman JA (2020) Climate finance. Rev Fin St 33:1011–1023. https://doi.org/10.1093/rfs/hhz146. Accessed 28 Oct 2021

Hooghiemstra SN (2020) The ESG Disclosure Regulation—New duties for financial market participants & financial advisers. https://ssrn.com/abstract=3558868. Accessed 28 Oct 2021

Huynh TD, Xia Y (2020) Climate change news risk and corporate bond returns. J Fin Quant 56:1985–2009. https://doi.org/10.1017/S0022109020000757. Accessed 28 Oct 2021

Ilhan E, Sautner Z, Vilkov G (2021) Carbon tail risk. Rev Fin St 34(3):1540–1571. https://doi.org/10.1093/rfs/hhaa071. Accessed 28 Oct 2021

Jebe (2019) The convergence of financial and ESG materiality: taking sustainability mainstream. Am Bus Law J 56:645–702

Joliet R, Titova Y (2018) Equity SRI funds vacillate between ethics and money: an analysis of the funds' stock holding decisions. J Bank Fin 97:70–86. https://doi.org/10.1016/j.jbankfin.2018.09.011. Accessed 28 Oct 2021

Kivisaari E (2021) Sustainable finance and prudential regulation of financial institutions. In: Fisher G (ed) Making the financial system sustainable. CUP, Cambridge, pp 75–103

Krueger P, Sautner Z, Starks LT (2020) The importance of climate risks for institutional investors. Rev Fin St 33:1067–1111. https://doi.org/10.1093/rfs/hhz137. Accessed 28 Oct 2021

Langenbucher K et al. (2020) What are the wider supervisory implications of the Wirecard case? Think Tank (europa.eu). https://www.europarl.europa.eu/thinktank/en/document/IPOL_STU(2020)651385. Accessed 28 Oct 2021

Larcker DF, Watts EM (2020) Where's the greenium? J Acct Econ 69(2–3):101312. https://doi.org/10.1016/j.jacceco.2020.101312. Accessed 28 Oct 2021

Liesen A et al. (2017) Climate change and asset prices: Are corporate carbon disclosure and performance priced appropriately? J Bus Fin Acct 44:35–62

Mancini M (2020) Nudging the financial system: a network analysis approach. UNEP Inquiry and FC4S. https://www.fc4s.org/publication/nudging-the-financial-system-a-network-analysis-approach

Moloney N, Ferran E, Payne J (2015) Introduction. In: Moloney N, Ferran E, Payne J (eds) The Oxford handbook of financial regulation. OUP 2015/2017, pp 1–10

Murfin J, Spiegel M (2020) Is the risk of sea level rise capitalized in residential real estate? Rev Fin St 33:1217–1255. https://doi.org/10.1093/rfs/hhz134. Accessed 28 Oct 2021

OECD (2020) Integrating ESG factors in the investment decision-making process of institutional investors, chapter 4. In: OECD Business and Finance Outlook 2020: Sustainable and Resilient Finance. OECD Publishing, Paris. https://doi.org/10.1787/eb61fd29-en. Accessed 28 Oct 2021

Painter M (2020) An inconvenient cost: the effects of climate change on municipal bonds. J Fin Econ 135:468–482. https://doi.org/10.1016/j.jfineco.2019.06.006. Accessed 28 Oct 2021

Pedersen LH, Fitzgibbons S, Pomorski L (2020) Responsible investing: the ESG-efficient frontier. J Financ Econ. https://doi.org/10.1016/j.jfineco.2020.11.001 (in press)

Riedl A, Smeets P (2017) Why do investors hold socially responsible mutual funds? J Fin 72:2505–2550

Rockström J et al. (2009) Planetary boundaries: exploring the safe operating space for humanity. Ecol Soc 14(2):32

Romano R (2014) Regulating in the dark and a postscript assessment of the iron law of financial regulation. Hofstra Law Rev 43(1):25–93

Rossi M et al. (2019) Household preferences for socially responsible investments. J Bank Fin 105:107–120. https://doi.org/10.1016/j.jbankfin.2019.05.018. Accessed 28 Oct 2021

Shive SA, Forster MM (2020) Corporate governance and pollution externalities of public and private firms. Rev Fin St 33:1296–1330. https://doi.org/10.1093/rfs/hhz079. Accessed 28 Oct 2021

Steffen W et al. (2015) Planetary boundaries:guiding human development on a changing planet. Science 347(6223). https://doi.org/10.1126/science.1259855

Thaler R, Sunstein C (2008) Nudge: improving decisions about health, wealth and happiness. Yale University Press, New Haven

Zetzsche DA, Buckley RP, Arner DW, Barberis JN (2017) Regulating a revolution: from regulatory sandboxes to smart regulation. Ford J Corp Fin Law 23:31–103

Zetzsche DA, Arner DW, RP Buckley, Kaiser-Yücel A (2020) Fintech toolkit: smart regulatory and market approaches to financial technology innovation. https://ssrn.com/abstract=3598142. Accessed 28 Oct 2021

Authors and Affiliations

Dirk A. Zetzsche[1] · Linn Anker-Sørensen[2]

Linn Anker-Sørensen
Linn.Anker-Soerensen@no.ey.com

[1] Professor of Law, ADA Chair in Financial Law (Inclusive Finance), Faculty of Law, Economics and Finance, and Coordinator, House of Sustainable Governance and Markets, University of Luxembourg, Luxembourg, Luxembourg

[2] PhD (University of Oslo), Head of Decentralized Finance, Ernst and Young Tax and Law Norway, Lecturer-in-Law, University of Oslo, Oslo, Norway

European Business Organization Law Review (2022) 23:87–123
https://doi.org/10.1007/s40804-021-00229-9

ARTICLE

The EU Sustainable Finance Agenda: Developing Governance for Double Materiality in Sustainability Metrics

Iris H-Y Chiu[1]

Accepted: 13 December 2021 / Published online: 31 January 2022
© The Author(s) 2022

Abstract

This article argues that the regulatory steers in the recent EU Sustainable Disclosure and Taxonomy Regulations rely heavily on the outworking of market-based governance to meet public interest goals in sustainable finance. Hence, additional work in sustainability metrics development that informs the investment sector of sustainable performance in companies would be of key importance. This article argues that there remain gaps in EU leadership for governing metrics development, and suggests that EU-level governance can be designed appropriately, especially in a multi-stakeholder manner, for metrics development and in relation to key information intermediaries in this space.

Keywords Sustainable finance · Sustainable taxonomy · Double materiality ·
Sustainable benchmark · Sustainable index

1 Introduction

One of the means for achieving sustainable policy goals[1] lies in mobilising the financial lever, i.e., to require financiers to make allocative decisions based on sustainable considerations, in order to steer economic activity towards sustainable outcomes. The financial lever is a meaningful one as private governance, often incentive-based, can steer behaviour in a manner that is also aligned with

---

[1] High-Level Expert Group on Sustainable Finance (HLEG) (2018).

✉ Iris H-Y Chiu
  hse-yu.chiu@ucl.ac.uk

[1] Professor of Corporate Law and Financial Regulation, University College London, London, UK

🌱 Springer · ASSER PRESS

the achievement of collective goals.[2] The financiers of corporate capitalism play a part in steering their debtor[3] or investee companies[4] towards behaviour that takes into account sustainability considerations.

The EU's sustainable finance reforms include the Sustainability Disclosure Regulation 2019[5] and Taxonomy Regulation 2020,[6] as well as follow-on initiatives for the regulation of investment firms, funds and benchmarks.[7] These reforms comprise (a) mandatory duties for regulated investment firms and fund managers to integrate sustainability risks;[8] (b) mandatory sale and ongoing disclosure obligations for marketing sustainable products;[9] and (c) defining sustainability objectives to prevent greenwashing.[10] However, the financial lever relies keenly on market forces to affect market participants' actions. Key to the success of the financial lever is arguably the measurement of sustainability impact and achievement which would enable investment intermediaries and their investors to make relevant decisions on that basis.

EU regulations have achieved much in terms of specifying and standardising the sustainable objectives and outcomes for the financial lever.[11] In particular, policy-makers embrace double materiality[12] in measuring investment outcomes. This

---

[2] Black (2003).

[3] Discussed in relation to banks' roles in monitoring sustainability impact in debt financing, such as in project finance, by means of implementing the voluntary Equator Principles, see https://equator-princ iples.com/about/ (accessed 15 Nov 2021); and Herbertson and Hunter (2007); critically, Sarro (2012).

[4] Socially responsible investors have been a driving force for influencing corporations in relation to socially responsible behaviour, either through portfolio selection processes or activism, see generally Gibson et al. (2018); Serafeim (2018); Kakeu (2017); Osthoff (2015). Investor trade bodies can also help promote best practices on the part of investors in responsible investment, see Yamahaki (2019). However, see critical discussions relating to passive investment and generally weak investment influence on corporate behaviour, Glac (2014), Grewal et al. (2016); Amba (2018).

[5] Regulation (EU) 2019/2088 of the European Parliament and of the Council of 27 November 2019 on sustainability-related disclosures in the financial services sector (Sustainability Disclosure Regulation 2019).

[6] Regulation (EU) 2020/852 of the European Parliament and of the Council of 18 June 2020 on the establishment of a framework to facilitate sustainable investment, and amending Regulation (EU) 2019/2088 (Taxonomy Regulation 2020). Other relevant legislation such as amendments to corporate reporting, regulation of investment firms and funds, as well as benchmark regulation will be discussed in the article.

[7] Communication from the Commission to the European Parliament, the Council, the European Economic and Social Committee and the Committee of the Regions: EU Taxonomy, Corporate Sustainability Reporting, Sustainability Preferences and Fiduciary Duties: Directing finance towards the European Green Deal (21 April 2021), https://eur-lex.europa.eu/legal-content/EN/TXT/?uri=CELEX:52021 DC0188 (accessed 15 Nov 2021).

[8] *Supra* n. 5 and *infra* n. 21.

[9] Regulations in nn. 5 and 6 *supra*.

[10] Art. 2, Sustainability Disclosure Regulation 2019, as well as environmentally sustainable objectives defined in the Taxonomy Regulation 2020 and the forthcoming social taxonomy envisaged by the Commission, https://ec.europa.eu/info/sites/default/files/business_economy_euro/banking_and_finance/ documents/finance-events-210226-presentation-social-taxonomy_en.pdf (accessed 15 Nov 2021).

[11] *Supra* nn. 5 and 6. See also Zetzsche and Sørensen (2021) in this volume.

[12] See ESMA's emphasis on double materiality in 'ESMA supports IFRS Foundation's efforts on international standardisation in sustainability reporting', 16 Dec 2020), https://www.esma.europa.eu/press-news/esma-news/esma-supports-ifrs-foundation%E2%80%99s-efforts-international-standardisation-in

means that sustainable outcomes matter not only for their relevance to financial performance of investments. The universe of sustainability outcomes is large and varied, with many aspects susceptible to qualitative evaluation. There is unfinished work in relation to the development of sustainability metrics. Metrics refer not only to the outcomes or objectives but also to the selection and identification of suitable indicators which provide a rubric for measuring attainment.[13] Further, the development of sustainability metrics must include choices about the tolerance level of the extent of attainment. Metrics development is important to facilitate the evaluations that need to be carried out by investment intermediaries in order to fulfil the newly introduced regulatory obligations. Further, metrics development goes beyond supporting the financial lever, as it provides for broader visibility and accountability for economic activity more generally, to stakeholders and society. Hence, in this article, we identify metrics governance as crucial to the EU's sustainable finance agenda and discuss how it may be further developed. Addressing such governance needs would likely be the next step in the evolution of the sustainable finance policy agenda.[14] In doing so, we do not forget that there have already been bottom-up developments in the investment industry focused on 'ESG' (environmental, social and governance) indicators over the years, raising the question to what extent the EU's attempts at redefining sustainability cohere with or contest against those developments.

However, this article acknowledges the obvious, which is that the financial lever cannot be the 'whole answer' to achieving economic behavioural change towards sustainability. Financial mobilisation towards sustainability is ultimately incentive-based, and the corporate sector needs to translate into actions and conduct economic activity that is sustainable. Investment influence upon the corporate sector is only one piece of the mosaic for transforming corporate behaviour,[15] and investors' behaviour is itself a subject of criticism and debate.[16] Nevertheless, the development of regulatory steers for investor behaviour can play a valuable part in the policy mosaic towards mobilising sustainable corporate behaviour.

Section 2 provides an overview of the sustainable finance policy in the EU. Section 3 discusses the role of regulatory governance in redefining sustainability and what it has achieved. It discusses the needs for metrics development and what governance needs remain unmet. Section 4 argues that the EU is well placed to address the governance needs for sustainability metrics development and the next steps policy-makers should consider. Section 5 concludes.

Footnote 12 (continued)
(accessed 15 Nov 2021).

[13] Tanzil and Beloff (2006).

[14] Maijoor (2020).

[15] See MacNeil and Esser (2021) in this volume.

[16] Gilson and Gordon (2013); Bebchuk and Hirst (2019); Fichtner and Heemskerk (2020).

2 The EU Sustainable Finance Agenda as Policy Lever

As the investment sector wields significant influence, with global assets under management growing year on year, estimated to be at USD\$145 trillion by 2025,[17] policy-makers have started looking to the gatekeeping capacities of the investment sector. This is so that these intermediaries in capital markets can play a useful part in the governance landscape for shaping economic behaviour towards alignment with sustainable goals.[18]

The EU's sustainable finance strategy has brought about reforms in capital markets regulation. The Sustainability Disclosure Regulation 2019 now compels all financial market participants engaging in portfolio management or fund management (whether as mainstream pension or collective investment schemes, or as alternative investments funds)[19] to make mandatory disclosure of how they integrate sustainability risks in their investment decision-making.[20] This also includes financial services providers that supply investment-based products as part of an insurance product. This mandatory disclosure obligation is to be upgraded shortly to a definitive duty to integrate sustainability risks into investment strategies, risk management and governance.[21] Further, a range of new mandatory disclosure obligations apply to large investment firms and to the marketing and ongoing review of sustainably labelled investment products.[22] In addition, and crucially, the redefinition of 'sustainability' has been legalised, proceeding from environmental sustainability[23] to social development sustainability, in order to prevent 'greenwashing' in investment products, a problem identified by critics of self-regulating and self-labelled ESG products.[24]

The EU's sustainable finance agenda has been built upon earlier policy nudging institutional investors towards becoming engaged shareholders in their investee companies. The EU Shareholders' Rights Directive 2017 introduced a regime of comply-or-explain for institutional investors[25] in order to nudge[26] them towards

---

[17] PwC (2017).

[18] https://sustainabledevelopment.un.org/?menu=1300 (accessed 15 Nov 2021).

[19] Sustainability Disclosure Regulation 2019, Art. 2.

[20] Ibid., Art. 3.

[21] Commission Delegated Regulation to amend the Alternative Investment Fund Managers Directive, https://ec.europa.eu/finance/docs/level-2-measures/aifmd-delegated-act-2021-2615_en.pdf (dated 21 April 2021) (accessed 15 Nov 2021); Commission Delegated Directive to amend the UCITs Directive, https://ec.europa.eu/finance/docs/level-2-measures/ucits-directive-delegated-act-2021-2617_en.pdf (dated 21 April 2021) (accessed 15 Nov 2021); Commission Delegated Directive to amend the Markets in Financial Instruments Directive, https://ec.europa.eu/finance/docs/level-2-measures/mifid-2-delegated-act-2021-2612_en.pdf (dated 21 April 2021) (accessed 15 Nov 2021).

[22] Sustainability Disclosure Regulation 2019, Arts. 4, 7, 8-11.

[23] Arts. 9-17, Taxonomy Regulation 2020.

[24] 'Unregulated "greenwashing"? ESG investing is under the microscope as the money rolls in', CNBC News, 14 Oct 2020, https://www.cnbc.com/2020/10/14/esg-investing-meaning-is-under-the-microscope-as-the-money-rolls-in.html (accessed 15 Nov 2021).

[25] Art. 3g.

[26] Madsen (2021).

more engaged behaviour, in the overall promotion of the long-term interests of ben-eficiaries.[27] Such shareholder engagement can take place in relation to companies' corporate governance as well as their footprint in ESG matters.[28] Earlier, to support investors' engagement role, the EU introduced regulation for listed companies to make relevant 'non-financial disclosures' in relation to environmental impacts, and impacts on employees, human rights, and anti-corruption matters.[29]

However, it can be argued that the shareholder engagement and corporate non-financial disclosure reforms suffer from a lack of connection to the public interest goals of sustainability. Shareholder engagement in response to corporate disclosure is very much in the nature of addressing the 'agency' problem, ultimately to steer companies towards being accountable to shareholders. These shareholders are also acknowledged to have their own private interests and mandates in relation to investment management. The nature of private corporate governance and the private nature of investment management duties may not sufficiently connect with the public interest goals of sustainability.[30] This is because private incentives are bound up in the need to generate financial return, on the part of companies for their shareholders and on the part of institutional shareholders for their asset owners and beneficiaries.[31] Although private incentives can be compatible with public interest goals, as empirical research has shown that investing in 'good' is largely compatible with investing 'well' in terms of financial performance,[32] trade-offs between generating financial return and committing to sustainable behaviour have also been observed.[33]

In this manner, the EU's sustainable finance reforms take a step further by introducing regulatory steers in the objectives of investment management so that public interest goals in sustainability have to be internalised. However, the Sustainable Disclosure and Taxonomy Regulations introduced in 2019 and 2020 cannot over-prescribe or over-intrude into the freedom to design investment mandates and continue to co-opt market forces, but in a manner that nudges towards the promotion of: (a) conventional investment that internalises sustainability considerations, and (b) specially designed sustainable investments that deliver sustainable outcomes alongside financial ones. The latter market is growing in relation to investors' pro-social preferences, on the part of many institutions and individuals,[34] and will be attractive for investment fund intermediaries.

---

[27] Arts. 3h and 3i.

[28] Arts. 3g and 3h in relation to non-financial performance. See also Principles 9-11, UK Stewardship Code, https://www.frc.org.uk/getattachment/5aae591d-d9d3-4cf4-814a-d14e156a1d87/Stewardship-Code_Dec-19-Final-Corrected.pdf (accessed 15 Nov 2021).

[29] Art. 19a, Non-financial Disclosure Directive 2014/95/EU.

[30] Sjåfjell et al. (2017).

[31] The fiduciary duty owed by funds to their beneficiaries is private in nature and centres on generating the necessary returns for the purpose of investment, although taking into account responsibility and sustainability issues is not per se irrelevant to the primary mandate, see UNEP FI (2019).

[32] Friede et al. (2015); Durán-Santomil et al. (2019); but see sceptical evidence in La Torre et al. (2020).

[33] Chen et al. (2017).

[34] See *infra* nn. 42-44.

2.1 Baseline Duty of Integrating Sustainability Risks

Under the Sustainability Disclosure Regulation, investment fund intermediaries are under a universal obligation to make mandatory disclosure of how they 'integrate sustainability risks'. 'Sustainability risk' is defined as an 'environmental, social or governance event or condition that, if it occurs, could cause an actual or a potential material negative impact on the value of the investment'.[35] Such a definition adopts a 'single materiality' approach of treating sustainability risk as salient only if it materially affects investment performance. At a baseline, this is not novel and is consistent with the interpretation of fiduciary duty in private investment management.[36] We will return to this point shortly to discuss whether an opportunity has been missed to embed double materiality in the baseline regulation of investment management conduct.

Next, investment intermediaries of a certain scale, defined as having 500 employees or above, or being a parent company of such an undertaking,[37] are mandated to account for principal adverse sustainability impacts (applying from 30 June 2021). This applies whether or not such financial services providers engage with sustainably labelled products. They must account for any adverse impact of their investment decision-making processes on sustainability objectives, for how adverse impacts are discovered and for the due diligence policies that are deployed.[38] Smaller providers may declare that they do not consider adverse sustainability impacts in their investment decision-making process but they must clearly explain why and whether this practice cuts across all their products.[39] This means that smaller providers are subject to the broad duty to integrate sustainability risks as discussed above, but not specifically to the prescribed mandatory disclosure of due diligence policies and measurement of adverse sustainability impact imposed on larger investment intermediaries. In this manner, larger investment intermediaries are under an obligation that is more socially-facing in nature, i.e., to account for sustainability cost *as such*.

Although this approach seems proportionate in order to reduce compliance obligations for smaller fund intermediaries, the bifurcation adopted suggests that smaller firms can elect to be principally 'private-facing' and potentially 'exempt', subject to their explanation, from the scope of socially-facing accountability imposed on larger firms. There is a large sector of investment firms that are medium-sized and employ under 500 employees. Hence, it is questioned as to whether the EU's legalisation has achieved much in terms of steering investment management conduct towards double materiality.

It may be argued that the more remarkable reforms are those pertaining to mandatory disclosure and transparency. These, however, crucially rely on market discipline to be effective.

---

[35] Art. 2(22), Sustainability Disclosure Regulation 2019.

[36] See Freshfields Bruckhaus Deringer (2005); UNEP FI (2019); Richardson (2011).

[37] Art. 4(3) and (4), Sustainability Disclosure Regulation 2019.

[38] Art. 4(1)(a), ibid.

[39] Art. 4(1)(b), ibid.

2.2 Mandatory Disclosure Obligations

It may be argued that mandatory disclosure of sustainability risk integration by all investment intermediaries is already a step forward, as, left to a self-regulatory state, only 'socially responsible' investment funds would be under a contractual expectation to have regard to single materiality. Further, by 30 December 2022, financial services providers mandated to disclose principal adverse sustainability impacts must also make that transparency available at the level of each financial product.[40] These disclosures are also regarded as pre-contractual in nature, therefore attracting market and legal discipline from investors.[41]

However, mandatory disclosure of material sustainability risks and principal adverse sustainability impacts will only change behaviour if asset owners and beneficiaries care about such information. There is increasing evidence that asset owners such as pension funds[42] and pro-social individuals value the avoidance of adverse sustainable impact in their investment allocations.[43] This is not necessarily the case with conventional institutions,[44] and investment beneficiaries have highly heterogenous preferences.[45] If market response is clear and effectively disciplines the investment management industry, such discipline can be much more effective than an extraction of compliance imposed by regulators. However, with the bifurcation in mandatory disclosure requirements applicable to larger and smaller investment intermediaries, investors arguably do not enjoy a level playing field for discipline effects to be transmitted. There would likely be mixed noise in relation to market discipline focused on material sustainability risks relating to investment performance and on adverse sustainability impact per se. In this manner, it may be preferable for policy-makers to consider whether to adopt double materiality as a universal standard. Smaller firms can be subject to less prescriptive governance, although they can be made to disclose how they manage double materiality, so that their priorities and processes can be subject to public scrutiny and accountability.[46] This is arguably proportionate for smaller firms in view of compliance costs.

Mandatory disclosure obligations for marketing sustainably labelled products have been enhanced considerably. The Sustainability Disclosure Regulation clarifies that sustainably labelled finance goes beyond 'harm-based analysis', and should reflect the achievement of positive sustainability outcomes and not merely the avoidance of negative ones. Indeed 'sustainable investment' is defined in two dimensions: it should positively achieve specified sustainable outcomes and do 'no significant harm' to environmental and social objectives as a whole.[47] The definition of 'sustainably labelled' relates to

---

[40] Art. 7, Regulation 2019/2088.

[41] Art. 6, ibid.

[42] Apostolakis et al. (2018); Delsen and Lehr (2019); de Haan et al. (2012).

[43] Wins and Zwergel (2016); Ammann et al. (2018).

[44] Jansson and Biel (2014); Ielasi and Rossolini (2019).

[45] Apostolakis et al. (2016); also pro-social individual investors remain a minority, see Christiansen et al. (2019).

[46] Parker (2000) in relation to the meta-regulatory technique.

[47] Derived from Art. 2(17), Sustainability Disclosure Regulation 2019.

an economic activity that contributes to an environmental objective, […] as measured by key resource efficiency indicators on the use of energy, renewable energy, raw materials, water and land, on the production of waste, and greenhouse gas emissions, or on its impact on biodiversity and the circular economy, or an investment in an economic activity that contributes to a social objective, […] [such as] tackling inequality or that fosters social cohesion, social integration and labour relations, or an investment in human capital or economically or socially disadvantaged communities, provided that such investments do not significantly harm any of those objectives and that the investee companies follow good governance practices, in particular with respect to sound management structures, employee relations, remuneration of staff and tax compliance.

Financial services providers who provide explicitly sustainably labelled products must explain how the environmental or social characteristics promoted by each product meet its characterisation, whether in active or in passive management. In an actively managed product, disclosure is to be made of the strategies designed to meet the relevant characteristics, including how the financial services provider defines the sustainability objective and how it measures its attainment or otherwise.[48] The European Securities and Markets Authority (ESMA) will prescribe a template[49] for such disclosure so that certain standards and comparability are attained.

In relation to passively managed products, financial services providers must disclose if the environmental or social characterisation is derived by benchmarking against indices for sustainable finance.[50] It is not sufficient that financial services providers merely refer to a designated index to be satisfied of a product's environmental or social characteristics. They must disclose how the index is aligned or consistent with those characteristics and how alignment with it differs from a broad market index.[51] Although financial services providers are in substance relying on an index provider's diligence and evaluation, there needs to be some level of intelligent engagement with indexers' methodologies[52] in order to demonstrate why the index has been selected and to show the difference to sustainable performance made by adhering to the index. As there are huge inflows into passively managed ESG products,[53] policy-makers have also set their sights on regulating index products adopted by investment funds in order to support the credibility of such products.[54] We take the view that although index provider governance is an important aspect of

---

[48] Arts. 8 and 10, ibid.

[49] Draft technical standards as of 23 April 2020, https://www.esma.europa.eu/press-news/esma-news/esas-consult-environmental-social-and-governance-disclosure-rules (accessed 15 Nov 2021).

[50] Arts. 8 and 9, Sustainability Disclosure Regulation 2019.

[51] Art. 9(1)(b), ibid.

[52] Bianchi and Drew (2012) on the differences between indices.

[53] 'ESG index funds hit $250 billion as pandemic accelerates impact investing boom', CNBC News, 2 Sep 2020, https://www.cnbc.com/2020/09/02/esg-index-funds-hit-250-billion-as-us-investor-role-in-boom-grows.html (accessed 15 Nov 2021).

[54] Benchmarks Regulation 2016/1011; amended by Regulation 2019/2089 (on EU Climate Transition Benchmarks, EU Paris-aligned Benchmarks and sustainability-related disclosures for benchmarks) dealing with 'low carbon' benchmarks for indexed funds.

the sustainable finance regulatory agenda, a more holistic agenda for metrics governance is needed, a point we canvass in Section 4.

The Sustainability Disclosure Regulation provides a gold standard for the labelling of sustainable financial products. Although the Taxonomy Regulation does not outlaw 'lower' labels such as 'ESG' or 'socially responsible' products,[55] the regulatory governance of the 'sustainable' label is intended to set standards as well as galvanise market choice. However, the effectiveness of such regulatory policy depends on the alignment between market choice and regulatory steering. If sustainably labelled products are more costly due to the more demanding compliance obligations, this could affect market choice and the demand side may be incentivised to settle for 'lower' labels.

In sum, the EU's sustainable finance reforms provide regulatory steers for the baseline integration of sustainability consciousness on the part of all investment intermediaries, as well as the market building of investment products that meet the purposes of *double materiality*, i.e., delivering on both investment and sustainable performance, hence avoiding greenwashing. We are of the view that although the EU has taken a step forward in legalising baseline investment management conduct in relation to sustainability risks, the conduct lever is relatively un-imposing on the majority of investment intermediaries not defined as 'large'. The obligation to integrate single materiality concerns merely consolidates bottom-up developments over the years, as many conventional investment firms are signatories to the UN Principles of Responsible Investment. It also remains to be seen how mandatory disclosure of principal adverse sustainability impact might change the behaviour of large investment intermediaries, who may then provide leadership for double materiality in conventional investment management. The more radical reform for now is the attempt to redefine sustainably labelled investment products and how this affects market interest and preferences.

In this respect, although EU policy-makers have achieved scientifically informed clarity in identifying the environmentally sustainable objectives in the Taxonomy Regulation and are developing a social taxonomy for social and governance objectives, these are objectives and outcomes which still require the support of measuring metrics in order to make sustainably labelled finance distinguishable and meaningful for the market. Although the Taxonomy Regulation provides environmentally sustainable outcomes, such as in relation to reduced emissions or the circular economy, it is questioned what level of granularity is defined for these outcomes[56] and whether they are aggregates of even more granular proxy indicators.[57] There may be a fine line between outcomes and proxy indicators, but outcomes often comprise a number of proxy indicators and how these are measured. Further, if double materiality is

---

[55] Art. 7, Taxonomy Regulation 2020.

[56] ESAs, Joint Consultation Paper: Taxonomy-Related Disclosures (17 March 2021), https://www.esma.europa.eu/press-news/esma-news/esas-consult-taxonomy–related-product-disclosures (accessed 15 Nov 2021).

[57] Karthik Ramanna, 'ESG accounting needs to cut through the greenwash', Financial Times, 17 Jan 2021, offers some insight into the type of 'accounting' or evaluative metrics that are needed for sustainability performance.

embraced as an ethos, this must be reflected in the nature of measurement. Indeed in relation to social and governance goals many of which are qualitative in nature, the selection of a range of suitable and proximate indicators which afford a rubric for measurement, and the determination of the tolerance level for attainment need to be precisely made. This is besides the issue of debatability in the selection of social outcomes and goals in terms of inclusion/exclusion choices[58] and how these reflect the social fabric in the EU as a whole, taking into account differences in social development and needs in different Member States.

The metrics for sustainable outcome evaluation remain an open field. However, this is a broader issue than for the purposes of investment intermediaries' product design, disclosures and conduct. The metrics for sustainable achievements or impact must fundamentally underpin economic activity generally, such as in corporate disclosures.[59] Sustainable investments are largely made in private sector corporate entities, whether in the form of debt or equity securities,[60] and corporate reporting forms an important cornerstone for investment intermediaries' evaluations, besides other sources of information such as those held by the World Bank, non-governmental organisations or media platforms.[61] In this manner, investors need to have increased confidence in paying[62] for the gold standard of 'sustainably labelled' investments, being sure that such investments are selected and evaluated on the basis of clear and suitable metrics. The governance of sustainability metrics can arguably go further in affecting investment choice architecture.[63]

This article argues that it is imperative that the EU develop follow-up governance in relation to sustainability metrics development. Metrics governance cuts across the spheres of corporate and financial institution reporting in order to enable market choice and discipline. As the sustainable finance reforms crucially rely on market

---

[58] The social taxonomy reflects international consensus such as consistency with international governance standards on anti-bribery and tax avoidance, international human rights standards, and labour standards.

[59] This is acknowledged to be in need of ongoing reform, see *supra* n. 7.

[60] Sustainable investments defined for the purposes of financial institutions' reporting include investments in equity, debt off-balance sheet exposures and other fee-generating services such as trade finance, see EBA, Advice to the Commission on KPIs and methodology for disclosure by credit institutions and investment firms under the non-financial reporting standards on how and to what extent their activities qualify as environmentally sustainable according to the EU Taxonomy Regulation (Feb 2021), https://www.eba.europa.eu/sites/default/documents/files/document_library/About%20Us/Missions%20and%20tasks/Call%20for%20Advice/2021/CfA%20on%20KPIs%20and%20methodology%20for%20disclosures%20under%20Article%208%20of%20the%20Taxonomy%20Regulation/963616/Report%20-%20Advice%20to%20COM_Disclosure%20Article%208%20Taxonomy.pdf (accessed 15 Nov 2021). Further, the integration of sustainability risk into prudential risk measurement by financial institutions would affect their incentives to allocate credit or investment to activities that may adversely affect such measurement, see EBA, Draft implementing standards on prudential disclosures on ESG risks in accordance with Article 449a CRR (Consultation Paper, Feb 2021), https://www.eba.europa.eu/sites/default/documents/files/document_library/Publications/Consultations/2021/Consultation%20on%20draft%20ITS%20on%20Pillar%20disclosures%20on%20ESG%20risk/963621/Consultation%20paper%20on%20draft%20ITS%20on%20Pillar%203%20disclosures%20on%20ESG%20risks.pdf (accessed 15 Nov 2021).

[61] Lucy Fitzgeorge-Parker, 'ESG data – mind the gaps', Euromoney, 27 Aug 2020.

[62] Corley (2019).

[63] Amel-Zadeh and Serafeim (2018); Pilaj (2017).

discipline for mandatory disclosures and on the market for sustainably labelled products, EU governance in metrics development seems unavoidable. In Section 3 we discuss the need for EU governance to be extended to the conceptual and implementational aspects of double materiality in order to secure clear, comparable and meaningful metrics development for users, so as to steer market choice in a manner aligned with public interest goals.

3 Double Materiality

Although EU policy-makers have signalled a preference for double materiality, the conceptual development of double materiality is only weakly evidenced and the implementation aspects of double materiality suffer from gaps. This Section critically explores where these areas require improvement in order to support governance for metrics development.

3.1 Conceptual Gaps in Double Materiality

First, in terms of what double materiality means, the Sustainability Disclosure Regulation provides examples of sustainable goals in its definition of 'sustainable investment', such as relating to efficient use of energy, enabling a circular economy, investing in human capital, and improving the position of socially disadvantaged communities. The Taxonomy Regulation provides more specific environmentally relevant goals in relation to climate change mitigation and adaptation, protection of water and marine resources, protecting biodiversity, and preventing pollution. These goals are valued per se rather than tied to their contribution to financial return.

The Taxonomy Regulation provides six environmentally sustainable goals and lists of indicators for each of the goals, but social goals are a work in progress.[64] The sustainable goals developed in the EU's sustainable finance policy overlap to an extent but do not map fully onto the United Nations' Sustainable Development Goals, for example.[65] Besides the issue of selection of goals and whether indicators for environmental and social goals are fully developed,[66] it is also not taken for granted that the indicators developed for environmental goals provide clear metrics.[67] Metrics are more granular in nature and provide a rubric for measuring attainment. Different metrics can also exist to show that an indicator of, for example, 'using sustainably sourced renewable materials' is met. We need metrics to measure

---

[64] See the EU's work on the social taxonomy, https://ec.europa.eu/info/sites/default/files/business_econo my_euro/banking_and_finance/documents/finance-events-210226-presentation-social-taxonomy_en.pdf (accessed 15 Nov 2021).

[65] https://www.undp.org/content/undp/en/home/sustainable-development-goals.html#:~:text=The% 20Sustainable%20Development%20Goals%20(SDGs,peace%20and%20prosperity%20by%202030 (accessed 15 Nov 2021). It is also opined that indicators for SDG goals are themselves emerging, Bebbington and Unerman (2018).

[66] Gibson et al. (2018).

[67] Cort and Esty (2020).

what 'sustainably sourced' means, such as by reference to certifications, origins or processes, and what degree of renewability or recyclability materials should meet in order to be regarded as 'renewable'. Must materials be wholly recycled to meet the criteria or would 'partly renewable' suffice? In this regard, the development of metrics that are salient and reliable for showing the achievement of an indicator is still a work in progress.[68] These metrics also have to be consistently applicable, within or across industries,[69] be independently verifiable,[70] and most of all, speak clearly to asset owners and beneficiaries in terms of choice framing.[71] It is further queried whether sustainability metrics have been more developed with regard to adverse impact such as carbon emissions or toxic release emissions in relation to pollutants, compared to positive sustainability contributions.[72] It may be more difficult to develop metrics for positive sustainability contributions as proxy indicators may be premature or selective, and it is uncertain what sort of timeframe is necessary to consider counterbalancing side effects. Finally, the Commission has also acknowledged that bottom-up feedback views the Taxonomy Regulation's categorisation of environmentally sustainable activities as being a somewhat narrow set, and a complimentary legislative initiative on a taxonomy for climate change mitigation activities is going to be developed.[73]

The governance for metrics development in the EU is faced with a number of challenges. To what extent would the EU engage with this comprehensively so as to provide a set of top-down metrics for standardisation purposes? Such work requires heavy lifting and may duplicate bottom-up developments in metrics, such as those relating to 'ESG'. There are already actors in this space that measure ESG performance, serving the universe of 'socially responsible' investment funds.[74] Nevertheless, the existing industry of ESG metrics development is arguably premised on portfolio risk management and more aligned with single materiality, i.e., how ESG metrics affect investment performance.[75] The key actors in this space include the Global Reporting Initiative,[76] Integrated Reporting Initiative,[77] Sustainability Accounting Standards Board[78] and more recently the International Financial Reporting Standards Foundation[79] that are developing sustainability reporting metrics aimed at companies. The reporting standards issued by the Task Force on

---

[68] Ibid.; Kotsantonis and Serafeim (2019).

[69] Esty and Karpilow (2019); Leuz (2020).

[70] Cort and Esty (2020).

[71] Pilaj (2017).

[72] Esty and Karpilow (2019).

[73] See *supra* n. 7, p 3.

[74] Based on techniques such as screening and exclusion, or stock-picking for 'best-in-class' performance, which means that ESG ratings are looked at in the relative and not absolute sense.

[75] Richardson and Cragg (2010); Schäfer (2012).

[76] https://www.globalreporting.org/ (accessed 15 Nov 2021).

[77] https://integratedreporting.org/resource/international-ir-framework/ (accessed 15 Nov 2021).

[78] https://www.sasb.org/ (accessed 15 Nov 2021).

[79] IFRS (2020).

Climate-related Financial Disclosures (TCFD)[80] and now adopted in the Listing Rules for premium-listed companies on the London Stock Exchange[81] are aimed at financial institution disclosures of transition and stranded asset risks, as well as corporate transparency. Further, there are many existing private sector specialists in ratings for environmental, social and governance performance, which support the industry of socially responsible investors, such as Viageo Eiris,[82] Robeco Sam[83] and Refinitiv.[84] Index providers have also developed partnerships[85] with ESG rating services or have built up in-house expertise[86] to carry out evaluations in order to develop socially responsible or sustainable indices as benchmarks for passive investment managers.

However, it may be argued that private sector-developed 'ESG' metrics have been sub-optimally self-regulatory as they cater for single materiality.[87] Hence, would not such metrics cater for the baseline duty to integrate material sustainability risks for all investment intermediaries? In this manner, the bifurcation of compliance imposed on larger and smaller firms, especially in relation to the disclosure of 'principal adverse sustainability impact', draws attention to the distinctness of the obligation for larger firms which necessitates evaluative and reporting metrics. Further, as the EU distinguishes the sustainably labelled financial product from other ESG labels, there is a need for metrics to be developed for the double materiality of the superior labelled products. In this manner, it is arguable that top-down provision is needed not only of doubly material outcomes but to extend more granularly into metrics. That said, it is queried whether the market should be allowed to develop double materiality metrics in response to the new measures for the market building of sustainably labelled products. We have not yet proved market failure. An attempt by the EU to completely re-write the metrics for double materiality not only requires heavy lifting but is easily susceptible to user criticism. We perceive the need for but also hazards of a top-down approach to the establishment of alternative double materiality metrics which will only gain traction if private sector actors and international markets adopt them. Although top-down metrics provision is not ruled out, we argue that EU governance for metrics development should first provide groundwork in terms of ideological choices and underpinnings, and take into account private sector innovations and implementational tendencies.

At a broader and more conceptual level, metrics development embeds choices in relation to what matters for measurement. Commentators have opined that over time corporations have developed various measures for environmental or social impact

---

[80] https://www.fsb-tcfd.org/ (accessed 15 Nov 2021).

[81] Financial Conduct Authority (2020).

[82] https://vigeo-eiris.com/ (accessed 15 Nov 2021).

[83] https://www.robeco.com/uk/about-us/robecosam.html (accessed 15 Nov 2021).

[84] https://www.refinitiv.com/en/financial-data/company-data/esg-data (accessed 15 Nov 2021).

[85] Such as the Dow Jones Sustainability Index in partnership with Robeco SAM, as well as the MSCI KLD index which is the product of acquiring KLD as an ESG ratings service provider.

[86] Such as the FTSE4Good / FTSE Russell Indices.

[87] Diez-Cañamero et al. (2020).

that are salient to them, usually in terms of economic cost,[88] but also in relation to reputational salience and perceived stakeholder pressures.[89] These are necessarily selective and corporate-centric,[90] but provide a good starting point for metrics development to be standardised across an industry, or even industries. It needs to be ascertained to what extent metrics development by private sector bodies is wedded to such corporate-centric development of ESG measurement, and whether there should be public policy intervention[91] that would compel other forms of measurement to be made to inform public interest of the sustainability footprint of corporate and economic activity.[92] It has been observed that metrics development based on stakeholder perspectives can change metrics design considerably.[93]

Further, choices of perspective also need to be made in developing sustainability metrics. For example, environmental impact can be measured or expressed as deterioration in natural capital. But this form of measurement embeds an implicit assumption that natural capital can be appropriated as private property and monetised.[94] Such a perspective need not be compatible with the sense of collective good in promoting sustainability objectives. It is arguable that metrics development implicates broader social and political choices in relation to sustainability goals and priorities.[95] Hence, metrics development gives rise to fundamental questions in relation to the premises upon which they are built and what actors or influencers are part of the landscape for such development. In this manner, metrics development is not merely a matter for private governance. There is also a need for public-led scrutiny to be involved in shaping the premises upon which metrics are generated and the purposes metrics serve.[96]

Next, EU policy-makers should clarify the connection between sustainable outcomes as defined in the Sustainability Disclosure Regulation and the characteristics of good governance in investee companies. The definition of 'sustainable investment' in the Regulation comes across as providing that good governance is a necessary condition for the definition of sustainable investment. The characteristics of good governance relate to sound management structures, employee relations and tax compliance. There is actually less support in empirical research to show that good governance characteristics support the attainment of sustainable outcomes by companies,[97] and no definitive causal correlations have been proposed, whether in terms

[88] De Benedetto and Klemes (2015).

[89] Alsayegh et al. (2020); Pitrakkos and Maroun (2020); Tadros and Magnan (2019).

[90] Beske et al. (2020).

[91] Such as mandatory conflict minerals disclosure under the EU Conflict Minerals Regulation 2017 in force from 2021 and the UK's Modern Slavery Act s54 on supply chain disclosure.

[92] There is however the danger that compliance-based disclosure and measurement would be minimalist and undertaken only to manage legal risk, see Park (2019).

[93] Diebecker et al. (2019).

[94] Barter (2015); Martineau and Lafontaine (2020).

[95] Nicholls (2020).

[96] Questions raised in Gibassier (2015).

[97] Dienes et al. (2016); Passador and Riganti (2019).

of sustainable performance affecting good governance or otherwise.[98] It is uncertain how this necessary condition works to frame sustainable investment choice. Could the conditions for good governance be treated as key or exclusive proxy indicators for sustainable investments? Has EU policy elevated the importance of governance factors so that other sustainability indicators may be outbalanced by these? Further, the metrics for good governance can be regarded as overly prescriptive, especially in relation to increasingly detailed corporate governance codes for listed companies.[99] Yet, many corporate governance codes apply on a comply-or-explain basis in order to accommodate the private bargaining processes between companies and their shareholders. Does the inclusion of the necessity of governance characteristics in sustainable investment elevate the need for *practically hard* corporate compliance with corporate governance codes, if companies need to appeal to their sustainability-conscious institutional investors? There is also a significant discrepancy between the level of detail and prescription in corporate governance codes for listed companies (such as the UK one) and voluntary codes for companies that may be private but significant in economic footprint.[100]

Hence, there is more clarification that EU policy-makers can provide regarding the materiality of governance characteristics and their connection with double materiality. With the lack of European harmonisation in matters regarding corporate governance codes, reference to good governance, a matter subject to national and divergent governance, also seems incompatible with the harmonised EU-level governance intended to be provided over the concept of sustainable investment.

In addition, EU policy-makers should clarify the extent of compatibility between single materiality metrics that are being developed significantly by private sector bodies and double materiality metrics catering for the obligations of adverse impact disclosure by larger investment firms and for evaluating sustainably labelled investment products. Market demand has brought about the development of more established ESG metrics, which may be regarded as a narrower set and premised upon assumptions that do not necessarily embrace a holistic or comprehensive conceptualisation.[101] ESG metrics meet the existing market demand for single materiality assessments, i.e., to measure for investors the sustainability performance of companies that matter for their financial performance.[102] This is consistent with investors' familiar ground in portfolio risk management for making allocational decisions.[103] Further, the use by credit rating agencies[104] and financial analysts[105] of financially material ESG ratings has also reinforced the trend towards developing metrics for single materiality.

---

[98] Ibid.

[99] Moore (2015).

[100] Such as the Wates Principles, critically discussed in Barker and Chiu (2020).

[101] Darton (2015); Fornasari (2020).

[102] Aureli et al. (2019); Rogers and Serafeim (2019).

[103] Hübel and Scholz (2020).

[104] Cubas-Díaz et al. (2018); Del Giudice and Rigamonti (2020); Jon Hay, 'Fitch joins ESG caravan with relevance scores', Global Capital, 10 Jan 2019.

[105] Hinze and Sump (2019); Kim et al. (2018).

There is arguably a lack of incentive on the part of private sector actors in metrics development to deviate too much from single materiality, whether on the part of corporations themselves or on the part of service providers in supporting the investment industry. Embracing authentic double materiality requires new mindsets, resources and processes for measurement and evaluation, and would generate conflict situations with single materiality that may not be easy to reconcile. Taïbi et al.[106] report on a project aimed at partnering with a corporation to develop strong sustainability metrics that extend, and in some respects depart, from economic and financial materiality. Perhaps to no surprise, the project was ultimately not adopted by the corporate partner. This explains why earlier endeavours such as the Integrated Reporting Initiative[107] and True Value Capital Accounting[108] have been adopted by some corporations based on single materiality. Of late, the Sustainability Accounting Standards, which focus on investor materiality, have become attractive to corporations and investors,[109] and the merger of the SASB and IIRC further reinforce the development of single materiality metrics.[110] The involvement of the IFRS in developing sustainability accounting standards that can be adopted globally,[111] based on the IFRS' expertise in providing financial accounting standards,[112] may also be geared towards single materiality drawing upon the IFRS' expertise. Further, it has been opined that although the GRI reporting standards that underlie many corporations' voluntary ESG reports are meant to appeal to a broad audience including shareholders and stakeholders, the nature of these standards has increasingly responded to investor materiality.[113] There also seems to be substantial support in US commentary for mandatory disclosure of ESG factors by companies based on a single materiality standard, to be incorporated into SEC-mandated disclosure.[114] In this manner, there may be significant international trends that support the introduction of a single materiality standard, as such a standard is more easily integrated within existing regulatory, legal and accounting frameworks.[115] Indeed, the single materiality standard is likely to be developed on the basis of corporate reporting, such as the work undertaken in relation to the Impact-Weighted Accounts reporting standards for different sectors.[116] In that manner, sustainability metrics that the investment community needs would not likely be developed in isolation from the movement

---

[106] Taïbi et al. (2020).

[107] Discussed in Akisik and Gal (2020); Mervelskemper and Streit (2017).

[108] See Hendriksen et al. (2016). Critique in Barter (2016), McElroy and Thomas (2015).

[109] Grewal et al. (2017); Busco et al. (2020).

[110] 'IIRC and SASB intend to merge', 25 Nov 2020, https://www.iasplus.com/en/news/2020/11/iirc-and-sasb-intend-to-merge (accessed 15 Nov 2021).

[111] IFRS (2020).

[112] Eroglu (2017); Klein (2017).

[113] Fornasari (2020) and Busco et al. (2020) continue to see the GRI standards as being more holistic and inclusive in relation to ESG perspectives and materiality.

[114] Fisch (2019); Harper Ho (2020); Saad and Strauss (2020).

[115] Congruence with law is discussed in Jebe (2019). The support for mandatory disclosure of material ESG factors by corporations within existing securities regulation is discussed in Christiansen et al. (2019).

[116] https://www.hbs.edu/impact-weighted-accounts/Pages/default.aspx (accessed 15 Nov 2021).

towards metrics development for corporate sustainability accounting and reporting. European policy-makers need to forge a more holistic policy in relation to metrics development, a point which we explore in greater detail in the next Section.

It is arguable that single materiality metrics may be under-inclusive for double materiality purposes and in some respects contesting in nature. However, it cannot be definitively argued that single materiality measurements completely contradict or are irrelevant for the purposes of sustainable investment. There is also an inevitable extent of convergence between single and double materiality. As the initiatives of the IIRC and True Value Capital Accounting have shown, single materiality is not unconnected with double materiality, but it is the extent of under-inclusiveness or contradiction that is not well articulated.[117] Would we leave it to investors with hybrid motivations, i.e., those interested in both financial and sustainable performance, to bring their demands to bear in order to shape metrics that would ultimately deliver hybrid signals,[118] therefore exceeding mere single materiality? Or should policy-makers provide guidance and steering in light of the natural lack of incentives on the part of industry and markets to value double materiality? This is a fundamental policy dilemma for EU policy-makers as regulatory steering to recharacterise the obligations of investment firms in relation to being socially-facing, such as in relation to the mandatory disclosure of principal adverse impact by larger firms, introduces 'beyond-market' obligations and the necessity of a discipline different from market discipline. This may mean that there is a limited extent to which bottom-up market-based developments can cater for the EU's governance needs in relation to metrics. However, as the regulatory policy hybridises incentive-based discipline and socially-facing accountability, it would likely be impractical for EU policy-makers to presume that they should be the only ones to undertake a re-write of metrics for double materiality. Further, commentators have argued that what investors value as material is dynamic in nature[119] and hybrid investors could play a part in shaping the development of more holistic metrics in due course.

In this complex landscape of public interest steers and private market incentives and developments, EU-level governance for metrics development should not be lacking, but should not be top-down either.[120] We see a role for policy engagement with the scrutiny of premises underlying metrics development, critical consideration of the salience and comprehensiveness of metrics,[121] and consideration of how balances between single and double materiality may be struck. Such governance roles encompass nuanced steering, oversight and market facilitation. In particular, the metrics development for adverse sustainability impact may be more mature than metrics development for measuring positive sustainable contribution. Metrics development

---

[117] On the divergence between financial materiality and sustainable performance, see Perez (2016); Lipton (2020).

[118] Some empirical research has mapped a positive correlation between investments in portfolios of ESG companies scored using the SASB standards and the attainment of UN SDG goals, see Antoncic et al. (2020); Betti et al. (2018).

[119] Rogers and Serafeim (2019).

[120] Maijoor (2020).

[121] Pagano et al. (2018).

for the latter runs the risk of being overly corporate-centric, such as looking at positive contribution from the lens of corporate opportunity. Metrics development for positive sustainability contribution is also fraught with issues relating to choice of success indicators and timeframes for evaluation. Policy-makers should harness the advantages of both convergence and competition amongst different private sector-based metrics frameworks,[122] and monitor the effectiveness of metrics frameworks for users. In this regard, policy-makers should also consider how third-party assurance providers[123] can play a role and be appropriately governed in this landscape. Section 4 sets out the steps for EU-level governance in metrics development.

3.2 Implementational Issues for Double Materiality

Besides conceptual issues regarding the clarity of double materiality as a concept and how they shape policy choices in supporting metrics development, EU policy-makers should extend oversight governance in relation to the implementational tendencies on the part of market participants. Market practice can deviate from policy intentions regarding how double materiality is used, even if such metrics are developed.[124] Market practice can shape the prioritisation of sustainable goals based on the market's allocational functions.

First, even if the sustainable performance of investments is compelled to be evaluated on a double materiality basis, if the investment market prioritises certain materiality evaluations and gives them greater weight in allocational decisions, then the practice of prioritisation will give rise to marginalisation of the importance of certain double materiality metrics. This results in a feedback loop for corporate reporting which then reinforces investors' allocational decisions. It is observed that in the current landscape where metrics development is still emerging, conventional institutional investors are already undertaking endeavours to filter information relevant to their preferences from the noise of voluminous ESG information reported by corporations.[125] Information users are behaviourally expected to choose and prioritise according to their interests and incentives. Some indications from empirical observations show that investors place emphasis on non-financial achievements such as gender diversity on boards or employee welfare, and have even demanded that these be built into chief executives' remuneration packages.[126] In this manner, policy-makers' mandating of double materiality in investment evaluations and disclosures would not prevent more granular market choices from being made in relation to the perceived salience of certain metrics over others. This could play a significant part in shaping selected corporate changes in behaviour[127] and allocative decisions

---

[122] Maijoor (2020).

[123] Del Giudice and Rigamonti (2020).

[124] Perez (2016).

[125] Betti et al. (2018); Mervelskemper and Streit (2017); Aureli et al. (2019). Lueg et al. (2019) look at risk salience of ESG reporting, for example.

[126] 'Half of FTSE 100 companies link executive pay to ESG targets', Financial Times, 17 March 2021.

[127] Le Roux and Pretorius (2019).

by the investment sector. Forces of isomorphism amongst conventional investment funds may thus converge on a narrower market-based selection of metrics development and prioritisation, and hence influence what is relatively more important in terms of environmental or social sustainability goals.

Industry practice in terms of prioritisation of certain sustainability metrics over others may influence the development of fund products, whether actively or passively managed, in favour of certain popular sustainability goals and metrics. Examples are the corporation's expense ratio for human capital training, the emission levels of greenhouse gases or pollutants, and the level of social or media attention on particular popular indicators.[128] In this manner, sustainable investment can develop in a selective manner prioritising support for certain sustainable objectives over others. Hence, the policy preference for double materiality may still not connect private investment holistically and comprehensively with the public interest goals of sustainability.

However, it can be argued that EU policy-makers should not expect the private investment sector to provide comprehensively for environmentally and socially sustainable development goals. The UN SDGs, for example, are envisaged to be achieved by a mixture of public and development finance[129] as well as private finance.[130] Hence, policy-makers should be prepared to observe and monitor market-led developments in terms of sustainable finance in order to discern the gaps in sustainability objectives that are not met by private sector finance. There is scope for policy-makers to consider the public goods nature of gaps and the need for public and development finance, or blended finance involving public-private partnership[131] to meet that need. The enrolment of private sector-led sustainable finance could be perceived as useful for policy-makers' determination of an optimal division of labour between market-driven provision and public provision. Policy-makers should not merely rely on private sector financial provision to meet sustainability goals in total.

However, contrary to the above argument, investors with particular preferences and investment funds with particular mandates, such as impact investment funds, could incentivise the development of specific metrics demonstrating specific impact to be delivered.[132] In niche quarters, new forms of double materiality may voluntarily arise and be developed. The needs of different investment quarters may exert different demands in terms of development of double materiality metrics.

Policy-makers and regulators should be attentive to market developments and be prepared to engage in a governance role in relation to the bottom-up development and implementation of sustainability metrics.

---

[128] Such as a convergence of investor interest upon human rights violations information, Bradford (2020).

[129] Georgeson and Maslin (2018).

[130] Walker et al. (2019).

[131] OECD (2018); see for critical discussion Tan (2019).

[132] Reeder et al. (2015). The difficulties of measuring impact and integrating this into financial materiality are canvassed in Brandstetter and Lehner (2015).

Finally, many conventional institutional investors make allocations to sustainable investments that are passively managed. Although the Sustainability Disclosure Regulation expects fund intermediaries to justify their choice of the benchmark index and to demonstrate sustainable performance, chiefly by comparing the sustainable benchmark index to a conventional broad-based index, the modus of performance demonstration in this manner results in the need to merely prove 'relative' but not absolute sustainable performance. Fund intermediaries only need to show that sustainably labelled funds improve on conventionally benchmarked funds' sustainable performance as a whole.[133] Relative improvement does not mean that sustainable goals have been achieved in significant measure. Further, sustainable indices often aggregate a range of sustainable metrics and scores, and smooth over detail in relation to different granular aspects of sustainable performance.[134] It is uncertain if the EU regime for benchmarks regulation fully addresses the information-signalling effects of sustainable indices, a point we return to in Section 4.

In sum, we see EU-level governance for metrics development as being essential in terms of underpinning ideological clarification and choices, as well as coordinating multi-stakeholder governance in public-private development. Some co-existence and co-development with single materiality metrics development is likely inevitable and to an extent can be productive. EU-level governance should also extend into implementational monitoring and considering how best to meet the gaps left by the market in terms of meeting certain sustainability objectives. Ultimately, the governance for metrics development should extend beyond the financial lever, and Section 4 offers some thoughts on next steps in securing a more holistic agenda for such governance.

4 EU Governance in Sustainability Metrics Development

We argue that EU-level governance should be extended to overseeing the development of sustainability metrics for consistent use in relation to the governance of economic activity generally, and not just pursuant to investment fund regulation. Such harmonisation is consistent with the policy agenda in the European Green Deal which seeks to situate economic growth pursuits within a sustainability framework.[135] The Green Deal focuses on environmentally sustainable goals, while social development policies are still emerging in the EU's '2030' agenda that endorses the UN Sustainable Development Goals.[136] In this context of wider policy agendas, sustainability metrics for investors should not be developed in isolation from

---

[133] Antoncic et al. (2020).

[134] Brakman Reiser and Tucker (2020) find that passive ESG funds pay lip service to substantive ESG performance, while 'aggregating' sustainability measurement can result in the obscuring of granular negative information, see Fiaschi et al. (2020).

[135] https://ec.europa.eu/info/strategy/priorities-2019-2024/european-green-deal_en (accessed 15 Nov 2021).

[136] https://ec.europa.eu/environment/sustainable-development/SDGs/index_en.htm (accessed 15 Nov 2021).

corporate[137] and financial regulation more generally, as these affect economic activities that relate to the achievement of the Green Deal or the 2030 agenda. Such a broader agenda is important in order to contextualise the financial lever as only one part of the policy mosaic. The financial lever's efficacy is likely incomplete if other complimentary policy levers that seek to change corporate behaviour are not developed.

4.1 Holistic Agenda for Governance of Metrics Development

First, there is a case for reforming the corporate disclosure regime for non-financial sustainability impact and performance, so as to shed light on the sustainability evaluation of economic activity. The reforms should target scope as well as metrics governance, incorporating the needs of the financial lever discussed above. In relation to scope, mandating[138] corporate reporting of sustainability performance across the corporate sector should extend beyond application to listed companies, which are currently the entities subject to mandatory non-financial reporting under the Non-financial Disclosure Directive 2014. There should not be a narrow focus to make sustainability matter only if fund-raising is in issue. The contribution of adverse or positive sustainable impact from all economic activities is relevant for the assessment of sustainability objectives achievement.[139] A more universal case is warranted for corporate transparency of the sustainability performance of private as well as publicly traded corporations. This is of relevance to investors in relation to new forms of capital formation, such as in equity crowdfunding for small and medium-sized enterprises, as well as for a broader range of stakeholders concerned about the impact of economic activity. After all, SMEs contribute to at least 50% of the EU economy and employ over 100 million people.[140]

The UK Government[141] is planning to introduce mandatory disclosure of climate impact risk and risk management by listed companies, companies traded on the Alternative Investment Market, large private companies and Limited Liability Partnerships with 500 employees and above. This measure recognises a wider scope of business and economic activity with potential climate impact. Although it may be argued this is proportionate for smaller companies in view of the regulatory burden, sustainability may be a collective good that should be shared by all,

---

[137] MacNeil and Esser (2021) and Sheehy (2021) in this volume.

[138] Also referring to fragmented and weak practices in voluntary reporting so far, Esty and Karpilow (2019); Sarfaty (2013).

[139] Lipton (2020).

[140] https://ec.europa.eu/growth/smes_en#:~:text=Small%20and%20medium%2Dsized%20enterprises%20(SMEs)%20are%20the%20backbone,every%20sector%20of%20the%20economy (accessed 15 Nov 2021).

[141] UK BEIS, 'Consultation on requiring mandatory climate-related financial disclosures by publicly quoted companies, large private companies and Limited Liability Partnerships (LLPs)', March 2021, https://assets.publishing.service.gov.uk/government/uploads/system/uploads/attachment_data/file/972422/Consultation_on_BEIS_mandatory_climate-related_disclosure_requirements.pdf (accessed 15 Nov 2021).

even the smallest businesses. The European Commission also now acknowledges that improved mandatory disclosure is needed for corporate reporting beyond the qualitative and principles-based approach in the 2014 Directive. It now proposes the contours of a Corporate Sustainability Reporting Directive envisaged to standardise sustainability disclosures for the entire corporate sector, including small and medium-sized enterprises but subject to proportionate application.[142]

It remains uncertain to what extent the recognition of the need to extend the scope of mandatory sustainability disclosures to the corporate sector includes policy endeavours for the governance of metrics development. In order to support consistent, comparable and meaningful corporate disclosure, the metrics against which sustainability impacts and achievements are reported should ideally be acceptable as proximate and measurable indicators for particular outcomes, and capable of being standardised. Mandating items for disclosure, such as those susceptible to qualitative disclosure, has often attracted criticism in relation to the lack of yardsticks for judging such disclosure. For example, in the UK, both private and publicly traded companies are subject to reporting obligations under the Modern Slavery Act[143] in order to provide transparency on corporate due diligence into supply chains and to prevent modern slavery and human trafficking. The Act did not extend into metrics governance and adopted a principles-based approach on the overall qualitative nature of the reporting. The principles-based approach under the Act is being reviewed[144] for greater prescription and consistency as flexibility and open-endedness have only resulted in vague development of indicators. Weak and fragmented reporting is also the experience in the US in relation to reporting on sourcing and due diligence policies for conflict minerals in the Democratic Republic of Congo,[145] without the specific development of clear metrics. These examples highlight a need for governance of metrics development, as the agenda for double materiality is to be a holistic one.

It is arguable that the Taxonomy Regulation has made a first attempt at metrics governance for non-financial corporate reporting. The Taxonomy Regulation includes an amendment to the EU Non-financial Disclosure Directive to compel listed companies to make disclosure of certain expenditure levels connected with sustainable activities.[146] These disclosures are intended to reflect real levels of commitment by companies to sustainable activities, 'if they put their money where their mouths are'. Corporations are to disclose three key financial indicators:[147] the proportion of turnover in products or services in economic activities that can be associated with environmentally sustainable activities as defined in the Taxonomy Regulation; the proportion of capital expenditure related to assets or processes associated

---

[142] *Supra* n. 7.

[143] Section 54 of the Modern Slavery Act 2015.

[144] UK Home Department (2019), pp 40-41, government consultation on reforms as of 22 Sep 2020, see   https://assets.publishing.service.gov.uk/government/uploads/system/uploads/attachment_data/file/919937/Government_response_to_transparency_in_supply_chains_consultation_21_09_20.pdf (accessed 15 Nov 2021).

[145] Sankara et al. (2019).

[146] Art. 8.

[147] ESMA, Final Report: Advice on Article 8 of the Taxonomy Regulation, Feb 2021.

with economic activities that can be classified as environmentally sustainable; and the proportion of operating expenses related to assets or processes associated with economic activities that are environmentally sustainable.

Capital expenditure relates to expenditure on planned projects or activities that are intended to yield sustainable outcomes in a 5-year timeframe or such other timeframe that may be justified. Operating expenditures are direct costs only and are usually shorter-term in nature and not to be duplicated with capital expenditure. These corporate disclosures, focusing on the level of financial commitment by corporations to sustainable outcomes, provide information at a 'harder' level than the qualitative reporting envisaged under the Non-financial Disclosure Directive. Although financial commitments do not perfectly translate into sustainable outcomes and performance, they can be treated as proxy metrics, and allow investors to probe further upon engagement, and also to make inferences and comparisons. There is however a hazard: such numerical disclosures can obscure qualitative disclosures or become unduly relied upon as shorthand information. Further, such disclosures seem too remote in relation to sustainability outcomes, and also do not reflect issue or outcome specificity.

Although the Commission's proposed Corporate Sustainability Reporting Directive looks promising in terms of scope, the approach is to leave to delegated legislation to develop sustainability indicators for corporate reporting. There is uncertainty as to whether this heralds an entirely public model of metrics prescription. Metrics development benefits from the expertise of epistemic communities of actors, hence private sector participation in metrics development would be valuable. A co-governance[148] framework could be optimal in ensuring that metrics development is subject to sufficient and inclusive debates and monitoring, so that single and double materiality needs can be addressed and reflected in metrics development. In this manner, a multi-stakeholder framework for metrics development, governed by regulatory oversight, could be the way forward, a point we elaborate below.

Further, we also consider that a blend of capital markets policy and company law may be relevant for fund-raising by small and medium-sized enterprises. For example, harmonised EU regulation[149] has been introduced for equity crowdfunding, entailing obligations for standardised key information disclosure[150] by issuers on crowdfunding platforms which are usually SMEs and unlisted private companies. The regulatory regime is proportionate and does not extend the gamut of mandatory securities disclosure to SME issuers on equity crowdfunding platforms. We suggest that further harmonised regulation can provide for the inclusion of sustainability performance in issuer disclosure, especially if relevant to their business models. Such a disclosure requirement could be enabling in nature, supporting the promotion of funding opportunities and channels for private companies. There is a risk that funding for private companies or SMEs to engage in sustainability initiatives

---

[148] Ackermann (2004); also see Finck (2018) in relation to governance of emerging blockchain technologies.

[149] Regulation (EU) 2020/1503 on crowdfunding service providers.

[150] Ibid., Arts. 23-24.

can become marginalised if institutional investors' allocations to sustainable finance are concentrated upon listed companies, since only listed companies are subject to the existing reporting obligations in the Non-financial Disclosure Directive and are included in stock exchange indices.

4.2 Relationship with Metrics Development by the Private Sector

It is yet unclear whether the Commission's proposed Corporate Sustainability Reporting Directive envisages a comprehensive policy-led 're-write' of sustainability metrics reflecting double materiality. There are hazards with such an approach to metrics governance. The top-down provision of sustainability metrics can more clearly reflect the public interest in double materiality, a phenomenon that can be insufficiently internalised in market-based developments. However, it can also be disengaged with market-based needs and result in prescriptions that compel private sector participants to reconcile competing needs for single materiality evaluations and double materiality compliance. Hence, this article prefers a governance approach for metrics development that is co-governance in nature where private sector development is not treated as irrelevant or separate from the regulatory regime. Complementarities and co-educational opportunities should be developed between public sector, private sector and stakeholder governance in a multi-stakeholder space.

This article proposes that the European Securities and Markets Authority (ESMA) can lead a multi-stakeholder framework or committee, besides its stakeholder panel that feeds into general policy and rule-making, to be dedicated to the monitoring of sustainability metrics development for the holistic agenda of regulating corporate disclosure and financial product evaluation.

ESMA can take leadership in engaging with key developers of metrics, such as the SASB/IIRC merged entity, IFRS and GRI, so that the multi-stakeholder committee may be consulted upon or have observer status at key policy meetings. Further, such a multi-stakeholder committee should comprise sufficient representation from non-commercially based stakeholders who are better able to give opinions on double materiality as distinguished from financial or economic materiality.[151] These may include experts such as drawn from the Stockholm Resilience Centre that have introduced the concept of planetary boundaries[152] for sustainable economic conduct, scientific experts on environmental and social developments, non-governmental organisations, and charitable groups with interests in social development. Inclusive and diverse governance groups are often better able to bring balanced perspectives and rich debates to issue areas, as a form of 'tripartite' governance model involving the pillars of public policy, industry and civil society.[153] Such input governance may evolve into more or less intense forms of formal or informal governance, but as a start, policy-makers and civil society should be engaged in the conceptual and

---

[151] Diebecker et al. (2019).

[152] https://www.stockholmresilience.org/ (accessed 15 Nov 2021).

[153] Omarova (2012).

🖄 Springer   ⬤ ASSER PRESS

implementational development of sustainability metrics, as many significant implications flow from such development. Metrics development should not be totally left to market-based forces.

In this manner, EU policy-makers can also consider developing a legislative framework for the endorsement of certain private-sector developed metrics, similar to the model adopted for the international accounting standards developed by the IFRS,[154] though not necessarily centring upon the IFRS per se. This would go beyond the issuance of non-binding guidelines such as has already been undertaken by the European Commission.[155] The adoption of the IFRS' international accounting standards was pursuant to the policy of enabling cross-border capital mobility in the Single Market[156] and also fostered a significant trend of international convergence upon the IFRS based on trading relations with the EU.[157] Of course, the IFRS had been sufficiently well-established at the point of the EU's adoption, and it can be argued that in a landscape of emerging sustainability metrics development, the EU should not prematurely endorse any particular standards or bodies in order to distort competition. However, there is already indication of soft endorsement of the TCFD's climate disclosure standards, which is based on single materiality.[158] This may be due to the international underpinnings of the TCFD led by the Financial Stability Board. Hence, the EU can benefit from a more formal and systematic framework for endorsement of sustainability metrics that should also benefit from multi-stakeholder input as discussed earlier.

Any endorsement framework should be inclusively informed and also be accountable for decision-making. In this manner, the governance framework at EU level can monitor the status of competition amongst sustainability metrics providers and pull levers in order to foster competition or innovation, as well as to offer convergence where that is timely. If, for example, certain metrics gain wide practical acceptance, then an endorsement that fosters convergence can be useful for industry and stakeholders. The endorsement mechanism further opens up channels for the EU governance framework to engage with leading providers of endorsed standards, in order to provide a form of continuing co-governance.

The endorsement framework and process are themselves a form of governance that can be exercised over sustainability metrics development and attracts private sector leaders to engage with policy-makers and ESMA in the EU. Although such a governance role for the EU in relation to endorsing IFRS standards has not been uncontroversial,[159] the bringing to bear of discourse and debate is crucial for the

---

[154] Directive 2013/34/EU.

[155] *Infra* n. 158.

[156] Armstrong et al. (2012).

[157] Ramanna and Sletten (2013).

[158] European Commission's non-binding guidelines for reporting under the Non-financial Disclosure Directive, see European Commission, Guidelines on reporting climate-related information (2019), https://ec.europa.eu/finance/docs/policy/190618-climate-related-information-reporting-guidelines_en.pdf (accessed 15 Nov 2021).

[159] Bischof and Daske (2016) on the tortuous journey for endorsing IFRS 9; also see Eroglu (2015, 2017); Hijink (2013).

shaping of sustainability metrics, which, as Section 3 has discussed, has conceptual implications beyond the financial sector.

4.3 Governing Information Intermediaries in Sustainable Metrics Development

Finally, this article suggests that EU-level governance for metrics development should be extended to information intermediaries of sustainability metrics generally. 'Informediaries' for sustainability or ESG information are often relied upon as they provide shorthand information for easy adoption[160] by active managers in socially responsible portfolios or by passive managers benchmarked to an index. Indeed, we predict elsewhere[161] that the EU sustainable finance agenda is likely to mobilise the passive investing sector more significantly, and providers of sustainability indices therefore wield great market influence.

It may be argued that index providers for passively managed investment funds are already regulated under the Benchmarks Regulation,[162] hence there is existing EU-level governance over these entities. Further, the EU introduced the 'Low Carbon Benchmarks' Regulation 2019[163] to set minimum standards for benchmarks that are labelled as 'climate transition' or 'Paris-aligned'. This is a good starting point for index providers who wish to use these labels for their benchmarks. Further developments in the social taxonomy and other benchmarks may be provided for in regulatory reform.

However, it is queried whether the Benchmarks Regulation addresses the issues specific to sustainability indices. The governance for the derivation of benchmarks is one issue, but this does not encompass all the issues in relation to metrics development as such. Granular metrics development is still relevant to active management and impact investing strategies, as well as to closer investor and stakeholder scrutiny into both corporate and investment allocation behaviour.

The Benchmarks Regulation was developed in the wake of the scandals relating to the manipulation of financial benchmarks for pricing variable interest rate contracts, i.e., the LIBOR and EURIBOR manipulation scandals.[164] Hence, the regulatory approach is to subject administrators of benchmarks to proper governance in relation to their conflicts of interest management, internal control, accountability functions, oversight of data collection and input into the derivation of benchmarks, as well as their oversight of submitters of such data.[165] Administrators are also to

---

[160] Vives and Wadhwa (2012).

[161] Chiu (2021).

[162] Regulation 2016/1011 on benchmark regulation.

[163] Regulation (EU) 2019/2089 on EU Climate Transition Benchmarks, EU Paris-aligned Benchmarks and sustainability-related disclosures for benchmarks.

[164] 'Libor scandal: the bankers who fixed the world's most important number', The Guardian, 18 Jan 2017, https://www.theguardian.com/business/2017/jan/18/libor-scandal-the-bankers-who-fixed-the-worlds-most-important-number (accessed 15 Nov 2021); 'Two former traders handed jail terms in Euribor manipulation case', Financial Times, 19 July 2018, https://www.ft.com/content/c970a0c0-8b53-11e8-b18d-0181731a0340 (accessed 15 Nov 2021).

[165] Regulation 2016/2011, Arts. 4-11, 15, 16.

develop robust, reliable and resilient methodologies for deriving benchmarks and to make these methodologies transparent.[166] Further, significant and critical benchmarks are subject to more intrusive regulatory supervision and requirements to maintain their integrity and continuity.[167] These provisions have been clearly aimed at the self-regulatory and opaque nature of bank panel submissions of hypothetical lending prices in order to derive the inter-bank offered rate benchmarks. However, the Regulation has broadened the definition of benchmarks to encompass indices adopted by investment funds to measure their performance, as indices function in a similar manner for financial evaluation and had been self-regulatory prior to the Regulation.

Although the broadly framed aspects of administrator governance in the Benchmarks Regulation can apply to index providers, the regulation of methodology may arguably be broad and under-inclusive. Different from the issues dogging price benchmarks, which is that there may be only hypothetical and small selections of data based on submitters' input, the issue with regard to sustainability indices is that index providers often have a wealth of information to manage, and there is opacity and variation in how they assess such information and aggregate it in order to derive the shorthand of the benchmark.[168]

The processes of aggregation by index providers of various sustainability data are underpinned by assumptions of salience and weight given to indicators.[169] The shorthand result does not usually offer transparency as to the prioritisation of objectives and metrics.[170] For example, empirical research has found little difference between socially-responsible labelled portfolios and conventional ones, where investments in oil and gas companies are routinely made in the former.[171] Further, empirical research has also found companies included in the Dow Jones Sustainability Index that have been fraught with scandals for regulatory non-compliance or that are polluters.[172] Rating and index differences can be ascribed to business model differences amongst informediaries, such as 'who pays for the ratings',[173] and ideological and methodological underpinnings[174] that differ amongst providers.

It is likely that specific governance requirements for methodologies of aggregation by sustainability index providers may be needed in terms of explaining their priorities, use of underlying metrics and trade-offs. This is not yet observed in the recent reforms introduced to the Benchmarks Regulation to clarify the meaning of 'low carbon' benchmarks. The reforms oblige index providers to be aligned with certain goals such as the EU's climate transition emission targets. This is outcome-focused and, arguably, index providers could curate the index based on

---

[166] Arts. 12 and 13, ibid.

[167] Arts. 20-25, ibid.

[168] Chiu (2010/2011).

[169] E.g., the Canberra aggregation method, see Brandi et al. (2014).

[170] Jitmaneeroj (2016); Esty and Cort (2017); Fiaschi et al. (2020).

[171] Nitsche and Schröder (2018).

[172] Arribas et al. (2019).

[173] Eccles et al. (2015).

[174] Chelli and Gendron (2013); Eccles and Stroehle (2019).

clear disclosures by companies that meet the targets. However, would companies included in such a low carbon index be regarded as generally 'sustainable'? How would the single issue of emission achievement sit with other sustainability indicators and metrics for the index construction? Index providers are likely more attracted to multi-issue sustainability, and the credibility of aggregation methodologies and their transparency remain in need of governance. Further, it is unlikely that a prescriptive approach to all possible index labels can practically be undertaken at the EU level, as this approach cannot prevent market innovations and developments for index labels that are not covered by the prescriptive approach.

We posit that the governance of informediaries for sustainability metrics development should be more encompassing and substantive. These include not only index providers but also ratings providers and analysts more broadly, as well as assurance providers for corporate sustainability reporting. Ratings providers and analysts are not all absorbed by index providers and there are independent entities in this space.[175] A regulatory focus only on benchmarks regulation would obscure the need for a more holistic and consistent framework for governing the roles of other actors in metrics development. Further, both input and output legitimacy for informediaries' and assurance work can be improved by engaging with multi-stakeholder governance including policy and civil society actors.

There are arguably three models for governing important financial sector informediaries, from which insights can be drawn for developing the governance of sustainability metrics developers and informediaries. One model is in the credit ratings regulatory regime, which is not dissimilar from the benchmarks regulatory regime, the other is in the disclosure regulation for proxy advisers implemented largely in soft law. For assurance providers, the model governing financial auditors can be consulted.

Credit rating agencies have been subject to pan-European regulation[176] after the global financial crisis of 2007-9, as they contributed to providing flawed creditworthiness assessments of structured financial products, which ultimately led to market and institutional stress in global financial systems.[177] Regulatory governance is extended to structural factors in credit rating business models that may affect objectivity[178] and the robustness and rigour of credit rating methodologies.[179] This is arguably similar to the regulation of benchmark administrators. Hence, the basic rubric of entity regulation can be considered for all sustainability metrics developers, but more refined consideration should be given to issues specific to the development of sustainability metrics. These issues are: the ideological underpinnings of metrics, how single and double materiality may be reconciled, and the need for

---

[175] Such as Bloomberg ESG or Viageo Eiris.

[176] Regulation (EC) No 1060/2009 on credit rating agencies.

[177] McVea (2010).

[178] As regards regulating conflicts of interest management, see also Bai (2010).

[179] Regulation 1060/2009, Art. 8; see also Commission Delegated Regulation (EU) 447/2012, Arts. 4-7. See critical discussion in Chiu (2013).

multi-stakeholder input. Further, supervisory governance is useful for backtesting rating methodologies and the effectiveness of metrics.

It may, however, be regarded as excessive that regulation is extended to sustainability metrics developers as significant problems have yet to surface. Nevertheless, the extension of regulatory governance for metrics developers in sustainability can foster a more level and credible playing field, and can be regarded as enabling in nature.

In the alternative, a more proportionate model for governing the role of another information intermediary can be found in the disclosure regulation for proxy advisers and ESMA's informal governance of them. Leading proxy advisers have significant market share[180] and there have been concerns that they would play a systemic role in shareholder voting and corporate governance trends.[181] Proxy advisers formed a collective group called the Best Principles Group to put forward a set of recommendations guiding their disclosures of research and house voting policies, their conflicts of interest management policies and how they communicate with their clients and relevant stakeholders.[182] ESMA conducted a review of proxy advisers' adherence to their best principles and did not find cause for more severe regulatory intervention, therefore indicating that disclosure-based regulation coupled with soft law in best practices can be sufficient for market discipline.[183] The EU Shareholder Rights Directive 2017 ultimately settled for this model of proportionate governance where proxy advisers should disclose if they adhere to a set of best practices in making their recommendations.[184] There is also empirical evidence that systemic reliance on proxy advisers is not found,[185] and therefore their influence is not so potent as to warrant direct regulatory intervention.

It may be warranted for sustainability metrics developers to be subject to a form of disclosure regulation that is proportionate and minimalist at first, like under the Shareholder Rights Directive 2017 for proxy advisers. Transparency can be required in relation to key issues that should be subject to policy-makers' and multi-stakeholders' scrutiny, such as research and methodological policies for sustainability data and data processing, the adoption and robustness of certain metrics, the conflicts of interest management policies that may affect ratings and index inclusion decisions, the use of automated technologies in data processing and policies employed against bias and for periodic review. Governance actors should monitor to what extent such disclosures affect metrics development, market adoption and reliance, so as to discern the effects of market discipline. A more proportionate approach to regulatory governance is an acceptable starting point.

---

[180] Choi et al. (2010).

[181] Ibid.

[182] Best Practice Principles for Providers of Shareholder Voting Research and Analysis (2014), https://bppgrp.info/wp-content/uploads/2014/03/BPP-ShareholderVoting-Research-2014.pdf (accessed 15 Nov 2021).

[183] ESMA, Report: Follow-up on the Development of the Best Practice Principles for Providers of Shareholder Voting Research and Analysis (2015).

[184] Art. 3j.

[185] 'Big investors ignore proxy advisers on controversial votes', Financial Times, 8 Feb 2020.

Regarding assurance providers, bottom-up developments indicate that there is a convergence upon assurance provision for corporate reporting using the GRI or AA1000 standards for non-financial voluntary reporting.[186] Indeed, the organisation AccountAbility, which has developed the AA1000 reporting standards, has issued its own assurance standard, the AA1000AS.[187] The International Federation of Accountants has also issued the ISAE3000 assurance standard for the accounting profession undertaking non-financial reporting assurance.[188] However, bottom-up developments currently support assurance for single materiality reporting, and there may be a need to develop assurance capabilities for double materiality metrics and reporting. This is an area where policy steering, multi-stakeholder governance and private sector development can engage with one another. Empirical research has generally found assurance for non-financial reporting to be useful,[189] e.g., motivating corporate restatements,[190] hence both policy support for the development of an assurance industry that can cater for double materiality and governance oversight of such an industry may be useful.

Drawing from regulatory oversight of the auditing industry, the governance development for this industry has moved from professional self-regulation to regulatory oversight, in the wake of corporate scandals the signs of which could not be usefully detected from earlier transparency.[191] Conflicts of interest management,[192] professional standards in auditing[193] and the lack of competition in the auditing industry[194] have been major concerns for a long time. Assurance providers in the audit industry would likely benefit from being covered by auditor regulation, as similar issues such as conflicts of interest management and industry oligopoly are present. However, it may be viewed as disproportionate to regulate ahead of market failures, and there is scope to explore a disclosure-based regime such as for proxy advisers who are bound by soft law for best practices in governance and conflicts of interest management to begin with. This can also apply to non-audit entities providing assurance for non-financial reporting. However, the more pressing issue for non-financial assurance is in relation to what professional standards of assurance are needed for newly emerging sustainability metrics. Emerging standards of assurance may also need to be forged with multi-stakeholder input in the face of the need to assure double materiality, as such assurance is unlike financial reporting assurance targeted at capital markets. There is a socially-facing dimension of assuring for public and stakeholder

---

[186] E.g., the Sustainability Report Assurance, https://www.sgs.com/en/sustainability/sustainability-repor ting/sustainability-report-assurance-sra (accessed 15 Nov 2021), is based on GRI or AA1000 reporting.

[187] https://www.accountability.org/standards/aa1000-assurance-standard/ (accessed 15 Nov 2021).

[188] https://www.iaasb.org/publications/international-standard-assurance-engagements-isae-3000-revised-assurance-engagements-other-audits-or-0 (accessed 15 Nov 2021).

[189] Sam and Tiong (2015); Chen et al. (2019).

[190] Chen et al. (2019).

[191] Such as the Enron scandal, discussed in Coffee (2002); more recently the UK's Carillion and Patisserie Valerie scandals, see House of Commons (2018).

[192] Ibid.

[193] Brydon (2019).

[194] Competition and Markets Authority (2018).

consumption, and the development of assurance standards should incorporate this dimension.

In sum, we see the extension of EU-level governance in sustainability metrics development as necessary and inevitable, although we caution against a completely top-down approach of re-writing metrics over existing private sector-based developments. Such governance should be holistic in terms of fostering credible metrics development for economic activity generally and should involve co-governance with private sector and stakeholder entities. Policy-makers may consider a spectrum of soft to legalised regimes for sustainability informediaries and metrics developers.

5 Conclusion

This article argues that the regulatory steers in the recent EU Sustainable Disclosure and Taxonomy Regulations rely heavily on the outworking of market-based governance to meet public interest goals in sustainable finance. Hence, additional work in sustainability metrics development that informs the investment sector of sustainable performance in companies would be of key importance. This article argues that there remain gaps in EU leadership for governing metrics development, and suggests that EU-level governance can be designed appropriately, especially in a multi-stakeholder manner, for metrics development and in relation to key information intermediaries in this space.

Acknowledgements I am grateful for the support of the Centre for Banking and Financial Law for facilitating the Sustainable Finance Conference between UCL and NUS on 16 April 2021. Comments from Iain MacNeil, Eva Micheler, David Rouch and Dirk Zetzsche are gratefully acknowledged. All errors and omissions are mine.

References

Ackermann J (2004) Co-governance for accountability: beyond 'exit' and 'voice.' World Dev 32:447–463
Akisik O, Gal G (2020) Integrated reports, external assurance and financial performance: an empirical analysis on North American firms. Sustain Account Manag Policy J 11:317–350
Alsayegh MF, Rahman AR, Homayoun S (2020) Corporate economic, environmental, and social sustainability performance transformation through ESG disclosure. Sustainability 12:1–20
Amba S (2018) Corporate sustainability: do executives and investors care? An empirical study. Int J Manag Mark Res 11:19–26
Amel-Zadeh A, Serafeim G (2018) Why and how investors use ESG information: evidence from a global survey. Finance Anal J 74:87–103

Ammann M, Bauer C, Fischer S, Müller P (2018) The impact of the Morningstar Sustainability Rating on mutual fund flows. https://ssrn.com/abstract=3068724. Accessed 15 Nov 2021

Antoncic M, Bekaert G, Rothenberg R, Noguer M (2020) Sustainable investment – exploring the linkage between Alpha, ESG, and SDG's. https://ssrn.com/abstract=3623459. Accessed 15 Nov 2021

Apostolakis G, Kraanen F, van Dijk G (2016) Pension beneficiaries' and fund managers' perceptions of responsible investment: a focus group study. Corp Gov 16:1–20

Apostolakis G, Van Dijk G, Blomme RJ, Kraanen F, Papadopoulos AP (2018) Predicting pension beneficiaries' behaviour when offered a socially responsible and impact investment portfolio. J Sustain Finance Invest 8:213–241

Armstrong CS, Barth ME, Jagolindzer AD, Riedl EJ (2012) Market reaction to the adoption of IFRS in Europe. http://ssrn.com/abstract=1265032. Accessed 15 Nov 2021

Arribas I, Espinós-Vañó MD, García F, Morales-Bañuelos PB (2019) The inclusion of socially irresponsible companies in sustainable stock indices. Sustainability 11:2047

Aureli S, Gigli S, Medei R, Supino E (2019) The value relevance of environmental, social, and governance disclosure: evidence from Dow Jones Sustainability World Index listed companies. Corp Soc Responsib Environ Manag 27:43–52

Bai L (2010) On regulating conflicts of interests in the credit rating industry. NYU J Legis Public Policy 13:253–312

Barker RM, Chiu IH-Y (2020) Examining the Wates Principles for large private companies as a social contract for business-society relations. Int Comp Corp Law J 14, chapter 3

Barter N (2015) Natural capital: dollars and cents/dollars and sense. Sustain Account Manag Policy J 6:366–373

Barter N (2016) A review of 'A New Vision of Value'—old wine, new bottle'. Sustain Account Manag Policy J 7:531–538

Bebbington J, Unerman J (2018) Achieving the United Nations Sustainable Development Goals. Account Audit Account J 31:2–24

Bebchuk L, Hirst S (2019) Index funds and the future of corporate governance: theory, policy and evidence. Columbia Law Rev 119:2029–2146

Beske F, Haustein E, Lorson PC (2020) Materiality analysis in sustainability and integrated reports. Sustain Account Manag Policy J 11:162–186

Betti G, Consolandi C, Eccles RG (2018) The relationship between investor materiality and the Sustainable Development Goals: a methodological framework. Sustainability 10:2248

Bianchi RJ, Drew ME (2012) Sustainable stock indices and long-term portfolio decisions. J Sustain Finance Invest 2:303–317

Bischof J, Daske H (2016) Interpreting the European Union's IFRS endorsement criteria: the case of IFRS 9. http://ssrn.com/abstract=2803567. Accessed 15 Nov 2021

Black J (2003) Enrolling actors in regulatory systems: examples from UK financial services regulation. Public Law 63-91

Bradford H (2020) Demand has more seeing inclusion of ESG metrics. Pensions and Investments 48:3. https://www.pionline.com/investing/demand-has-more-seeing-inclusion-esg-metrics. Accessed 15 Nov 2021

Brakman Reiser D, Tucker A (2020) Buyer beware: variation and opacity in ESG and ESG index funds. Cardozo L Rev 41:1921–2018

Brandi HS, Daroda RJ, Olinto AC (2014) The use of the Canberra metrics to aggregate metrics to sustainability. Clean Technol Environ Policy 16:911–920

Brandstetter L, Lehner OM (2015) Opening the market for impact investments: the need for adapted portfolio tools. Enterprise Res J 5:87–107

Brydon, Sir Donald (2019) The quality and effectiveness of audit: independent review. https://www.gov.uk/government/publications/the-quality-and-effectiveness-of-audit-independent-review. Accessed 15 Nov 2021

Busco C, Consolandi C, Eccles RG, Sofra E (2020) A preliminary analysis of SASB reporting: disclosure topics, financial relevance, and the financial intensity of ESG materiality. https://ssrn.com/abstract=3548849. Accessed 15 Nov 2021

Chelli M, Gendron Y (2013) Ratings and the disciplinary power of the ideology of numbers. J Bus Ethics 112:187–203

Chen P-C, Ballou B, Grenier JH, Heitger DL (2019) Sustainability assurance's link to reporting quality. J Account. https://www.journalofaccountancy.com/news/2019/oct/sustainability-assurance-link-to-reporting-quality-201919354.html. Accessed 15 Nov 2021

Chen RCY, Hung S-W, Lee C-H (2017) Does corporate value affect the relationship between corporate social responsibility and stock returns? J Sustain Finance Invest 7:188–196

Chiu IH-Y (2010/2011) Standardization in corporate social responsibility reporting and a universalist concept of CSR? A path paved with good intentions. Florida J Int Law 22:361–400

Chiu IH-Y (2013) Regulatory governance of credit rating agencies in the EU: the perils of pursuing the holy grail of rating accuracy. Eur J Risk Regul 4:209–226

Chiu IH-Y (2021) Building a single market for sustainable finance in the EU – mixed implications and the missing link of digitalisation. European Company and Financial Law Review, forthcoming

Choi SJ, Fisch JE, Kahan M (2010) The power of proxy advisors: myth or reality? Emory Law J 59:869–918

Christensen HB, Hail L, Leuz C (2019) Adoption of CSR and sustainability reporting standards: economic analysis and review. ECGI Working Paper No. 623/2019. http://ssrn.com/abstract_id=3427748. Accessed 15 Nov 2021

Christiansen C, Jansson T, Kallestrup-Lamb M, Noren V (2019) Who are the socially responsible mutual fund investors? http://ssrn.com/abstract=3128432. Accessed 15 Nov 2021

Coffee JC Jr (2002) Gatekeepers. OUP, Oxford

Competition and Markets Authority (2018) Statutory Audit Market Study. https://www.gov.uk/cma-cases/statutory-audit-market-study. Accessed 15 Nov 2021

Corley E (2019) Sustainable investment: the golden moment. In: London Institute of Banking and Finance (ed) Banking on change: the development and future of financial services. John Wiley & Sons, Chichester, ch 6

Cort T, Esty D (2020) ESG standards: looming challenges and pathways forward. Organ Environ 33:491–510

Cubas-Díaz M, Sedano MÁM (2018) Do credit ratings take into account the sustainability performance of companies? Sustainability 10:4272

Darton RC (2015) Setting a policy for sustainability: the importance of measurement. In: Klemes J (ed) Assessing and measuring environmental impact and sustainability. Elsevier, ch 14

De Benedetto L, Klemes J (2015) The Environmental Performance Strategy Map: an integrated life cycle assessment approach to support the strategic decision-making process. In: Klemes J (ed) Assessing and measuring environmental impact and sustainability. Elsevier, ch 11

de Haan M, Dam L, Scholtens B (2012) The drivers of the relationship between corporate environmental performance and stock market returns. J Sustain Finance Invest 2:338–375

Del Giudice A, Rigamonti S (2020) Does audit improve the quality of ESG scores? Evidence from corporate misconduct. Sustainability 12:5670

Delsen L, Lehr A (2019) Value matters or values matter? An analysis of heterogeneity in preferences for sustainable investments. J Sustain Finance Invest 9:240–261

Diebecker J, Rose C, Sommer F (2019) Spoiled for choice: does the selection of sustainability datasets matter? https://ssrn.com/abstract=3359508. Accessed 15 Nov 2021

Dienes D, Sassen R, Fischer J (2016) What are the drivers of sustainability reporting? A systematic review. Sustain Account Manag Policy J 7:154

Diez-Cañamero B, Bishara T, Otegi-Olaso JR, Minguez R, Fernández JM (2020) Measurement of corporate social responsibility: a review of corporate sustainability indexes, rankings and ratings. Sustainability 12:2153

Durán-Santomil P, Otero-González L, Correia-Domingues RH, Reboredo JC (2019) Does sustainability score impact mutual fund performance? Sustain J 11:2972

Eccles RG, Stroehle JC (2019) Exploring social origins in the construction of ESG measures. http://ssrn.com/abstract=3212685. Accessed 15 Nov 2021

Eccles RG, Herron J, Serafeim G (2015) Reliable sustainability ratings. In: Hebb T, Hawley JP, Hoepner AGF, Neher AL, Wood D (eds) The Routledge handbook of responsible investment. Routledge, Oxford, ch 48

Eroglu ZGK (2015) Whose Trojan horse? Dynamics of resistance against IFRS. Univ Pa Int Law J 36:89–190

Eroglu ZGK (2017) The political economy of international standard setting in financial reporting: how the United States led the adoption of IFRS across the world. Northwest J Int Law Bus 37:457–512

Esty DC, Cort T (2017) The data challenges that remain. In: Kronsinsky C, Purdom S (eds) Sustainable investing: revolutions in theory and practice. Routledge Earthscan, ch 9

Esty DC, Karpilow Q (2019) Harnessing investor interest in sustainability: the next frontier in environmental information regulation. Yale J Reg 36:625–692

Fiaschi D, Giuliani E, Nieri F, Salvati N (2020) How bad is your company? Measuring corporate wrong-doing beyond the magic of ESG metrics. Bus Horiz 63:287–299

Fichtner J, Heemskerk EM (2020) The new permanent universal owners: index funds, patient capital, and the distinction between feeble and forceful stewardship. Econ Soc 49:493–515

Financial Conduct Authority (2020) Proposals to enhance climate-related disclosures by listed issuers and clarification of existing disclosure obligations, 21 Dec 2020. https://www.fca.org.uk/publicatio ns/policy-statements/ps20-17-proposals-enhance-climate-related-disclosures-listed-issuers-and-clarification-existing. Accessed 15 Nov 2021

Finck M (2018) Blockchain regulation and governance in Europe. CUP, Cambridge

Fisch JE (2019) Making sustainability disclosure sustainable. Geo LJ 107:923–966

Fornasari F (2020) Knowledge and power in measuring the sustainable corporation: stock exchanges as regulators of ESG factors disclosure. Wash U Global Stud L Rev 19:167–233

Freshfields Bruckhaus Deringer (2005) A legal framework for the integration of environmental, social and governance issues into institutional investment. Report for the UNEP Finance Initiative. https://www.unepfi.org/fileadmin/documents/freshfields_legal_resp_20051123.pdf. Accessed 15 Nov 2021

Friede G, Busch T, Bassen A (2015) ESG and financial performance: aggregated evidence from more than 2000 empirical studies. J Sustain Financ Invest 5:210–233

Georgeson L, Maslin M (2018) Putting the United Nations sustainable development goals into practice: a review of implementation, monitoring, and finance. Geograph Environ. https://doi.org/10.1002/geo2.49.Accessed15Nov2021

Gibassier D (2015) The corporate reporting landscape: a market for virtue or the virtue of marketization? Sustain Account Manag Policy J 6:527–536

Gibson R, Krüger P, Mitali SF (2018) The sustainability footprint of institutional investors. ECGI Working Paper No. 571/2018. https://ssrn.com/abstract=2918926. Accessed 15 Nov 2021

Gilson RJ, Gordon JN (2013) The agency costs of agency capitalism activist investors and the revaluation of governance rights. Columbia Law Rev 113:863–928

Glac K (2014) The influence of shareholders on corporate social responsibility. Econ Manag Financ Mark 9:34–72

Grewal J, Hauptmann C, Serafeim G (2017) Material sustainability information and stock price informativeness. https://ssrn.com/abstract=2966144. Accessed 15 Nov 2021

Grewal J, Serafeim G, Yoon A (2016) Shareholder activism on sustainability issues. Harvard Business School Working Paper No. 17-003. https://www.hbs.edu/faculty/Pages/item.aspx?num=51379. Accessed 15 Nov 2021

Gutsche G, Ziegler A (2019) Which private investors are willing to pay for sustainable investments? Empirical evidence from stated choice experiments. J Bank Finance 102:193–214

Haar B (2012) Civil liability of credit rating agencies – regulatory all-or-nothing approaches between immunity and over-deterrence. http://ssrn.com/abstract=2198293. Accessed 15 Nov 2021

Harper Ho V (2020) Disclosure overload? Lessons for risk disclosure & ESG reform from the Regulation S-K Concept Release. Vill L Rev 65:67–91

Hendriksen B, Weimer J, McKenzie M (2016) Approaches to quantify value from business to society: case studies of KPMG's True Value methodology. Sustain Account Manag Policy J 7:474–493

Herbertson K, Hunter D (2007) Emerging standards for sustainable finance of the energy sector. Sustain Dev. L. & Pol'y 7:4–9

High-Level Expert Group on Sustainable Finance (HLEG) (2018) Financing a sustainable European economy. https://ec.europa.eu/info/sites/info/files/180131-sustainable-finance-final-report_en.pdf. Accessed 15 Nov 2021

Hijink S (2013) Towards European accounting law? http://ssrn.com/abstract=2233089. Accessed 15 Nov 2021

Hinze A-K, Sump F (2019) Corporate social responsibility and financial analysts: a review of the literature. Sustain Account Manag Policy J 10:183–207

House of Commons (2018) Carillion plc. https://publications.parliament.uk/pa/cm201719/cmselect/cmworpen/769/76902.htm. Accessed 15 Nov 2021

Hübel B, Scholz H (2020) Integrating sustainability risks in asset management: the role of ESG exposures and ESG ratings. J Asset Manag 21:52–69

Ielasi F, Rossolini M (2019) Responsible or thematic? The true nature of sustainability-themed mutual funds. Sustain J 11:3304

IFRS (2020) Consultation paper on sustainability reporting. https://www.ifrs.org/content/dam/ifrs/proje ct/sustainability-reporting/consultation-paper-on-sustainability-reporting.pdf. Accessed 15 Nov 2021

Jansson M, Biel A (2014) Investment institutions' beliefs about and attitudes toward socially responsible investment (SRI): a comparison between SRI and non-SRI management. Sustain Dev 22:33–41

Jebe R (2019) The convergence of financial and ESG materiality: taking sustainability mainstream. Am Bus Law J 56:645–702

Jitmaneeroj B (2016) Reform priorities for corporate sustainability: environmental, social, governance, or economic performance? Manag Decis 54:1497–1521

Kakeu J (2017) Environmentally conscious investors and portfolio choice decisions. J Sustain Finance Invest 7:360–378

Kim S, Maas K, Perego P (2018) The effect of publication, format and content of integrated reports on analysts' earnings forecasts. In: Boubaker S (ed) Research handbook of finance and sustainability. Edward Elgar, Cheltenham, ch 28

Klein I (2017) A change in accounting, a change in law. Del J Corp l CHK 42:51–76

Kotsantonis S, Serafeim G (2019) Four things no one will tell you about ESG data. J Appl Corp Financ 31:50–58

La Torre M, Mango F, Cafaro A, Leo S (2020) Does the ESG index affect stock return? Evidence from the Eurostoxx50. Sustainability 12:6387

Le Roux C, Pretorius M (2019) Exploring the nexus between integrated reporting and sustainability embeddedness. Sustain Account Manag Policy J 10:822–843

Leuz C (2020) Keynote speech, ECGI Webinar on Sustainable Finance, 4 Dec 2020

Lipton AM (2020) Not everything is about investors: the case for mandatory stakeholder disclosure. Yale J on Reg 37:499–572

Lueg K, Krastev B, Lueg R (2019) Bidirectional effects between organizational sustainability disclosure and risk. J Clean Prod 229:268–277

MacNeil IG, Esser I-m (2021) From a financial to an entity model of ESG. European Business Organization Law Review, this volume

Madsen MB (2021) Behavioural economics in European corporate governance—much ado about nudging? Eur Bus Law Rev 32:295–316

Maijoor S (2020) The three (apparent) paradoxes of sustainability reporting and how to address them. Keynote speech, 8 December 2020. https://www.esma.europa.eu/sites/default/files/library/esma32-67-765_speech_steven_maijoor_-_the_three_paradoxes_of_sustainability_reporting_and_how_to_addre ss_them.pdf. Accessed 15 Nov 2021

Martineau R, Lafontaine J-P (2020) When carbon accounting systems make us forget nature: from commodification to reification. Sustain Account Manag Policy J 11:487–504

McElroy MW, Thomas MP (2015) The MultiCapital Scorecard. Sustain Account Manag Policy J 6:425–438

McVea H (2010) Credit rating agencies, the subprime mortgage debacle and global governance: the EU strikes back. ICLQ 59:701–730

Mervelskemper L, Streit D (2017) Enhancing market valuation of ESG performance: is integrated reporting keeping its promise? Bus Strateg Environ 26:536–549

Moore MT (2015) 'Whispering sweet nothings': the limitations of informal conformance in UK corporate governance. J Corp Law Stud 15:95–138

Nicholls JA (2020) Integrating financial, social and environmental accounting. Sustain Account Manag Policy J 11:745–769

Nitsche C, Schröder M (2018) Are SRI funds conventional funds in disguise or do they live up to their name? In: Boubaker S, Cumming D, Khuong Nguyen D (eds) Research handbook of investing in the triple bottom line. Edward Elgar, Cheltenham, ch 19

OECD (2018) Making blended finance work for the Sustainable Development Goals. https://www.oecd.org/ dac/making-blended-finance-work-for-the-sustainable-development-goals-9789264288768-en.htm. Accessed 15 Nov 2021

Omarova S (2012) Bankers, bureaucrats, and guardians: toward tripartism in financial services regulation. J Corp Law 37:621–674

Pagano MS, Sinclair G, Yang T (2018) Understanding ESG ratings and ESG indexes. In: Boubaker S (ed) Research handbook of finance and sustainability. Edward Elgar, Cheltenham, ch 18

Park SK (2019) Social responsibility regulation and its challenges to corporate compliance. Brook J Corp Fin Com L 14:39–52

Parker C (2000) The open corporation. CUP, Cambridge

Passador ML, Riganti F (2019) Less is more in the age of information overload: the paradigm shift from a shareholder- to a stakeholder-oriented market. NYU JL Bus 15:567–651

Osthoff Peer (2015) What matters to SRI investors? In: Hebb T, Hawley JP, Hoepner AGF, Neher AL, Wood D (eds) The Routledge handbook of responsible investment. Routledge, Oxford, ch 54

Perez O (2016) The green economy paradox: a critical inquiry into sustainability indexes. Minn JL Sci Tech 17:153–219

Pilaj H (2017) The choice architecture of sustainable and responsible investment: nudging investors toward ethical decision-making. J Bus Ethics 140:743–753

Pitrakkos P, Maroun W (2020) Evaluating the quality of carbon disclosures. Sustain Account Manag Policy J 11:553–589

PwC (2017) Asset & wealth management revolution: embracing exponential change. https://www.pwc.com/ng/en/press-room/global-assets-under-management-set-to-rise.html. Accessed 15 Nov 2021

Ramanna K, Sletten E (2013) Network effects in countries' adoption of IFRS. Harvard Business School Working Paper No. 10-092. http://ssrn.com/abstract=1590245. Accessed 15 Nov 2021

Reeder N, Colantonio A, Loder J, Rocyn Jones G (2015) Measuring impact in impact investing: an analysis of the predominant strength that is also its greatest weakness. J Sustain Finance Invest 5:136–154

Richardson B (2011) From fiduciary duties to fiduciary relationships for socially responsible investing: responding to the will of beneficiaries. J Sustain Finance Invest 1:5–19

Richardson B, Cragg W (2010) Being virtuous and prosperous: SRI's conflicting goals. J Bus Ethics 92:21–39

Rogers J, Serafeim G (2019) Pathways to materiality: how sustainability issues become financially material to corporations and their investors. Harvard Business School Working Paper No. 20-056. https://ssrn.com/abstract=3482546. Accessed 15 Nov 2021

Saad AI, Strauss D (2020) A new 'reasonable investor' and changing frontiers of materiality: increasing investor reliance on ESG disclosures and implications for securities litigation. Berkeley Bus LJ 17:391–433

Sam CY, Tiong PNC (2015) An investigation of the corporate responsibility report assurance statements of the Big Four banks in Australia. Journal of Economics Library 2:3–14

Sankara J, Patten DM, Lindberg DL (2019) Mandated social disclosure: evidence that investors perceive poor quality reporting as increasing social and political cost exposures. Sustain Account Manag Policy J 10:208–234

Sarfaty GA (2013) Regulating through numbers: a case study of corporate sustainability reporting. Va J Int'l L 53:575–622

Sarro D (2012) Do lenders make effective regulators? An assessment of the Equator Principles on project finance. German Law J 13:1525–1558

Schäfer H (2012) Sustainable finance. http://ssrn.com/abstract=2147590. Accessed 15 Nov 2021

Serafeim G (2018) Investors as stewards of the commons? Journal of Applied Corporate Finance 30:8-17. https://ssrn.com/abstract=3014952. Accessed 15 Nov 2021

Sheehy B (2021) Sustainability, justice and corporate law: redistributing corporate rights and duties to meet the challenge of sustainability. European Business Organization Law Review, this volume

Sjåfjell B, Rapp Nilsen H, Richardson BJ (2017) Investing in sustainability or feeding on stranded assets: the Norwegian Government Pension Fund Global. Wake Forest L Rev 52:949–979

Tadros H, Magnan M (2019) How does environmental performance map into environmental disclosure?: a look at underlying economic incentives and legitimacy aims. Sustain Account Manag Policy J 10:62–96

Taïbi S, Antheaume N, Gibassier D (2020) Accounting for strong sustainability: an intervention-research based approach. Sustain Account Manag Policy J 11:1213–1243

Tan C (2019) Creative cocktails or toxic brews? Blended finance and the regulatory framework for sustainable development. In: Gammage C, Novitz T (eds) Sustainable trade, investment and finance: toward responsible and coherent regulatory frameworks. Edward Elgar, Cheltenham, ch 13

Tanzil D, Beloff BR (2006) Assessing impacts: overview of sustainability indicators and metrics. Environ Qual Manag 15:41–56

Thaler R, Sunstein C (2009) Nudge: improving decisions about health, wealth and happiness. Penguin

UK Green Finance Taskforce (2018) Accelerating green finance. https://assets.publishing.service.gov.uk/government/uploads/system/uploads/attachment_data/file/703816/green-finance-taskforce-accelerating-green-finance-report.pdf. Accessed 15 Nov 2021

UK Home Department (2019) Independent Review of the Modern Slavery Act 2015: Final Report. https://assets.publishing.service.gov.uk/government/uploads/system/uploads/attachment_data/file/803406/Independent_review_of_the_Modern_Slavery_Act_-_final_report.pdf. Accessed 15 Nov 2021

UNEP FI (2019) Fiduciary duty in the 21st century. https://www.unepfi.org/wordpress/wp-content/uploads/2019/10/Fiduciary-duty-21st-century-final-report.pdf. Accessed 15 Nov 2021

Vives A, Wadhwa B (2012) Sustainability indices in emerging markets: impact on responsible practices and financial market development. J Sustain Finance Invest 2:318–337

Walker J, Pekmezovic A, Walker G (2019) Sustainable development goals: harnessing business to achieve the SDGs through finance, technology, and law reform. John Wiley & Sons, Chicester

Wins A, Zwergel B (2016) Comparing those who do, might and will not invest in sustainable funds: a survey among German retail fund investors. Bus Res 9:51–99

Yamahaki C (2019) Responsible investment and the institutional works of investor associations. J Sustain Finance Invest 9:162–181

Zetzsche DA, Anker-Sørensen L (2021) Regulating sustainable finance in the dark. European Business Organization Law Review, this volume

Publisher's Note Springer Nature remains neutral with regard to jurisdictional claims in published maps and institutional affiliations.

European Business Organization Law Review (2022) 23:125–141
https://doi.org/10.1007/s40804-021-00233-z

The Use of Technology in Corporate Management and Reporting of Climate-Related Risks

Andrea Miglionico[1]

Accepted: 13 December 2021 / Published online: 24 January 2022
© The Author(s) 2022

Abstract

Sustainable finance and climate change have emerged as areas of renewed interest in the wake of the global financial crisis, when the assessment of companies' risk management was shown to be the key to the prevention of systemic disruption. While many aspects of corporate disclosures were radically and quickly revised following the crisis, even several years later commentators have pointed to a continuing pressure for improvement to regulatory requirements in relation to financial statements. Much of the debate focuses on the need for expedited operational execution of reporting information. Over the past decade significant advances have taken place in digital technologies, especially with respect to the security and processing of granular data. This article examines how these new technologies can be deployed in a manner that will address the need to eliminate the vulnerabilities of the climate risk management process, which requires standardisation of data in order to improve managerial decision-making and the desired outcomes. It further explores the use of technology to enhance the evaluation of climate change impact on company exposures, and to advance transparency in regulatory reporting for financial institutions. Technology applications such as automated language systems offer opportunities to align corporate disclosure with climate change policy objectives, which in turn can increase sustainability in the performance of companies' activities.

Keywords Climate risk · Corporate disclosure · Regulatory reporting · Automated language systems · Standardisation of data · Climate litigation

1 Introduction

The use of technology to coordinate corporate governance mechanisms (e.g., board structures) has become attractive for monitoring compliance with climate change policies. Digital technologies offer opportunities to automate complex and manual

✉ Andrea Miglionico
    a.miglionico@reading.ac.uk

[1]   Lecturer, School of Law, University of Reading, Reading, UK

🖄 Springer   ● ASSER PRESS

investment analysis, the key challenge of sustainable decision-making. The Financial Stability Board (FSB) has launched a Task Force to mandate companies to incorporate information about the potential impact of climate change in their risk management process.[1] This regulatory initiative has been complemented by the European Commission's Guidelines on Reporting Climate-related Information which aim to support corporations in managing sustainable reporting in financial statements.[2] The FSB's Task Force together with the Commission's Guidelines marked a step forward in the transparency and accountability of corporations, although they did bring to light a gap in data sharing which makes it difficult to succeed in having quantitative information about climate risks. Companies lack adequate methodologies and clear indicators for the assessment of environmental issues: the absence of an international consensus on green investments creates information imbalances that limit the effectiveness of monitoring systems.

This article examines the use of digital technologies, specifically standardised representation of climate risk granular data, to aid the achievement of sustainable objectives in corporate disclosure. It discusses how automated language systems such as Natural Language Processing (NLP) can be deployed to improve the measurement of granular data and the provision of meaningful information. It then considers whether the application of NLP methods can promote effective compliance processes, while ensuring standardisation of data together with contractual certainty and predictability of enforcement actions in order to avoid losses on the part of companies. Climate risk disclosures can be expedited through modern technologies, which, in turn, can enhance the transparency of reporting outcomes. Information providers continue to improve quality and availability, although data continues to be one of the largest impediments to climate risk assessment. Technology offers the possibility of 'algorithmic' regulation by substantially automating financial reporting, which means that the real-time calculation of future exposure based on data and simulation of risk factors is now feasible in order to detect environment-related events.[3]

The article proceeds as follows. Section 2 outlines the regulatory responses to climate change and sustainability: a copious set of recommendations have been published in the international arena with the aim of equipping companies with adequate tools for mitigating the implications of environmental externalities for financial activities.[4] The pressure of global regulators has encouraged firms to reduce the scarcity of climate information and ensure consistency in reporting requirements.

---

[1] Financial Stability Board (2020), pp 49–50. The Task Force provides a classification of climate risks into physical risks and transition risks. Transition risks arise from the transition to a low-carbon and climate-resilient economy and affect the value creation and reputation of the company. Physical risks arise from the adverse effects of climate change, such as material events that cause disruptions and financial damages. Those risks are sources of financial losses and lead to exposure to credit default.

[2] European Commission (2019).

[3] Ryan-Collins (2019).

[4] United Nations Framework Convention on Climate Change (2015). https://unfccc.int/process-and-meetings/the-paris-agreement/the-paris-agreement (accessed 25 May 2021).

Several initiatives focus on the possibility of establishing green finance objectives in sustainability reports, which represents a challenge for climate economic policies.

Section 3 examines the rationales for companies managing their climate risk and impact. It discusses the use of technology both in the disclosure of firms' activities with regard to climate and in the evaluation of the risks that climate change imposes on the firm. This Section also explores whether automation of climate disclosures is 'algorithm ready' and presented in a way that allows automated software-based compliance. It further argues that the application of technological solutions in climate data analysis may not be sufficiently complete to fulfil the reporting requirements. As a result, climate change litigation represents a significant indicator which enables companies' behaviour to be analysed and the risks of harmful environmental events to be audited.

Section 4 addresses how companies manage their climate risk, which involves an analysis of the achievements and potential downsides of algorithmic systems for processing granular climate information. Technology can improve information sharing and access to large volumes of climate data, which will allow firms to obtain a more insightful view of sustainable activities.[5] The broader challenge is standardisation. Data should be held in consistent formats, or at least should be translatable into consistent formats, across all institutions. Standardisation will include a variety of granular data: agreement and support by regulators for standardised representations of contracts will support greater efficiencies in many aspects of regulatory reporting and oversight.[6]

The last Section sets out conclusive remarks and summarises the discussion about the potential of using new technologies to achieve desired regulatory outcomes in climate change financial risk disclosure.

2 The Regulatory Landscape of Climate Change

Tackling the impact of climate risk in order to preserve financial stability has become the main priority on the agenda of global regulators and national supervisory authorities. The Task Force on Climate-related Financial Disclosures (TCFD) formed by the FSB provides guidance to companies for the reporting of climate change implications for investment decisions.[7] The TCFD aims to standardise climate change reporting requirements by providing a set of voluntary recommendations to be incorporated in companies' business models and the regulatory monitoring process. These reporting standards mark a shift towards a common framework of climate change disclosures. Specifically, it is recommended to disclose the models and data used to assess and manage relevant climate risks so as to make it easier for participants to acquire information about the potential vulnerabilities of a given company's management and oversight by the board.

---

[5] Macchiavello and Siri (2021), pp 23-25.
[6] Gal and Rubinfeld (2019), pp 752–753.
[7] Financial Stability Board (2016), pp 10–11.

In the UK, the Financial Conduct Authority (FCA) has proposed introducing binding rules requiring premium listed companies to disclose climate change financial risks in line with the TCFD.[8] In a similar vein to the FCA's policy goals, HM Treasury[9] and the Financial Reporting Council[10] have promoted mandatory best practices to implement TCFD disclosure obligations for UK corporations with the objective of addressing the lack of information about the financial impact of climate change. The UK Government has launched a consultation to require mandatory TCFD-aligned climate-related financial disclosures from publicly quoted companies, large private companies, and Limited Liability Partnerships.[11] This consultation aims to develop the programme set in the 'Green Finance Strategy'[12] and to mandate listed firms to commit themselves to sustainable managerial actions. Further improvements in climate change regulation are recorded at EU level, where the Commission adopted the Action Plan on Financing Sustainable Growth, which was followed by the Taxonomy Regulation,[13] an innovative piece of legislation which provides for harmonisation of the climate and energy targets set in the UN 2030 Agenda and the Paris Agreement.[14]

The Taxonomy Regulation adopts a binary approach (i.e., an activity is considered either compliant or not) and requires credit institutions and investment firms to comply with the reporting requirements for environmentally sustainable activities according to the non-financial disclosure (NFRD) obligations.[15] The NFRD introduced mandatory rules for companies to incorporate non-financial statements in their annual reports in relation to the corporate social responsibility and environmental, social and governance (ESG) criteria.[16] These reforms represent a step forward in the development of a mandatory reporting framework, although the measures face challenges on account of the scant incentives to establish sustainable corporate business strategies. Despite the evident progress in designing a sustainability agenda in the EU regulatory landscape, the successful achievement of a sufficient degree of harmonisation needs a significant change in the corporate governance model, which, in parallel, will require a level playing field of climate change rules.

---

[8] FCA (2021). See also FCA (2020).

[9] HM Treasury (2020).

[10] Financial Reporting Council (2020), pp 6–7.

[11] UK Department for Business, Energy & Industrial Strategy (2021).

[12] HM Treasury (2019).

[13] EU Regulation No 2020/852 (Taxonomy) on the establishment of a framework to facilitate sustainable investment (OJ L 198/2020), p 13.

[14] European Commission (2018).

[15] EU Taxonomy Regulation (2020), Art. 8.

[16] Directive 2014/95/EU of the European Parliament and of the Council of 22 October 2014 amending Directive 2013/34/EU as regards disclosure of non-financial and diversity information by certain large undertakings and groups (OJ L 330/2014), p 1.

3 Automation of the Climate Risk Assessment Process

The use of technology in the corporate sector generally refers to algorithms in business decision-making, both in investment contracts and in business strategy.[17] Automated mechanisms have the potential to assist with the governance of internal controls which are relevant for minimising reputational risk, legal risk and operational risk for companies.[18] Automation of the climate risk assessment process can improve the accuracy and comparability of information, which would also enhance the ability of senior management to monitor report disclosures. In this context, the algorithmic climate risk assessment can advance the collection and classification of data in order to facilitate decision-making procedures.

Sophisticated algorithms trained to analyse legal rules can help businesses gather, process and analyse granular operational information relevant to the compliance with mandatory reporting requirements. By employing digital solutions, such as a distributed shared ledger, a company can more rapidly assess the potential harms of climate change and adverse sustainability impacts. Automated practices can support corporate compliance processes through the use of natural language processing and cognitive computing. However, as Armour et al. have observed, 'automated systems must be designed, customized, set up, maintained, and overseen',[19] which requires human capital. The below demonstrates how these systems work, but the article is mindful that human engagement and supervision remain necessary in order to manage systemic biases or failures in algorithmic systems.[20]

Machine-learning programmes such as Natural Language Generation and NLP can be used to automate regulatory reports and detect environmental externalities.[21] These artificial systems are classified as deep-learning applications which rely on neural networks to predict climate risk.[22] NLP can extract regulations and decipher regulatory and control requirements (i.e., legislation 'gap' analysis tools).[23] It is a computation tool designed to optimise prediction and classification tasks: the NLP system resembles the structure of the brain with the purpose of elaborating an objective function, e.g., the best combination between inputs and outputs.[24] Using NLP-based systems, firms can improve operational and organisational awareness of information, as unstructured text can be swiftly converted into a formal representation which computers can interpret: this methodology can address the data challenges and increase climate risk detection and management accuracy.[25] NLP techniques involve predictive approaches for identifying climate losses in corporate

---

[17] Yeung (2019), pp 24–25.

[18] Lui and Lamb (2018), pp 268–269.

[19] Armour et al. (2020), p 14.

[20] Johnson et al. (2019), p 511.

[21] NLP is an application of AI that helps computers understand and interpret human language. Luccioni and Palacios (2019).

[22] Gensler and Bailey (2020), p 2.

[23] Gotthardt et al. (2020), pp 92–93.

[24] Gensler and Bailey (2020), p 9.

[25] Stein (2020), pp 899–900.

disclosures and for analysing climate information: the categorised sections of the reports addressing specific climate risk serve to create accessible datasets for advancing compliance with regulatory requirements. Specifically, NLP tools help to understand what type of information should be disclosed, in what manner, with what frequency, and the extent to which the data needs to be verified. This can improve board management oversight and avoid confusion in classifying the categories of climate exposures. It is a valuable approach to detect potential climate-related disclosures and solve the ambiguity of textual information (e.g., different meanings of climate taxonomy) identified in corporate reports. Language-based algorithms can reduce uncertainties in the available metrics and increase comparability between score estimates: this can improve the standardisation of granular data in climate risk disclosure which is a major source of divergences.[26]

Corporations have started to produce reporting information in machine-readable form so that granular data processing can be expedited.[27] Regulatory requirements (financial statements and periodic filings) are also adapted to machine readership, so that detection for regulatory non-compliance is also automated to an extent. This results in a strong relationship with AI applications, which influences managers' decision-making and affects desired outcomes.[28] The use of algorithms and machine learning has become important at the level of corporate governance in facilitating corporate decision-making as well as improving corporate compliance such as with mandatory disclosure. In the banking sector, algorithmic systems for climate information processing can also assist with banks' prudential assessments and regulatory compliance: technological solutions to calculate risk weights have the potential to make transparent the metrics and targets applied in the internal models for climate risk.[29]

The automated processing of granular climate-related data at firm level also assists with the valuation of all of a firm's assets, liabilities and off-balance-sheet commitments, possibly near real time. Improved standardisation would then help to facilitate the climate risk assessment process for firms and their investors, who could have access to transparent data to which to apply their own risk modelling and valuation techniques.

3.1 Technology and the Disclosure of Firms' Activities That Impact the Climate

There is growing concern about the implications of environmental risks in companies' business models, which show limitations in establishing a governance framework designed to ensure compliance with climate reporting.[30] Corporations are in need of expedited organisational systems and effective measurement of climate

---

[26] Hain et al. (2021), pp 7–8.

[27] Lewis and Young (2019), pp 587–589.

[28] Björkegren et al. (2020).

[29] Broeders and Schlooz (2021), pp 126–127.

[30] Ferrarini (2020).

Springer   ASSER PRESS

data[31] in order to consider non-financial information in their business strategy. The shift towards sustainability reporting is the new frontier of companies' performance as well as regulatory compliance. It is commonly considered that financial reporting reflects a backward-looking and judgment-based approach to information, which raises concerns as regards the achievement of long-term sustainability goals.[32] A key area of climate disclosure that needs improvements and consistency is strategic resilience in companies' business strategies.[33] Considerable attention is being paid to enhancing this part of disclosure owing to lack of consolidation of global regulatory standards.

Technological advancements in the disclosure of firms' activities that impact the climate can be deployed to improve data standardisation and granularity of climate information. The use of technology to gather data can help companies demonstrate that their activities are sustainable for the environment and society. For instance, software applications (e.g., data mining and machine learning) can assist the management board to extract valuable information from climate data and identify which section of the annual report needs to account for environmental risks.[34] This can also reduce firms' opportunistic behaviour to disclose climate information selectively. There is a prevalent sentiment among policy makers and shareholders on the need to introduce mandatory sustainability reporting for financial organisations. It is observed that disclosure of climate risk is a significant factor for investors and directors in their strategic management as they prefer standardised and mandatory obligations with regard to climate reporting.[35] Ioannou and Serafeim have analysed the extent to which mandatory sustainability disclosure regulations have an impact on corporate disclosure practices, as it is unclear whether the ESG metrics would improve the transparency of firms.[36] Integrating sustainability reporting in managerial decision-making entails the costs of gathering ESG information from professional data providers and the costs of changing organisational processes.

The European Commission study on directors' duties and sustainable corporate governance observed that 'companies lack a strategic perspective over sustainability and current practices fail to effectively identify and manage relevant sustainability risks and impacts'.[37] Specifically, it is reported that corporate decision-making and board management do not adequately promote sustainable goals within the governance framework. The Commission emphasises the need to improve companies' social performance through legislation on directors' duties and sustainability under EU company law.[38] This should enhance the sustainable values of corporate governance and foster sustainable corporate practices. However, efforts to mitigate the

---

[31] Johnston (2018), p 29.
[32] Lusk (2021), pp 7–8.
[33] Sustainability Accounting Standards Board (2021), p 5.
[34] Balch (2021).
[35] Bresnahan et al. (2021), pp 13–15.
[36] Ioannou and Serafeim (2019), pp 452–453.
[37] European Commission (2020), p 42.
[38] Ferrarini et al. (2021), pp 16–17.

implications of climate change for financial institutions and interventions to foster organisational changes seem a déjà vu in the regulatory policy options.

National regulations do not establish mandatory obligations for companies to adopt and disclose sustainable objectives, which makes it difficult to align the corporate disclosure regime with climate reporting.[39] The various guidelines on climate risks issued by the global regulators add layers of complexity and do not clarify the sustainability requirements to be incorporated in financial reporting. This voluntary set of soft law measures have created more uncertainty for shareholders and investors with the result that the perimeter of climate disclosures is left undefined.

The EU legislation standardises the sustainability impact under the principle of 'double materiality', which calculates sustainable outcomes (social and environmental values), but it does not indicate the sustainability metrics for measuring the impact of sustainable activities in corporate governance. Chiu argues that the metrics on sustainable impact constitute an essential indicator for evaluating the sustainability risks in a corporate's decision-making on investment.[40] The regulation on sustainable disclosure requirements identifies the environmental and social objectives as a benchmark indicator for periodic financial reports.[41] The Sustainable Finance Disclosure Regulation adopts a 'comply or explain' approach to promote harmonisation of climate disclosure standards, although it does not address the issues of limited availability of ESG data and the lack of a central supervisor.[42] Another concern is the absence of a degree of liability with respect to market participants and financial institutions for breach of the sustainability disclosure rules and management (i.e., oversight) duties. It can be argued that investors' desire for social responsibility on the part of companies seems constrained by the undefined materiality of climate change impact on corporate disclosures.

The identification and quantification of the material factors of climate change are inherently dependent on publicly available information, which offers little evidence of direct physical and non-physical effects on business activities.[43] The question is: to what extent do corporations have to indicate the amount of materiality which is necessary for inclusion in the financial report? Corporations would not have particular incentives to disclose items of information which involve negative exposure to investors and shareholders: it is likely that they would avoid analyses of materiality parameters because of the high costs of accessing this information. In the absence of mandatory disclosure obligations, financial firms have an appetite to limit the volume of reporting in order to reduce the burdensome procedures of internal control systems. Further, corporations are not required to update their measurement methodologies, making the assessment process particularly vulnerable when it comes to capturing climate risks. The classification of material climate risk drivers and their

---

[39] Schoenefeld et al. (2018), pp 121–122.

[40] Chiu (2021).

[41] For a commentary, see Gortsos (2020).

[42] EU Regulation 2019/2088 on sustainability-related disclosures in the financial services sector (OJ L 317/2019), p 1; see Busch (2021).

[43] Burton (2010), p 1296.

concentration in financial activities depends on the availability of relevant data, which affects the management decision to disclose hazard events.

3.2 Automated Models of Climate Risk Management for Firms

The rapid transition to environmental policies is challenging the paradigm of companies' business models as regards the way to assess the level of exposure to climate risk factors.[44] Accurate estimation of climate exposures lowers the costs of tracking pollution emissions and contributes to the mitigation of endogenous financial shocks arising from environmental damages. Although ESG criteria are being refined by industry and rating providers, firms are in need of integrating key and accepted parameters into their business strategies.[45] By modelling well-accepted ESG criteria into corporate climate risk data and management systems, companies can be assisted in re-orienting their internal operational systems. This may even have an impact upon the nature of corporate governance, corporate purpose and business model. Stakeholder engagement can be improved too.[46] Corporate decision-making can be informed by forward-looking predictions as to the climate impact on corporate governance.[47] Möslein and Engsig argue that certification schemes provide a means for sustainable corporations to signal their good behaviour to the market with the aim of promoting a sustainable corporate governance framework.[48]

Evaluating financial risks associated with climate change involves the application of technological solutions that have the potential to improve the quality of information by translating granular metrics into accurate predictions. Avgouleas points out that '*spatial finance* can offer a valuable measure of the impact of sustainable investments' through the use of machine-learning technology for climate change evaluation.[49] The digitalisation of the corporate sector has been faced with an increasing use of automated processes, e.g., machine learning, neural networks and adaptive algorithms that display intelligent behaviour by taking actions to advance process innovation.[50] The deployment of technology has resulted in the automation of firms' operating systems by supporting both risk assessment and peer comparison. Machine learning software can assist manual intervention, although automatic procedures rely on algorithms which, if the software is not perfectly designed, can lead to problems.[51] Making climate data machine readable entails accurate control and permissioning for access to and screening of data: artificial intelligence (AI) and cognitive computing can enhance real-time information and provide evidence about

---

[44] Carney (2015), pp 5–6.
[45] Inderst et al. (2012), p 13.
[46] Lund and Pollman (2021), pp 47–48.
[47] Zenghelis and Stern (2016).
[48] Möslein and Engsig Sørensen (2021), pp 8–9.
[49] Avgouleas (2021), p 57 [emphasis added].
[50] Enriques and Zetzsche (2020), pp 59–60.
[51] Chiu and Lim (2021), pp 13–15.

the climate impact on financial assets.[52] However, the lack of available data on companies' exposure to environmental hazards (e.g., natural disasters, weather disruptions, concentration of greenhouse gases) constitutes a barrier for companies and their investors alike who find it difficult to evaluate companies' strategies towards climate change issues.

A key challenge for corporations is to identify a suitable modelling approach for each company's needs in assessing the material factors of climate change relevant to them. Different models have been proposed among regulators focused on estimating foreseeable transition costs and losses, such as by adopting scenario analysis, sensitivity analysis and stress tests.[53] Although these models still require refinement, such as in relation to data gaps,[54] more sophisticated stress-testing and scenario analysis approaches for corporate climate risk management are emerging. Eley proposes transition capacity testing as an alternative model for the classification of the exposures that are most vulnerable to climate change.[55] These methodologies incorporate forward-looking information complemented by historical data and provide an assessment of the varying degrees of environmental risk. However, the main question relates to the credibility and reliability of such approaches, given the fact that they are essentially based on market information and the backward-looking materiality of risk, which do not guarantee accurate long-term forecasts.[56] Climate risk modelling and stress-testing processes can support increased processing of granular information in order to achieve the required precision and to support swifter corporate decision-making to address the effects of environmental adversities.

3.3 Climate Litigation as a New Taxonomy of Corporate Exposures

One area of climate risk management crucial for corporations is climate risk litigation management. The increasing attention paid to climate cases filed against corporations has given rise to considerable debate about enforcing 'brown activities' (carbon emissions mainly dependent on fossil fuels) and addressing non-sustainable behaviours.[57] Violations of social and human rights are at the centre of climate litigation, although the outcomes of disputes have been marginal with respect to the pressure that international movements against climate change and global warming have created with regard to environmental concerns.[58] This is also linked to the perception that climate litigation is in its infancy and there is widespread scepticism on the part of the courts about entertaining any arguments sympathetic to the social effects of climate hazards. As Wilensky observed, 'climate change has been treated in the courts much like any other environmental issue and has not resulted

---

[52] Brunetti et al. (2021).
[53] Basel Committee on Banking Supervision (2021), pp 17–18.
[54] Monnin (2018).
[55] Eley (2021), p 9.
[56] Chenet (2019), p 19.
[57] Solana (2020), p 105.
[58] Posner (2007), pp 9–10.

in the development of a distinct climate-change jurisprudence'.[59] However, there have been recent developments with regard to climate protection in the shape of successful lawsuits and unexpected judicial activism in the legal proceedings relating to environmental issues. This the case with the German Federal Constitutional Court, which declared partially unconstitutional the Federal Climate Change Act on the ground that it failed to indicate greenhouse gas (GHG) emission reduction targets, resulting in a breach of the country's binding commitment under the Paris Agreement.[60]

A similar conclusion is found in the ruling in *The Netherlands vs. Urgenda*, where the Dutch Supreme Court held that a country's inadequate action on climate change may constitute a violation of human rights.[61] The judges recognised the legally binding target and the deadline for the Dutch government to reduce GHG emissions, de facto imposing a duty to protect citizens' rights in the face of climate change. Most interestingly, the Hague District Court made an unprecedented order against Shell, ruling that the oil company needs to drastically reduce its carbon emissions and take robust steps towards sustainability.[62] This decision is likely to create a precedent for other oil majors, which could face similar lawsuits and be required to change their business models.[63] Despite the positive attitude of courts in the aforementioned cases, climate litigation is subject to hurdles when it comes to accessing available remedies for holding a company liable for poor sustainable standards.[64]

The harmful effects of climate litigation on companies' reputational capital and the value of assets can stimulate courts to rethink the existing legal arguments concerning corporate accountability for environmental damages and open up new judicial avenues for successful private lawsuits. The increase of successful cases in environmental litigation is remarkable and litigants seem less deterred by the thresholds required to initiate a climate claim which involve burdensome proofs, such as the causal nexus between the firm's behaviour in causing climate threats and the injury resulting from the harmful act. It is worth considering that the material risk for corporations can be the high costs of litigation and the reputational impact on markets arising from the public scrutiny, which can lead to a downgrade from rating agencies.[65] Corporates need to manage climate risk because of their own economic futures, mandatory disclosure compliance and climate risk litigation. Automated information processing systems can support corporates to prevent and mitigate material risk on the basis of textual sources about environmental exposures.

---

[59] Wilensky (2015), p 178.

[60] See BVerfG (2021).

[61] Case 19/00135 *The State of the Netherlands (Ministry of Economic Affairs and Climate Policy) v. Stichting Urgenda*, ECLI:NL:HR:2019:2007.

[62] Case C/09/571932/ HA ZA 19-379 *Milieudefensie et al. vs Royal Dutch Shell PLC*, ECLI:NL:RBDHA:2021:5339.

[63] Raval (2021).

[64] For a discussion on tort law remedies in climate change litigation see Hunter and Salzman (2007), pp 1750–1751.

[65] Ganguly (2018), pp 865–866.

4 The Use of Algorithmic Systems for Processing Granular Climate Information

The application of AI systems for processing granular climate information has the potential to support companies with their mandatory reporting requirements and risk management. Achieving the full benefits of technology requires standardised access to corporations' operating systems and the data they contain. However, data management requirements for regulatory reporting present challenges such as poor data quality and poor data integration. An organisation's data management framework requires effective data governance, e.g., treatment of data as an asset, agreements between those who create data and those who use the data, and processes and controls of data collection. AI and machine learning offer a solution to fill the gaps of voluntary climate disclosures: they ensure measurable material risks and standardised auditing practices. This involves a risk management strategy which needs to adopt automated systems for extracting information about harmful events and engendering change in corporate behaviour.[66]

The opportunities provided by technology can be used in transformative ways which will yield far wider benefits than are sometimes envisaged. Valuation, while involving an inherent subjective element, can still be carried out using more standardised procedures; and the underlying data and risk factor simulations can be made available to external parties seeking to reach their own judgments on the valuation of assets and other exposures. Technological solutions can be deployed to improve the elaboration of annual company reports: they reduce the risk of bias and can assist in the analysis of 'structured' (reports) and 'unstructured' (statistical data) texts on climate.[67] Specifically, NLP can classify the variety of metrics elaborated in the corporate reporting. The potential of cognitive technologies to improve the analysis of climate risk for firms is manifest: they extract information and translate it into knowledge in real time, which, at the same time, expedites data sharing. Basically, NLP techniques allow structured information to be extracted from natural language text. The structured information extracted by the NPL algorithm can potentially be used to populate a data model of a regulatory reporting system. NLP can also be used to uncover hidden patterns and anomalies in large quantities of text. AI tools can help make sense of unstructured texts, although much of the most relevant data held within a company and required for automation of operational tasks is structured but blocked. To unlock data, labelling or standardising it, corporations need to develop automated processing and intelligence. This also means there can be scale barriers: potentially only the largest companies are adequately placed to manage their data and take advantage of the technology opportunities. These challenges are even greater for sharing of data between firms because each firm has its own individual processes and definitions.

A valuable NLP application is ClimateBert (Bidirectional Encoder Representations from Transformers), an algorithm which elaborates textual data of companies'

---

[66] Solomon et al. (2011), p 1119.
[67] Antoncic (2020), pp 109–110.

annual reports.[68] It is a language representation software that excerpts specific wording from company disclosures into an accessible dataset in order to assess compliance with TCFD requirements.[69] Risk management practices should enable automated processes for analysing large volumes of data to achieve real-time granular information. For climate reporting to be automated, data should be provided in a standardised format, but the fact that firms' data are stored in different systems requires allocating those data into a single standardised platform. Ensuring that the format used to standardise data can be reused across multiple climate reporting methods can create a potential downside to the efficiency of NLP applications. Regular changes to the format or maintaining several different formats for different regulatory reporting methods will significantly reduce the potential cost efficiencies of reports under algorithmic systems. Corporations should provide data in a number of different formats that are defined for each regulatory report while at the same time needing to ensure the data is correct before feeding it to automated processes.

5 Conclusion

To improve accuracy and clarity in climate risk reporting, corporations should engage with technological applications which can expedite the standardisation of data and the comparability of scores. Automation of climate risk assessment can reduce incentives for managerial opportunism and increase reliability of corporate sustainable management tools. The practical applications of technology can assist in accessing real-time granular data, leading to the improved disclosure of climate-related financial risks and a better evaluation of climate impact. More specifically, the use of technology to better assess the climate risk requires greater standardisation of data, which will in turn enhance the transparency of firms' exposures and regulatory actions. The working of NLP methods can assist firms in improving their climate risk assessment process. Various cognitive computing systems have developed language representation models which enable companies to operationalise their instructions or responses to the climate regulatory requirements into compliance activities using NLP with machine learning techniques.

The deployment of technology holds out the promise of improving the assessment of climate risk and level of corporate exposures, and to enhance the transparency of monitoring processes. The main downside is the risk that the application of sophisticated machine-learning systems will exacerbate the possibility of technology malfunctioning and will fail to achieve its stated purposes.[70] The potential benefits of technological innovation in climate change should be weighed carefully against the risks. In the long term, there is scope for AI to be used as a service provider for network interconnectedness and as a tool to monitor the ESG conduct of corporations.

---

[68] Bingler et al. (2021), pp 2–3.
[69] Devlin et al. (2019), p 4171.
[70] Scherer (2016), p 359.

Acknowledgements The author is grateful to the anonymous reviewer for the useful comments provided on an early draft. Any errors or omissions remain the sole responsibility of the author. I would like to dedicate this article to my dad, who gave me the strength to write during his illness.

References

Antoncic M (2020) Uncovering hidden signals for sustainable investing using Big Data: artificial intelligence, machine learning and natural language processing. J Risk Manag Financ Inst 13:106–113

Armour J, Parnham R, Sako M (2020) Augmented lawyering. ECGI Law Working Paper No. 558/2020. https://ssrn.com/abstract=3688896. Accessed 25 May 2021

Avgouleas E (2021) Resolving the sustainable finance conundrum: activist policies and financial technology. Law Contemp Probl 84:55–73

Balch O (2021) Big data helps put numbers on sustainability. Financial Times, 25 January 2021. https://www.ft.com/content/2a405cf6-9592-4de2-960b-4c3e5d0df030. Accessed 25 May 2021

Basel Committee on Banking Supervision (2021) Climate-related financial risks—measurement methodologies. https://www.bis.org/bcbs/publ/d518.htm. Accessed 25 May 2021

Bingler JA, Kraus M, Leippold M (2021) Cheap talk and cherry-picking: what ClimateBert has to say on corporate climate risk disclosures. https://ssrn.com/abstract=3796152. Accessed 25 May 2021

Björkegren D, Blumenstock JE, Knight S (2020) Manipulation-proof machine learning. CEGA Working Paper Series No. 123. https://escholarship.org/uc/item/6tp4q9zv. Accessed 25 May 2021

Bresnahan K, Frankenreiter J, L'Helias S, Hinricks B, Hodzic N, Nyarko J, Pandya S, Talley EL (2021) Global investor-director survey on climate risk management. Columbia Law and Economics Working Paper No. 650. https://ssrn.com/abstract=3722958. Accessed 25 May 2021

Broeders D, Schlooz M (2021) Climate change uncertainty and central bank risk management. J Risk Manag Financ Inst 14:121–130

Brunetti et al. (2021) Climate change and financial stability. FEDS Notes. Board of Governors of the Federal Reserve System, Washington

Burton CD (2010) An inconvenient risk: climate change disclosure and the burden on corporations. Adm Law Rev 62:1287–1305

Busch D (2021) Sustainable finance disclosure in the EU financial sector. EBI Working Paper Series 2021—No. 70. https://ssrn.com/abstract=3650407. Accessed 25 May 2021

BVerfG (2021) Beschluss des Ersten Senats vom 24. März 2021. https://www.bundesverfassungsgericht.de/SharedDocs/Downloads/DE/2021/03/rs20210324_1bvr265618.pdf?__blob=publicationFile&v=1. Accessed 25 May 2021

Carney M (2015) Breaking the tragedy of the horizon—climate change and financial stability. Speech given at Lloyd's of London. https://www.bankofengland.co.uk/speech/2015/breaking-the-tragedy-of-the-horizon-climate-change-and-financial-stability. Accessed 25 May 2021

Chenet H (2019) Climate change and financial risk. https://ssrn.com/abstract=3407940. Accessed 25 May 2021

Chiu I (2021) The EU sustainable finance agenda—developing governance for double materiality in sustainability metrics. European Business Organization Law Review, this volume

Chiu I, Lim E (2021) Technology vs ideology: how far will artificial intelligence and distributed ledger technology transform corporate governance and business? Berkeley Bus Law J 18:1–64

Devlin J, Chang M-W, Lee K, Toutanova K (2019) BERT: pre-training of deep bidirectional transformers for language understanding. In: Proceedings of the 2019 Conference of the North American Chapter of the Association for Computational Linguistics: Human Language Technologies. https://doi.org/10.18653/v1/N19-1423

Eley S (2021) Testing capacity of the EU banking sector to finance the transition to a sustainable economy. EBA Staff Paper Series No. 13. https://www.eba.europa.eu/sites/default/documents/files/document_library/1010012/Testing%20capacity%20of%20the%20EU%20banking%20sector%20to%20finance%20the%20transition%20to%20a%20sustainable%20economy.pdf. Accessed 25 May 2021

Enriques L, Zetzsche DA (2020) Corporate technologies and the tech nirvana fallacy. Hastings Law J 72:55–98

European Commission (2018) Action plan: financing sustainable growth. COM (2018) 97 final

European Commission (2019) Guidelines on reporting climate-related information. https://ec.europa.eu/finance/docs/policy/190618-climate-related-information-reporting-guidelines_en.pdf. Accessed 25 May 2021

European Commission (2020) Study on directors' duties and sustainable corporate governance. https://op.europa.eu/en/publication-detail/-/publication/e47928a2-d20b-11ea-adf7-01aa75ed71a1/language-en. Accessed 25 May 2021

FCA (2020) Proposals to enhance climate-related disclosures by listed issuers and clarification of existing disclosure obligations. Policy Statement PS20/17. https://www.fca.org.uk/publication/policy/ps20-17.pdf. Accessed 25 May 2021

FCA (2021) Climate-related reporting requirements. https://www.fca.org.uk/firms/climate-change-sustainable-finance/reporting-requirements#international. Accessed 14 May 2021

Ferrarini G (2020) Corporate purpose and sustainability. ECGI Working Paper 559/2020. http://ssrn.com/abstract_id=3753594. Accessed 25 May 2021

Ferrarini G, Siri M, Zhu S (2021) The EU sustainable governance consultation and the missing link to soft law. ECGI Law Working Paper No. 576/2021. https://ssrn.com/abstract=3823186. Accessed 25 May 2021

Financial Reporting Council (2020) Climate thematic. https://www.frc.org.uk/getattachment/ab63c220-6e2b-47e6-924e-8f369512e0a6/Summary-FINAL.pdf. Accessed 25 May 2021

Financial Stability Board (2016) Recommendations of the Task Force on Climate-related Financial Disclosures. https://www.fsb.org/wp-content/uploads/Recommendations-of-the-Task-Force-on-Climate-related-Financial-Disclosures.pdf. Accessed 25 May 2021

Financial Stability Board (2020) Task Force on Climate-related Financial Disclosures. 2020 Status Report. https://assets.bbhub.io/company/sites/60/2020/09/2020-TCFD_Status-Report.pdf. Accessed 25 May 2021

Gal MS, Rubinfeld DL (2019) Data standardization. NYU Law Rev 94:737–770

Ganguly G (2018) If at first you don't succeed: suing corporations for climate change. Oxf J Leg Stud 38:841–868. https://doi.org/10.1093/ojls/gqy029

Gensler G, Bailey L (2020) Deep learning and financial stability. Working Paper. https://ssrn.com/abstract=3723132. Accessed 25 May 2021

Gortsos C (2020) The Taxonomy Regulation: more important than just as an element of the capital markets union. European Banking Institute Working Paper Series 2020 No. 80. https://ssrn.com/abstract=3750039. Accessed 25 May 2021

Gotthardt M, Koivulaakso D, Paksoy O, Saramo C, Martikainen M, Lehner O (2020) Current state and challenges in the implementation of robotic process automation and artificial intelligence in accounting and auditing. ACRN Oxford J Finance Risk Perspect 9:90–102

Hain LI, Kölbel JF, Leippold M (2021) Let's get physical: comparing metrics of physical climate risk. https://ssrn.com/abstract=3829831. Accessed 25 May 2021

HM Treasury (2019) Green finance strategy. https://www.gov.uk/government/publications/green-finance-strategy. Accessed 25 May 2021

HM Treasury (2020) Interim Report of the UK's Joint Government-Regulator TCFD Taskforce. https://assets.publishing.service.gov.uk/government/uploads/system/uploads/attachment_data/file/933782/FINAL_TCFD_REPORT.pdf. Accessed 25 May 2021

Hunter D, Salzman J (2007) Negligence in the air: the duty of care in climate change litigation. Univ Pa Law Rev 155:1741–1794

Inderst G, Kaminker C, Stewart F (2012) Defining and measuring green investments: implications for institutional investors' asset allocations. OECD Working Papers on Finance, Insurance and Private Pensions No. 24. https://doi.org/10.1787/5k9312twnn44-en

Ioannou I, Serafeim G (2019) The consequences of mandatory corporate sustainability reporting. In: McWilliams A et al. (eds) The Oxford handbook of corporate social responsibility: psychological and organizational perspectives. OUP, Oxford

Johnson K, Pasquale F, Chapman J (2019) Artificial intelligence, machine learning, and bias in finance: toward responsible innovation. Fordham Law Rev 88:499–530

Johnston A (2018) Climate-related financial disclosures: what next for environmental sustainability? University of Oslo Faculty of Law Legal Studies Research Paper Series No. 2018-02. https://ssrn.com/abstract=3122259. Accessed 25 May 2021

Lewis C, Young S (2019) Fad or future? Automated analysis of financial text and its implications for corporate reporting. Account Bus Res 49:587–615

Luccioni A, Palacios H (2019) Using natural language processing to analyze financial climate disclosures. https://www.climatechange.ai/papers/icml2019/34/paper.pdf. Accessed 25 May 2021

Lui A, Lamb GW (2018) Artificial intelligence and augmented intelligence collaboration: regaining trust and confidence in the financial sector. Inf Commun Technol Law 27:267–283

Lund DS, Pollman E (2021) The corporate governance machine. ECGI Law Working Paper No. 564/2021. https://ssrn.com/abstract=3775846. Accessed 25 May 2021

Lusk G (2021) Looking forward and backward at extreme event attribution in climate policy. Ethics Policy Environ 24:1–15. https://doi.org/10.1080/21550085.2020.1848195

Macchiavello E, Siri M (2021) Sustainable finance and Fintech: can technology contribute to achieving environmental goals? A preliminary assessment of 'Green FinTech'. EBI Working Paper Series 2020—No. 71. https://ssrn.com/abstract=3672989. Accessed 25 May 2021

Monnin P (2018) Integrating climate risks into credit risk assessment. CEP Discussion Note 2018/4. https://ssrn.com/abstract=3350918. Accessed 25 May 2021

Möslein F, Engsig Sørensen K (2021) Sustainable corporate governance: a way forward. ECGI Law Working Paper No. 583/2021. http://ssrn.com/abstract_id=3761711. Accessed 25 May 2021

Posner EA (2007) Climate change and international human rights litigation: a critical appraisal. Coase-Sandor Institute for Law & Economics Working Paper No. 329. http://ssrn.com/abstract_id=959748. Accessed 25 May 2021

Raval A (2021) Dutch court orders Shell to accelerate emissions cuts. Financial Times, 26 May 2021. https://www.ft.com/content/340501e2-e0cd-4ea5-b388-9af0d9a74ce2?emailId=60ae5ebe4ab84000040e79d7&segmentId=3d08be62-315f-7330-5bbd-af33dc531acb. Accessed 26 May 2021

Ryan-Collins J (2019) Beyond voluntary disclosure: why a 'market-shaping' approach to financial regulation is needed to meet the challenge of climate change. SUERF Policy Note Issue No 61. https://www.suerf.org/docx/f_a821a161aa4214f5ff5b8ca372960ebb_4805_suerf.pdf. Accessed 27 May 2021

Scherer MU (2016) Regulating artificial intelligence systems: risks, challenges, competencies, and strategies. Harvard J Law Technol 29:354–398

Schoenefeld JJ, Hildén M, Jordan AJ (2018) The challenges of monitoring national climate policy: learning lessons from the EU. Clim Policy 18:118–128

Solana J (2020) Climate litigation in financial markets: a typology. Transnatl Environ Law 9:103–135. https://doi.org/10.1017/S2047102519000244

Solomon JF, Solomon A, Norton SD, Joseph NL (2011) Private climate change reporting: an emerging discourse of risk and opportunity? Account Auditing Account J 24:1119–1148. https://doi.org/10.1108/09513571111184788

Stein AL (2020) Artificial intelligence and climate change. Yale J Regul 37:890–939

Sustainability Accounting Standards Board (2021) Climate risk. Technical Bulletin. https://www.sasb.org/knowledge-hub/climate-risk-technical-bulletin/. Accessed 25 May 2021

UK Department for Business, Energy & Industrial Strategy (2021) Consultation on requiring mandatory climate-related financial disclosures by publicly quoted companies, large private companies and Limited Liability Partnerships (LLPs). https://www.gov.uk/government/consultations/mandatory-climate-related-financial-disclosures-by-publicly-quoted-companies-large-private-companies-and-llps. Accessed 25 May 2021

United Nations Framework Convention on Climate Change (2015) The Paris Agreement. https://unfccc.int/process-and-meetings/the-paris-agreement/the-paris-agreement. Accessed 25 May 2021

Wilensky M (2015) Climate change in the courts: an assessment of non-U.S. climate litigation. Duke Environ Law Policy Forum 26:131–179

Yeung K (2019) Why worry about decision-making by machine? In: Yeung K, Lodge M (eds) Algorithmic regulation. OUP, Oxford

Zenghelis D, Stern N (2016) The importance of looking forward to manage risks: submission to the Task Force on Climate-related Financial Disclosures. Policy paper. The London School of Economics and Political Science, Grantham Research Institute on Climate Change and the Environment, London. http://eprints.lse.ac.uk/67133/1/Zenghelis-and-Stern-policy-paper-June-2016.pdf. Accessed 25 May 2021

Publisher's Note Springer Nature remains neutral with regard to jurisdictional claims in published maps and institutional affiliations.

European Business Organization Law Review (2022) 23:143–185
https://doi.org/10.1007/s40804-021-00231-1

ARTICLE

Developing a Green Bonds Market: Lessons from China

Lin Lin[1] · Yanrong Hong[2]

Accepted: 13 December 2021 / Published online: 21 February 2022
© T.M.C. Asser Press 2022

Abstract

Since its launch in 2016, China's green bonds market has amassed a significant size and is currently ranked as the second largest in the world. This paper takes a pioneering step to analyze how a transitional economy can develop a burgeoning green bonds market within a short period, using China as a case study. It concludes that the Chinese government plays an instrumental but also evolving role in this process. The carefully designed use of government mechanisms in the context of unique government structures can constructively facilitate the growth of a green bonds market. At the emerging stage of this unique market, the government can play an active role in designing a conducive regulatory environment through law and policy, providing the necessary financial infrastructure and appropriate incentives for investors and green bond issuers. Government intervention is warranted at this stage, given the special characteristics of the green market, in particular, the desired positive externalities on environmental protection and climate change. In China, such a regime is implemented with a focus on inter-ministerial, central-local and international collaboration, centralized policy-making, and alignment of green goals with performance assessment of local officials. However, as the green bonds market matures, this paper suggests a transition towards a market-oriented model where the government should assume a limited role, providing funding and monitoring, and letting market forces play a greater role in achieving market efficiency. Unleashing the potential of market forces can mitigate several of the challenges faced by a top–down approach. This paper also examines the challenges that have surfaced in China, including low-quality information disclosure and under-utilization of green bonds financing by private enterprises. In response, several solutions are proposed to address these specific challenges.

Keywords China's green bonds market · Role of government · Sustainability · Green finance · Green bond standard · Sustainability information disclosure

✉ Lin Lin
   lawll@nus.edu.sg

✉ Yanrong Hong
   hyr@pku.edu.cn

Extended author information available on the last page of the article

🍂 Springer ⬤ ASSER PRESS

1 Introduction

According to the International Capital Market Association (ICMA) green bonds are 'any type of bond instrument where *the proceeds will be exclusively applied to finance or re-finance in part or in full new and/or existing eligible green projects* and which are aligned with the four core components of the Green Bond Principles'.[1] The same definition is applied in the Climate Bonds Standard and Certification Scheme developed by the Climate Bonds Initiative (CBI), which also provides certifications to green bonds based on pre-issuance and post-issuance requirements.[2] The EU Green Bond Standard defines an EU Green Bond in a similar way requiring that the proceeds shall be exclusively used to finance or refinance in part or in full new and/or existing Green Projects.[3]

A vibrant green bonds market is desirable for China because it promotes environmental protection and sustainability even amid rapid economic development and introduces diversified portfolios into the capital market to alleviate climate risks. Over the past 40 years of reform and opening up, economic development in China has made world-renowned achievements. China's GDP exceeded RMB 100 trillion for the first time in 2020.[4] However, along with rapid economic development, China is also facing serious damage to the living environment.[5] In recent years, the government has resolved to pursue environmental protection and sustainable development as an important national strategy and to mitigate some of the negative impacts brought about by decades of rapid growth. As a result, China specifically proposed the national strategy of achieving 'ecological civilization' in 2015[6] and incorporated a green philosophy into the five major development concepts.[7] It then began to explore reforms geared towards green and low-carbon economic development, becoming an active implementer of the climate control goals[8] proposed by the United Nations Framework Convention on Climate Change, the Paris Agreement, and other related international conventions.

---

[1] International Capital Market Association (2018), p 3 [emphasis added]. The four core components are: (1) use of proceeds; (2) process for project evaluation and selection; (3) management of proceeds; and (4) reporting.

[2] CBI (2019), p 8.

[3] EU Technical Expert Group on Sustainable Finance (2019a), Annex 1, Section 3 Definition of an EU Green Bond.

[4] State Council (2021).

[5] See, for instance, Kan (2009).

[6] The Opinions of the Central Committee of the Communist Party of China and the State Council on Accelerating the Construction of Ecological Civilization [中共中央、国务院关于加快推进生态文明建设的意见], Central Committee of the CPC (25 Apr 2015); General Plan for the Reform of the Ecological Civilization System [生态文明体制改革总体方案], Central Committee of the CPC (21 Sep 2015); this became the top-level design plan to guide China's development of the green economy.

[7] The 13th 5-year plan for the National Economic and Social Development of the People's Republic of China [中华人民共和国国民经济和社会发展第十三个五年规划纲要], National People's Congress (3 March 2016), hereinafter referred to as the '13th 5-Year Plan', puts forward the five new development concepts, i.e., 'innovation, coordination, green economy, openness and sharing'.

[8] I.e., to meet the objectives enshrined in the Paris Agreement, limiting the global temperature increase this century to below 2 °C above pre-industrial levels.

In September 2020, President Xi Jinping announced the '30/60 goal' at the United Nations General Assembly, according to which China aims to peak carbon emission by 2030 and reach carbon neutrality by 2060.[9] More specifically, at the 5th Anniversary of the Paris Agreement at the Climate Ambition Summit on 12 December 2020 he announced that

> China will lower carbon dioxide emissions per unit of GDP by 65% from 2005 levels, increase the share of non-fossil fuels in primary energy consumption to around 25% by 2030, increase forest stock by 6 billion cubic meters above 2005 levels and bring the total installed capacity of wind and solar power to over 1200 GW by 2030.[10]

At the same time, a report by the Climate Policy Initiative suggests that a sizeable investment of RMB 3–4 trillion per year is needed for China to meet its commitments under the Paris Agreement.[11]

In order to implement China's '30/60 goal', the 14th 5-year plan that started in 2021 aims to accelerate low-carbon development in China.[12] The State Council's Guiding Opinions on Accelerating the Establishment of a Sound Green, Low-Carbon Circular Economic System released on 2 February 2021 reiterate the importance of establishing a sound green, low-carbon circular economic system, and includes comprehensive guidelines.[13] The guidelines include the accelerated development of green finance, the strengthening of legal and regulatory support, and the improvement of green standards, the green certification system and the statistical monitoring system.[14] The setting of such high-level policy goals sends a strong signal to the market and spurs market participants to actively initiate green projects and raise funds in green finance.[15] The State Council further issued the Guidance for Carbon Dioxide Peaking, and Carbon Neutrality in Full and Faithful Implementation of the New Development Goals on 22 September 2021, detailing the principles and methods for achieving the '30/60 goal'.[16]

---

[9] Myers (2020).

[10] World Resources Institute (2020).

[11] Climate Policy Initiative (2020b), p 1.

[12] The Proposal of the Central Committee of the Communist Party of China on Formulating the 14th Five-Year Plan for National Economic and Social Development and the Visionary Goals for 2035 [中共中央关于制定国民经济和社会发展第十四个五年规划和二〇三五年远景目标的建议], Central Committee of the CPC (29 Oct 2020), proposed goals and initiatives such as 'achieving new progress in ecological civilization construction' and 'accelerating the promotion of green and low-carbon development'.

[13] State Council's Guiding Opinions on Accelerating the Establishment of a Sound Green, Low-Carbon Circular Economic System [国务院关于加快建立健全绿色低碳循环发展经济体系的指导意见], State Council (2 Feb 2021), State Council No. 4 of [2021].

[14] See for an English analysis Wang and Huang (2021).

[15] Ma (2017); see also Wilkins (2021).

[16] Guidance for Carbon Dioxide Peaking, and Carbon Neutrality in Full and Faithful Implementation of the New Development Goals [中共中央、国务院关于完整准确全面贯彻新发展理念做好碳达峰碳中和工作的意见], Central Committee of the CPC and State Council (22 Sep 2021).

Under this context, the establishment of the green bonds market assumes cru-cial significance in China's ongoing economic transformation from an energy-and-pollution-intensive economy to a resource-conserving and environment-friendly economy. With the accelerating pace of adopting low-carbon economic activities, the improvement of the green financial system, including green bonds, and its cor-responding market operation mechanism becomes increasingly urgent. Accord-ingly, green bonds are considered by the Chinese government as an effective financial instrument to facilitate this economic transformation. As a result, develop-ing the green bonds market has been a part of the central government's top-level green finance initiative.[17] CGN Wind Power Co., Ltd. first issued a RMB 1 billion medium-term note (i.e., a debt financing instrument of non-financial enterprises), with interest rates linked to carbon emission reduction benefits, in the Interbank Bond Market in May 2014.[18] In January 2016, the Industrial and Commercial Bank of China was approved to issue RMB 10 billion of green financial bonds in the Inter-bank Bond Market,[19] marking the official launch of green bonds in China.[20]

Despite its relative youth compared to its counterpart in the EU, where the Euro-pean Investment Bank issued the first green bonds in the world - the Climate Aware-ness Bonds—in 2007,[21] China's green bonds market developed at a rapid pace in the past few years.[22] In 2016, China became one of the largest issuers of green bonds in the world.[23] According to statistics from the CBI and China Central Depository and Clearing Research Centre (CCDC Research), Chinese issuers issued a total of RMB 386.2 billion (US\$ 55.8 billion) of labeled green bonds in 2019 in both domestic and international markets, making China the largest source of labeled green bonds.[24] By the end of 2019, China's domestic green bonds market had a total outstanding

---

[17] China proposed the strategic initiative of 'establishing a green finance system' in the General Plan for the Reform of the Ecological Civilization System in 2015, see *supra* note 6. In 2016, the People's Bank of China (PBOC) and six ministries and commissions jointly issued the Guiding Opinions on Building a Green Financial System [中国人民银行、财政部、发展改革委等关于构建绿色金融体系的指导意见] (31 Aug 2016), which were enacted to establish a green finance system. See, in general, Green Chi-na's Financial System Study Group of DRC (2016), stating that 'green bonds have become an important vehicle for green finance, as they are more easily incorporated into investment portfolios by institutional investors as a medium and long-term financial product'.

[18] Hong (2016).

[19] Zheng (2016).

[20] The operation of these green financial bonds follows the Green Bond Principles issued by the ICMA and the Climate Bonds Standard.

[21] International Finance Corporation (2016), p 1.

[22] Zhang (2020), p 1.

[23] Shi and Wang (2018), p 32.

[24] CBI and CCDC Research (2020), p 3. According to the CBI, an aligned green bond in the Chinese market is a green bond that has been approved for issuance by the regulator or has been registered on the bond exchange with a full name that includes the word 'green' in the label. Green bonds are considered to be aligned green bonds as defined by the CBI only if they invest at least 95% of the funds raised in green assets or projects that are consistent with the Climate Bonds Taxonomy. Verification of Certified Climate Bonds involves third-party assessments that are conducted by approved verifiers authorized by the CBI in accordance with the Climate Bonds Standard and industry standards, certifying that the funds raised are used to limit global warming to below 2 °C.

amount of RMB 977.2 billion (US$140 billion).[25] As of March 2021, China leads the world in the value of outstanding green loans at about US$ 2 trillion.[26] It is also the second largest green bonds market in the world ranking only after the United States.[27] Such a rapid expansion of the green bonds market contributed significant investment to important sectors such as energy, transport and environmental protection, paving the way for China's transition to a low-carbon green economy (Fig. 1).[28]

However, the government-led approach in building a green bonds market in China comes in contrast with the laissez-faire approach which entrusts market forces alone to develop the green bonds market.[29] For instance, scholars have argued that the governance regime of the green bonds market in the United States is largely established by private ordering.[30] Meanwhile, the approach in the EU is somewhere in between government intervention and private ordering. This is demonstrated by the enactment of the EU Taxonomy Regulation[31] and the EU Sustainable Finance Disclosure Regulation,[32] where the regulators set certain bounds and rules for market activities to take place in a guided way. Going forward, while it is unlikely for China to straightly switch to the US style focusing primarily on private ordering, it does have a lot to learn from the EU experience.

These varying approaches beg the paradoxical question of what the limitations and drawbacks of industrial policies and centralized government strategies are. Against this backdrop, this paper takes a pioneering step to analyze how a transitional economy can develop a burgeoning green bonds market within a short period, using China as a case study. Although there is some literature discussing the role

---

[25] RMB 628.2 billion (US$90 billion) of the total outstanding amount meets both the CBI definition and the Chinese green bonds definition, and another RMB 349 billion ($50 billion) of bonds only meet the Chinese green bonds definition. Exchange rate conversions for the above data may vary, as the CBI uses the actual exchange rate on the date of issuance for each bond. See CBI and CCDC Research (2020), p 12.

[26] Brown (2021).

[27] CBI and CCDC Research (2021), p 3.

[28] Kidney et al. (2015), pp 249–253.

[29] Ma (2017).

[30] See, for example, Park (2018) (arguing that the green bonds market in the United States is largely a legacy of private governance and the role of government regulators is largely missing); see for another example MacLeod and Park (2011) (describing the role of investor-based coalitions in environmental governance based on political science scholarship).

[31] Regulation (EU) 2020/852 of the European Parliament and of the Council of 18 June 2020 on the establishment of a framework to facilitate sustainable investment, and amending Regulation (EU) 2019/2088.

[32] Regulation (EU) 2019/2088 of the European Parliament and of the Council of 27 November 2019 on sustainability-related disclosures in the financial services sector.

of government in the green bonds market,[33] there is little legal literature analyzing this issue in the context of China.[34] While there are a number of factual reports by research institutes shedding light on this issue, relatively less academic analysis is available.[35] This paper therefore aims to fill this literature gap. It also provides a timely reflection on the desirability of a government-steered green bonds market versus private ordering and their relative pros and cons.

To do this, three pressing questions need to be answered. First, why and how is China able to effectively develop a green bonds market within a short period of time? Second, what are some of the challenges in developing its green bonds market, and how might these be addressed through regulatory reform? Third, which parts of this analysis are unique to the Chinese context and what is the general advice applicable to other growing markets? These questions will be of special importance to policymakers and legislators in countries looking to develop their green bonds market or encountering difficulties in developing their green bonds market.

This paper suggests that a government can help to develop a green bonds market by playing an instrumental but also evolving role. First, at the emerging stage of this unique market, the government can play a more active role in designing a conducive regulatory environment through law and policy, providing the necessary financial infrastructure and appropriate incentives for investors and green bond issuers. Government intervention is warranted at this stage, given the unique features of the green market, in particular, the desired positive externalities on environmental protection and climate change. In China, such a regime is implemented with a focus on inter-ministerial, central-local collaboration, centralized policy-making, and alignment of green goals with performance assessment of local officials. Second, as the green bonds market matures with sophisticated market players and a well-established institutional and financial infrastructure, the government should assume a limited role, providing funding and monitoring, and letting market forces play a greater role in achieving market efficiency. Unleashing the potential of market forces can mitigate several of the challenges faced by a top–down approach.

The framework of this paper is as follows. Section 2 introduces the unique Chinese experience in developing a green bonds market in China through a top–down approach, inter-ministerial synergy, and central-local cooperation. Section 3 analyzes the special characteristics of China's green bonds market, highlighting the existing differences with international standards in important aspects such as the use of proceeds, sustainability information disclosure, and credit ratings, while making

---

[33] See, for example, Park (2018) (examining governance gaps in the green bonds market where there is an absence of government regulation); Freeburn and Ramsay (2020) (examining legal and policy issues present in the green bonds market and identifying how some of these issues could potentially be solved by the government and law).

[34] Some positive examples that have been written on this topic include Zhang (2020) (analyzing the definitional divergence in Chinese regulations governing China's green bonds market), Kidney et al. (2015) (highlighting the importance of green bonds in China and making a few policy recommendations to develop the market in China) and Ma et al. (2019) (discussing key features of China's green bonds market and the role of the government in developing the market). However, in general there is a shortage of academic writing on this topic and such positive examples are limited in number.

[35] See, for example, CBI (2017), CBI and CCDC Research (2020) and Climate Policy Initiative (2020b).

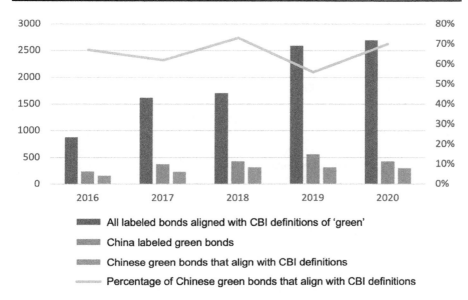

Fig. 1 Amount of China's green bond issuance in 2016–2020 (in billion USD). The data is compiled by the authors according to the CBI green definition and China's domestic green definition. It is also based on the statistics from CBI, Lianhe Equator Environmental Impact Assessment and China Bond Rating. The sources include CBI and CCDC Research (2017), CBI and CCDC Research (2018), CBI and CCDC Research (2019), CBI and CCDC Research (2020), and Jones (2021).

the case for greater convergence. Section 4 further examines the challenges that have surfaced in China, including under-utilization of green bonds financing by private enterprises, potential misallocation and waste of resources, and the need for greater retail investor education. It proposes several solutions to these specific challenges and, lastly, makes the case for a gradual transition from a government-oriented approach towards a market-oriented one. Section 5 concludes.

2 The Unique Chinese Experience in Establishing a Government-led Green Bonds Market

This Section explores in detail the unique Chinese experience in establishing a green bonds market with the help of high-level government policy guidance and intervention. It begins by introducing the different types of green bonds in China and goes on to explain how China is able to tap into a combination of top–down and bottom–up approaches in terms of top-level design, inter-ministerial synergy, and central-local coordination in taking a concerted approach in developing the green bonds market. In addition, the importance of tying sustainability goals with the performance evaluation of officials and the evolving role of the courts are also analysed. The authors note here that the Chinese experience is *sui generis* due to its political and social constructs and not easily transferable to other jurisdictions where, for example, the government does not have a strong influence or incentive to guide the development of the market.

2.1 Multiple Types of Green Bonds in China

There are various types of green bonds in China and they are launched and administered by different regulatory agencies.[36] There are broadly three categories, namely green corporate bonds administered by the China Securities Regulatory Commission (CSRC), green enterprise bonds administered by the National Development and Reform Commission (NDRC), and green medium-term notes administered by the People's Bank of China (PBOC) and registered by the National Association of Financial Market Institutional Investors (NAFMII).[37] Unlike financial institution bonds, these three types of green bonds are ordinary corporate bonds financed on the basis of the issuer's commercial credit.

Chinese financial institutions have also issued green bonds securitized by credit assets in the Interbank Bond Market.[38] Non-financial corporations have issued green asset-backed securities and green asset-backed notes in exchange markets and the Interbank Bond Market respectively.[39] These green asset-backed financial instruments are based on assets that can generate cash flow returns in the future, and they are different from financial institution bonds or general green corporate bonds financed on the basis of issuers' credit.

Some local government financing vehicles (LGFVs, i.e., financing firms) have issued green bonds, which are often referred to as LGFV green bonds, in the market under the domestic bonds system.[40] On 18 June 2019, Ganjiang New Area of Jiangxi Province issued its first RMB 300 million green bond with a fixed maturity of 30 years, the first labeled municipal green bond from China,[41] further enriching the type of green bonds and their issuers in China.

In addition, the Chinese government has also established various channels to facilitate greater access to the domestic bonds market by foreign investors. At

---

[36] There is a large non-labeled green bonds market in China, i.e., bonds that are not specifically labeled as green bonds but raise funds for green industries. In this market, local governments (including local state-owned enterprises and local government financing platform companies) are the most important issuers, and the funds raised are mainly invested in the clean transportation sector. According to statistics, from 2009 to 2020, a total of 3,368 non-labeled green bonds were issued in China's bond market, with an issue size of about RMB 10.32 trillion, RMB 6.12 trillion of which was used for green project investment. See Yun (2021).

[37] The green project standard set by the Green Finance Professional Committee of the Chinese Society of Finance applies to the former two types, while the green project standard set by the Development and Reform Commission applies to the last type. See also Climate Policy Initiative (2020a), p 5, Table 2.

[38] See, for example, CBI and SynTao Green Finance (2017), p 4.

[39] Ibid., p 6.

[40] The volumes of LGFV green bonds have increased by four times since the inaugural issuance by Jiangsu Guoxin Investment, an investment and holding company of the State-owned Assets Supervision and Administration Commission of Jiangsu Province, in 2016. The surge was primarily driven by provincial LGFVs. See CBI and CCDC Research (2020), p 5.

[41] Jiang and Lei (2019).

present, the main channels for international investors to invest in China's green bonds market include: (1) Qualified Foreign Institutional Investors (QFII); (2) Renminbi Qualified Foreign Institutional Investors (RQFII);[42] (3) direct access to the Chinese Interbank Bond Market;[43] and (4) the Bond Connect programme.[44]

Since Goldwind Science and Technology Co., Ltd. issued its first green bond of US$ 300 million with a maturity of 3 years on the Hong Kong Stock Exchange (HKEx) on 18 July 2015,[45] China's overseas green bonds market has achieved a steady growth. As of 2019, Chinese entities have issued 66 green bonds overseas for a total amount of about RMB 212.995 billion, the issuers being policy banks, commercial banks, non-financial corporates, etc.[46] At a news conference on 19 July 2021, the NDRC reported 16 overseas green bonds issuances, with a total amount of about US$ 8.5 billion in 2020, marking a significant increase.[47] For the exchange market, a number of international trading centers are included, such as the HKEx, the Luxembourg Stock Exchange, the London Stock Exchange and the Singapore Exchange, with the US dollar as the main issuance currency.[48] In terms of the use of funds raised, in addition to meeting the requirement of being green, they also feature targeted support for China's national strategies, such as the 'Belt and Road' bonds and Guangdong-Hong Kong-Macao Greater Bay Area bonds.[49]

Among the channels used, the Bond Connect programme is currently the most convenient channel for international investors to invest in the domestic green bonds market.[50] The Hong Kong–Mainland Bond Market Connect allows investors from mainland China and overseas to trade bonds in each other's markets through an infrastructure link established in Hong Kong, which includes the 'Northbound Connect' and the 'Southbound Connect'.[51] This means international investors can invest in bonds in the domestic Interbank Bond Market through an account opened for them by a custodian in Hong Kong, which in turn will open a corresponding account in mainland China through a domestic custodian.[52] Given the proximity of Hong

---

[42] The People's Bank of China and the Foreign Exchange Administration issued a document in September 2020 to abolish the restrictions on the investment quota of QFII and RQFII, while the restrictions on the pilot countries and regions of RQFII were also abolished, and the policies regarding different channels for foreign institutional investors to invest in the interbank market were, in principle, basically converged. See State Administration of Foreign Exchange (2020).

[43] See People's Bank of China Announcement [2016] No. 3 [中国人民银行公告 (2016) 第3号], PBOC (24 Feb 2016), http://www.pbc.gov.cn/tiaofasi/144941/144959/3021203/index.html (accessed 31 Nov 2021). This announcement stated that the 'direct access to the Chinese Interbank Bond Market' route requires investors to first register with the People's Bank of China and then invest through a qualified domestic correspondent bank.

[44] Bond Connect (2021a).

[45] Renewables Now (2015).

[46] Liao and Yun (2020), Section II.

[47] National Development and Reform Commission (2021).

[48] See *supra* note 46, Section II (2).

[49] Ibid., Section II (3).

[50] Qian and Lu (2018), p 84.

[51] People's Bank of China (2017).

[52] Bond Connect (2021b).

Kong's existing market infrastructure to the international market, through the Bonds Connect programme, international investors can make use of Hong Kong's market infrastructure to invest in China's domestic bond market. This programme not only reduces the burden on international investors to understand and follow the specific rules and procedures of the Chinese Interbank Bond Market, but also avoids transaction costs.[53]

The relaxation of investor eligibility requirements under the Bonds Connect programme means that more small and medium-sized foreign investors are able to access the domestic market.[54] There are also no investment quotas for small and medium-sized foreign investors under the Bond Connect programme. Through the programme, more international investors have direct access to the primary and secondary markets, increasing the liquidity of China's green bonds market.[55] It also allows mainland investors easy access to foreign bonds in Hong Kong, providing them with additional means to diversify their portfolios.[56]

2.2 A Top-Level Design

The Chinese government takes the lead in developing the green financial system, which includes green bonds.[57] The central government believes that adopting a top–down approach and the so-called 'forced institutional change' in establishing the green bonds market in China is necessary.[58] First, it can help China to efficiently establish a green financial system for the transformation to a green low-carbon economy and the construction of ecological civilization, instead of waiting for the market to develop organically. Second, China has a vast land with different and complex energy structures, industrial structures and regional development status. The policy and regulatory guidance on green finance are conducive to forming a consensus on green development and unifying the institutional standards.[59] Nevertheless, it is noteworthy that this does not mean that the 'invisible hand' of the government replaces the invisible hand of the market in resource allocation. Instead, government policies help to construct the basic framework of green finance and leverage on tax incentives, financial subsidies and financial policies to support the development of green industries.

Following the policy goals of building the ecological civilization, achieving a green economy as one of the five major development concepts in the 13th 5-year plan, and vigorously encouraging green and low-carbon development, China has rapidly started the construction of a green financial system.[60] So far, the policy

---

[53] CBI (2017), p 26, Appendix 2.

[54] Ibid.

[55] Ibid.

[56] Yeung (2021).

[57] Ba et al. (2019).

[58] Mai and Xu (2015) and Ba et al. (2018).

[59] See Table 1 below for more details.

[60] Ibid.

Table 1 Institutional framework of China's green bonds market

Issuing body and date	Regulations/guidelines	Significance
15 Dec 2015 People's Bank of China	Announcement on Issues concerning the Issuance of Green Financial Bonds on the Interbank Bond Market (《关于在银行间债券市场发行绿色金融债券有关事宜公告》) together with the China Green Bond Endorsed Project Catalogue (2015 Edition) prepared by the Green Finance Committee, China Society for Finance and Banking	Allowed financial institutions to issue green bonds and provided a range of green industry projects for reference. They became the first industries in China allowed to issue green bonds
13 Dec 2015 National Development and Reform Commission	Guidelines for the Issuance of Green Bonds (《绿色债券发行指引》)	Used as a guide for the issuance of green corporate bonds and to clarify the scope of green projects
16 March 2016 Shanghai Stock Exchange	Notice on Launching the Pilot Programme of Green Corporate Bonds (《关于开展绿色公司债券试点的通知》)	Used as a guide for the issuance and trading of green corporate bonds in the exchange market, with reference to the China Green Bond Endorsed Project Catalogue (2015 Edition) for the scope of green projects
22 Apr 2016 Shenzhen Stock Exchange	Notice on Launching the Pilot Programme of Green Corporate Bonds (《关于开展绿色公司债券业务试点的通知》)	Used as a guide for the issuance and trading of green corporate bonds in the exchange market, with reference to the China Green Bond Endorsed Project Catalogue (2015 Edition) for the scope of green projects
31 Aug 2016 People's Bank of China and six Ministries[a]	Guidelines for Establishing a Green Financial System (《关于构建绿色金融体系的指导意见》)	Clarified the meaning of building a green financial system. The roadmaps and policies of green financial investment and financing tools in the guidelines are the overall institutional frameworks guiding China's green finance
2 March 2017 China Securities Regulatory Commission	Guiding Opinions of the China Securities Regulatory Commission on Supporting the Development of Green Bonds (《中国证监会关于支持绿色债券发展的指导意见》)	Used as a guide for the issuance and trading of green corporate bonds on the exchange market
22 March 2017 National Association of Financial Market Institutional Investors[b]	Guidelines for the Issuance of Green Debt Financing Instruments for Non-Financial Enterprises (《非金融企业绿色债务融资工具业务指引》) and the attached Green Debt Financing Instrument Disclosure Form and Green Assessment Report Disclosure Form	Used as a guide for the issuance and trading of green medium-term notes in the Interbank Bond Market, with reference to the China Green Bond Endorsed Project Catalogue (2015 Edition) for the scope of green projects

Table 1 (continued)

Issuing body and date	Regulations/guidelines	Significance
26 Oct 2017 People's Bank of China, China Securities Regulatory Commission	Interim Guidelines for Green Bond Assessment and Certification (《绿色债券评估认证行为指引（暂行）》)	Unified and guided the assessment and certification of green bonds
26 Dec 2017 China Securities Regulatory Commission	Guidelines on the Content and Format of Information Disclosure by Companies Issuing Public Securities No. 2—content and Format of Annual Reports (《公开发行证券的公司信息披露内容与格式准则第2号·年度报告的内容与格式》)	The CSRC requires listed companies, or their significant subsidiaries included in the list of key emission companies announced by the Ministry of Ecology and Environment, to disclose information on emissions, the construction of pollution prevention and control facilities and their operation, and environmental impact assessments of construction projects[c]
5 Feb 2018 People's Bank of China	Notice on Strengthening of Supervision and Management of Green Financial Bonds During the Term of the Bond (《关于加强绿色金融债券存续期监督管理有关事宜的通知》) Code on Information Disclosure During the Term of the Bond (《绿色金融债券存续期信息披露规范》)	Rules for the regulation and information disclosure requirements of green financial bonds during the term of the bond
14 Feb 2019 People's Bank of China and six Ministries[d]	Catalogue of Green Industries (2019 Edition) (《绿色产业指导目录（2019年版）》)	Revision and refinement of the China Green Bond Endorsed Project Catalogue (2015 Edition) to better suit development needs
26 Apr 2019 People's Bank of China	Notice on Supporting the Issuance of Green Debt Financing Instruments in Green Finance Reform and Innovation Pilot Zones (《关于支持绿色金融改革创新试验区发行绿色债务融资工具的通知》)	Since 2017, China has been setting up pilot zones in several regions in six provinces (Zhejiang, Guangdong, Guizhou, Jiangxi, Xinjiang and Gansu) and has achieved significant results
20 Oct 2020 People's Bank of China and four Ministries[e]	Guiding Opinions on Promoting Climate Change Financing (《关于促进应对气候变化投融资的指导意见》)	Keeps up with China's Intended Nationally Determined Contributions by implementing financing initiatives to address climate change. It is considered an update and expansion upon the 2016 Guidelines for Establishing a Green Financial System

Table 1 (continued)

Issuing body and date	Regulations/guidelines	Significance
27 Nov 2020 Shanghai Stock Exchange	Guideline No. 2 on the Application of the Rules Governing the Examination and listing of corporate bonds—specific types of corporate bonds—Green Corporate Bonds (《公司债券发行上市审核规则适用指引第2号——特定品种公司债券》之"绿色公司债券")	Repeals the 2016 Notice on Launching the Pilot Programme of Green Corporate Bonds and treats green corporate bonds as a specific type of corporate bonds
27 Nov 2020 Shenzhen Stock Exchange	Guideline No. 1 of the Shenzhen Stock Exchange on Innovative Corporate Bond Business—Green Corporate Bonds (《深圳证券交易所公司债券创新品种业务指引第1号——绿色公司债券》)	Repeals the 2016 Notice on Launching the Pilot Programme of Green Corporate Bonds and treats green corporate bonds as a specific type of corporate bonds
2 Apr 2021 People's Bank of China, National Development and Reform Commission, China Securities Regulatory Commission	Notice on the Issuance of the Green Bonds Endorsed Project Catalogue (2021) (关于印发《绿色债券支持项目目录 (2021年版)》的通知)	Introduces the latest version of the Green Bonds Endorsed Project Catalogue, taking into account public consultation on the 2020 draft. Improves alignment with international standards, for example, by excluding fossil energy-related projects
24 May 2021 Ministry of Ecology and Environment	Notice on the Issuance of the Plan for the Reform of the Legal Disclosure System of Environmental Information (关于印发《环境信息依法披露制度改革方案》的通知)	Mandates environmental information disclosure for key pollution units and other specified categories of entities. Requires that environmental information disclosure must be carried out in a timely, comprehensible and easily searchable manner and must be uploaded to a centralized, comprehensive system

The Table reflects the policy and regulations as of the end of April 2021

[a] Including the Ministry of Finance, the National Development and Reform Commission, the Ministry of Environmental Protection, the China Banking Regulatory Commission, the China Securities Regulatory Commission, and the China Insurance Regulatory Commission

[b] The National Association of Financial Market Institutional Investors is a self-regulatory organization under the supervision of the People's Bank of China and is responsible for the registration and management of bond issuance in the Interbank Bond Market

[c] Guidelines on the Content and Format of Information Disclosure by Companies Issuing Public Securities No. 2—Content and Format of Annual Reports (Revised 2017) [公开发行证券的公司信息披露内容与格式准则第2号——年度报告的内容与格式 (2017年修订)], CSRC (26 Dec 2017), Article 44

[d] This included the National Development and Reform Commission, Ministry of Industry and Information Technology, Ministry of Natural Resources, Ministry of Ecology and Environment, Ministry of Housing and Urban–Rural Development, and National Energy Administration

[e] This included the National Development and Reform Commission, the Banking and Insurance Regulatory Commission, the Securities Regulatory Commission and the Ministry of Ecology and Environment

scheme of green development in China has basically covered all green development fields and has formed a relatively comprehensive systematic policy hierarchy.[61] [See Table 1 above for a summary of major domestic regulations about green finance (including green bonds)]. It should be noted that laws and regulations have different levels of hierarchy in China and the Table mainly presents those at the national level with the highest significance and authority, whereas laws and regulations at the local level will also be canvassed in the following sub-sections.

2.3 Inter-ministerial Synergy

The issuance and regulation of green bonds cover a wide range of aspects, including natural resources, environmental protection, energy deployment, economics of people's livelihood, financial management and information sharing. The positive externality of green bonds is difficult for the market alone to internalize within a short period without the help of favorable state financial, fiscal and tax policies.[62] Inter-ministerial cooperation mechanisms are necessary to facilitate communication, cooperation and coordination among different ministries and regulatory agencies in a nation. This is particularly crucial in the context of China due to the segmentation of the financial regulation system (the so-called 'one bank, two commissions and one committee' system), as well as the co-existence of three corporate credit bonds regimes.[63]

To achieve 'inter-ministerial synergy', different regulators need to jointly discuss and decide on vital matters in the green field and share information on low-carbon development. For example, the PBOC issued the Plan for the Division of Work in the Implementation of the Guiding Opinions on Building a Green Financial System 2017, deciding on the leading ministries and examining the progress of construction article by article, setting a timetable and roadmap for the construction of the green financial system and holding symposiums to ensure implementation.[64] For another example, the National Leading Group to Address Climate Change was established by the State Council as an important deliberative and coordinating body in the green field.[65] It studies and formulates major strategies, guidelines and policies for addressing climate change and unifying the active responses to climate change. Such inter-ministerial collaboration is necessary and beneficial in the context of China's facilitating an efficient and fast-paced growth of the green bonds market.

---

[61] China Center for International Economic Exchanges (2013), p 70.

[62] Ma (2016), pp 2–3, and Dai and Kidney (2016), p 10.

[63] Hong (2010), pp 9–10.

[64] Green Finance Dynamics of the Research Bureau of the People's Bank of China: Further Promotion of the Symposium on the 'Division of the Work Plan for the Implementation of the Guidance on Building a Green Financial System [落实〈关于构建绿色金融体系的指导意见〉的分工方案], People's Bank of China (12 Oct 2018), http://www.greenfinance.org.cn/displaynews.php?id=2334 (accessed 31 Nov 2021).

[65] See, for example, Xinhua News (2019).

2.4 Central-Local Unification

China is a vast country with differences in resource endowments, energy structures and economic development levels among provinces and municipalities in the east, centre and west. Since 2016, China has been taking the central-local unifying approach to set up a systematic framework at the central level, incentivizing local government officials and market players at all levels.[66] Similarly, central-local unification plays a pivotal role in making sure that targets set by the central government are met or even exceeded at the local level.

Since June 2017, China has selected nine cities in six eastern, central and western provinces to establish green financial reform and innovation pilot zones.[67] Such pilot zones explore green financial development models with regional characteristics, pilot new green financial regulations and standards, provide green financial services for the green transformation of the regional economy and gain a number of replicable beneficial experiences while making remarkable achievements.[68] As of the end of 2020, the stock amount of green bonds in the above-mentioned pilot zones was RMB 135.05 billion.[69]

Local governments with more resources and showing greater economic progress should step forward in experimenting with green finance regulations and setting a role model for the other regions to follow. Take Shenzhen for instance: the Shenzhen Special Economic Zone Green Finance Regulations were issued on 5 November 2020 and became effective on 1 March 2021.[70] The Green Finance Regulations provide the legal basis in terms of standards and procedures, investment evaluations, information disclosure, monitoring and governance, as well as responsibilities and liabilities in relation to green finance.[71] They are the first green finance regulations in China and provide the legal basis for regulatory actions against misbehaving market participants.[72]

The implementation of the Green Finance Regulations is subject to sufficient market and infrastructure conditions in Shenzhen. Shenzhen has a relatively large share of green bonds. By the end of 2020, the balance of green loans from depository financial institutions in Shenzhen was nearly RMB 350 billion, accounting for 5.1% of the balance of various loans.[73]The financial institutions in Shenzhen have

---

[66] People's Bank of China Research Bureau (2019), p 3.

[67] Ibid. For example, the Standing Committee of Shenzhen People's Congress issued the Shenzhen Special Economic Zone Green Finance Regulations in 2020 in order to promote the development of green finance, enhance the ability of green financial services to contribute to the real economy, promote the construction of a sustainable financial centre in Shenzhen, and promote sustainable economic and social development, according to the basic principles of relevant laws and administrative regulations, combined with the actual situation in the Shenzhen Special Economic Zone.

[68] Ibid.

[69] People's Bank of China (2021a).

[70] Shenzhen Special Economic Zone Green Finance Regulations, issued by Shenzhen People's Congress on 5 Nov 2020 and effective from 1 March 2020.

[71] Ibid., Chapters II, IV, V, VII and VIII.

[72] Shenzhen Municipal Financial Regulatory Bureau (2021).

[73] Ibid.

also gradually started systematic sustainability information disclosure, as over half of the sample financial institutions involved in a study by the Green Finance Committee of the Institute of Finance in the Special Economic Zone had begun making public disclosure of sustainability information.[74] Additionally, due to its rapid economic progress, Shenzhen has the requisite private capital to invest in green bonds and the relevant expertise to monitor the health of the green bonds market and detect malpractices such as green-washing.[75]

The financial institutions in Shenzhen are also well prepared for the implementation of the Green Finance Regulations.[76] The Industrial Bank, as the first Equator Bank in China, and a pioneer in green finance, has set up an internal governance structure to adapt to the development of green finance and actively participated in the building of the green financial system in Shenzhen. Another example is the Shenzhen branch of the China Development Bank, which also actively supports the Green Finance Regulations and played a major role in the formation of the Green Finance Committee.[77]

As can be seen from the Shenzhen example, some municipalities are better prepared to take more progressive steps in developing the green bonds market due to the relative abundance of resources, expertise and environmental education. They should therefore implement relevant laws and regulations in advance of nationwide implementations. Such pilot projects can lend valuable experience and learning points for national roll-out at a later stage.

2.5 Integrating Sustainability Goals with Official Performance Evaluation

In order to provide a powerful incentive for local officials to faithfully and efficiently implement national policies on green finance, the Chinese government tied sustainability goals to the performance evaluation and promotion process for officials. Since 2005, China has been actively promoting the assessment of the environmental performance of leading officials in their respective jurisdictions to strengthen environmental protection measures by targeting the governmental organization.[78] Four indicators of environmental protection, namely enforcement of environmental protection laws, pollution emission intensity, change in environmental quality, and public satisfaction, were included in the assessment system for local government officials of all levels.[79] This fundamentally changes the phenomenon of local officials unilaterally pursuing GDP growth without paying attention to environmental indicators and links the problem of the deteriorating environmental quality directly to the power of officials. Among the four new indicators, pollution emission intensity is a qualitative index to comprehensively measure pollutant emissions. Changes in environmental

---

[74] Ibid.

[75] Ibid.

[76] Xinhua News (2021a).

[77] Ibid.

[78] Sina News (2005).

[79] Ibid.

quality are measured by regular environmental tests conducted by local environmental monitoring agencies to reflect changes in environmental quality at different times. The other two indicators—enforcement of environmental laws and public satisfaction—are relatively difficult to quantify. Environmental law enforcements are determined by reviewing enforcement records to determine whether the departments have complied with the environmental laws. Public satisfaction is determined by the number of public complaints about environmental problems.

Additionally, on 6 December 2013, the Organization Department of the CPC Central Committee issued the Notice on Improving the Performance Appraisal of Local Party and Government Bodies and Leading Officials.[80] This includes more comprehensive content regarding the local party leadership's and government officials' target performances, as well as a change in the format of the review and inspection of their performance. In addition to economic indicators, such performance indicators now include political, cultural, social and ecological progress and other aspects that showcase 'actual effectiveness'.[81] In 2016, the General Office of the CPC Central Committee and the General Office of the State Council issued the Ecological Progress Target Evaluation and Assessment Methods.[82] Subsequently, the National Development and Reform Commission, the National Bureau of Statistics, the Ministry of Environmental Protection and the Organization Department of the CPC Central Committee formulated the Green Development Index System and the Ecological Progress Assessment System as the basis for the evaluation and assessment of ecological progress.[83] On 24 October 2020, the Organization Department of the CPC Central Committee issued a circular on improving performance appraisals to promote high-quality development.[84] It stipulates that the 'comprehensive performance evaluation of high-quality development' is an important part of the performance evaluation of local party units and government bodies, and of leading officials of all levels. It also provided that, in response to the demand for innovative, coordinated, green, open and shared development, key indicators should be set precisely and assessments should be conducted on a tiered and classified basis.

Local governments have also cooperated with the central government's officials assessment reform. For example, in September 2017, Jiangsu Province introduced the Implementation Measures for the Ecological Progress Target Evaluation and Assessment in Jiangsu Province, the Jiangsu Province Green Development Index System and the Jiangsu Province Ecological Progress Assessment System.[85] These policies require that the party committee and government of each district and city

---

[80] Notice on Improving the Performance Appraisal of Local Party and Government Bodies and Leading Officials, issued by the Organization Department of the CPC Central Committee (6 Dec 2013).

[81] Ibid., point 1.

[82] Goals Evaluation and Assessment Methods for the Construction of Ecological Civilization [生态文明建设目标评价考核办法], State Council (2 Dec 2016).

[83] Xinhua News (2017).

[84] Notice of the Organization Department of the Central Committee of the CPC on Improving the Performance Assessment for Promoting High-quality Development [中共中央组织部关于改进推动高质量发展的政绩考核的通知], Organization Department, Central Committee of CPC (24 Dec 2020).

[85] People.cn (2017).

will implement the '1-year evaluation and 5-year assessment' mechanism for ecological progress targets. The assessment of whether targets are achieved is based on a score out of 100 marks, and categorized into four grades, namely excellent, good, qualified and unqualified. The leading appraisal department collates the scores of each district or city and their relevant situations, proposes the appraisal grading, and handles the appraisal results. This is combined with the formulation of assessment reports based on the audited results of the inspection of outgoing leading officials' natural resources and assets usage, environmental protection responsibilities and environmental protection. The assessment reports are published to the public after being examined and approved by the Jiangsu Provincial Party Committee and the Provincial Government.

The assessment results serve as an important basis for the comprehensive assessment and evaluation of the party and government bodies and leading officials in each district or city, as well as the reward, punishment, appointment and removal of officials.[86] The Jiangsu Province Green Development Index System is mainly used to measure the dynamic progress of the local ecological progress each year, covering seven primary indicators, i.e. resource utilization, environmental management, environmental quality, ecological protection, growth quality, green life and public satisfaction, as well as 56 secondary indicators.[87] The Jiangsu Province Ecological Progress Assessment System includes 24 indicators in 5 aspects, i.e., resource utilization, ecological and environmental protection, annual evaluation results, public satisfaction, and ecological environmental events, among which 16 indicators are resource and environmental constraint indicators. The assessment grade of the region is determined unqualified if three or more of such constraint indicators are not satisfied. Meanwhile, 'adverse ecological and environmental events' result in score deductions. Each occurrence of a major environmental emergency, a major source of environmental pollution that causes severe social impact, or an incident that causes serious ecological damage results in a deduction of 5 points, up to a maximum deduction of 20 points. Both systems emphasize public participation, not only allowing people to have a say in the evaluation and assessment process, but also striving to harmonize the assessment results with public opinion. Therefore, 'public satisfaction' is an important indicator that is included in the Jiangsu Province Ecological Progress Assessment System, amounting to 10 points.

Similarly, in February 2021, Shenzhen completed the Gross Ecosystem Product (GEP) accounting '1 + 3' system, led by the GEP accounting implementation plan and supported by technical specifications, the statistical reporting system and the automatic accounting platform.[88] This means that GDP will no longer be the only indicator to measure development, and GEP will become the 'green baton' to lead Shenzhen's future development. In terms of the local standard for GEP accounting, the Shenzhen Administration for Market Regulation issued the Technical Specification for the Gross Ecosystem Product (GEP) Accounting in Shenzhen, which establishes a two-level indicator system for GEP accounting, as well as the technical

---

[86] Ibid.

[87] Ibid.

[88] Xinhua News (2021b).

parameters and accounting methods for each indicator.[89] Amongst the indicators, three are primary indicators, namely material products, regulation services and cultural tourism services. There are 16 secondary indicators, including, e.g., agriculture, forestry, animal husbandry and fishery products, climate regulation, water conservation, air purification, tourism and leisure services. Under the GEP accounting statistical reporting system, more than 200 accounting data are divided into 4 categories: ecosystem monitoring, environment and meteorological monitoring, socio-economic activities and pricing, and geographic information. Data sources and filling requirements are comprehensively regulated, involving 18 departments and 48 forms. Lastly, the GEP automatic accounting platform can facilitate online data filling and generate accounting results with one click, which greatly improves the efficiency and accuracy of the accounting.

It can be seen from the preceding analysis that efforts have been made at both the national and municipal level to integrate environmental protection with the performance evaluation of officials. Such moves are applaudable as they provide the appropriate incentive structure for officials to emphasize sustainability and pursue economic progress in a sustainable way.

2.6 The Role of the Courts

In the transition towards a low-carbon green economy, it is foreseeable that certain types of legal disputes will increase in number due to adjustment by companies under new regulations and a surge in the number of green investments. Accordingly, courts need to be forward-thinking and prepared to adjudicate such disputes when they arise.

To achieve carbon neutrality by 2060, related laws, regulations and policies will be gradually introduced and implemented in China.[90] As a result, a large number of enterprises will face production reduction, shutdown, default on contracts, or even restructuring and bankruptcy as a result of mandatory capacity reduction, being assigned the air pollution control catalogue, or not falling under the Green Industry Guidance Catalogue. Cases involving contractual disputes arising from industrial restructuring in key industries, green credit disputes, green bond disputes, administrative penalties, administrative compulsory measures, among other things, will likely increase. In 2021, the Ministry of Ecology and Environment issued the Management Measures for Carbon Emission Trading, and disputes and controversies will inevitably arise during the trading process.[91]

The Supreme People's Court has already proposed to make good forecasts, publish leading judgments in due course, formulate judicial policies and propose judicial solutions.[92] This especially applies to cases involving climate change response

---

[89] Ibid.

[90] See Table 1 above.

[91] Notice of the Supreme People's Court on the Issuance of the Type and Statistical Specification of Environmental Resources Cases (for Trial Implementation) [最高人民法院关于印发《环境资源案件类型与统计规范（试行）》的通知], Supreme People's Court (4 Feb 2021), SPC Order No. 9 of [2021].

[92] Xu and Su (2020).

triggered by the development of renewable energy, reduction of energy consumption, carbon emission transformation, sustainable transportation, construction, etc. It also covers new types of green finance and carbon finance-related cases, with factual scenarios involving the provision of financial services to promote green low-carbon development, industrial transformation, and the application of new energy-saving and environmental protection technologies, equipment and product research.

On 4 August 2017, the Supreme People's Court proposed to explore the possibility of specialized financial trial institutions on the basis of the characteristics of financial disputes and cases.[93] In his speech at the World Judicial Conference on the Environment that took place at Kunming, Yunnan, on 26 May 2021, Zhou Qiang, the Chief Justice of the SPC, reiterated China's resolve to strengthen the environmental rule of law.[94] He emphasized three important aspects of the SPC's endeavor, namely specialized courts and tribunals for the adjudication of environment-related disputes, public participation in and monitoring of environmental issues, and the use of technology in dispute resolutions.[95]

Courts have a role to play in contributing towards sustainability for a few reasons.[96] For instance, green finance courts can play a part in reducing financial risks and in promoting the sustainable development of financial institutions by strengthening the risk control norms of financial institutions in anticipation of potential lawsuits. Moreover, green finance courts assume their conventional role of deterrence.[97] Judicial decisions and punishments not only increase the cost of non-compliance and illegal activities that damage the environment, but also guard against systemic risk in the green finance system.[98] The use of a blacklist of institutions with records of litigation or dishonest behavior in tapping into green bonds (e.g., green-washing or fraudulent disclosure) discourages short-termism and prevents markets for lemons.[99] Furthermore, green finance courts and public prosecutors could actively prosecute companies that violated environmental protection laws and therefore send a strong signal to the market of the importance and seriousness of environmental protection. In this respect, much more can be undertaken and gradually implemented as such green finance courts are currently limited in number and still at their infancy stage.

3 Special Characteristics of the Green Bonds Market in China and Recent Trends Towards International Convergence

Currently, China's green bonds market has a number of characteristics that differ from other major market and international standards. Most importantly, these include the profile of major issuers, requirements on the use of proceeds, sustainability

---

[93] Ibid.

[94] Zhou (2021).

[95] Supreme People's Court (2021).

[96] Ibid.

[97] Wang (2021).

[98] Ibid.

[99] Ibid.

information disclosure and credit ratings. Some of these features that create difficulties and cause hindrance for the long-term growth of China's green bonds market are examined closely in this Section. But before delving into the specific features, the authors would like to acknowledge a general trend towards greater consistency, standardization and international convergence in China's green bonds standard.

Inconsistency and lack of standardization in green projects potentially hinder the evaluation and comparison of green projects. This risk is not unique to the Chinese market. As alluded to earlier, there are three sets of independent green bonds regulatory and supervision systems in China.[100] Previously, there used to be a lack of unified standards in green project classifications and no common set of indicators such as carbon emission. As a result, investors found it hard to effectively assess and compare green projects. The issuers of green bonds could also take undue advantage in terms of green-washing, aggravating the moral hazard problem in this context.

In recent years, the international green bond standards have undergone a widespread update. The ICMA, which first proposed the four principles of green bonds, updated the contents of the Green Bond Principles in June 2018 and of the Green Bond Impact Reporting in December 2020.[101] Additionally, the ICMA's Handbook of Harmonized Framework for Impact Reporting refines and explains the disclosure methods and indicators for major categories of green projects and provides guidelines and templates for issuers to prepare impact reports, so as to further enhance the transparency and comparability of information on green bonds.[102] The CBI, the main designer of climate bond standards, released version 3.0 of the Climate Bonds Standard in December 2019. This new version strengthens public disclosure requirements and timeliness for green bonds, advocates for more pre-issuance disclosure and further clarifies the certification requirements and use.[103]

Since 2018, the EU has accelerated the pace of development of sustainable financing. The EU Green Bond Standard released in March 2019 shares similar features with the Green Bond Principles and the Climate Bonds Standard.[104] Additionally, the Report on EU Green Bond Standard issued in March 2020 specified that green economic activities should contribute to one of six environmental objectives,[105] including climate change mitigation, climate change adaptation, and adhering to the requirement of 'doing no significant harm' to any of the other environmental objectives.[106] These new criteria are expected to become the next international benchmarks for green bonds.

---

[100] See text accompanying note 37 *supra*.

[101] See *supra* note 1 for the four principles.

[102] International Capital Market Association (2021).

[103] See CBI (2019).

[104] EU Technical Expert Group on Sustainable Finance (2019a), p 13, Table 1.

[105] EU Technical Expert Group on Sustainable Finance (2019b), p 19. It also includes the following four major goals: sustainable use and protection of water and marine resources, transition to a circular economy, waste prevention and recycling, and pollution prevention control and protection of healthy ecosystems, p 16.

[106] Lu (2020), pp 77–78. See also Ma (2021).

In this light, in recent years, China has begun to harmonize its regulations and standards with the new international standards. Some progress has already been made. The Green Bonds Standards Committee was set up as a new self-regulatory authority and coordination mechanism for green bonds in December 2017.[107] In July 2020, the People's Bank of China, the National Development and Reform Commission and the Securities Regulatory Commission jointly released the China Green Bond Endorsed Project Catalogue (2020 Version) (Draft for Comments) for the first time for public consultation.[108] The 2020 version of the Catalogue is highly compatible with the Catalogue of Green Industries (2019 Edition) and inherits the basic principles of the China Green Bond Endorsed Project Catalogue (2015 Version). It unifies the domestic green bonds market in terms of the projects and fields endorsed, making significant progress for the standardization of green finance.[109] The 2020 version of the Catalogue also expands the green bonds market by increasing the categories of endorsed green consumption and trade projects and by extending the scope of endorsed projects to areas such as agriculture and ecological protection.[110] Compared to the original two green project Catalogues, the new version eliminates projects involving the clean use of fossil energy and includes climate-friendly projects, which is an important step forward in the alignment with international standards.[111] Most recently, the Green Bond Endorsed Project Catalogue (2021 Version) was introduced in April 2021, having taken into account public opinions in response to the 2020 draft.[112]

Furthermore, China actively participates in bilateral and multilateral international exchange platforms, such as the International Platform for Sustainable Finance (IPSF) which it established together with the European Commission.[113] China is also taking steps to establish a working group on green classification terminologies, and is conducting a study, organized by the People's Bank of China and its European counterparts, in exploration of the similarities and differences between the green

---

[107] Whiley (2018).

[108] Notice on the Public Consultation and the Issuance of the Green Bonds Endorsed Projects Catalogue (2020) (Draft for Public Consultation) [《绿色债券支持项目目录 (2020年版)》 (征求意见稿)], issued by the PBOC, CSRC and NDRC (8 July 2020). See further Response to the Public Consultation on the Announcement of the Issuance of Green Bonds Endorsed Projects Catalogue (2020) (Draft for Public Consultation) [关于《绿色债券支持项目目录 (2020年版) (征求意见稿)》公开征求意见的反馈], issued by the PBOC, CSRC and NDRC (27 Apr 2021).

[109] Ma (2020).

[110] Ibid.

[111] Taking into account China's economic and social development, its industry development and characteristics of its biodiversity and ecological environment, the new version of the catalogue retains many characteristics of a developing country. This is so as to provide a reference path for the development of green finance in developing countries along the 'Belt and Road' initiative. See Ma et al. (2020), p 16.

[112] Notice on the Issuance of the Green Bonds Endorsed Project Catalogue (2021) [关于印发《绿色债券支持项目目录 (2021年版)》的通知], issued by the PBOC, CSRC and NDRC on 2 Apr 2021 and effective from 1 July 2021, PBOC Order No. 96 of [2021]; Response to the Public Consultation on the Announcement of the Issuance of the Green Bonds Endorsed Projects Catalogue (2020) (Draft for Public Consultation) [关于《绿色债券支持项目目录 (2020年版) (征求意见稿)》公开征求意见的反馈], issued by the PBOC, CSRC and NDRC (27 Apr 2021).

[113] SWITCH Asia (2019).

financing standards in China and Europe with the intent of harmonizing their standards in 2021.[114] Importantly, China is working with the EU to push for greater convergence of taxonomies of green finance and investments. On 21 March 2021, the People's Bank of China announced that China was working with the EU to adopt a China-EU Shared Classification Catalogue for Green Finance.[115] The PBOC's announcement followed related milestones in the EU, namely the debut of the EU Sustainable Finance Disclosure Regulation and the EU Taxonomy Climate Delegated Act in March to April 2021.[116] To push this harmonization even further, the adoption and incorporation of a globally recognized green taxonomy, reporting and disclosure regime was discussed at the G20 Summit in Rome in October 2021.[117] All these efforts culminated in the Common Ground Taxonomy—Climate Change Mitigation Instruction Report, issued by the IPSF Taxonomy Working Group on 4 November 2021.[118]

At the PBOC-IMF High-Level Seminar on Green Finance and Climate Policy held on 15 April 2021, Yi Gang, the Governor of the PBOC, noted that, to achieve the '30/60' goal, China will need to invest RMB 2.2 trillion per year to reduce carbon emissions by 2030, and RMB 3.9 trillion per year from 2030 to 2060, and private capital participation is indispensable in this process.[119] To encourage the participation of private capital, he noted the importance of information disclosure and the provision of policy incentives. In terms of information disclosure, the PBOC plans to set up a mandatory disclosure regime with uniform standards, and to promote greater information sharing between financial institutions and companies.[120] The importance of harmonization with international green taxonomy standards is again emphasized. Regarding policy incentives, the PBOC plans to launch a set of facilitative mechanisms to provide low-cost funds for carbon emission reduction, and to strengthen its support of green finance through measures such as commercial credit ratings, deposit insurance rates, and open market operations.[121]

China has actively sought other venues of international cooperation on green finance. For instance, China took the opportunity of its G20 presidency in 2016 to introduce green finance into G20 motions for the first time, leading the creation of the G20 Green Finance Study Group and promoting the formation of a global consensus on green finance.[122] To date, this mechanism has exerted significant influence. In December 2017, China co-launched the Green Finance Network (NGFS) of central banks and regulators, focusing on the impact of climate change on macro-finance stability and macroprudential regulation, aiming to strengthen the risk management of the financial system and to mobilize capital for green and low-carbon

---

[114] People's Bank of China (2021a).

[115] Latham and Watkins LLP (2021), Chen Jia (2021).

[116] Doyle (2021).

[117] Latham and Watkins LLP (2021).

[118] IPSF (International Platform on Sustainable Finance) Taxonomy Working Group (2021).

[119] People's Bank of China (2021b).

[120] Ibid.

[121] Ibid.

[122] International Institute for Sustainable Development (2016).

investments.[123] At the end of 2018, the Green Finance Professional Committee of the Chinese Society of Finance and the City of London jointly launched the Green Investment Principles (GIP) which introduced green and sustainable development into the investment and financing activities of the Belt and Road, and 39 Chinese and foreign financial institutions have signed the GIP.[124] In addition, China has carried out various forms of international dialogues and cross-border efforts on green finance through bilateral platforms, such as the Sino-British Economic and Financial Dialogue and the Sino-French High-Level Economic and Financial Dialogue.[125]

As can be seen from the preceding analysis, the Chinese government has gained some momentum in terms of the unification of its domestic green bond standards and the convergence with international standards. It is of crucial importance that this endeavour be carried out in a thorough and consistent manner, paying special attention to the different aspects highlighted in the following sub-sections, including, most importantly, requirements regarding the use of proceeds, sustainability information disclosure and credit ratings. Following the international standards would help to resolve some of the hindrance created by the above-mentioned unique features of China's green bonds market. China's green bonds market stands to benefit from this convergence process as not only domestic but also overseas private capital would flow into the market when investors become more confident of its standardization and governance. Where applicable, recent reforms and recommended changes are included for a holistic analysis.

3.1 Profile of Major Issuers

In contrast with other markets where private issuers play a significant role, the major issuers of green bonds in China have been state-related entities so far. While there has been a change in the profile of major issuers of green bonds over the years, the main groups of issuers remain state-dominated or state-associated. Since 2016, policy banks and large commercial banks have been the main issuers of green financial bonds, with increased participation from small and medium-sized financial institutions (e.g., urban commercial banks) in recent years.[126] Non-financial enterprises became the largest group of issuers of green bonds in 2019.[127] Nevertheless, these non-financial enterprises still comprise mostly state-owned enterprises and a relatively smaller number of private enterprises. This situation is less than optimal as it leaves untapped the potential of private enterprises in China's green bonds market. Further recommendations on how the government can adjust the incentives and

---

[123] See, for example, Yi (2020). The initial institutions include the People's Bank of China, the Central Bank of the Netherlands, the Bank of France, the Bank of England, the German Central Bank, the Swedish Monetary Authority, the Monetary Authority of Singapore, and the Central Bank of Mexico, and now the membership has expanded to 83 institutions.

[124] Green Belt and Road Initiative Centre (2021).

[125] UK Treasury (2019) and CGTN (2020).

[126] China Green Bonds and Credits (2018).

[127] CBI & CCDC Research (2020), p 4.

constraints in the market to encourage participation by private enterprises can be found in Section 4 below.

3.2 Use of Proceeds

The Chinese requirements on the use of proceeds for green bonds also differ from international standards. The rule is that 100% of green financial bonds and medium-term notes, at least 70% of green corporate bonds and 50% of green enterprise bonds are to be invested in green projects.[128] In comparison, this threshold can be as high as 95% in the international rules.[129] The low threshold applied in China causes concerns about misuse of proceeds and green-washing. In practice, a portion of the capital is used for repaying debts, supplementing operation expenses, and other non-green purposes. For this reason, the Green Bonds Database managed by the CBI excluded USD 6.6 billion (RMB 46 billion) worth of purported green bonds in 2019.[130] While allowing the use of a large proportion of green bonds financing for peripheral purposes helps to meet the needs of green bond issuers and boosts the supply and scale of green bonds, it undermines the intended effect of green investment, weakening investor confidence, the appeal of green bonds and their valuations.

Another related concern is the major area of green bonds investment. In practice, the funds raised are mainly invested in clean transportation and clean energy projects, with a relatively smaller percentage of raised funds invested in ecosystem-based adaptation projects or pollution prevention and energy efficiency projects.[131] As such, the focus is on the reduction of energy consumption per unit, the elimination of environmental pollution and the curtailment of environmental damage, and on directing the limited policy supports and grants to transforming the industries that have the greatest impact on the environment and display the highest urgency in promoting green development.[132] As mentioned earlier, it is only until recently that fossil-based green energy projects have been excluded from the scope of green bonds; unlike international green standards, such projects used to qualify for green bonds in China.[133] The problem with this old arrangement was that although it fit the needs of China in the industrialization process, it limited the potential growth of green bonds, the alignment of the Chinese green standards with international ones, and the utilization of foreign funds.

The authors argue that, similar to the exclusion of fossil-based green energy projects, China can put in greater efforts aimed at the alignment of scope. For instance,

---

[128] Climate Policy Initiative (2020a), p 5, Table 2.

[129] CBI & CCDC Research (2020), p 13.

[130] CBI and SynTao Green Finance (2020), p 18.

[131] CBI & CCDC Research (2020), p 9.

[132] Lu (2020), p 78.

[133] Xinhua News (2021c). This news article cited the Notice on the Issuance of the Green Bonds Endorsed Project Catalogue (2021) [关于印发《绿色债券支持项目目录（2021年版）》的通知], issued by the PBOC, CSRC and NDRC on 2 Apr 2021 and effective from 1 July 2021, PBOC Order No. 96 of [2021]. See also Ng (2021).

China currently places emphasis on the new energy vehicle industry[134] while the international standards take a cautious approach in this sector.[135] Similarly, China does not set carbon emission targets for its green projects[136] whereas the international standards exclude all projects related to fossil energy sources without carbon capture mechanisms.[137] Alignment of these areas would help to place China on the same track as other major global players. In this regard, China's guiding philosophy is expected to shift more towards climate change mitigation and adaptation, similar to international standards such as the EU Green Bond Standard.[138]

3.3 Sustainability Information Disclosure

In China, sustainability information disclosure is required only to a limited extent. Except for listed companies and a few other specified categories, bond issuers need not disclose information regarding the use of funds or the performance of green projects.[139] Any information disclosed is mostly descriptive and not quantitative.[140] The frequency, however, is significant. Chinese banks are required to provide quarterly reports on how the green bonds are used, while corporate issuers must provide annual or semi-annual reports, which is more frequent than stipulated by international standards, which require annual reporting.[141] In contrast, a number of international green bond standards require bond issuers to disclose reports on the use of funds and information on environmental benefits.[142] They also recommend that issuers use qualitative performance indicators and/or quantitative performance indicators to measure the environmental impact of projects.[143]

It is recommended that the disclosure of environmental information on green bonds should be mandated alongside the provision of a standardized format for disclosure and the quantification of environmental indicators. This provides

---

[134] Yin (2020), p 66.

[135] Ibid.

[136] Guo (2021), pp 45–46.

[137] Ibid.

[138] See *supra* note 104.

[139] China Central Depository and Clearing Co., Ltd. (2018), p 31. The specified categories include 'key emission units; enterprises subject to compulsory clean production audit obligations; listed companies, or debt-issuing companies subject to criminal liability or significant administrative penalties due to ecological and environmental violations; and other enterprises as required by laws and regulations', see Notice on the Reform Programme for the Environmental Information Disclosure System [关于印发《环境信息依法披露制度改革方案》的通知], Ministry of Ecology and Environment (24 May 2021), Ministry of Ecology and Environment Order No. 43 of [2021], Article 2(1) (1).

According to the latest rules, issuers are required to disclose information concerning the intended usage of funds raised from green bonds issuance. See SSE Corporate Bond Issuance and Listing Rules Application Guideline No. 2—Corporate Bonds of Specific Types [上海证券交易所公司债券发行上市审核规则适用指引第2号—特定品种公司债券], Shanghai Stock Exchange (27 Nov 2020), Article 4.4.

[140] Ibid., China Central Depository and Clearing Co., Ltd. (2018), p 32.

[141] Climate Policy Initiative (2020a), p 5, Table 2.

[142] Hong (2017), p 128.

[143] Ibid.

transparency and sufficient information for domestic and foreign investors to make their investment decisions, thereby enhancing investor confidence and increasing investments in China's green bonds market.

In fact, China has been accelerating the process of mandating the disclosure of green bond information. For example, in addition to green financial bonds and green medium-term notes, the fund usage and actual environmental benefits of which must be disclosed, carbon neutral bonds launched in 2021 on the Interbank Bond Market are also subject to the provision of information on their carbon emission reduction and other environmental benefits.[144] Meanwhile, the Securities Regulatory Commission has also included environmental protection in the scope of voluntary disclosure by companies listed on the Science and Technology Innovation Board.[145] Moreover, the People's Bank of China organized and developed a green financial information management system to promote information sharing and enhance regulatory effectiveness.[146] On 24 May 2021, the Ministry of Ecology and Environment issued the Notice on the Reform Programme for the Environmental Information Disclosure System.[147] The Reform Programme mandates environmental information disclosure for key pollution units, enterprises subject to clean production auditing obligations, listed companies and bond-issuing enterprises subject to criminal liability or major administrative penalties due to ecological and environmental violations, and other enterprises or institutions as required by laws and regulations.[148] It further requires that environmental information disclosure must be carried out in a timely, comprehensible and easily searchable manner and must be uploaded to a centralized, comprehensive system.[149]

Additionally, at the international level, the pilot work on climate and environmental information disclosure for Sino–British financial institutions (there are already 13 such pilot institutions) continues to advance.[150] These 13 Sino-British financial institutions have made environmental information disclosures according to the recommendations of the Task Force on Climate-related Financial Disclosure (TCFD) and the Climate and Environmental Information Disclosure Framework set up by China, with clear results and demonstratable effects.[151]

The green bond disclosure system should identify green bond issuers as the primary party responsible for green bond disclosure. They should be encouraged to disclose the carbon footprint of raised funds in a multi-dimensional and

---

[144] National Association of Financial Market Institutional Investors (2021a).

[145] SSE Guideline No. 2 on the Application of Self-Regulatory Rules for Listed Companies on the STAR Market – Voluntary Information Disclosure [上海证券交易所科创板上市公司自律监管规则适用指引第2号—自愿信息披露], Shanghai Stock Exchange (25 Sep 2020), Article 4.14.

[146] UN Partnership for Action on Green Economy (2016).

[147] Notice on the Reform Programme for the Environmental Information Disclosure System [关于印发《环境信息依法披露制度改革方案》的通知], Ministry of Ecology and Environment (24 May 2021), Ministry of Ecology and Environment Order No. 43 of [2021].

[148] Ibid., Section II (1) (1).

[149] Ibid., Section II (1) (4).

[150] UNPRI (2019).

[151] See Energy Foundation (2020), p 3.

comprehensive manner. Additionally, the system should enable external evaluation agencies to prudently verify the content of such disclosures,[152] and complement the regulatory authorities in ensuring strict enforcement and accountability in order to fulfill China's green bond environmental information disclosure obligations. While certain efforts have been made in this respect, more extensive reforms are required to deliver optimal impact.

3.4 Credit Ratings and Environmental Risk Analysis

Finally, green bond credit ratings in China are generally above AA+, with most receiving AAA ratings.[153] The bonds are mostly certified by domestic third-party evaluation agencies, with a small portion being certified by overseas agencies.[154] However, there is also a large proportion of bonds that are unrated, and the proportion of green bonds that are certified is currently not as high as desired.[155] Furthermore, China's green bond standard does not mandate third-party certification. There is no unified or recognized certification process,[156] with the process varying from institution to institution. This differs greatly from the international green bond standards, which emphasize the importance of third-party certification, requiring the quantification of environmental benefits as a basic criterion for certification.[157]

It is therefore recommended that more efforts be put into the effective assessment of a project's greenness and the establishment of trustworthy credit-rating agencies. The determination of the green attributes prior to the issuance of green bonds also requires active monitoring of the use of raised funds during their subsequent operation and measurement of the environmental benefits they generate. In September 2020, the NGFS released two important documents, i.e., the Overview of Environmental Risk Analysis by Financial Institutions and the Case Studies of Environmental Risk Analysis Methodologies, calling for a concerted effort to promote the use of environmental risks analysis in the financial industry.[158] As one of the founders of the NGFS, China should take this opportunity to make full use of the expertise of market institutions to accelerate the construction of a statistical database on environmental benefits, to develop and share environmental risk analysis methods and assessment models, and to complete work on green financial investment analysis tools. As the green bonds market becomes increasingly popular, the government should lead the way by redirecting local government subsidies or concessions for individual green bond issuers into various forms of green funds (e.g., green industry funds, green guarantee funds, green M&A funds, green guidance funds, green

---

[152] China Government Securities Depository Trust and Clearing Co. Ltd. and CECEP Consulting Co. Ltd. (2018), p 113.

[153] Ibid.

[154] Ibid.

[155] Ibid. Non-public issuance of bonds does not need to be rated.

[156] Shi (2019), p 93.

[157] CBI (2019), Part B and Part D.

[158] Network for Greening the Financial System (2020).

development funds, etc.) in order to guide the development of green industries.[159] In doing so, market participants in China should attempt to align with international developments, such as the NGFS guidelines, as much as possible in order to secure international confidence in their environmental risk assessment methodologies right from the start.

Additionally, in-depth use of financial technology in the field of green bonds will arguably improve the accuracy and automation of the systematic measurement of the environmental performance of green enterprises and projects.[160] For instance, the use of big data analysis may improve the accuracy and sensitivity of external evaluations based on data such as green bond ratings and certifications and promote information sharing. Other forms of measurement technologies such as earth observations via satellites or drones, and spatial finance can help overcome the difficulty with independent verification of sustainability information disclosure.[161] China has already begun adopting fintech for green finance in some pilot regions. For example, in Huzhou city, the local government makes use of the internet, big data and other technologies to build a comprehensive green finance service platform to reduce environmental and climate-related information asymmetries and to quickly match green enterprises and projects with financial institutions.[162]

4 Lessons Learnt and Ways Forward

After canvassing the unique policies and features in China's green bonds market, this Section identifies several problems arising from the top–down approach taken by the Chinese government as well as from the fact that the green bonds market is still at its emerging stage. Such problems include potential misallocation and waste of resources, resource and manpower constraints on the regulators, and the lack of investor education. Targeted recommendations are made accordingly. The last part of this Section makes the case for the evolving role of the government as the green bonds market matures and the approach shifts from a government-oriented to a more market-oriented one.

4.1 Adjustment of Incentives and Constraints to Ensure Efficient Allocation

As it stands, there is a disproportionate allocation of capital in China's green bonds market in favor of state-owned enterprises (SOEs). This means that private companies find it harder to secure financing through green bonds and accordingly have a small share in the green bonds market. In 2019, while the number of times that green bonds had been issued by private enterprises had increased to 11, an 83.33% increase compared to 2018, the actual amount of green bonds issued by private

---

[159] An et al. (2018), pp 76–78.

[160] Yin (2020), p 67; see also Avgouleas (2021).

[161] Avgouleas (2021), pp 68–72.

[162] Shanghai Branch of the State Administration of Foreign Exchange (2020).

enterprises (RMB 5 billion, comprising 2% of the market) was still far lower than that issued by SOEs (RMB 194.937 billion, comprising 79.90% of the market).[163] This is still the prevailing situation as at the date of this paper.

As a result, private enterprises that lack a government background or government connections, or have a low credit rating, tend to find it hard to secure a favorable interest rate even though they might have good-quality green projects with significant environmental impact. The lack of participation by private enterprises is undesirable in the long term as it stifles competition, limits the long-term potential of the market and creates potential concerns about the waste of resources or unaccountability of SOEs.

Chinese local policies primarily focus on green projects with high credit ratings, a large scale and relatively mature technology.[164] However, a number of projects with vast potential in promoting green low-carbon growth may not receive funding because they did not fulfill the local requirements. The issuers of green bonds that are backed by government support enjoy several advantages.[165] They get quicker approval for issuance from regulatory authorities. They can also use a higher proportion of the capital raised for purposes other than supporting their green projects, as explained above. As some of the companies controlled by local governments find it hard to issue ordinary corporate bonds, they may switch to issuing green bonds for financing.[166] At the same time, companies in industries heavily regulated by macroeconomic policies may also tend to raise funds by issuing green bonds or even seek undue advantages from the green bond standards yet to be standardized, adding more risks to the system.[167]

On top of inefficient allocation of resources, corruption, fraud and green-washing are potential vices hidden in a top–down approach. As mentioned previously, sustainability information is still a weak link in China's green bonds market.[168] Because the quality of information disclosure cannot be adequately determined, problems such as fraudulent disclosure and green-washing tend to be present.[169] In addition, local officials may be influenced by bribery and nepotism to provide green bonds-related subsidies and grants in an unfair manner, although it should be noted that corruption by officials in China has been strongly subdued in recent years.[170] Rent seeking is also an area where companies issuing green bonds may accrue undue advantages and benefits by selecting a more favorable regulatory environment,[171] and such regulatory arbitrage is particularly likely in China, where there used to be different sets of standards governing green bonds.[172] In this regard, it should be

---

[163] United Equator Bonds Research Institute (2020).

[164] Climate Bonds Initiative and SynTao Green Finance (2020), p 18.

[165] Ibid.

[166] Ba et al. (2019), p 102.

[167] Xiao and Yan (2018), p 85.

[168] See Section 3.3 above.

[169] See, for example, Harlan (2019).

[170] See, for example, Ting (2020).

[171] Park (2018), p 31.

[172] See Climate Policy Initiative (2020a), p 5, Table 2.

noted that the standardization has significantly improved after the PBOC, NDRC and CSRC jointly issued the Green Bonds Endorsed Project Catalogue (2021).[173]

These issues could be aggravated by the resource and manpower constraints of regulators. As regulators face challenges in allocating sufficient resources to the regulation of such matters, the risks associated with under-regulation of illegal activities and non-compliance loom large.[174] Compared to ordinary bonds, green bonds attract positive attention because of their positive impact on the environment. However, it is much more difficult to quantitatively assess the green nature and environmental impact of such projects.[175] Regulation of green bonds therefore requires greater manpower, resources and money. Suitable monitoring tools and techniques are needed for each industry.[176] These requirements far exceed the resource and capability constraints faced by conventional financial regulators. This dilemma brings unprecedented challenges for regulators and results in practical problems such as the difficulty to deal with green-washing in a timely manner. All of these complications make it difficult for regulators to perform their role of safeguarding and promoting the healthy development of the green bonds market.

In this regard, on top of the conventional role of regulators, enforcers and courts,[177] it is important to contemplate the roles of other market players, such as financial institutions and third-party service providers like law firms, auditing firms and credit-rating agencies. Financial institutions can act as checks and balances of the quality of sustainability information disclosure.[178] Similarly, credit rating agencies should uphold fairness and be held to their task of quality control, and not be unduly influenced by conflicts of interests.[179] Law firms should also properly advise their clients on the requirements of the laws and regulations and the risks of non-compliance or green-washing. In this sense, regulations and monitoring are a systematic design instead of a one-sided effort.

Accordingly, China should adjust the incentives and constraints of green bond investment and financing, promote the internalization of the positive externalities of green bonds through market-based mechanisms, and design a suitable environment for the development of green bonds by complementing the market's functions with the government's functions. In this regard, as illustrated in Fig. 2 below, the government's role is to provide sufficient incentives to market players and eventually allow market mechanisms to promote the development of the green bonds market. In doing so, it should provide the institutional framework for issuers to issue green bonds in

---

[173] See *supra* note 112.

[174] Ba et al. (2019), pp 102–103.

[175] Climate Policy Initiative (2020a), p 3.

[176] For instance, the SASB framework devised by the Sustainability Accounting Standards Board provides sector-specific standards and guidance for ESG disclosure in 77 industries, Sustainability Accounting Standards Board (2021).

[177] See Section 2.6 for a discussion on the role of the courts.

[178] Chang et al. (2019).

[179] Climate Policy Initiative (2020a), pp 9–10.

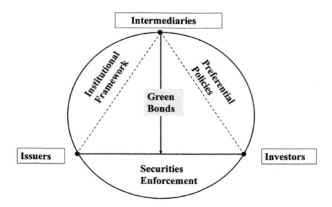

Fig. 2 Government measures to facilitate effective market mechanisms

a conducive regulatory environment,[180] introduce preferential policies such as tax exemptions and investor education to attract investors to invest in green bonds, and act as an enforcer and a conduit for dispute settlement between issuers and investors to maintain investor confidence in the market.

Government policies can help to construct a favorable institutional framework for green bond issuers in a number of ways. In terms of financing, as of end 2020, the market capitalization of China's green bonds market, which is the world's second largest, only amounted to RMB 813.2 billion. This is much lower than the market size of China's green loans market, which is the world's largest, with a market capitalization of RMB 12 trillion.[181] As compared to green credit, the financing model of green securities is more direct, and green industries can obtain funds at a lower cost and through a simpler process.[182] Therefore, it is necessary to increase policy support for green bonds in the future. Achieving a low-carbon green economy requires investment by the masses. In the future, China needs to stimulate private enterprises' interest in joining the green cause and the government should divert more financial concessions and subsidies to such private enterprises as well as to green projects with greater potential environmental benefits. Since private enterprises face certain disadvantages in seeking green financing in the current context, it is recommended that such difficulties should be removed by reforms for the benefit of diversification and healthy competition in the green bonds market.

At the same time, China must guide green bond issuers in investing more raised funds in green projects, release a greater variety of green bonds in accordance with China's economic transition, support the development of not only dark green projects but also medium and light green projects, and develop transition bonds to help

---

[180] Such an institutional framework would encompass the key recommendations in this paper, such as greater standardization and consistency of green bonds, and more stringent requirements on information disclosure and use of proceeds.

[181] People's Bank of China (2021a).

[182] Wang and Ma (2020), p 75.

brown industries transit to becoming green ones. Since green bonds no longer have any advantage in the issuance approval process after the implementation of the new Securities Law as of 1 March 2020, mandating that all corporate bonds comply with the 'registration system', the rules in that law should be adjusted.[183] A suitable market mechanism and legal liability framework should be formulated for the rational evaluation of green bond prices. These measures, together with market intermediaries that assist green bond issuers with green certification and environmental information disclosure, will raise the costs of environmental damage, hence incentivizing green bond issuers to improve the environmental benefits of green bonds in order to enhance their attractiveness.

4.2 Improvement of Retail Investor Education

From the investor's perspective, the lack of investor education means that investors do not have a strong sustainability mindset while the market demands sophisticated retail investors.[184] In recent years, the negative impact of climate change on socioeconomic conditions has been increasingly felt, particularly amidst COVID-19, and has become an inevitable source of financial risk.[185] At the same time, the demand for and interest in sustainable investment by retail investors has increased and should be tapped into for further growth of the green bonds market. However, because green bonds carry both the credit risks of ordinary bonds and the environmental risks associated with their environmental goals, investors are required to have relevant knowledge about environmental risks and the methodology to identify, evaluate and manage such risks in their portfolios.[186]

According to statistics, the majority of green bond (medium-term) buyers in 2020 are institutional investors.[187] There is limited participation by other enterprises and retail investors. Retail investors are still primarily concerned with the financial returns of their investment and not with information disclosure concerning the public welfare goals and the sustainable impact of the use of the funds.[188] The situation is a far cry from having investors with proper techniques to evaluate and manage environmental risks in their investments. Because of the lack of analytical tools, many investors cannot identify and quantify the credit and market risks arising from environmental factors, and therefore underestimate the risks in unsustainable assets and overestimate the risks in green investment.[189] As such, the lack of incorporation of concepts and tools for managing environmental risks covered by the Principles

---

[183] The Measures for the Administration of the Issuance and Trading of Corporate Bonds (2021 Revision) [公司债券发行与交易管理办法(2021修订)], Order No. 180 of the CSRC [2021] (26 Feb 2021), consolidated the reform of the registration system concerning the public issuance of corporate bonds.

[184] See, for example, Daeniken (2020) and Standard Chartered (2020), p 10.

[185] Lau (2020).

[186] Hong (2017), p 134.

[187] National Association of Financial Market Institutional Investors (2021b).

[188] Liu (2018), p 110.

[189] Ma (2019), p 8.

for Responsible Investment (PRI)[190] may further limit the sustainable growth of the green bonds market in China.

With regard to further incentivizing investors to invest in green bonds, there is a need to further publicize, and educate people on the importance of a green and low-carbon circular economy, to encourage investors to use the ESG criteria to screen potential investments, to guide financial resources toward a green, low-carbon circular economy and to enhance investors' preferences for and sensitivity to green attributes. Ideally, green and sustainable development or social welfare should gradually become the main investment objective of investors and the areas that China's domestic markets focus on.[191] An important pre-condition for attracting sophisticated retail investors to enter the green bonds market is adequate investor protection, demonstrated by enhanced requirements on the use of proceeds, continuous monitoring and certification, and information disclosure, as recommended in this paper.

After investors put their money into the green bonds market, the government's role continues in terms of enforcing green bond issuers' compliance with their obligations and adjudicating disputes between investors and issuers. Much ink has already been spilt about guarding against malpractices, such as fraud and greenwashing, that undermine investor confidence. The role of courts has been canvassed earlier as well.[192] Ultimately, investors will only stay in the green bonds market when they have enough confidence that the issuers stay true to their commitment to sustainability and any disputes can be resolved in an efficient and fair manner. The government can do much in this respect in terms of regulatory design and boosting judicial expertise in this area.

4.3 Evolving Role of the Government and Gradual Transition Towards a Market-oriented Model

On the one hand, China, with a transition economy, has impressed many in pioneering the establishment of a government-led green bonds market that fulfills the goals of green bonds. However, on the other hand, the hidden challenges brought about by China's top–down development model and new pressures arising from the green development at home and abroad render it necessary to recharacterize the government's involvement from that of a government-oriented model with a limited role for the market to a market-oriented model with a limited role for the government. The authors therefore argue that the role of the government should not be a stagnant one where the green bonds market is concerned but requires evolution in response to the level of maturity of the market.

---

[190] The Six Principles for Responsible Investment promulgated by the United Nations Environment Programme are as follows: (1) incorporate ESG issues into investment analysis and decision-making processes; (2) be active owners and incorporate ESG issues into our ownership policies and practices; (3) seek appropriate disclosure on ESG issues by the entities in which we invest; (4) promote acceptance and implementation of the Principles within the investment industry; (5) work together to enhance our effectiveness in implementing the Principles; and (6) each report on our activities and progress towards implementing the Principles.

[191] Feng et al. (2019), p 502.

[192] See Section 2.6 above.

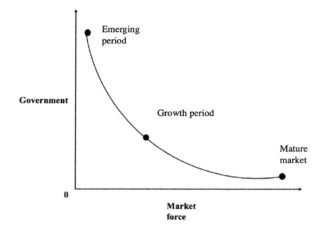

Fig. 3 Evolving role of the government in developing a green bonds market

As illustrated in Fig. 3 above, at the emerging stage of the market the government has a greater role to play. Such a role would involve setting up a conducive institutional and regulatory framework, creating preferential policies to attract investors, and providing reliable dispute resolution mechanisms, as explained earlier. Overall, these government interventions are not an end in themselves, but rather a means to reach desirable ends such as diversification, reliability and competence of green bond issuers, sophistication of investors and expertise of the courts. It is not difficult to see that these end goals all drive towards a more mature market where market forces alone can distribute resources in an efficient and environment-friendly way. Similarly, scholars have identified the signs of a mature market as including proper management of information asymmetry, strong investor protection (particularly for minority investors), and continuous monitoring of company directors and managers.[193]

Once there are observable signs of a mature market, the extent of government intervention should be significantly curtailed, letting market forces take the leading role in shaping its development.[194] At this later stage, the role of government as a limited participant should be reduced to the provision of necessary funding and of efficient dispute resolution mechanisms, and monitoring of the performance of green bond issuers. In fact, overregulation at this stage risks stifling the attractiveness and competitiveness of a market.[195] By letting market forces take a predominant role, the government will also be mitigating some of the issues related to the top–down approach, such as inefficient allocation of resources. Overall, while at the present stage the government still has a major role to play in terms of putting in place a robust regulatory regime that properly incentivizes different stakeholders to

---

[193] See, for example, Black (2001) (although in the context of stock markets the concepts are transferrable).

[194] Chen (2014), p 45.

[195] Coffee (2007), pp 233–247.

enter the green bonds market, eventually its role is going to diminish to a facilitative monitor in the long run as the market matures.

5 Conclusion

China has progressed from a high-energy consumption, high-pollution economic model to a green and low-carbon economic model in its attempt to build an ecological civilization. In the process, China established the world's second largest green bonds market in a short period of time through top–down government-led reforms. This is a significant example of how a country with a transitional economy can build a vibrant green bonds market. The top–down design, unified deployment and efficient implementation of its green bond system and operation mechanisms have empowered China to overcome certain market failures and thereby shorten the natural evolutionary process of the market. This highlights the government's positive role as the institutional force that mandates change. However, despite the initial successes of its green bonds market, China also faced challenges brought about by its government-led reform model that varied between regions and eras. Additionally, China also realized the importance of allowing the market to work hand-in-hand with the government, the importance of giving effect to market mechanisms for resource allocation and the importance of establishing efficient incentive and constraint mechanisms for the market.

In response to the new changes in international green standards and the need to fulfill its '30/60 goal', China must reform and improve on the mechanism and institutional framework of its green bonds market with the aim of unifying its domestic practices and aligning them with international standards. It should further strengthen sustainability information disclosure requirements and cultivate a group of sophisticated retail investors. The role of courts as a bridge between black-letter laws and actual stakeholders such as issuers and investors should be enhanced as well. In implementing these measures, the government needs to be guided by the ultimate goal of constructing an efficient and independent green bonds market driven by market forces with an appropriate institutional design. All these policy reforms will eventually allow the market to further develop and to more effectively promote the making of a green, low-carbon circular economy so as to realize the vision of building a better home on earth.

Acknowledgements This article is supported by the Centre for Banking and Finance Law, National University of Singapore. We thank Iris Chiu, Virginia E. Harper and Xia Mian for valuable comments on an earlier draft.

References

An G et al. (2018) Research on global and China's green funds/国内外绿色基金发展研究. China Finance Publishing House, China
Avgouleas E (2021) Resolving the sustainable finance conundrum: activist policies and financial technology. Law Contemp Probl 84:55–73

Ba S, Cong Y, Zhu W (2019) Analysis of green bond theory and market development in China/绿色债券理论与中国市场发展分析. J Hangzhou Normal Univ (Soc Sci Edn) 1:91–106

Ba S, Yang C, Yao S (2018) Review of the progress of green finance research in China/中国绿色金融研究进展述评. Finan Dev Res 6:3–11

Black B (2001) The legal and institutional preconditions for strong stock markets: the nontriviality of securities law. UCLA Law Rev 48:781–856

Bond Connect (2021a) About Bond Connect Company Limited (BCCL). https://www.chinabondconnect.com/en/About-Us/Company-Introduction.html. Accessed 31 Nov 2021

Bond Connect (2021b) Trading mechanisms. https://www.chinabondconnect.com/en/Trading/Trading-Bc/Trading-Mechanism.html. Accessed 31 Nov 2021

Bonds Market Research Team (2021) Lianhe Credit Ratings Report on Green Bonds (2021Q1). China Lianhe Credit Rating Co., Ltd. (WeChat official account), 23 Apr 2021. https://mp.weixin.qq.com/s/E4i83xMXbgddNpVCeCskIA. Accessed 31 Nov 2021

Brown M (2021) 'China's Central Bank Governor outlines green finance priorities'. Lexology, 25 March 2021. https://www.lexology.com/library/detail.aspx?g=29538399-a5db-443c-83ba-7b33c061093e&utm_source=lexology+daily+newsfeed&utm_medium=html+email+-+body+-+general+section&utm_campaign=lexology+subscriber+daily+feed&utm_content=lexology+daily+newsfeed+2021-03-26&utm_term. Accessed 31 Nov 2021

CBI (2017) Facilitating cross-border capital flows to grow the China green bond market. https://www.climatebonds.net/files/reports/china_intracountry_2017-01d_da_en_28nov17_a4.pdf. Accessed 31 Nov 2021

CBI (2019) Climate Bonds Standard Version 3.0. https://www.climatebonds.net/files/files/climate-bonds-standard-v3-20191210.pdf. Accessed 31 Nov 2021

CBI and CCDC Research (2017) China Green Bond Market 2016. https://www.climatebonds.net/resources/reports/china-green-bond-market-2016. Accessed 31 Nov 2021

CBI and CCDC Research (2018) China Green Bond Market 2017. https://www.climatebonds.net/resources/reports/china-green-bond-market-2017. Accessed 31 Nov 2021

CBI and CCDC Research (2019) China Green Bond Market 2018. https://www.climatebonds.net/resources/reports/china-green-bond-market-2018. Accessed 31 Nov 2021

CBI and CCDC Research (2020) China Green Bond Market: 2019 Research Report. https://www.climatebonds.net/system/tdf/reports/2019_cbi_china_report_en.pdf?file=1&type=node&id=47441&force=0. Accessed 31 Nov 2021

CBI and CCDC Research (2021) China Green Bond Market Report 2020. https://www.climatebonds.net/files/reports/cbi_china_sotm_2021_06d.pdf. Accessed 31 Nov 2021

CBI and SynTao Green Finance (2017) Study of China's local government policy instruments for foreign green bonds. https://www.climatebonds.net/system/tdf/reports/chinalocalgovt_02_13.04_final_a4.pdf?file=1&type=node&id=31001. Accessed 31 Nov 2021

CBI and SynTao Green Finance (2020) Report on the Opportunities and Challenges Facing the Issuance of Green Bonds in China/中国的绿色债券发行与机遇报告. https://www.climatebonds.net/resources/reports/China_GBIO_CN. Accessed 31 Nov 2021

CGTN (2020) 'China, France vow to promote finance, economic cooperation amid Covid-19 battle', 21 July 2020. https://news.cgtn.com/news/2020-07-21/China-France-vow-to-promote-finance-economic-cooperation-SjwhmRhJWU/index.html. Accessed 31 Nov 2021

Chang WF, Amran A, Iranmanesh M, Foroughi B (2019) Drivers of sustainability reporting quality: financial institution perspective. Int J Ethics Syst 35:632–650

Chen J (2021) 'China, EU lead "green revolution" with finance standards', China Daily, 29 Apr 2021. https://www.chinadaily.com.cn/a/202104/29/WS608a0eeca31024ad0babb2c0.html. Accessed 31 Nov 2021

Chen S (2014) Functional positioning of government and market in the commercial law mechanisms/商法机制中政府与市场的功能定位. China Legal Sci 5:41–59

China Center for International Economic Exchanges (2013) Research on public policies for implementing green development in China. China Economic Press, China

China Central Depository and Clearing Co., Ltd. (2018) Research Report on Green Bond Environmental Benefit Information Disclosure System and Indicator System. https://www.chinabond.com.cn/cb/cn/yjfx/zybg/20190610/151734197.shtml. Accessed 31 Nov 2021

China Government Securities Depository Trust and Clearing Co. Ltd. and CECEP Consulting Co. Ltd. (2018) Research Report on a Green Bond Environmental Benefit Information Disclosure System

and Indicator System. https://www.chinabond.com.cn/cb/cn/yjfx/zybg/20190610/151734197.shtml. Accessed 31 Nov 2021

China Green Bonds and Credits (2018) Annual overview of green bonds 2017. Investment Database (WeChat official account), 19 Jan 2018. https://mp.weixin.qq.com/s/1GT6TBksC6Qcl02vd_LflQ. Accessed 31 Nov 2021

Climate Policy Initiative (2020a) MRV system design: recommendations for Chinese green bonds. http://climatepolicyinitiative.org/wp-content/uploads/2020/06/MRV-System-Design-Recommendations-for-Green-Bonds-in-China.pdf. Accessed 31 Nov 2021

Climate Policy Initiative (2020b) The state and the effectiveness of the green bond market in China. https://www.climatepolicyinitiative.org/wp-content/uploads/2020/06/The_State_and_Effectiveness_of_the_Green_Bond_Market_in_China.pdf. Accessed 31 Nov 2021

Coffee J (2007) Law and the market: the impact of enforcement. Univ PA Law Rev 156(2):229–311

Daeniken D (2020) 'Sustainability: investor education can lead to long-term resilient growth', Emerging Market Views, 28 Oct 2020. https://em-views.com/sustainability-investor-education-can-lead-to-long-term-resilient-growth. Accessed 31 Nov 2021

Dai W, Kidney S (2016) Roadmap for China: using green securitisation, tax incentives and credit enhancements to scale green bonds. Climate Bonds Initiative. https://cn.climatebonds.net/files/files/CBI-IISD-Paper3-EN.pdf. Accessed 31 Nov 2021

Dong X, Liu X, Lin Q (2020) Green Bonds Operation Report 2019—Green bonds market in China continued to improve and the amount of green bonds issuance increased substantially. China Lianhe Credit Rating Co., Ltd. (WeChat official account), 16 March 2020. https://mp.weixin.qq.com/s/KDiPr9VO6gUpP07xTRC_Dg. Accessed 31 Nov 2021

Dou R, Zhang W (2019) A study on the effect of green factors on bond yield spreads—an analysis based on PSM method / 绿色因子对债券收益利差的影响研究——基于PSM法的分析. J Shanghai LiXin Univ Account Finan 6:47–57

Doyle DH (2021) What is the impact of the EU Sustainable Finance Disclosure Regulation (SFDR)? S&P Global, 1 Apr 2021. https://www.spglobal.com/marketintelligence/en/news-insights/blog/what-is-the-impact-of-the-eu-sustainable-finance-disclosure-regulation-sfdr. Accessed 31 Nov 2021

Energy Foundation (2020) Climate and Environmental Disclosure Pilot Initiative for UK and China Financial Institutions: 2019 Annual Progress Report. https://www.efchina.org/Reports-zh/report-lceg-20201103-zh. Accessed 31 Nov 2021

EU Technical Expert Group on Sustainable Finance (2019a) Report on EU Green Bond Standard. https://ec.europa.eu/info/sites/default/files/business_economy_euro/banking_and_finance/documents/190618-sustainable-finance-teg-report-green-bond-standard_en.pdf. Accessed 31 Nov 2021

EU Technical Expert Group on Sustainable Finance (2019b) Taxonomy Technical Report. https://www.ecologic.eu/sites/default/files/publication/2021/3567-190618-sustainable-finance-teg-report-taxonomy_en.pdf. Accessed 31 Nov 2021

Feng G et al. (2019) Green development and green assessment/绿色发展与绿色评估. China Finance Publishing House

Freeburn L, Ramsay I (2020) Green bonds: legal and policy issues. Cap Mark Law J 15(4):418–442

Green Belt and Road Initiative Centre (2021) The Green Investment Principle (GIP) for the Belt and Road Initiative (last updated 30 Apr 2021). https://green-bri.org/green-investment-principle-gip-belt-and-road-initiative/#:~:text=The%20Green%20Investment%20Principle%20(GIP)%20is%20a%20set%20of%20principles,in%20the%20Belt%20and%20Road.&text=As%20of%20April%202025%2C%202019,for%20the%20Belt%20and%20Road. Accessed 31 Nov 2021

Green Bonds Research Team (2021) Green bonds in 2020—a review (second half). China Bonds and Credits (WeChat official account), 27 Jan 2021. https://mp.weixin.qq.com/s/AaebaMEfGltZ2RlU9v-nQg. Accessed 31 Nov 2021

Green China's Financial System Study Group of DRC (2016) The developmental logic and framework of China's green finance/发展中国绿色金融的逻辑与框架. Financ Forum 2:17–28

Gregory HJ, Palmer H, Wood L (2020) 'Emerging ESG disclosure trends highlighted in GAO Report', Harvard Law School Forum on Corporate Governance, 15 Aug 2020. https://corpgov.law.harvard.edu/2020/08/15/emerging-esg-disclosure-trends-highlighted-in-gao-report/. Accessed 31 Nov 2021

Guo X (2021) Vigorous development of green finance to help achieve the goal of carbon neutrality/大力发展绿色金融 助力实现碳中和目标. Tsinghua Financ Rev 1:44–46

Harlan T (2019) Green development or greenwashing? A political ecology perspective on China's green Belt and Road. Eurasian Geogr Econ 62(2):202–226

Hong Y (2010) Multi-pronged regulation, path dependence and future development plan of corporate bonds. Secur Mark Her 4:9–16

Hong Y (2016) Challenges and improvements of green corporate bonds in China/中国绿色公司债券的制度挑战与改进. Secur Mark Her 9:4–12

Hong Y (2017) International rules and insights on the operational mechanism of green bonds/绿色债券运作机制的国际规则与启示. Law Sci 2(2):124–134

International Capital Market Association (2018) Green bond principles—voluntary process guidelines for issuing green bonds. https://www.icmagroup.org/assets/documents/Regulatory/Green-Bonds/Green-Bonds-Principles-June-2018-270520.pdf. Accessed 31 Nov 2021

International Capital Market Association (2021) Impact reporting. https://www.icmagroup.org/sustainable-finance/impact-reporting/. Accessed 31 Nov 2021

International Finance Corporation (2016) Mobilizing private climate finance—green bonds and beyond. https://openknowledge.worldbank.org/bitstream/handle/10986/30351/110881-BRI-EMCompass-Note-25-Green-Bonds-FINAL-12-5-PUBLIC.pdf?sequence=1&isAllowed=y. Accessed 31 Nov 2021

International Institute for Sustainable Development (2016) 'China's G20 Presidency holds green finance, energy sustainability meetings', 22 Feb 2016. http://sdg.iisd.org/news/chinas-g20-presidency-holds-green-finance-energy-sustainability-meetings/. Accessed 31 Nov 2021

IPSF (International Platform on Sustainable Finance) Taxonomy Working Group (Co-chaired by the EU and China) (2021) Common Ground Taxonomy—Climate Change Mitigation. Instruction report, 4 Nov 2021. https://ec.europa.eu/info/sites/default/files/business_economy_euro/banking_and_finance/documents/211104-ipsf-common-ground-taxonomy-instruction-report_en.pdf. Accessed 31 Nov 2021

Jiang Y, Lei N (2019) 'Ganjiang New Area issues the first municipal green bond in China', Ganjiang New Area official website, 21 June 2019. http://www.gjxq.gov.cn/art/2019/6/21/art_42022_26601 45.html. Accessed 31 Nov 2021

Jones L (2021) 'Record $269.5bn green issuance for 2020: late surge sees pandemic year pip 2019 total by $3bn', Climate Bonds Initiative, 24 Jan 2021. https://www.climatebonds.net/2021/01/record-2695bn-green-issuance-2020-late-surge-sees-pandemic-year-pip-2019-total-3bn. Accessed 31 Nov 2021

Kan H (2009) Environment and health in China: challenges and opportunities. Environ Health Prospect 117(12):A530-531

Kidney S, Oliver P, Sonerud B, Climate Bonds Initiative (2015) Chapter 10: greening China's bond market. In: Halle M (ed) Greening China's financial system. International Institute for Sustainable Development, pp 249–253

Latham and Watkins LLP (2021) 'China and EU to collaborate on green investment standards', Lexology, 12 Apr 2021. https://www.lexology.com/library/detail.aspx?g=9031e27b-bc47-4210-b8e5-c4887 8773309#:~:text=The%20People's%20Bank%20of%20China,two%20markets%20later%20this% 20year. Accessed 31 Nov 2021

Lau KY (2020) 'COVID-19: what does it mean for climate change? Lessons from responding to the immediate threat of COVID-19', KPMG. https://home.kpmg/sg/en/home/insights/2020/04/covid-19-what-does-it-mean-for-climate-change.html. Accessed 31 Nov 2021

Liao Z, Yun Z (2020) Analysis of green bonds issued overseas by Chinese entities in 2019. Source: International Institute of Green Finance of CUFE. Sina News, 29 July 2020. https://finance.sina.cn/esg/2020-07-29/detail-iivhvpwx8120629.d.html. Accessed 31 Nov 2021

Liu T (2018) Where does China fall short in cultivating green bond investors?/培育绿色债券投资者, 中国还差在哪里? China Bank 6:108–110

Lu W (2020) Comparative analysis of standardization and consistency in green finance standards between China and Europe/中欧绿色金融标准一致性的比较与分析. China Bonds 4:75–80

Lu W, Wang Y (2016) Seeking a clear definition of green bonds projects/明确界定绿色债券项目. China Financ 6:54–55

Ma J (2016) Building a theoretical framework for green finance. Financ Mark Res 2:2–8

Ma J (2017) Green finance and the role of government, UN Environment Programme, 13 Oct 2017. https://unepinquiry.org/blogs/green-finance-and-the-role-of-government/. Accessed 31 Nov 2021

Ma J (2019) Preface for green finance series/《绿色金融丛书》序言. In: Jin H (ed) Research on green finance evaluation system—green evaluation of enterprises, assets and supply chain / 绿色金融评价体系研究——企业,资产与供应链的绿色评价. China Finance Publishing

Ma J (2021) 'Improving the green financial system with the goal of carbon neutrality', Financial Times, 18 Jan 2021. https://h5.newaircloud.com/detailArticle/15048522_28236_jrsb.html?app=1& source=1. Accessed 31 Nov 2021

Ma J, Liu J, Chen Z, Xie W (2019) Chapter 7: green bonds. In: Schipke A, Rodlauer M, Zhang L (eds) The future of China's bond market. International Monetary Fund

Ma J et al. (2020) How to construct a financial service system that supports green technological innovation/构建支持绿色技术创新的金融服务体系. China Finance Publishing House

Ma M (2020) 'Harmonization of domestic green bond standards praised by international authorities', Hexun.com, 10 July 2020. http://bank.hexun.com/2020-07-10/201686705.html. Accessed 31 Nov 2021

MacLeod M, Park J (2011) Financial activism and global climate change: the rise of investor-driven governance networks. Global Envtl Pol 11:54–74

Mai J, Xu F (2015) Research on the impact factors of green finance in China based on joint analysis/基于联合分析的我国绿色金融影响因素研究. Macroecon Res 5:23–27

Myers SL (2020) 'China's pledge to be carbon neutral by 2060: what it means', The New York Times, 23 Sep 2020. https://www.nytimes.com/2020/09/23/world/asia/china-climate-change.html. Accessed 31 Nov 2021

National Association of Financial Market Institutional Investors (2021a) Innovative launch of carbon neutral bonds to help achieve the 30-60 goals/创新推出碳中和债, 助力实现30/60目标. http://www.nafmii.org.cn/xhdt/202102/t20210209_84483.html. Accessed 31 Nov 2021

National Association of Financial Market Institutional Investors (2021b) Statistics on the volume of debt financing instruments in 2020/2020年债务融资工具业务量统计. http://www.nafmii.org.cn/scyjfx/ywltj/202101/P020210121612536685896.pdf. Accessed 31 Nov 2021

National Development and Reform Commission (2021) Press Conference of 19 July 2021 on macroeconomic conditions and other important topics/国家发展改革委举行7月份新闻发布会 介绍宏观经济运行情况并回应热点问题, 19 July 2021. https://www.ndrc.gov.cn/xwdt/xwfb/202107/t20210719_1290743.html?code=&state=123. Accessed 31 Nov 2021

Network for Greening the Financial System (2020) Overview of environmental risk analysis by financial institutions. https://www.ngfs.net/sites/default/files/medias/documents/overview_of_environmental_risk_analysis_by_financial_institutions.pdf, and case studies of environmental risk analysis methodologies. https://www.ngfs.net/en/case-studies-environmental-risk-analysis-methodologies. Both accessed 31 Nov 2021

Ng E (2021) 'Earth Summit 2021: China excludes fossil fuel projects from green bonds, taking a step towards global standards on the path to 2060', South China Morning Post, 22 Apr 2021. https://www.scmp.com/business/companies/article/3130643/earth-summit-2021-fossil-fuel-exclusion-chinese-green-bonds. Accessed 31 Nov 2021

Park S (2018) Investors as regulators: green bonds and the governance challenges of the sustainable finance revolution. Stanf J Int Law 54:1–47

People.cn (2017) 'Jiangsu: "Green GDP" formally included in the appraisal report for officials published to the public', 5 Sept 2017. http://politics.people.com.cn/n1/2017/0905/c1001-29514670.html. Accessed 31 Nov 2021

People's Bank of China (2017) Joint announcement of the People's Bank of China and Hong Kong Monetary Authority, 2 July 2017. http://www.pbc.gov.cn/en/3688110/3688181/3699007/index.html. Accessed 31 Nov 2021

People's Bank of China (2021a) Transcript of the briefing on green finance at the State Council Information Office of China, 9 Feb 2021. http://www.pbc.gov.cn/goutongjiaoliu/113456/113469/4191657/index.html. Accessed 31 Nov 2021

People's Bank of China (2021b) 'Governor Yi Gang attended the PBC-IMF High-Level Seminar on Green Finance and Climate Policy and delivered opening remarks', Hong Kong Green Finance Association, 16 Apr 2021. https://www.hkgreenfinance.org/governor-yi-gang-attended-the-pbc-imf-high-level-seminar-on-green-finance-and-climate-policy-and-delivered-opening-remarks/. Accessed 31 Nov 2021

People's Bank of China Research Bureau (2019) China green finance development report 2018. China Finance Press

Qian L, Lu Z (2018) New opportunities and challenges in China's green bonds market. China Bank 9:83–85

Renewables Now (2015) 'Update 1—Goldwind's USD—300m green bond 5 times oversubscribed', Renewables Now, 21 July 2015. https://renewablesnow.com/news/update-1-goldwinds-usd-300m-green-bond-5-times-oversubscribed-484885/. Accessed 31 Nov 2021

Shanghai Branch of the State Administration of Foreign Exchange (2020) Green finance and low-carbon development—Video speech by Yi Gang, Governor of the People's Bank of China, at the Singapore Fintech Festival. http://www.safe.gov.cn/shanghai/2020/1210/1420.html. Accessed 31 Nov 2021

Shenzhen Municipal Financial Regulatory Bureau (2021) 'Shenzhen Special Economic Zone Green Finance Regulations came into effect', 2 March 2021. http://jr.sz.gov.cn/sjrb/xxgk/gzdt/content/post_8577732.html. Accessed 31 Nov 2021

Shi Y (2019) Green Finance International Research Institute's China Green Bond Market Development Report 2019/中央财经大学绿色金融国际研究院《中国绿色债券市场发展报告 (2019)》. China Finance Press

Shi Y, Wang Y (2018) Green bonds. China Financial Press

Sina News (2005) 'Environmental performance assessment of leading officials pilot this year', 17 March 2005. https://news.sina.com.cn/c/2005-03-17/08025383989s.shtml. Accessed 31 Nov 2021

Standard Chartered (2020) Standard Chartered Sustainable Investing Review 2020 – Growing sustainable investments through knowledge. https://av.sc.com/corp-en/content/docs/Sustainable-Investing-Review-2020.pdf. Accessed 31 Nov 2021

State Administration of Foreign Exchange (2020) 'PBOC & SAFE remove QFII/RQFII investment quotas and promote further opening-up of China's financial market', 7 May 2020. https://www.safe.gov.cn/en/2020/0507/1677.html. Accessed 31 Nov 2021

State Council (2021) 'China's GDP tops 100 trillion yuan in 2020', 18 Jan 2021. http://english.www.gov.cn/archive/statistics/202101/18/content_WS60052129c6d0f72576944049.html. Accessed 31 Nov 2021

Supreme People's Court (2021) 'Zhou Qiang: promote environmental rule of law and the harmonious co-existence between human beings and nature', Supreme People's Court, 26 May 2021. http://www.court.gov.cn/zixun-xiangqing-305331.html. Accessed 31 Nov 2021

Sustainability Accounting Standards Board (2021) Download SASB Standards. https://www.sasb.org/standards/download/. Accessed 31 Nov 2021

SWITCH Asia (2019) International Platform on Sustainable Finance (IPSF). https://www.switch-asia.eu/resource/international-platform-on-sustainable-finance-ipsf/#:~:text=The%20International%20Platform%20on%20Sustainable,the%20world's%20greenhouse%20gas%20emissions. Accessed 31 Nov 2021

Ting C (2020) 'Has Xi Jinping's anti-corruption campaign been effective? China's land transactions provide one answer', South China Morning Post, 20 Aug 2020. https://www.scmp.com/comment/opinion/article/3097830/has-xi-jinpings-anti-corruption-campaign-been-effective-chinas-land. Accessed 31 Nov 2021

UK Treasury (2019) UK-China 10th Economic and Financial Dialogue: policy outcomes. https://www.gov.uk/government/publications/uk-china-10th-economic-and-financial-dialogue-policy-outcomes. Accessed 31 Nov 2021

United Equator Bonds Research Institute (2020) 2019 Report on Green Bonds in China/2019年绿色债券运行报告. http://www.lianhecreditrating.com.cn/userfiles/2019%E5%B9%B4%E5%BA%A6%E7%BB%BF%E8%89%B2%E5%80%BA%E5%88%B8%E8%BF%90%E8%A1%8C%E6%8A%A5%E5%91%8A.pdf. Accessed 31 Nov 2021

UN Partnership for Action on Green Economy (2016) 'The People's Bank of China issued the "Guidelines for Establishing the Green Financial System" ', 31 Aug 2016. https://www.un-page.org/people%E2%80%99s-bank-china-issued-%E2%80%9Cguidelines-establishing-green-financial-system%E2%80%9D. Accessed 31 Nov 2021

UNPRI (2019) UK–China Climate and Environmental Information Disclosure Pilot—2019 Progress Report. https://www.unpri.org/download?ac=10546. Accessed 31 Nov 2021

US Government Accountability Office (2020) Public companies. Disclosure of environmental, social and governance factors and options to enhance them. https://www.gao.gov/assets/gao-20-530.pdf. Accessed 31 Nov 2021

Wang C (2021) 'What can environmentally conscious judiciary do to support green finance', China Environmental News, 19 March 2021. https://www.cenews.com.cn/opinion/plxl/202103/t20210319_972072.html. Accessed 31 Nov 2021

Wang CN, Huang H (2021) Interpretation of guiding opinions on green and low-carbon circular development (State Council, February 2021), 27 Feb 2021. https://green-bri.org/interpretation-of-guiding-opinions-on-green-and-low-carbon-circular-development-state-council-february-2021/. Accessed 31 Nov 2021

Wang Y, Ma Q (2020) Local green finance development index and assessment report 2019/地方绿色金融发展指数与评估报告 (2019). China Finance Publishing House

Whiley A (2018) 'Chinese regulators introduce supervisory scheme for green bond verifiers—further step in building market frameworks', Climate Bonds Initiative, 15 Jan 2018. https://www.climatebonds.net/2018/01/chinese-regulators-introduce-supervisory-scheme-green-bond-verifiers-further-step-building. Accessed 31 Nov 2021

Wilkins RC (2021) 'China urges "market forces" to fill gap in green bond program', 22 March 2021. https://www.bloomberg.com/news/articles/2021-03-22/china-urges-market-forces-to-fill-gap-in-green-bond-program. Accessed 31 Nov 2021

World Resources Institute (2020) 'Statement: China commits to stronger climate targets at Climate Ambition Summit', World Resources Institute, 12 Dec 2020. https://www.wri.org/news/statement-china-commits-stronger-climate-targets-climate-ambition-summit. Accessed 31 Nov 2021

Xiao J, Yan X (2018) Status quo and comparative analysis of green finance standards and recommendations/绿色金融标准体系现状, 国际比较及建议. Financ Perspect J 5:81–87

Xinhua News (2017) 'China's first green development index released to evaluate the quality of development in local regions', 26 Dec 2017. http://www.stats.gov.cn/tjsj/sjjd/201712/t20171226_1567038.html. Accessed 31 Nov 2021

Xinhua News (2019) 'Li Keqiang leads the meeting of National Leading Group to address climate change, energy saving and emission reduction', 11 July 2019. http://www.xinhuanet.com/politics/2019-07/11/c_1124741769.htm. Accessed 31 Nov 2021

Xinhua News (2021a) 'The Shenzhen Special Economic Zone Green Finance Regulations came into effect, 1 Mar 2021. http://www.gd.xinhuanet.com/newscenter/2021-03/01/c_1127153864.htm. Accessed 31 Nov 2021

Xinhua News (2021b) 'Shenzhen launches the GEP accounting "1+3" system', 24 Mar 2021. http://www.szzengjin.com/caij/214103.html. Accessed 31 Nov 2021

Xinhua News (2021c) 'Coal and other fossil-based energy clean use projects will no longer be included in the scope of green bonds', 22 Apr 2021. http://www.xinhuanet.com/2021-04/22/c_1127358663.htm. Accessed 31 Nov 2021

Xu T, Su F (2020) 'Providing judicial support for green finance and environmental protection', Xinhua Finance, 29 Apr 2020. http://greenfinance.xinhua08.com/a/20200429/1933781.shtml. Accessed 31 Nov 2021

Yeung K (2021) 'China's opening of Hong Kong bond market for mainlanders signals Beijing hastening efforts to open capital account', South China Morning Post, 5 May 2021. https://www.scmp.com/economy/china-economy/article/3132379/chinas-opening-hong-kong-bond-market-mainlanders-signals. Accessed 31 Nov 2021

Yi G (2020) Supporting low carbon development with green finance. Speech at the Singapore FinTech Festival, Bank for International Settlements, 9 Dec 2020. https://www.bis.org/review/r201222g.htm. Accessed 31 Nov 2021

Yin H (2020) Development of global green classification standards/全球绿色分类标准及发展. China Financ 9:65–67

Yun Z (2021) China's Green Bond Market 2020 Annual Analysis Brief. International Institute of Green Finance, Central University of Finance and Economics (WeChat official account), 19 Jan 2021. https://mp.weixin.qq.com/s/_pMK6aphJSOK2E7gtnWHiw. Accessed 31 Nov 2021

Zhang H (2020) Regulating green bonds in the People's Republic of China: definitional divergence and implications for policy making. ADBI Working Paper 1072.

Zheng Y (2016) The current situation and prospects of China's green bond development in the context of economic transformation. Contemp Econ Manag 6:77–78

Zhou Q (2021) Strengthening environmental rule of law for sustainable development. Speech prepared for delivery at the World Judicial Conference. UN Environmental Programme, 26 May 2021. https://www.unep.org/news-and-stories/speech/strengthening-environmental-rule-law-sustainable-development. Accessed 31 Nov 2021

Publisher's Note Springer Nature remains neutral with regard to jurisdictional claims in published maps and institutional affiliations.

Authors and Affiliations

Lin Lin[1] · Yanrong Hong[2]

[1]   Associate Professor, Faculty of Law, National University of Singapore, Singapore, Singapore

[2]   Associate Professor, School of Law, Peking University, Beijing, China

🖄 Springer ⬤ ASSER PRESS

European Business Organization Law Review (2022) 23:187–216
https://doi.org/10.1007/s40804-021-00238-8

ARTICLE

Venture Capital in the Rise of Sustainable Investment

Lin Lin[1]

Accepted: 16 December 2021 / Published online: 17 February 2022
© T.M.C. Asser Press 2022

Abstract

In recent years, the world has witnessed a soaring inflow of capital into sustainable investment. This is particularly so following the devastating COVID-19 pandemic. However, while a growing amount of literature has been deliberating debt financing in sustainable investment, less ink has been spilt on equity financing in this area, and even less scholarship has explored the role of government and law in supporting sustainable venture capital ('VC') funds. This paper proposes a dualist approach towards facilitating the development of sustainable VC funds encompassing a contractarian strategy with government support. The contractarian approach includes effective contracting covering the entire VC cycle in sustainable investment. It aims to provide strong incentives for all participants, ranging from investors, entrepreneurs and fund managers, to credit-rating agencies and evaluation firms. In the same vein, this paper seeks to craft a role for regulators that facilitates the simultaneous availability of several factors in a sustainable VC cycle (i.e., fund raising, investment and exit). In the fund-raising stage, governments can play an active role by expanding the source of financing for sustainable VC funds and enacting detailed and targeted legislation. In the VC investment stage, sustainable VC funds should make full use of their strong corporate governance rights and monitoring tasks to ensure that start-ups deliver on their sustainable promises. In the exit stage, a specialised sustainability board is strongly recommended to offer viable exit options, together with greater standardisation and comparability in sustainability information disclosure, and regulatory support for trustworthy sustainable impact rating agencies to sustain investor confidence.

Keywords Venture capital · Sustainable investment · Green financing · ESG · Equity investment · VC cycle

✉ Lin Lin
 lawll@nus.edu.sg

[1]   Associate Professor, Faculty of Law, National University of Singapore, Singapore, Singapore

1 Introduction

There has been a surge in the amount of capital flowing into funds practising sustainable investing in recent years, corresponding to heightened investor awareness of issues related to environmental, social and corporate governance ('ESG'). This phenomenon of increasing capital inflow into sustainable investing has occurred both in specific markets, such as the U.S. and Europe, and on a global scale.

The significant increase in the amount of capital flowing into sustainable funds in major markets in recent years is an exciting phenomenon which bodes well for the sector. Unfortunately, while contemporaneous literature on debt financing in green finance is abundant, the same cannot be said about equity financing.[1] Legal literature is marked by a dearth of coverage concerning green equity financing. Hence, this paper fills a literature lacuna by analysing the roles that VC funds play in sustainable investing, how this works, what the loopholes are and the ways forward from a legal perspective.

Compared to other forms of financing, VC is particularly ideal for sustainable investment given its characteristics. Firstly, VC is uniquely compatible with the needs of sustainable projects. VC funds typically have a long lock-in period,[2] which aligns well with the need of sustainable start-ups to secure investment for an extended formation period. VC funds are also able to value-add to sustainable start-ups by providing technical knowledge, industry relationships or management skills, therefore bringing additional benefits to the monetary contribution.[3] It enables the portfolio company to commercialise cutting-edge science to achieve the innovation needed for sustainable development and accelerates the availability of sustainable solutions, heralding various environmental and social benefits.[4]

Secondly, and more importantly, VC offers strong and unique investor protection mechanisms that are urgently needed in the sustainable investment space given its many uncertainties. VC investment normally comes with strong continuous monitoring and contractual mechanisms to guard against uncertainty and information asymmetry.[5] For instance, staged financing is often utilised to close information gaps. Knowing that the next round of financing will only be released if key objectives in the business plan are met, entrepreneurs have an incentive to get an accurate valuation of their projects and work hard to attain their goals.[6] The VC community also runs on an implicit reputation mechanism, where alternative investors would find the project unattractive if existing investors ceased to provide funding in subsequent rounds. VC funds also acquire more control in the portfolio companies and their de

---

[1] For example, see Breen and Campbell (2017), Talbot (2017) or Wang (2018). In comparison, there is scant literature on green equity financing at the time of writing. At best, research on this subject has been conducted in other disciplines such as economics but not necessarily from a legal perspective, see Punzi (2018), Krämer-Eis and Pelly (2011), or Ahmad et al. (2018).

[2] Lin (2021), p 10.

[3] Ibid., p 2.

[4] Bocken (2015).

[5] Gilson (2003), p 1078.

[6] Ibid., pp 1078–1081.

facto influence over decision-making is often disproportionately larger than the voting rights associated with their equity holdings.[7] Accordingly, VC fund managers often become directly involved in the corporate governance of portfolio companies and steer them towards sustainability. This also provides an extra incentive for entrepreneurs to properly manage their companies in order to regain their control rights. There are also other contractual mechanisms designed for investor protection, such as drag along rights, tag along rights, and right of first refusal.[8]

Against this backdrop, this paper proposes a contractarian strategy in facilitating the development of sustainable VC funds and seeks to craft a role for government that promotes the simultaneous availability of several factors in a sustainable VC fund cycle (fund raising, investment and exit). The contractarian approach includes effective contracting covering the entire VC cycle in sustainable investment. It aims to provide strong incentives for all participants, ranging from investors, entrepreneurs and fund managers, to credit-rating agencies and evaluation firms. The two-pronged approach suggested here would address the need to mobilise entrepreneurship, innovation as well as private sector funding capacity to support the growth of the sustainable VC market. The proposed strategy involves the following 3 stages:

(1) At the fund-raising stage, sustainable VC funds could adopt a different approach when negotiating with investors as compared to previously rigid standard practice. Furthermore, governments can play an active role by expanding the source of financing for sustainable VC funds through relaxed regulations for institutional investors, the provision of a clear and authoritative definition of sustainable investment and the consolidation of sustainable standards. Concurrently, stakeholders may consolidate sustainable standards. Ultimately, these would craft a role for the government that facilitates the VC market premised on private contracting rather than on heavy government intervention in the capital allocation decision.

(2) During the VC investment stage, greater comparability in sustainability information disclosure by green projects is required. This would need to be supervised and enforced.

(3) In the exit stage, educating investors to pique their interest in green portfolio companies and broadening exit options is crucial for the successful exit of sustainable VC funds. Junior markets or flexible listing rules may be introduced for sustainable start-ups and this could be supported with enhanced disclosure measures. In sum, the suggestions made in this paper could be valuable to countries or regions that are attempting to promote the formation and growth of sustainable investments through equity financing.

This paper proceeds as follows. Section 2 gives an overview of venture capital in the rise of sustainable investment and several similar concepts relating to sustainable investment. Section 3 discusses the different kinds of sustainable fund structures,

---

[7] Ibid., p 1082.
[8] Lin (2021), pp 163–175.

backed by examples. Subsequently, Section 4 provides detailed recommendations to improve the legal and regulatory framework for VC green investment commensurate to the problems identified, spanning the fund-raising, investment and exit stages. Section 5 concludes.

2 Venture Capital in the Rise of Sustainable Investment

According to the 2020 Global Sustainable Investment Review, a biannual report published by the Global Sustainable Investment Alliance (GSIA),[9] the total sustainable investing assets in the five major global markets studied (Europe, U.S., Canada, Japan and Australasia)[10] stood at USD$ 35.3 trillion at the start of 2020, a 55% jump from four years earlier in 2016. At the start of 2020, sustainable investing assets already commanded a sizeable share of 35.9% of professionally managed assets in these five major markets.[11]

Figure 1 below represents the growth in total sustainable investing assets in the five major markets studied in the GSIA's biannual reports from 2012 to 2020. A clear upward trend can be observed in terms of both the total amount of sustainable investing assets and their share of the total professionally managed assets.

It is reasonable to infer that the size of total sustainable investing assets on a global scale is larger than the value reported by the above GSIA Review, since there are many other sustainable investment markets in developing countries such as China and India that are not covered by the Review. Regrettably, statistics are often incomplete in those countries. For example, in China, the amount of publicly held ESG funds alone is reported to be RMB 48.6 trillion (USD$ 7.55 trillion), whereas there is no complete set of data on private funds at national level.[12]

At the outset, there are a few similar concepts that need to be discussed and distinguished. These concepts include sustainable investing, socially responsible investing, ESG investing, impact investing and green finance. Figure 2 below presents a chart illustrating the definitions and relationship of these concepts.

In this paper, the term 'sustainable investing' is used as an overarching concept that covers socially responsible investing, ESG investing and impact investing. This term is chosen for its deliberately broad and inclusive scope, and corresponds well with the actual practices of VC funds which, except for very specialised funds, by and large do not make minute distinctions between these concepts and often lump them under the title of sustainable investment.

---

[9] The Global Sustainable Investment Alliance (GSIA) is an international collaboration of membership-based sustainable investment organisations, including the European Sustainable Investment Forum (Eurosif), US SIF, Responsible Investment Association Canada, Responsible Investment Association Australasia and Japan Sustainable Investment Forum.

[10] Global Sustainable Investment Alliance (2021).

[11] Ibid.

[12] China Social Investment Forum (2019).

Fig. 1 Growth of global sustainable investing assets from 2012 to 2020 (The Figure has been drawn by the author based on data from Global Sustainable Investment Alliance (2013), Global Sustainable Investment Alliance (2015), Global Sustainable Investment Alliance (2017), Global Sustainable Investment Alliance (2019) and Global Sustainable Investment Alliance (2021))

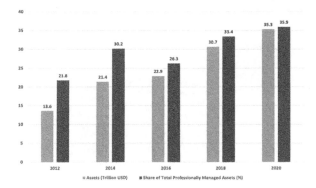

The GSIA defines sustainable investing as 'an investment approach that *considers environmental, social and governance (ESG) factors in portfolio selection and management*'.[13] Similarly, BlackRock recognises that sustainable investing is achieved through a combination of traditional investment approaches with ESG insights.[14] Furthermore, the Sustainable Funds U.S. Landscape Report published by Morningstar broadly places sustainable funds in three categories: (1) ESG Focus, (2) Impact/Thematic, and (3) Sustainable Sector.[15]

According to the EU Sustainable Investment Taxonomy Regulation of 18 June 2020,[16] 'environmentally sustainable investment' means an investment in economic activities that qualify as 'environmentally sustainable' under the Regulation.[17] The criteria for qualifying as an environmentally sustainable economic activity include:[18] (1) substantial contribution to one or more of the environmental objectives;[19] (2) absence of significant harm to one or more of the environmental objectives;[20] (3)

[13] Global Sustainable Investment Alliance (2019), p 7 [emphasis added].

[14] BlackRock (undated a).

[15] Hale (2020). ESG Focus refers to funds that intentionally make ESG factors a central consideration in portfolio selection and construction, while Impact/Thematic refers to funds that seek to create a positive impact alongside financial returns. The third category, Sustainable Sector, refers to funds that invest in 'green economy' industries such as renewable energy and environmental protection. Noticeably, funds that merely mention ESG considerations in their analysis but omit details on how these ESG considerations are central or material to their portfolio selection and construction are excluded from the Landscape Report's definition of sustainable funds.

[16] European Union, Regulation (EU) 2020/852 of the European Parliament and of the Council of 18 June 2020 on the establishment of a framework to facilitate sustainable investment, and amending Regulation (EU) 2019/2088.

[17] EU Sustainable Investment Taxonomy Regulation, Article 2(1), definition of 'environmentally sustainable investment'.

[18] Ibid., Article 3: Criteria for environmentally sustainable economic activities.

[19] Ibid., Article 9 sets out the environmental objectives, i.e., climate change mitigation and adaptation, the sustainable use and protection of water and marine resources, the transition to a circular economy, pollution prevention and control, and the protection and restoration of biodiversity and ecosystems.

[20] Ibid., Article 17 provides the definition of significant harm to environmental objectives, including significant greenhouse gas emissions, and an increased adverse impact of the current climate and the expected future climate, among others.

Fig. 2 Definition of concepts related to sustainable investing (For the sources of the definitions of these closely associated concepts, see the text accompanying notes 13 to 30)

compliance with the minimum safeguards;[21] and (4) compliance with technical screening criteria.[22]

In this regard, some closely related concepts are defined in ways largely similar to sustainable investing. For instance, the UN Principles for Responsible Investment (PRI) set out a voluntary and aspirational set of six investment principles that enable the incorporation of ESG issues into investment practice.[23] The six principles include, *inter alia*: (1) incorporation of ESG issues into investment analysis and decision-making; (2) active ownership and incorporation of ESG issues into ownership policies and practices; and (3) appropriate disclosure on ESG issues by portfolio companies.[24]

As for impact investing, the Global Impact Investing Network defines it as 'investments made with the intention to generate positive, measurable social and environmental impact alongside a financial return', addressing urgent issues such as sustainable agriculture and renewable energy.[25] It can target both developing and developed markets, with a rate of return equal to or lower than market rate.[26] It should also be noted that some studies tend to categorise impact investing as a strategy of sustainable investing, together with other strategies such as negative screening and ESG integration.[27]

---

[21] Ibid., Article 18 sets out the minimum safeguards, most importantly in terms of compliance with the OECD Guidelines for Multinational Enterprises and the UN Guiding Principles on Business and Human Rights, including the principles and rights set out in the eight fundamental conventions identified in the Declaration of the International Labour Organisation on Fundamental Principles and Rights at Work, and the International Bill of Human Rights.

[22] Ibid., Articles 10(3), 11(3), 12(2), 13(2), 14(2) and 15(2) set out the technical screening criteria.

[23] UN Principles for Responsible Investment (2021). See also for a similar definition of responsible investing AXA Investment Managers (2021) and Fidelity International (2021).

[24] UN Principles for Responsible Investment (2021).

[25] Global Impact Investing Network (2021).

[26] Ibid.

[27] See, for example, Global Sustainable Investment Alliance (2019), p 9.

Green finance broadly refers to efforts by the financial community to mitigate the global environmental challenge, while bearing in mind risk-return priorities as usual.[28] More precisely, the definition of green finance requires clarification of two separate aspects: first, of sectors or activities that can be financed by green funds, including but not limited to contributions to climate change mitigation and adaptation; and second, of the specific operational standards that must be followed before certain financial products can be considered green finance.[29]

Figure 2 above summarises the definitions of overlapping terms canvassed above, and is modified from a conceptual mind map developed by the China Alliance of Social Value Investment.[30]

3 Evolving Sustainably Focused Funds

There exists a broad array of different types of funds that make sustainable investments. There are market-oriented private funds, public–private collaboration funds, and public funds based on their sources of funding. This Section examines the differences in terms of sources of funding, organisational structure, portfolio selection and construction, and exit strategies between these various types of sustainable funds. These key differences are summarised in Figure 3 below, and further explained in the subsequent description.

3.1 Market-oriented Private Fund

3.1.1 Basic Characteristics

Similar to conventional VC funds, market-oriented sustainable VC funds[31] source their committed capital from accredited investors and institutional investors.[32] A typical structure of such a fund based on a limited partnership is provided in Fig. 4. In order to materialise the returns of their investments in portfolio companies, their exit strategies generally involve listing the portfolio companies via IPOs, or Mergers & Acquisitions (M&A) by larger corporations.[33] In terms of selection and construction of portfolio companies, they use ESG integration while adopting other

---

[28] Berrou et al. (2019), pp 3–4.

[29] Ibid., pp 31–32.

[30] Zhang and Lu (2020).

[31] It should be noted that there is a growing trend amongst broader private equity (PE) and VC funds to integrate ESG factors and considerations into their investment policies. Some examples include KKR and Blackstone. However, for reasons of prudence, the focus of this paper remains centred on VC funds.

[32] Lin (2019), pp 563–594. See further, e.g., my interview with Ms Lv from Impact Hub Shanghai, 29 Oct 2020 (script with author), in which she mentioned that a bulk part of their LPs included sophisticated investors from wealthy families.

[33] An et al. (2018), p 24. See further, e.g., my interview with Mr Cui Fang from UOB Venture Management, 29 Oct 2020 (script with author), and my interview with Mr Bai Bo, CEO from Asia Green Fund, 28 Oct 2020 (script with author), in which they both mentioned that the exit strategies are similar to those of conventional VC funds and primarily included IPOs and M&As.

traditional selection methods.[34] Market-oriented private sustainable funds are generally established in either of two ways: (1) by creating a new fund specifically catered to sustainable investing; or (2) by expanding an existing fund into the sustainable sector. Examples of these two approaches are provided in the following sub-sections.

3.1.2 New Fund vs Expanding an Existing Fund

Setting up a new fund specially catered to sustainable investing helps to signal the fund's commitment to and speciality in sustainable investing as a unique point of attraction for conscientious investors.[35] Many of these funds display their exclusive commitment to sustainable investing on the frontpage of their website. For instance, SET Ventures is the only fund in Europe that is 100% focused on transitioning the carbon-intense energy system to a robust sustainable energy system.[36] Similarly, ETF Partners—the Environmental Technologies Fund—invests in early-stage European companies that deliver sustainability through innovation.[37] U.S. examples include DBL Partners, which imposes a 'double bottom line' of top tier VC financial returns and positive ESG impacts in its portfolio selection,[38] and Social Impact Capital.[39] In China, such examples are also emerging, e.g., Green Leaves Investment, the first Chinese fund that invests in early-stage green start-ups,[40] and Tsing Capital.[41]

Alternatively, instead of setting up a new fund, many established funds simply expand a portion of their portfolio selection so as to incorporate sustainable investing concepts. BlackRock, for instance, has specifically created a 'sustainable investing' category among its investment strategies.[42] It offers its clients a spectrum of sustainable investing styles, from 'avoiding' portfolio companies with negative ESG characteristics to 'advancing' portfolio companies with positive ESG characteristics.[43] ESG integration is also made possible with a strategy that involves actively implementing ESG-friendly approaches in the process of selecting and developing portfolio companies.[44] Other major funds have followed this trend as reports have shown that 11% of VC firms in the U.S. now invest through an ESG lens.[45]

---

[34] Global Sustainable Investment Alliance (2019), p 9.

[35] Examples of such funds can be found in major markets around the world. In Europe, general partners (GPs) of successful sustainable VC funds are invited to speak at the EcoSummit Conferences held on a monthly basis. See EcoSummit (undated). See their past events' speakers list for an almost comprehensive collection of sustainable VC funds in Europe.

[36] SET Ventures (undated). By investing in energy transition, it also fulfils the UN Sustainable Development Goals (SDG) of affordable and clean energy (SDG 7) and industry, innovation and infrastructure (SDG 9).

[37] ETF Partners (undated).

[38] DBL Partners (undated).

[39] Social Impact Capital (undated).

[40] Green Startups (undated).

[41] Tsing Capital (undated).

[42] BlackRock (undated a).

[43] BlackRock (undated b).

[44] BlackRock (undated c).

[45] Different Funds (2020).

Springer   ASSER PRESS

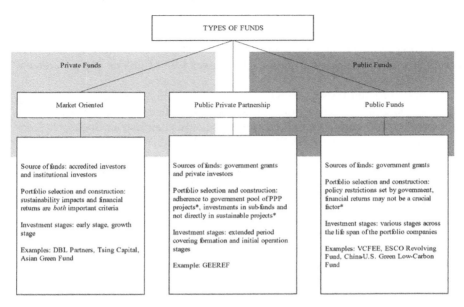

Fig. 3 Types of sustainable funds and characteristics (See for a more detailed explanation and citation of sources the following text accompanying notes 31 to 83. While only short forms of the funds are provided in this Table, their full names can be found in the following text. Asterisks (*) indicate optional features)

Fig. 4 Structure for limited partnership—type sustainable VC funds

3.2 Public–Private Partnership

3.2.1 Basic Characteristics

A Public–Private Partnership (PPP) is designed for situations where government funds or private funds are themselves insufficient or restricted in providing financing to massive infrastructure projects with a sustainable focus (e.g., transport, energy, healthcare). A PPP normally involves collaboration between state organs and private funds through the pooling of funds, management and collective decision-making in terms of portfolio selection and construction.[46] Compared to private market-oriented funds, a PPP has numerous advantages including, among others, stronger credibility due to government support, a longer investment period covering the extended formation and initial operation stages, and a larger pool of private and government resources and networks.[47]

However, one must also be cognisant of the potential drawbacks of the PPP model. As observed in Canada, the PPP model has resulted in issues such as crowding out, and overcharging for underperformance. Canadian Labour-Sponsored Venture Capital Corporations (LSVCCs) have even been criticised for reducing the amount of venture capital supply in Canada. As a result, this hindered the maturation of the Canadian VC industry and 'set [it] back ... by many years'.[48] At the same time, the selection of portfolio companies by PPPs is often limited by policy considerations stipulated by the government, curtailing the free reign of the fund managers.[49] For example, the selection of portfolio companies by the China Public-Private Partnership Investment Fund Co., Ltd (China PPP Fund) requires some form of recognition by the government in its PPP Project Databases.[50] Therefore, it may appear ostensibly true that underperformance as observed by Cumming et al.'s research (in the Canadian context) may materialise. Nevertheless, this may not necessarily be true for sustainability-oriented VC and it remains an open question as to whether such sustainable PPP models have the propensity to tend towards underperformance.[51]

A typical PPP may follow either of the following three structures.[52] First, it could be a stand-alone fund where the investment is pooled from state organs, financial institutions and other investors.[53] Second, it could be a fund of funds (FoF) where the sub-funds receive investment not only from the parent fund but also from other sources of investment, similarly consisting of state organs, financial institutions and other investors.[54] The second structure is the most useful when the central or federal government controls and invests in the parent fund while local or provincial governments control and invest in the sub-funds specifically designed for each local area. Third, it could adopt a FoF structure where the sub-funds only receive investment from the parent fund.

---

[46] An et al. (2018), p 79.

[47] Ibid., pp 82–83.

[48] Cumming et al. (2017).

[49] Ibid.

[50] China PPP Fund (2016). The exact requirements are (1) listing by the Ministry of Finance in its Comprehensive Information Platform PPP Project Management Database, or by the China Development and Reform Commission in its PPP Project Database, and/or (2) inclusion in the special plans for national economic and social development, infrastructure and public services, or otherwise determined as major projects by the State Council.

[51] Cumming et al. (2017).

[52] An et al. (2018), pp 85–87.

[53] See, for instance, the European Investment Fund 2/3rd of which consists of private money on top of state funds.

[54] Nassiry and Wheeler (2011), p 4.

3.2.2 Prominent Examples

One prominent example of a PPP fund is the China PPP Fund, whose 11 shareholders include the Ministry of Finance, the National Social Security Fund, the People's Bank of China, and other financial institutions.[55] The China PPP Fund was established in March 2016 with the endorsement of the State Council, while its management company, the China PPP Fund Management Co., Ltd, was set up shortly after, in July 2016. As of 31 December 2019, the China PPP Fund manages a total investment of RMB 1.3 trillion (USD$ 203 billion) in 155 projects, and supports infrastructure development, environmental protection and public service projects in 28 provinces.[56] An outstanding example of an international PPP fund is the China-U.S. Green Fund. First conceived in 2015, when China's President Xi Jinping visited the United States, and formally registered in 2017, the China-U.S. Green Fund is a joint creation of the governments and business communities in China and the U.S.[57] Its first round of VC investment amounted to more than two billion RMB, and soon after exceeded three billion RMB in 2018.[58]

The China-U.S, Green Fund uniquely adopts the P.R.I.M.E model: Policy, Research, Integration, Money and Execution.[59] This model effectively means that under the guidance and facilitation of government policies, the fund is executed by professional management teams, who have integrated money, technology and commercial considerations in managing the portfolio.[60] In terms of operations, the fund adopts a purely market-oriented approach, as strongly encouraged by the Guiding Opinions on Building a Green Financial System issued in 2016.[61] Adopting a purely market-oriented approach means that the fund relies entirely on its professional management teams to generate positive returns and cannot rely on government subsidies to cover losses. Furthermore, the China-U.S. Green Fund has set up a Green Fund Research Centre for the purpose of evaluating the ESG impact of portfolio companies.[62] Successful portfolio companies managed by the fund include the Horen Group, which developed a recyclable industrial packing system based on the internet of things, and AIpark, which provides AI-based unmanned management of urban parking lots.[63] The China-U.S. Green Fund also has a FoF structure and has a number of high-profile sub-funds, such as the Four Rivers Investment Management Company.[64] This company in turn owns China's first steel industry structure adjustment fund aimed at achieving greater energy efficiency and cleanliness in the

---

[55] China PPP Fund (2016). Such other financial institutions include, for example, the China Construction Bank and China International Trust and Investment Corporation.

[56] China Public Private Partnership Centre (2020).

[57] An et al. (2018), pp 221–222.

[58] Lu (2018).

[59] China-U.S. Green Fund (2021).

[60] An et al. (2018), pp 224–231.

[61] People's Bank of China (2016), §4.19.

[62] Sohu (2020). The author notes that the China-U.S. Green Fund is managed by the Asian Green Fund.

[63] Asia Green Fund (undated).

[64] Four Rivers Investment (undated).

steel industry.[65] Another example is the Three Gorges Green Fund, which focuses on investing in clean energy, environmental protection and a green production line.[66]

The PPP structure can be found in major markets such as the U.S. and the EU as well. For instance, the Global Energy Efficiency and Renewable Energy Fund (GEEREF), initiated by the European Commission and advised by the European Investment Bank Group, adopts a PPP and FoF structure by leveraging public sector funds to invest in specialist renewable energy and energy efficiency private equity funds in emerging markets.[67] As a PPP, the GEEREF is able to obtain funding from both the public and private sector, having received a €112 million contribution from the European Union, and the German and Norwegian governments in 2008, and another €112 million from private investors in 2015.[68] Adhering to a triple bottom line of people, planet and profit, GEEREF invests in 79 developing countries across Africa, Central and South America, as well as South-East Asia.[69] In a similar vein, the European Investment Fund (EIF), an EU-sponsored development fund, will only invest if sustainability criteria are taken into account, even though the EIF is not a 'sustainable only' fund. Furthermore, it should be observed that most, if not all, EU vehicles do adhere to such similar sustainability criteria further to the EU Sustainable Finance Action Plan 2018.[70] A U.S. example is P4G—Pioneering Green Partnerships, Investing in Impact—which is headquartered in Washington D.C. and collaborates with government ministries in a number of countries to promote five of the UN SDGs.[71]

Lastly, no discussion would be complete without mention of certain forms of matching funds. Such matching funds facilitate the matching of public and private capital in a particular sustainable investment in accordance with a defined ratio. Some notable examples include France's Ecotechnologies Fund and Argentina's Fiduciary Fund for the Development of Venture Capital (FONDCE).[72]

3.3 Public Fund

3.3.1 Basic Characteristics

In order to overcome the difficulties in obtaining private financing for sustainable projects, a number of governments and international organisations have set up public funds to support such projects. Most of these public funds are conceptually broader than a typical VC fund, as they invest across different stages of the life span of the portfolio companies and utilise an array of investment tools covering equity

---

[65] Xinhua News Agency (2017).

[66] Sina Finance (2020).

[67] GEEREF (2021a).

[68] GEEREF (2021b).

[69] GEEREF (2021c).

[70] Communication from the Commission to the European Parliament, the European Council, the Council, the European Central Bank, the European Economic and Social Committee and the Committee of the Regions. Action Plan: Financing Sustainable Growth, COM/2018/097 final.

[71] Zabarenko et al. (2018), pp 3 and 28.

[72] Ahmad et al. (2018), p 25.

investment, debt investment or even a combination of both.[73] Nevertheless, a number of these public funds are exclusively focused on the VC stage of investment, and some examples are cited in the following sub-section. Unlike market-oriented private funds or PPP funds, public funds tend to rely heavily or exclusively on government grants or subsidies.[74] Sometimes, there are also stricter limitations on the type of projects that can be funded.[75]

3.3.2 Prominent Examples

Examples of public funds set up by the government for the purpose of sustainable development can be found in numerous countries around the world. For instance, the Venture Capital Fund for Energy Efficiency (VCFEE) was set up by the Indian Bureau of Energy Efficiency in 2017.[76] It provides last-mile equity support to selected energy efficiency projects, limited to 15% of total equity required by the projects.[77] It is noteworthy to point out that in the first phase of the VCFEE, investments can only be made in government buildings and in energy efficiency projects supported by municipalities.[78] In Thailand, the ESCO Revolving Fund was established in 2008 and has undergone four phases so far.[79] It aims to encourage private investments in renewable energy and energy efficiency projects. The arsenal of financial services offered by the fund include equity investment, venture capital and equipment leasing.[80]

In China, it has gradually become a trend for provincial governments to set up green development funds and environmental protection funds.[81] In particular, as a joint initiative between the Beijing Environment Exchange and the China-U.S. Green Fund, the China-U.S. Green Low-Carbon Fund was set up in the Xiong'an New Area in 2017.[82] With the estimated size of the fund exceeding RMB 10 billion (USD$ 1.5 billion), it seeks to boost liquidity in China's national carbon emission trading market, and assists green development funds in the quantification, collection and commercialisation of carbon assets.[83] Additionally, the fund also invests in domestic and overseas projects with a focus on low-carbon energy efficiency, green smart cities and green villages.

---

[73] An et al. (2018), pp 41–44.
[74] Ibid., p 223. See also the explanation of the examples cited below.
[75] See, for example, text accompanying notes 76 to 78, stating that the VCFEE fund in India is limited to only investing in 'government building or municipality projects'.
[76] Bureau of Energy Efficiency (undated a & b).
[77] An et al. (2018), at p 2.
[78] An et al. (2018).
[79] Energy for Environment Foundation (2021).
[80] Ibid.
[81] An (2017), p 73.
[82] Beijing Daily (2017).
[83] Ibid.

4 Legal and Regulatory Needs for Mobilising Sustainable VC

The unique advantages of VC funds in financing sustainable projects, in terms of fulfilling the needs of green start-ups and offering distinctive investor protection mechanisms, have been canvassed in Section 2 above. Nevertheless, despite these advantages and a soaring interest from investors in sustainable investing in recent years, particularly in the midst of the COVID-19 pandemic, there remains a significant amount of apprehension in this relatively new and underdeveloped area which deters investors from actually committing their capital.[84] Apart from the conventional contracting problems in financing start-ups (i.e., uncertainty, information asymmetry) and the familiar agency problems, parties involved in sustainable VC funds face a set of specific problems. In general, such challenges can be summarised as how to incubate and maintain investor interest and confidence through contractual and regulatory means, how to ensure that portfolio companies stay true to and deliver on their sustainable promises, and how to construct credible mechanisms to verify the environmental impact of sustainable projects. This article examines the specific challenges in each stage of sustainable VC funds and makes recommendations to address these challenges.

4.1 Fund-raising Stage

There remains a multitude of problems experienced by sustainable VC funds during the fund-raising stage. These can pertain to the perception of investors towards sustainable VC funds, a mismatch in maturity between sustainable and traditional VC funds, and the lack of norms, laws or regulations necessary to internalise environmental externalities and to provide a uniform approach and uniform sustainability standards for sustainable VC funds.

In relation to sustainable VC funds, there exists a perception that sustainable green VC funds have a less attractive risk-to-return profile as compared to other, traditional VC funds. This is due to 'long holding periods, illiquidity, additional investment restrictions, and limited exit prospects' or even additional costs that might be incurred to comply with any prevailing sustainability requirements.[85] These factors make sustainable VC funds a 'less commercially attractive [proposition]'[86] as compared to traditional VC funds. In furtherance of this comparison with traditional VC funds, this perception may be further exacerbated by a 'maturity mismatch' where most traditional VC funds operate in more developed capital markets and invest in companies with more familiar growth cycles or investment horizons as compared to sustainable VC funds.[87] Investors may also be deterred by the new attendant risks that come with investing in 'nascent industries' such as whether such technology could indeed prove effective, and even if it is effective, whether it will be scalable.[88]

---

[84] Standard Chartered PLC (2020), p 10.
[85] Ahmad et al. (2018), p 40.
[86] Ahmad et al. (2018).
[87] Ibid.
[88] Ibid., p 41.

The future of such industries with technology in its infancy is often clouded with uncertainty, which may compromise their commercial viability. Ostensibly, these considerations could possibly weigh down on investors' minds, thus contributing towards their hesitancy towards sustainable VC funds.

There is also a lack of knowledge regarding the norms of sustainable investing, including ESG risk management standards and practices. Financial intermediaries also have inadequate instruments and incentives to price and internalise environmental externalities which reduce 'the financial returns of sustainable projects'.[89] Such inability to internalise these externalities may be attributable in part to the lack of a 'carbon market' or to 'inadequate laws and regulations penalising pollution and emission',[90] or even to the sheer lack of sustainability standards and data for screening sustainable projects or assets.

At present, sustainable finance is shrouded by a general state of ignorance engendered by a 'lack of data on [the] profitability of sustainable investments', a lack of 'broadly acknowledged theoretical insights … into the co-relation and causation of sustainability factors with financial data' which 'hinder … a rational, calculated approach to allocating funds with a view to sustainability' which is normally associated with 'finance'.[91] This lack of data which leads to the inability to come to a consensus on an agreed standard has consequently stemmed the flow of 'public and private capital' to 'finance sustainable growth'.[92]

As a result, there currently remains a lack of a clear, authoritative and consistent definition and conception of 'sustainability framework' in many countries, even though a broad consensus regarding a generic idea has emerged.[93] This is yet another problem that plagues the fund-raising stage of sustainable VC funds. The European Sustainable Funds Report issued by Morningstar in 2019 observed that as both conventional and sustainable funds have increased the usage of ESG language in their prospectuses, the description of ESG contributions in their legal and marketing documents is often ambiguous, incomplete and unstandardised.[94] Investors may also be interested to find out exactly under which of the ESG limbs the company falls. Equally importantly, a set of benchmark standards should be created for investors to appreciate the different extent to which funds and companies commit themselves to sustainability issues.

While the present practice is that some more established funds have created their own research centres and ESG assessment guidelines,[95] these measures are limited in their applications as funds tend to devise divergent standards that best suit their own investment objectives. Also, not every VC firm has such resources or capacity to set up an internal research centre to conduct sustainable due diligence of portfolio

---

[89] Ibid., p 40.
[90] Ibid., p 40.
[91] Zetzsche (2021).
[92] Ahmad et al. (2018), p 40.
[93] Bioy et al. (2019).
[94] Ibid., pp 21–22.
[95] For example, the China-U.S. Green Fund set up its own Green Fund Research Centre, see text accompanying note 62. In my interview with Mr Cui Fang from UOB Venture Management, 29 Oct 2020 (script with author), he mentioned that UOB engages with third-party service providers to conduct ESG due diligence.

companies. Further, it is costly and less efficient for VC firms to outsource such work to third-party specialists, such as sustainability credit-rating agencies, whose role is explained in the next Section. In this research centre scenario, the problems of asymmetric information and agency costs are hidden between the investors and the sustainability research centre run by the funds.[96] Driven by the interest to attract more sustainability-friendly investors and to highlight the impact of their sustainable investment, fund managers may be incentivised to paint a rosier picture of what their portfolio companies achieved than is actually the case. Potential investors would hesitate to invest without a clear sign of certainty and recognition, hindering fund raising for sustainable VC funds.[97]

Hence, it is imperative that these issues which pose an obstacle to fund raising for sustainable VC funds be addressed. This paper thus provides some recommendations to address the aforementioned concerns. To be fair, it would be difficult to change an investor's perception towards fund raising for sustainable funds. Even if one were to argue for some form of educational effort, its ostensible impact would be difficult to measure and evaluate. Therefore, changing an investor's perception is a long-term endeavour. Hence, a more appropriate approach would be to prioritise the other issues that sustainable VC funds face during fund raising—not only are these issues more pertinent, but solving them would arguably have positive implications for investor perception as well for boosting investor confidence. These issues are the maturity mismatch and attendant risks that come with investing in a nascent industry, the lack of norms, laws or regulations necessary to internalise environmental externalities, and the lack of data for constructing applicable uniform standards linking sustainability and finance.

This paper's recommendation can be understood in two ways, based on the *entity* which takes the requisite action: either the sustainable VC fund itself, or the government of the country where the fund is domiciled.

As regards sustainable VC funds themselves, it is suggested that they may look towards adapting their approach to the sustainable investing sector so as to better attract capital in the fund-raising process through amending previously strict contractual terms[98] between themselves and their investors. A similar approach was proposed by Lerner, albeit in the context of venture capital in financing innovation.[99] Notwithstanding this contextual difference, his observations remain compelling and it is submitted that a similar approach may be adopted in the fund-raising process for sustainable VC funds. Indeed, Lerner himself alludes to the innovative industries including renewable energy technology,[100] which would more likely than not be

---

[96] Christie (2021).

[97] As a matter of last resort, sustainable VC funds could also rely on contractual mechanisms such as representations and warranties, and indemnifications to guard against the negative repercussions arising from poor-quality, or even fraudulent, disclosures.

[98] Such as terms mandating the lifetime of the fund in which case the fund would seek to exit from its investment, or the potential degree of involvement that the VC fund would have in the portfolio company. With a more suitable exit timeframe tailored to the specific sector, as well as the reassurance that investors may get from knowing that fund managers would be active investors instead of being overly passive, this may have a confidence-boosting effect advancing the fund-raising process.

[99] Lerner and Nanda (2020).

[100] Ibid., p 248.

considered as a form of sustainable finance and in this context could possibly be the scope of applicability for sustainable VC funds.

This contractual approach would also address the maturity mismatch raised by the IFC Report.[101] Appropriate contractual amendments and tweaks can be made between the sustainable VC fund and the investors to address the attendant risks found in investing in such nascent industries, and variation in the maturity period for sustainable VC funds may be included to cover funds which require this, such as funds with different investment foci in a myriad of sustainable sectors.[102] This is a good opportunity to 'rethink' VC partnerships as Lerner suggests,[103] and sustainable VC funds may be just the appropriate candidates to kickstart the process.

Separately, respective governments may also play an active role and take the lead in attempting to facilitate a conducive setting for sustainable VC funds. This may be done in three key ways: (1) crafting an autochthonous and workable definition of sustainable finance in line with what governments are able to provide; (2) enacting effective policies to expand the source of funding and diversify the types of investors available; and (3) exploring and getting involved with PPP projects which could collaborate with sustainable VC funds.

First, governments may attempt to develop a clear definition and a set of targeted regulations or legislation concerning relevant matters such as qualifications as sustainable company and sustainability information disclosure. In this respect, this paper does not attempt to instruct *how* governments should do so, but merely recommends that this is *what* governments could do to facilitate fund raising for sustainable VC funds. This is because it would be impractical to provide suggestions as to how a government should compile this definition since each government would necessarily have to incorporate its own domestic considerations (which differ amongst countries with varying needs) in order to formulate a definition of sustainability suitable for its own country. However, as evidenced by efforts made by the EU, it is possible for such a definition to be formulated despite the fact that this appears to be an insurmountable task.

On this score, the EU provides a role model through the clear and detailed EU Taxonomy Regulation accompanied by its surrounding regulations[104] and has even promised to issue a 'social sustainable investment' definition in the near future. Presently, the EU Taxonomy Regulation not only provides a clear definition of 'environmentally sustainable investment'[105] but also requires that an environmentally sustainable investment must substantially contribute towards one of the six environmental objectives,[106] and goes on to articulate the types of activities that fall under each of the six objectives.[107] For instance, if an economic activity claims to substantially contribute towards climate change mitigation, it must be able to prove that its activities are aligned with the long-term temperature goal

---

[101] Ahmad et al. (2018), p 40.

[102] Lerner and Nanda (2020), p 253.

[103] Ibid., pp 253–255.

[104] EU Sustainable Investment Taxonomy Regulation, *supra* n. 16.

[105] Ibid.

[106] Ibid., Article 9: Environmental objectives.

[107] Ibid., Articles 10–15.

of the Paris Agreement and fall under one of the pre-defined categories, including but not limited to renewable energy, energy efficiency, and clean mobility.[108] It is also observed that various other jurisdictions have also embarked on developing their own domestic sustainable taxonomy. Some examples include Canada, Kazakhstan and Indonesia.[109] While this remains a long way from the desired goal of international standards and certainty, it is admittedly a much welcomed improvement on the status quo.

Such definitions would also go some way in bringing about much needed clarity for sustainable VC funds. It also eliminates the possibility of funds abusing the 'sustainability' label when it is actually not sustainable at all. This form of abuse manifests itself most through the phenomenon of greenwashing, which lately has been an issue of concern.[110] Having a definition of what is sustainable investment would minimise the possibility of such abuse and would be useful in addressing the uncertainty which has hindered fund raising for a considerable period of time.

Second, it is also recommended that governments facilitate the raising of capital for sustainable VC funds. There are a number of ways governments can do so. For instance, through policies and changes in regulations, government efforts may help to expand the sources of funds and diversify the types of investors that invest in sustainable VC funds.

Presently, certain local regulatory restrictions may hinder domestic investors from investing in sustainable VC funds. As such, sustainable VC funds end up being suffocated by a 'natural source of long-term local capital'.[111] Some developing countries also remain beset by insular regulatory frameworks and investment guidelines that could pose further obstacles to domestic investors investing in such sustainable VC funds as are typically based offshore.[112] This may even be more true if sustainable VC funds have a focus on the country which itself imposes such restrictions. For instance, this was previously the case in China, where certain institutional investors faced prohibitions which straitjacketed their ability to make such equity investments. Policy constraints and applicable quotas imposed by regulations were obstacles that restricted VC investment by institutional investors.[113] This meant that VC as an effective vehicle in promoting sustainable investing would be unduly inhibited. However, the restrictive effect of this policy was recognised and regulators have, since 2008, been taking the necessary actions to correct this, thereby promoting long-term investments in VCs by institutional investors and foreign investors. On this score, special attention should be paid to the relaxation of restrictions placed on institutional investors raising VC funds, including sustainable VC funds.

Third, governments could explore more channels of public-private collaboration in the sustainable VC space. The PPP structure explored in Section 3 is one such example. In addition, governments could consider business incubators collaboratively set up by government agencies and sustainable VC funds.[114] Such business

---

[108] Ibid., Article 10: Substantial contribution to climate change mitigation.
[109] OECD (2020), 2.4.
[110] O'Mahony and Awan (2021).
[111] Ahmad et al. (2018), p 40.
[112] Ahmad et al. (2018).
[113] Lin (2017), p 173.
[114] Baker (2014).

incubators help sustainable VC funds to add more value to portfolio companies through expertise and connections in the public and private sectors. Governments could also intentionally cultivate a greater talent pool in sustainable investing by updating curricula for higher education. This idea was also mooted by Lerner, albeit conservative in noting that such collaboration may not necessarily guarantee success unless it is 'executed correctly'. In particular, the example of FONDCE mentioned above was inspired by Israel's Yozma Fund. While this is an impact fund, the lessons it provides would similarly be applicable to sustainable funds. The Yozma Fund utilises a modified waterfall structure and meets the appropriate 'golden mean' to incentivise private capital in tandem with public capital.[115] This requires an appropriate public to private capital ratio which does not prohibitively inhibit fund raising. The simple fact that the Yozma Fund is an impact fund does not detract from the plausible chances of such an approach facilitating fund raising by sustainable VC funds. The lessons learnt should be considered seriously by governments in efforts to create a more facilitative environment for raising capital.

In conclusion, considered from an entity approach, there are two main players that could do more to advance the fund-raising process: VC funds, which could adapt traditional and sometimes rigid practices through contractual mechanisms to better suit the sustainable sector; and governments, which could play a more active role in facilitating a fund-raising environment. Lastly, it is also worth noting that a tangential method whereby governments may further improve funding for VC funds is to adopt a broader approach rather than being myopic and focusing solely on funds alone. For the sake of completeness, it is worth mentioning that governments should also consider facilitating the development of potential portfolio companies through accelerators.[116] This would serve to minimise risk or uncertainty that investors may perceive on the part of potential portfolio companies, which would hopefully reassure them and facilitate the fund-raising process.

4.2 Investment Stage

The biggest challenge for sustainable VC fund managers in constructing a successful sustainable portfolio concerns their ability to identify portfolio companies and entrepreneurs that can faithfully adhere to the sustainable goals and at the same time generate a positive profit.

In this respect, this paper submits that sustainable VC funds could take full advantage of their stronghold in corporate governance rights to promote the sustainability of its portfolio companies. Corporate engagement and shareholder activism have been identified as key strategies of sustainable investment, whereby the fund makes use of its shareholder power to gear portfolio companies towards making sustainable corporate decisions.[117] Sustainable VC funds are particularly well positioned to make use of corporate engagement and governance mechanisms compared

---

[115] Lerner (2012).

[116] Ahmad et al. (2018), p 28.

[117] Global Sustainable Investment Alliance (2019), p 7.

to other forms of financing. It has been well noted that VC funds tend to assume greater de facto influence than the voting rights associated with their equity stake in the portfolio companies.[118] Such control takes the form of board representation, veto rights and informal influence over corporate decisions.[119]

Staged financing also provides greater control to sustainable VC funds as subsequent rounds of financing will not materialise if key business objectives are not met. Such objectives can be set with a sustainable focus to ensure that portfolio companies deliver on their sustainable promises. Staged financing, together with the reputational mechanism in the VC community, acts as a strong vanguard against greenwashing and poor quality of sustainability information disclosure. If the existing investors choose to step out from start-ups in subsequent rounds of financing, the reputational mechanism works in such a way as to preclude alternative investors as they are warned of potential loopholes and non-trustworthiness in these particular start-ups. Furthermore, the continuous monitoring conducted by VC fund managers[120] means that they are more familiar with the actual operations of the start-ups and whether they indeed deliver on their sustainable promises. Sustainable start-ups who truly want to make a success of their business would therefore be incentivised to keep working hard and stay truthful, preventing a market for lemons.

On this note, it is valuable to observe how the content of investors' fiduciary duties has shifted in recent years to include an obligation to incorporate ESG considerations alongside financial returns. An important illustration is the modern fiduciary duty introduced by the Final UNEP Report issued by the PRI and UNEP FI in 2019.[121] The Final UNEP Report justifies the modern fiduciary duty through three key limbs: first, ESG incorporation is now an investment norm; second, ESG issues are financially material; and lastly, policy and regulatory frameworks are changing to require ESG incorporation. As identified and labelled by MacNeil and Esser,[122] this is the financial 'intermediary' fiduciary duty operating within the investment chain which has evolved from a 'permissive' model where one *may* incorporate ESG considerations, to the 'mandatory' model where one *has to* incorporate ESG considerations into the investment process.

Such a shift in the content of fiduciary duty is valuable for the growth of sustainable VC funds as it encourages and justifies fund managers' incorporation of ESG considerations in their portfolio selection. This paves the way for more generic VC funds to opt for a sustainable focus. Moreover, the Final UNEP Report is comprehensive enough to acknowledge the differences between jurisdictions where 'obligations equivalent to "fiduciary duties"' manifest themselves as 'statutory provisions' in civil law jurisdictions despite their common law roots. It identifies 'common themes' amongst the various civil law jurisdictions and concludes that fiduciary duties in both common and civil law jurisdictions exist such that ESG considerations are included.

Overall, the investment stage is where sustainable VC funds should make full use of their edge in terms of tailored contractual designs, greater corporate governance rights and continuous monitoring to make sure that start-ups achieve their

---

[118] Gilson (2003), pp 1081–1083.

[119] Lin (2021), pp 1–43.

[120] Gilson (2003), p 1072.

[121] Sullivan et al. (2019).

[122] MacNeil and Esser (2021).

sustainable goals. This stage makes VC particularly valuable for sustainable investing, since it offers special vantage points to tackle the heightened uncertainty and information asymmetry present in the emerging sustainable investing market.

4.3 Exit Stage

VC investments exit at a time when the fund managers are confident that the start-ups have achieved a certain level of maturity, with increased value, ability to attract further rounds of financing through IPOs, M&As or other means, and a firm business structure to contribute towards sustainable economic activities. Accordingly, at the exit stage, the main issue pertains to the lack of suitable exit mechanisms for sustainable VC funds. A wide range of exit options available to VCs remain important as they ensure that VCs are able to realise the fruits of their investments. As astutely pointed out by the IFC, respondents in the GIIN's Annual Impact Investor Survey 2018 reflected that the lack of suitable exit options remained 'a challenge in the impact investment industry'.[123] In this regard, structural reforms in terms of institutional design may be necessary to support viable exits and eventual realisation of returns on investment in the following ways.

First, following the same logic of a specialised technology and innovation board to be set up by stock exchanges around the world,[124] it is suggested that a specialised stock market board be created for companies that focus on sustainability or have a strong sustainability practice (a 'sustainability board'). The idea of separating stocks with strong sustainability performance from their peers is a familiar concept in the market. Secondary boards with a focus on innovation or technology include the Shanghai Stock Exchange's STAR Market, or even the Hong Kong Exchange's Sustainable and Green Exchange (STAGE).[125] Beyond just establishing a specialised sustainability board, regulators may consider reforming or introducing more flexible rules to facilitate exits by green sustainable funds and start-ups. These rules can apply either to the main boards, but also to the said specialised secondary boards.[126]

In contrast to the complexity of listing requirements for the main board, companies to be listed on a sustainability board should enjoy the same benefits and conveniences as start-ups on technology and innovation boards. This approach would mean that the securities regulator and the stock exchange themselves pay less attention to the documentation submitted in the IPO process, but rely more on checks and verifications carried out by the underwriters or sponsors of the issuer. An example of this expedited process can be seen in China's reform from the existing time-consuming

---

[123] Ahmad et al. (2018), p 39.
[124] Examples of technology and innovation boards include the NASDAQ in the U.S., the Science and Technology Innovation Board at the Shanghai Stock Exchange in China, the Growth Enterprise Market at the Hong Kong Stock Exchange and the Catalist Board at the Singapore Stock Exchange.
[125] Lin (2021), pp 213–304.
[126] Ibid., p 235.

approval-based IPO regime to a registration-based IPO regime.[127] Stringent listing requirements such as the profitability requirement and the cash-flow requirement should also be lowered for companies and especially start-ups with a strong sustainable impact.[128]

In exchange for expedience and efficiency offered to IPO on the sustainability board, greater attention should be paid to the importance of ongoing disclosure obligations,[129] as well as to investor education in terms of cultivating a 'buyer beware' mentality. Overall, the introduction of a specialised sustainability board would make clear the exit venue for sustainable VC investments and therefore boost investor confidence in sustainable investing.

Second, the standardisation and comparability of sustainability information should be enhanced to make the sustainability board more credible and attractive for investors so that VC exits can be made in a more viable way. As it currently stands, sustainability information disclosures made by listed companies themselves suffer from incompleteness, inconsistency and incompatibility.[130] A report published by the U.S. Government Accountability Office in July 2020 concluded that because companies often use self-devised, varying and divergent methods and criteria in disclosing their sustainable impact, investors found it extremely hard to make comparisons over time and across companies.[131] This problem is exacerbated when companies make overly generic disclosures, disclose only the measures but not the results, or selectively disclose sections of their business with a more positive ESG outlook.[132] Such observations are generally applicable to major markets such as China.[133]

In this regard, the EU is taking the lead with a detailed set of regulations concerning the classification of ESG disclosures and disclosure obligations introduced under the EU Taxonomy Regulation and the EU Regulation on Sustainability-related Disclosures.[134] In tightening the standard of sustainability information disclosure, legislators could borrow salient ideas from established standards of professional organisations. For instance, the SASB framework devised by the Sustainability Accounting Standards Board, a non-profit organisation, provides sector-specific standards and guidance for ESG disclosure in 77 different industries.[135] These ESG issues are carefully selected by the SASB based on the materiality of their impact on the financial performance of companies.[136] Another viable framework can be found

---

[127] Ibid., pp 234–239.

[128] Ibid., at pp 222–230, for an example of how the stringent listing requirements are relaxed for technology and innovation companies seeking an IPO on the STAR board.

[129] See explanation below.

[130] Palmer et al. (2020).

[131] Government Accountability Office, U.S.A. (2020), pp 32–33. Note that while this report focuses on public companies, it is safe to assume that these issues are even more serious with private start-up companies that are less heavily regulated in terms of disclosure obligations.

[132] Ibid., at pp 17–31.

[133] Pirovska et al. (2019).

[134] EU Sustainable Investment Taxonomy Regulation, *supra* note 16; European Union, Regulation (EU) 2019/2088 of the European Parliament and of the Council of 27 November 2019 on sustainability-related disclosures in the financial services sector.

[135] Sustainability Accounting Standards Board (2021a).

[136] Sustainability Accounting Standards Board (2021b).

in the Recommendations of the Task Force on Climate-related Financial Disclosures (TCFD).[137] The TCFD standard differs from the SASB standard in the sense that it only concerns climate-related topics and provides both general and sector-specific guidance. Noticeably, the TCFD framework has already been incorporated by the EU, the UK and Hong Kong in their mandatory ESG disclosure regimes.[138] Hence, specialist second tier boards should adopt, for the sake of clarity, a standard set of sustainable disclosure measures instead of leaving companies to choose.

Meanwhile, the appropriate use of technology such as machine learning and artificial intelligence in data collection and processing could significantly improve the capacity and efficiency of sustainability impact measurement.[139] The Spatial Finance Initiative is one example of the application of state-of-the-art technology in measuring sustainability risks and impacts.[140] This Initiative focuses on the integration of geospatial data (including but not limited to Earth Observation Data from the National Aeronautics and Space Administration (NASA), remote sensing, payment systems, and telecommunications) with financial theories and practice to develop applications related to climate risk, ESG transparency and verification.[141] Technological processes of this kind are greatly beneficial for the purpose of cross-checking and verifying the sustainability impact of companies.

It is crucial for government policies to promote the growth of third-party sustainability rating agencies to boost investors' confidence in investing in sustainable business on the secondary market. Current examples of such agencies include the ESG Evaluation Framework Developed by S&P Global Ratings[142] and the ESG Relevance Scores developed by Fitch Ratings.[143] However, it should be cautioned that, as the number of such rating agencies is growing, government agencies should also intervene at the appropriate timings to make sure that there is some form of standardisation of the impact assessment criteria used by these agencies, lest investors will again be confronted by a plethora of varying standards. In developing a common set of impact assessment standards, governments could borrow from existing matrices developed by credible international organisations. For instance, the World Economic Forum has released a set of 21 sustainability matrices for ESG impact assessment.[144] The Organisation for Economic Co-operation and Development (OECD) has also developed a set of 'well-being metrics' that measure a company's impact on current and future well-being and sustainability.[145] In implementing a

---

[137] Task Force on Climate-related Financial Disclosures (2017).

[138] Clarkin et al. (2020).

[139] Avgouleas (2021), pp 18–22.

[140] Spatial Finance Initiative (undated a & b).

[141] Avgouleas (2021).

[142] S&P Global Ratings (2020). This ESG Evaluation Framework is 'a cross-sector, relative analysis of an entity's capacity to operate successfully in the future and is grounded in how ESG factors could affect stakeholders, potentially leading to a material direct or indirect financial impact on the entity'.

[143] Irving and Dwyer (2020). The ESG Relevance Scores present the relevance and materiality of ESG risks with respect to the rating decision.

[144] World Economic Forum (2020).

[145] OECD (2018), chapter 9.

common set of standards, the government could make the incorporation or adoption of such standards, in full or in part, by the rating agencies a pre-requisite for issuing their licence.

While promoting the development of such sustainability credit-rating agencies, governments should be prepared to come up with a set of holistic regulations concerning such groups ab initio. Such regulations should be particularly concerned with the issue of conflict of interest that plagued the credit-rating industry in the 2007–2008 financial crisis.[146] Since credit-rating agencies have an interest in maintaining a healthy commercial relationship with the companies paying them to conduct credit ratings, they may be incentivised to inflate or glorify the ratings. In fact, there have already been news reports of rating agencies colluding with pollutive companies to issue fraudulent sustainability reports.[147] On this aspect, regulatory mechanisms should be designed to encompass ex-ante qualification and licensing, ongoing monitoring and supervision, and ex-post punishment for abuse of such agencies.[148]

Third, compatible with the suggestion of creating a sustainability-focused stock market is the idea of constructing an eco-system for sustainable investing. Such an eco-system would include the three key players in the VC cycle, namely investors who provide funding, fund managers who select and add value to the portfolio companies, and portfolio companies that operate a sustainable business, and form a closed loop for the flow of capital.[149] Figure 5 below sets out a possible conception of the sustainable VC cycle from fund raising to exit. Capital enters the eco-system through investments made by investors, and is then invested in sustainable projects handpicked by the VC fund managers.

The value of the capital increases with appropriate management by the VC fund managers and advice from commercial and industrial experts who often value-add to the portfolio companies. The investment eventually realises its returns via exit strategies such as IPOs or M&As, and can be subsequently channelled back into the eco-system for another round of financing.

It can be observed from Figure 5 that sustainability education and the cultivation of sustainability awareness is crucial in every step of the cycle. Investors with the intention to finance sustainable companies are more likely to seek out sustainable VC funds.[150] Sustainable VC funds can only construct a successful portfolio if there is a sufficient number of environmentally conscious entrepreneurs who faithfully operate their businesses in ways that contribute towards a sustainable future. There is also a need for a group of specialists with the requisite knowledge of the industry in which specific portfolio companies operate and of how sustainability can

---

[146] Efing and Hau (2015), pp 46–60.

[147] Zhen (2019).

[148] See, for example, International Organization of Securities Commissions (2017), Section F: Principles for Auditors, Credit Rating Agencies, and other Information Providers, Principle 22.

[149] Salzmann (2013), pp 568–572.

[150] Newburger (2020).

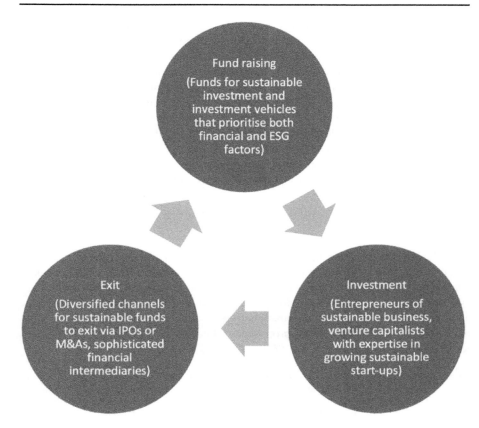

Fig. 5 The cycle of sustainable VC investing

be incorporated into their business operations.[151] Finally, a greater chance of a successful exit of a sustainable portfolio company can only be guaranteed if the market in general embraces such an idea. Such a positive market environment requires a greater willingness and proactivity of mega-corporations to acquire sustainable start-ups through M&As,[152] and of stock market investors to actively purchase stock in listed companies with a strong record of sustainability. A well-designed sustainability education policy can be a rising tide that lifts up the entire eco-system for sustainable VC investment. The regulatory bodies can play an instrumental role in facilitating the link between fund raisers and green project investors.

As such, it is crucial for the government to design a sustainability education programme that reaches out to every potential stakeholder in the eco-system. This programme could encompass public policy communications on the mass media targeted at the public, revamped university curricula targeted at fresh graduates entering the work force, and professional training sessions targeted at professionals and experts.

---

[151] Weinreb (2018).
[152] Rajeev (2019).

One essential aspect of sustainability education is investor education, where investors should be informed of the urgency and importance of sustainability matters on the one hand, and be equipped with the necessary knowledge to appropriate the right type of sustainable investment for themselves on the other.[153] Doing so should also reduce the currently prevalent sentiment of apprehension among investors with regard to sustainable investing.[154] While VC investment is mostly open to institutional investors and not retail investors, greater interest by retail investors (e.g., in buying stocks of sustainable listed companies) is still beneficial for the sustainable VC industry by making exit options more viable. Overall, with the help of a carefully designed sustainability education programme, the sustainable VC eco-system stands to evolve in terms of maturity, self-sufficiency and vibrancy.

5 Conclusion

In conclusion, the immense inflow of capital into sustainable investment is a phenomenon that should be welcomed. To this end, VCs are also well poised to take advantage of and further buttress its continued growth. However, more could possibly be done to ensure that VCs do so. Hence, this precipitates a dualist strategy encompassing a contractarian approach with government support. Ultimately, it is hoped that the recommendations proposed in this paper will help to develop the sector and craft a stronger role for VCs in the field of sustainable investing.

Acknowledgements I thank the interviewees who have generously shared their knowledge and insights with me. I am grateful to Mr Bai Bo and Ms Liao Jia from the Asian Green Fund and Mr Li Ting from the ECO Fund. I thank Iris Chiu, Dirk Zetzsche, Xia Mian and Chan You Quan for their valuable comments on earlier drafts of this paper. The research is supported by the Centre for Banking and Finance Law of the National University of Singapore. All errors remain my own.

References

Ahmad RA, Reed L, Zhang R (2018) Private equity and venture capital's role in catalysing sustainable investment. International Finance Corporation, World Bank Group
An G (2017) Broad prospect of green fund development in China. Financ Market 8:72–74
An G et al. (2018) 国内外绿色基金发展研究 [Studies on the development of domestic and foreign green funds]. China Finance Publications, Beijing
Asia Green Fund (undated) http://www.asiagreenfund.com/html/en_portfolio/. Accessed 13 May 2021
Avgouleas E (2021) Resolving the sustainable finance conundrum: activist policies and financial technology. Law Contemp Probl 84:15–18
AXA Investment Managers (2021) Responsible investing. https://www.axa-im.com.sg/responsible-investing. Accessed 13 May 2021
Baker B (2014) '5 incubators that are shaping the future of green business'. EcoWatch. https://www.ecowatch.com/5-incubators-that-are-shaping-the-future-of-green-business-1881859789.html. Accessed 28 Jan 2021

---

[153] von Daeniken (2020).
[154] Standard Chartered PLC (2020), p 10.

Beijing Daily (2017) 百亿低碳基金落户雄安 助推碳市场流动性增强 ['Low-carbon fund worth ten billion RMB settled in Xiong'an to boost carbon market liquidity']. Xinhua News, 11 Nov 2017. http://www.xinhuanet.com/fortune/2017-11/11/c_129738204.htm. Accessed 6 Jan 2021

Berrou R, Dessertine P, Migliorelli M (2019) An overview of green finance. In: Migliorelli M, Dessertine P (eds) The rise of green finance in Europe: opportunities and challenges for issuers, investors and marketplaces. Palgrave Macmillan, Switzerland

Bioy H, Stuart E, Boyadzhiev D (2019) European sustainable funds landscape. Morningstar, Chicago

BlackRock (undated a) Sustainable Investing. https://www.blackrock.com/us/individual/investment-ideas/sustainable-investing. Accessed 6 Jan 2021

BlackRock (undated b) Sustainable Investment Solutions. https://www.blackrock.com/us/individual/investment-ideas/sustainable-investing/sustainable-solution. Accessed 6 Jan 2021

BlackRock (undated c) ESG Integration. https://www.blackrock.com/us/individual/investment-ideas/sustainable-investing/esg-integration. Accessed 6 Jan 2021

Bocken NMP (2015) Sustainable venture capital—catalyst for sustainable start-up success? J Clean Prod 108:647–658. https://doi.org/10.1016/j.jclepro.2015.05.079

Breen S, Campbell C (2017) Legal considerations for a skyrocketing green bond market. Nat Resour Environ 31:16–20

Bureau of Energy Efficiency, India (undated a) VCFEE-Achievements. https://beeindia.gov.in/content/vcfee-acheivements. Accessed 6 Jan 2021

Bureau of Energy Efficiency, India (undated b) Venture Capital Fund for Energy Efficiency. https://beeindia.gov.in/content/vcfee-acheivements. Accessed 6 Jan 2021

China PPP Fund (2016) 关于我们 [About us]. http://www.cpppf.org/investment/index.html. Accessed 6 Jan 2021

China Public Private Partnership Centre (2020) China PPP Fund drives forward the guided, healthy and sustainable PPP development. http://www.cpppc.org/en/szyw/999262.jhtml. Accessed 6 Jan 2021

China Social Investment Forum (2019) 中国责任投资年度报告 2019 [China Sustainable Investment Review 2019]. http://www.syntaogf.com/Uploads/files/%E4%B8%AD%E5%9B%BD%E8%B4%A3%E4%BB%BB%E6%8A%95%E8%B5%84%E5%B9%B4%E5%BA%A6%E6%8A%A5%E5%91%8A2019.pdf. Accessed 31 Nov 2021

China-U.S. Green Fund (undated) 基金投资理念与策略 [Investment model and strategies]. http://www.china-usgreenfund.com/p/touziguanli.html. Accessed 6 Jan 2021

Christie AL (2021) The agency costs of sustainable capitalism. University of Cambridge Faculty of Law Legal Studies Research Paper No. 7/2021. https://papers.ssrn.com/sol3/papers.cfm?abstract_id=3766478

Clarkin C, Levin J, Sawyer M (2020) The rise of standardized ESG disclosure frameworks in the United States. The Harvard Law School Forum on Corporate Governance. https://corpgov.law.harvard.edu/2020/06/22/the-rise-of-standardized-esg-disclosure-frameworks-in-the-united-states/. Accessed 28 Jan 2021

Cumming D, Johan S, MacIntosh JG (2017) A drop in an empty pond: Canadian public policy towards venture capital. Econ Polit Ind 44:103–117. https://doi.org/10.1007/s40812-016-0063-4

DBL Partners (undated) We are venture capitalists and impact investors. http://www.dblpartners.vc. Accessed 6 Jan 2021

Different Funds (2020) The rise of ESG in venture capital. https://differentfunds.com/esg/rise-of-esg-venture-capital. Accessed 6 Jan 2021

EcoSummit (undated) About. https://ecosummit.net/about. Accessed 6 Jan 2021

Efing M, Hau H (2015) Structure debt ratings: evidence on conflicts of interest. J Financ Econ 116:46–60

Energy for Environment Foundation (2021) ESCO Revolving Fund. http://www.efe.or.th/escofund.php?task=8. Accessed 6 Jan 2021

ETF Partners (undated) The Environmental Technologies Fund. https://etfpartners.capital/. Accessed 6 Jan 2021

European Investment Fund (2021) EIF for venture capital & private equity funds : how to submit an investment proposal. https://www.eif.org/EIF_for/venture_capital_equity_funds/index.htm. Accessed 22 Jun 2021

Fidelity International (2021) Understanding ESG investing. https://www.fidelity.com.sg/beginners/esg-investing. Accessed 21 May 2021

Four Rivers Investment (undated) 公司介绍 [About us]. https://www.fourriversinvestment.com/gongsijieshao.html. Accessed 6 Jan 2021

GEEREF (undated a) What GEEREF does. https://geeref.com/about/what-geeref-does.html. Accessed 6 Jan 2021

GEEREF (undated b) What GEEREF is. https://geeref.com/about/what-geeref-is.htm. Accessed 6 Jan 2021

GEEREF (undated c) Portfolio. https://geeref.com/portfolio.html. Accessed 6 Jan 2021

Gilson R (2003) Engineering a venture capital market: lessons from the American experience. Stanf Law Rev 55:1067–1103

Global Impact Investing Network (2021) What you need to know about impact investing. https://thegiin.org/impact-investing/need-to-know/. Accessed 13 May 2021

Global Sustainable Investment Alliance (2013) 2012 Global Sustainable Investment Review. http://gsiareview2012.gsi-alliance.org/pubData/source/Global%20Sustainable%20Investement%20Alliance.pdf. Accessed 11 Dec 2021

Global Sustainable Investment Alliance (2015) 2014 Global Sustainable Investment Review. http://www.gsi-alliance.org/wp-content/uploads/2015/02/GSIA_Review_download.pdf. Accessed 11 Dec 2021

Global Sustainable Investment Alliance (2017) 2016 Global Sustainable Investment Review. http://www.gsi-alliance.org/wp-content/uploads/2017/03/GSIR_Review2016.F.pdf. Accessed 11 Dec 2021

Global Sustainable Investment Alliance (2019) 2018 Global Sustainable Investment Review. http://www.gsi-alliance.org/wp-content/uploads/2019/03/GSIR_Review2018.3.28.pdf. Accessed 31 Dec 2021

Global Sustainable Investment Alliance (2021) Global Sustainable Investment Review 2020. http://www.gsi-alliance.org/wp-content/uploads/2021/08/GSIR-20201.pdf. Accessed 11 Dec 2021

Government Accountability Office, U.S.A. (2020) Public companies disclosure of environmental, social and governance factors and options to enhance them (July 2020)

Green Startups (undated) 什么是绿叶投资? [What is Green Leaves Investment?]. http://www.greenstartups.cn/about-us/green-leaf-fund/. Accessed 6 Jan 2021

Hale J (2020) Sustainable funds U.S. Landscape Report—record flows and strong fund performance in 2019. Morningstar, Chicago

International Organization of Securities Commissions (2017) Objectives and principles of securities regulation. https://www.iosco.org/library/pubdocs/pdf/IOSCOPD561.pdf. Accessed 31 Nov 2021

Irving S, Dwyer M (2020) What investors want to know: ESG relevance scores for corporates. Fitch Ratings. https://www.fitchratings.com/research/corporate-finance/what-investors-want-to-know-esg-relevance-scores-for-corporates-20-02-2020. Accessed 28 Jan 2021

Krämer-Eis H, Pelly R (2011) Creating a better business environment for financing business, innovation and green growth. OECD J Financ Market Trends 2011:129–140. https://doi.org/10.1787/fmt-2011-5kg55qw0x7xx

Lerner J (2012) Boulevard of Broken Dreams: why public efforts to boost entrepreneurship and venture capital have failed—and what to do about it. California Princeton Fulfillment Services

Lerner J, Nanda R (2020) Venture capital's role in financing innovation: what we know and how much we still need to learn. J Econ Perspect 34:237–261. https://doi.org/10.1257/jep.34.3.237

Lin L (2017) Engineering a venture capital market: lessons from China. Columbia J Asian Law 30:160–220

Lin L (2021) Venture capital law in China, 1st edn. Cambridge University Press

Lin L (2019) Private equity in Singapore: In: Booysen S et al. (eds) Financial services law and regulation. SAL, Singapore

Lu W (2018) 发改委官员加盟中美绿色基金:如何绿动中国发展? [Officials from the National Development and Reform Commission joined the China-US Green Fund: how to push for China's green development?]. Sina, 3 Nov 2018. https://finance.sina.com.cn/chanjing/gsnews/2018-11-05/doc-ihmutuea6531209.shtml. Accessed 6 Jan 2021

MacNeil I, Esser I-M (2021) From a financial to an entity model of ESG. Social Science Research Network, Rochester

Nassiry D, Wheeler D (2011) A green venture fund to finance clean technology for developing countries. Center for Global Development

Newburger E (2020) Amid climate crisis, investors are starting to put their money towards a sustainable future. CNBC, 25 Jan 2020. https://www.cnbc.com/2020/01/24/climate-crisis-investors-putting-money-towards-sustainable-future.html. Accessed 28 Jan 2021

OECD (2018) For good measure: advancing research on well-being metrics beyond GDP

OECD (2020) Developing sustainable finance definitions and taxonomies

O'Mahony D, Awan M (2021) ESG: greenwashing and the EU Taxonomy Regulation—Part 1—Greenwashing, what is it? https://www.matheson.com/insights/detail/greenwashing-and-the-eu-taxonomy-regulation-part-one. Accessed 6 Jun 2021

Palmer H, Gregory H, Wood L (2020) Emerging ESG disclosure trends highlighted in GAO Report. The Harvard Law School Forum on Corporate Governance. https://corpgov.law.harvard.edu/2020/08/15/emerging-esg-disclosure-trends-highlighted-in-gao-report/. Accessed 28 Jan 2021

People's Bank of China et al. (2016) 中国人民银行、财政部、发展改革委等关于构建绿色金融体系的指导意见 [Guiding Opinions of the People's Bank of China, the Ministry of Finance, the National Development and Reform Commission, and other Departments on building a green financial system]

Pirovska M et al. (2019) ESG data in China—recommendations for primary ESG indicators. UN Principles for Responsible Investment. https://www.unpri.org/download?ac=6500. Accessed 31 Nov 2021

Punzi MT (2018) Role of bank lending in financing green projects: a dynamic stochastic general equilibrium approach. Asian Development Bank Institute (ADBI), Tokyo

Rajeev P (2019) Can start-ups help big business become sustainable? Eco-Business. https://www.eco-business.com/news/can-start-ups-help-big-business-become-sustainable/. Accessed 28 Jan 2021

S&P Global Ratings (2020) ESG evaluation—sustainable practices. Sustainable returns. https://www.spglobal.com/ratings/en/research/pdf-articles/190401-esg-evaluation-brochure. Accessed 31 Nov 2021

Salzmann AJ (2013) The integration of sustainability into the theory and practice of finance: an overview of the state of the art and outline of future developments. J Bus Econ 83:555–576

SET Ventures (undated) Investing in the energy system transition. https://www.setventures.com. Accessed 6 Jan 2021

Sina Finance (2020) 三峡资本发起设立三峡绿色产业 (山东) 基金 [China Three Gorges Corporation initiated and set up the Three Gorges Green Industry (Shandong) Fund], 16 May 2020. https://finance.sina.com.cn/enterprise/central/2020-05-16/doc-iirczymk1916982.shtml. Accessed 6 Jan 2021

Social Impact Capital (undated) Social impact + venture capital = social impact capital. https://social-impact-capital.com/. Accessed 6 Jan 2021

Sohu (2020) 绿动资本白波:技术赋能绿色影响力投资,创造可持续资本回报 [Asia Green Fund Baibo: technology empowers green impact investment and creates sustainable capital returns]. https://www.sohu.com/a/414978894_413933. Accessed 6 Jan 2021

Spatial Finance Initiative (undated a) GeoAsset. https://spatialfinanceinitiative.com/geoasset-project/. Accessed 28 Jan 2021

Spatial Finance Initiative (undated b) The initiative. https://spatialfinanceinitiative.com/. Accessed 28 Jan 2021

Standard Chartered PLC (2020) Standard Chartered Sustainable Investing Review 2020—Growing sustainable investments through knowledge

Sullivan R et al. (2019) Fiduciary duty in the 21st century: final report. UN Principles for Responsible Investment and UNEP Finance Initiative

Sustainability Accounting Standards Board (2021a) Download SASB Standards. https://www.sasb.org/standards/download/. Accessed 28 Jan 2021

Sustainability Accounting Standards Board (2021b) Standards overview. https://www.sasb.org/standards/. Accessed 28 Jan 2021

Talbot KM (2017) What does green really mean?: How increased transparency and standardization can grow the green bond market. Villanova Environ Law J 28:127–145

Task Force on Climate-related Financial Disclosures (2017) Final report—recommendations of the task force on climate-related financial disclosures

Tsing Capital (undated) About us. http://www.tsingcapital.com/index.php?file=chindex.html. Accessed 6 Jan 2021

UN Principles for Responsible Investment (2021) What are the Principles for Responsible Investment? https://www.unpri.org/pri/what-are-the-principles-for-responsible-investment. Accessed 21 May 2021

von Daeniken D (2020) Sustainability: investor education can lead to long-term, resilient growth. Emerging Market Views, 28 Oct 2020. https://em-views.com/sustainability-investor-education-can-lead-to-long-term-resilient-growth. Accessed 28 Jan 2021

Wang EK (2018) Financing green: reforming green bond regulation in the United States. Brooklyn J Corp Financ Commer Law 12:467–491

Weinreb E (2018) Sustainability careers of the future require depth and breadth. https://www.greenbiz.com/article/sustainability-careers-future-require-depth-and-breadth. Accessed 28 Jan 2021

World Economic Forum (2020) Measuring stakeholder capitalism: towards common metrics and consistent reporting of sustainable value creation—White Paper. https://www3.weforum.org/docs/WEF_IBC_Measuring_Stakeholder_Capitalism_Report_2020.pdf. Accessed 31 Nov 2021

Xinhua News Agency (2017) 国内首只钢铁产业结构调整基金签署框架协议 [Structural agreement signed for the First Domestic Steel Industry Structure Adjustment Fund]. http://www.xinhuanet.com/fortune/2017-04/07/c_1120770734.htm. Accessed 6 Jan 2021

Zabarenko D, Walter F, Danielsen K (2018) Accelerating public-private partnerships for sustainable development growth. P4G Partnering for Green Growth and the Global Goals 2030, Washington DC

Zetzsche DA (2021) Regulating sustainable finance in the dark. European Business Organization Law Review, this volume

Zhang R, Lu K (2020) 当我们在聊可持续发展金融,我们究竟在聊什么? [What are we really talking about when we speak of sustainable finance?]. CASVI, 16 March 2020. https://www.casvi.org/h-nd-905.html. Accessed 31 Nov 2021

Zhen H (2019) 警惕第三方环保服务机构成为污染帮凶 [The police warns third-party sustainability service agencies against colluding with pollutive companies]. http://opinion.people.com.cn/n1/2019/0514/c1003-31083051.html. Accessed 28 Jan 2021

Publisher's Note Springer Nature remains neutral with regard to jurisdictional claims in published maps and institutional affiliations.

European Business Organization Law Review (2022) 23:217–239
https://doi.org/10.1007/s40804-021-00232-0

ARTICLE

Investor Capitalism, Sustainable Investment and the Role of Tax Relief

Dionysia Katelouzou[1] · Eva Micheler[2]

Accepted: 13 December 2021 / Published online: 31 January 2022
© The Author(s) 2022

Abstract

This contribution examines the connection between investor capitalism and sustainable investment. It will be observed in this article that investor capitalism has gone through a structural change. Individual investors have been replaced by funds. Financial service providers have emerged that assist investors in managing and holding investments. This development coincided and was arguably facilitated by the growth in workplace and personal pensions. Pensions are subsidised by the government through tax relief. This financial contribution of the government is justified on social policy grounds. But it has the effect that pension savers, who receive substantial return by saving tax, are deprived of a reason to take an interest in how their money is invested. This not only deprives the service providers assisting pension savers from oversight from their ultimate customers. It also can help to explain why pension savers do not actively select investment products but rely on the default settings suggested by their employers. If the government is serious about encouraging investor capitalism to bring about sustainable business it should start with its own financial contribution, which has coincided with the emergence of the current model of investor capitalism, and connect pension tax relief to sustainable investment practices.

Keywords Sustainable investment · Green investment · Social investment · Pension tax relief · ESG · Stewardship · Sovereign wealth funds · Retail investors · Workplace pensions · Personal pensions · Pension trustees · Independent governance committees · Auto-enrolment · NEST · Disclosure · Kay Review

✉ Eva Micheler
  e.micheler@lse.ac.uk

  Dionysia Katelouzou
  dionysia.katelouzou@kcl.ac.uk

1 The Dickson Poon School of Law, King's College London, London, UK

2 Department of Law, London School of Economics, London, UK

1 Introduction

The aim of this contribution is to examine the connection between investor capitalism and sustainable business. We view investor capitalism broadly as encompassing not only institutional investors dominating corporate governance – as Useem's
book famously promulgated[1] – but also retail investors. Investor capitalism, thereby,
refers to all types of investors and their direct or indirect relations with directors and
managers rather than merely focusing on intermediaries as a new kind of 'engaged
owners'.[2] We do not take a normative view on the conventional wisdom that investor
capitalism has an agency-cost-minimising effect,[3] but we aim to place it within sustainable finance. It is observed that investor capitalism – the ascendant of managerial capitalism in the US and the UK – has gone through a structural change. In the
1960s investors were predominantly individuals, who were assisted by brokers and
invested with a strategy that matched their individual preferences. Today investors
are mostly nominee companies acting for funds. Since the mid-twentieth century
financial service providers – defined broadly as encompassing investment companies, fund managers, pension funds, brokers, proxy advisors, ESG data providers,
investment consultants etc. – have emerged that assist investors in managing and
holding investments. This development coincided and was arguably facilitated by
the growth in workplace and personal pensions. The UK Competition and Markets
Authority (CMA) observed in 2018 that 90% of the revenues of investment consultants and fiduciary managers is derived from pensions.[4] Pensions are subsidised
by the government through tax relief. This financial contribution of the government
is justified on social policy grounds. But it has the effect that pension savers, who
receive substantial return by saving tax, are deprived of a reason to take an interest
in how their money is invested. This not only deprives the financial service providers assisting pension savers from oversight from their ultimate customers. It also
can help to explain why pension savers do not actively select investment products
but rely on the default settings suggested by their employers. If the government is
serious about encouraging investor capitalism to bring about sustainable business it
should start with its own financial contribution, which has coincided with the emergence of the current model of investor capitalism, and connect pension tax relief to
sustainable investment practices.

The paper is structured as follows. In Sect. 2 we will examine two factors motivating investment decision: financial return and altruism. We will see that the
empirical evidence as to whether sustainable investment practices enhance return
is mixed. This suggests that, while there is no clear financial case for investors to
favour sustainable investment products, a bias towards such products also does not

---

[1] Useem (1996).

[2] See also Katelouzou (2018).

[3] But see Gilson and Gordon (2013).

[4] Competition & Markets Authority, Investment Consultants Market Investigation, Final Report (2018),
https://assets.publishing.service.gov.uk/media/5c0fee5740f0b60c8d6019a6/ICMI_Final_Report.pdf
(accessed 3 Oct 2021), p 29, para. 1.14.

appear to cause significant financial harm. This is encouraging from the perspective of a governmental decision on how tax relief should be best designed. Sustainable investment practices can also be justified on the basis of altruism. Ecological and social consideration play an increasing role in the public discourse and it is possible to justify a decision of the government to bring pension tax relief in line with environmental, social, and corporate governance (ESG) goals.

In Sect. 3 three groups of investors and their investment preferences will be examined. We will distinguish large portfolio end-investors, small portfolio end-investor and beneficiaries of workplace and personal pensions and conclude that in the UK the vast majority of these investors fall into the third category.

Section 4 will discuss the role of the intermediaries serving these investors. We will see that they are bound by contracts that require them to deliver financial results. They are required to integrate sustainability as a risk factor but that does not permit them to prioritise sustainability over return.

In Sect. 5 we will examine the role of the government as a regulator but also as a financial investor and conclude with the suggestion that the government should fully appreciate its role in pension investments and design tax relief in a way that integrates sustainability criteria.

2 Motivations for Sustainable Investment

Sustainable investment is rising in popularity and growing in volume, but a clear and universal definition is still missing.[5] The Global Sustainable Investment Alliance – a collaboration of membership-based sustainable investment organisations worldwide – defines sustainable investment as an 'investment approach that considers environmental, social and governance (ESG) factors in portfolio selection and management'.[6] The EU Sustainable Finance Disclosure Regulation adopts an all-round definition of sustainable investment as an 'economic activity that contributes to' an 'environmental' or 'social' 'objective', but the 'G' of ESG seems to be excluded.[7] Others use the terms sustainability investment, responsible investment, socially responsible investment (SRI), impact investment and ESG investment interchangeably.[8]

In this paper we understand sustainable investment broadly as referring to the consideration of environmental, social but also governance factors in all investment decisions. Sustainable investment includes strategies that seek to improve ESG policies or prevent bad decisions through active (but not necessarily activist) monitoring, voting and engagement.[9] This is often referred to as 'active ownership' or

---

[5] See, e.g., Sandberg et al. (2009) for an early discussion of the 'heterogeneity' of SRI.

[6] http://www.gsi-alliance.org/wp-content/uploads/2019/03/GSIR_Review2018.3.28.pdf, p 3 (accessed 4 Oct 2021).

[7] Article 2(17).

[8] For a literature review see Talan and Sharma (2019).

[9] Katelouzou (2022).

'shareholder stewardship'.[10] But sustainable investment also encompasses a broad remit of investment strategies beyond shareholder stewardship, including ESG integration, screening and thematic/impact investing.[11] Sustainable investment, therefore, is a part and parcel of investor stewardship, a term developed in the UK and now adopted across more than 20 jurisdictions around the world.[12]

There are two reasons why investors would be interested in parting with their money to invest in sustainable shareholder stewardship: financial return and altruism. These will be examined in turn below.

2.1 Financial Return

The literature examining the relationship between ESG activism, on the one hand, and financial return for investors, on the other, does unfortunately not support a general claim that ESG activism leads to better returns for investors over time. The evidence is mixed.[13] Some studies conclude that ESG activism is associated with financial benefit for investors. For example, a 2015 study on corporate social responsibility (CSR) engagements focused on a single investment firm in the US finds positive abnormal returns but only for successful engagements.[14] Another recent study concludes that coordinated engagements targeting environmental or social issues are value-enhancing (in the sense of significant abnormal stock returns), especially when they are headed by a lead investor and are successful.[15] On the other hand, another recent study examines 847 engagements around the globe and finds that ESG activism comes only with modest financial returns during the engagement period from the perspective of the activist fund.[16] For index funds, in particular, academic contributors increasingly question whether engagement and stewardship are cost-effective and meaningful from the perspective of beneficiaries.[17] But there is also recent evidence on ESG index fund activism which portray a different and more positive picture of index funds' role as purported leaders of sustainable shareholder stewardship.[18]

Another body of the empirical literature compares the performance of funds that invest in ESG – previously referred to as socially responsible investment (SRI) funds[19] – with their conventional competitors. The conclusions on the whole are that both types achieve similar returns and that there are at best negligible gains for ESG

---

[10] For the varieties of shareholder stewardship see Katelouzou and Puchniak (2022).

[11] See further Katelouzou (2022).

[12] Katelouzou and Siems (2022).

[13] For a general review of the literature on the relationship between shareholder activism and firm performance, see Denes et al. (2017).

[14] Dimson et al. (2015).

[15] Dimson et al. (2019).

[16] Barko et al. (2018).

[17] Fisch (2020).

[18] Barzuza et al. (2020).

[19] For the shift from SRI to ESG funds, see Schanzenbach and Sitkoff (2020), pp 395–397.

funds.[20] There is some evidence that sustainable investment acts as a 'risk mitiga-tion' tool.[21] But, the overall conclusion from the empirical literature seems to be that 'at the worst case, investors in ESG mutual funds can expect to lose nothing compared to conventional fund investments'.[22] In addition, there are less favourable empirical studies regarding 'E' and 'S' factors compared to 'G' factors where the link between better governance and firm performance is stronger.[23]

More generally, the CMA has recently investigated the market for investment consultants andconcluded that it is not possible to claim that once fees have been taken into account managed funds do better than index trackers.[24]

This creates a situation where there seems to be no clear evidence that ESG activ-ism and sustainable investment more broadly is good for investors, but where there also is no clear evidence that it is bad for them. This is bad and good news. It is bad news because we cannot point to strong financial reasons justifying a sustainable investment strategy. It is good news because such a strategy does also not appear to cause harm to financial results. It will be observed below that these mixed empiri-cal results could explain why beneficiaries and end-investors are generally passive.[25] It will also be suggested that the government is a financial contributor to pension investments.[26] If the government is seriously interested in promoting sustainable investments it should connect its own financial investment to sustainability criteria.

2.2 Altruism

In addition to financial return altruism can be a motivating factor inspiring sustain-able investment. We have experienced how in our lifetime attitudes towards plas-tic waste have changed from indifference to a situation where the government now requires plastic bags to be associated with a charge. We also know that smoking atti-tudes changed from students and staff smoking in offices and corridors to a situation where they are now banished to specific areas outside of public buildings.

We will see below that there exists a group of suppliers of sustainable investment products who believe that their market will grow in the future. They are encouraged by the fact that younger pension beneficiaries and retail individuals say in surveys that they are interested in using their investment to further the common good. For the time being that wholly altruistic investment market is, however, relatively small.[27] In

---

[20] For comprehensive literature reviews, see Margolis et al. (2009); Barko and Renneboog (2016), pp 268–290; see also Hartzmark and Sussman (2018).

[21] See Gibson et al. (2019). For earlier evidence focusing on the US market see Gibson and Krueger (2018).

[22] Friede et al. (2015), p 226.

[23] For a review of the literature, see Schanzenbach and Sitkoff (2020), p 436.

[24] Competition & Markets Authority, Investment Consultants Market Investigation, Final Report (2018), https://assets.publishing.service.gov.uk/media/5c0fee5740f0b60c8d6019a6/ICMI_Final_Report.pdf (accessed 3 Oct 2021), p 16, para. 50.

[25] Section 3.3.

[26] Section 5.2.

[27] Section 3.3.

addition, there exists a group of investors with large portfolios who actively pursue altruistic aims.[28] In the next three sections end-investors will be divided into three categories and for each of these the respective motivation in relation to sustainable investment will be examined.

3 Investors

3.1 Large Portfolio End-Investors

There exists a group of end-investors who have portfolios that are sufficiently large for them to be able to attract the attention of financial services providers. Examples are endowment funds and sovereign wealth funds (SWFs). These are potential candidates from which demand for sustainable investment can emerge.

Empirical evidence systematically surveying the attitudes of these investors in relation to sustainable investment is, however, scarce.[29] A 2019 Schroder survey among institutional investors (pension funds, insurance companies, foundations, endowments and SWFs) confirms that sustainable investing gains traction globally. 50% of the respondents state that they have increased their sustainable investments over the last five years, while 75% believe that 'sustainability will play a more important role in the next five years'. But performance concerns and a lack of transparency are reported as institutional investors' biggest sustainability challenges. In fact, 49% of the respondents (up from 34% in 2018) consider performance as the most important driver for future adoption of sustainable investing.[30]

While this survey is not limited to endowment funds and SWFs, it suggests that the extent to which large portfolio end-investors engage in sustainable investment depends on their respective investment strategy. If their focus is on generating a financial return, they will take a view on how this is best achieved. This may lead to interest in sustainable investment products as long as they generate risk-adjusted returns.[31] It may, however, also lead to the conclusion that their financial goals are best served by adopting a neutral strategy. Either way the fact that there is no clear evidence that sustainable investment leads to better financial results means that financial return is hardly going to be a motivator encouraging this group to embark sustainable investment activity.

There are, of course, some large portfolio beneficiaries who pursue investment strategies that, in addition to financial return, are also influenced by wider aims. This has been coined by Schanzenbach and Sitkoff as 'collateral benefits ESG investing'

---

[28] Section 3.1.

[29] There is, of course, a body of literature analysing family-controlled businesses but these are not the focus of this paper.

[30] Schroders, Institutional Investor Study: Sustainability (2019), https://www.schroders.com/en/sysgl obalassets/digital/institutional-investor-study/sustainability/pdf/Schroder2019_SIIS_Sustainabilityv2.pdf (accessed 3 Oct 2021).

[31] There is evidence that SWFs do take climate change and sustainability seriously. See, for instance, the One Planet Sovereign Wealth Funds: https://oneplanetswfs.org/ (accessed 3 Oct 2021).

because it aims to improve ESG for moral or ethical reasons without considering the financial interests of beneficiaries.[32] The Norwegian Government Pension Fund Global, the world's largest sovereign wealth fund, is an example of an early adopter of altruistic sustainable investing practices.[33] Charitable organisations with a large investment portfolio also fall in this category.[34] But charities only own a very small percentage of public equity in the UK and their role as sustainable shareholder stewards is therefore very limited.

It is also important to note that end-investors with large portfolios are not necessarily motivated by solely altruistic considerations. A survey including 75 non-profits in the US finds that while sustainable investing strategies are gaining traction (38% invest in sustainability and a further 12% plan to do so in 2019), 60% of the respondents cite 'concerns about performance' as the key factor preventing them from investing in sustainable investments.[35] Some of them receive scrutiny from the public. In the UK, the Church of England falls in this category.[36] Another UK example is the Duchy of Cornwall which funds the public, charitable and private activities of the Prince of Wales and his family. Investments held by the Duchy of Cornwall have been publicly scrutinised against the values promoted by the current holder of the office.[37]

For end-investors with large portfolios we can assume that, given the empirical evidence, financial return is likely to be a weak factor motivating sustainable investment. Some in this group are nevertheless motivated by altruistic aims. It is doubtful, however, how far their efforts on their own can bring about a shift to more sustainable shareholder stewardship encouraging issuers to adopt sustainable business practices in turn.

---

[32] Schanzenbach and Sitkoff (2020), p 390.

[33] For the investment approach adopted by the Norwegian Government, see https://www.nbim.no/en/the-fund/about-the-fund/. For how stewardship is exercised in Norway, see generally Mähönen et al. (2020).

[34] It is notable that, based on recommendations by the Law Commission, the duties of charitable trustees in relation to social investment have recently been clarified (Law Commission, Social Investment by Charities, The Law Commission's Recommendations (2014); The Charities (Protection and Social Investment) Act 2016, 2016 c 4).

[35] SEI Institutional Investors Sustainable Investment Survey 2018, https://seic.com/sites/default/files/inline-files/SEI%20Sustainable%20Investing%20Survey%202018.pdf (accessed 3 Oct 2021).

[36] For the approach adopted by the Church of England, see https://www.churchofengland.org/more/media-centre/news/finance-news/church-commissioners-england-achieve-positive-return-18-2018 (accessed 3 Oct 2021). On social shareholder engagement by religious organisations in general, see Goodman (2015), p 201.

[37] Hilary Osborne, 'Prince Charles's estate made big profit on stake in friend's offshore firm', The Guardian, 7 November 2017, https://www.theguardian.com/news/2017/nov/07/prince-charles-profit-best-friend-hugh-van-cutsem-offshore-firm-paradise-papers (accessed 3 Oct 2021).

3.2 Small Portfolio End-Investors

Small portfolio end-investors are individuals who hold financial investments. In 2016, the BIS conducted a study on the intermediated shareholding model.[38] They found that 76% of individual investors had a low interest in voting or attending annual general meetings although there were equity investors who valued their share-holder rights.[39] There exists, however, a group of investors who belong to share-holder representative organisations such as the Shareholders Society (ShareSoc) and the UK Shareholders Association (UKSA). For this group shareholder rights are important. They frequently describe their investment as a 'hobby' suggesting that they do not expect the time spent in researching companies and engaging with them to be compensated by returns.[40] Such investors articulate demand for sustainable shareholder stewardship.[41] The study commissioned by the BIS focused on engage-ment for governance purposes. It did not ask questions about ecological and social motives for engagement.

The market for ESG-active retail investment appears to be currently relatively small. There exists research examining the attitude of retail investors towards altru-istic investment strategies. A study making recommendations on how to encourage social impact investing, for example, found that only 13% of respondents have previ-ously invested in impact investments and that only 18% of respondents were more than moderately interested in such investments.[42] A number of suppliers of what can loosely be termed 'responsible investment products' have conducted empirical research predicting substantial future growth in the market for responsible invest-ing. Younger respondents appear to be more willing than older individuals to forgo financial return in favour of positive social or environmental outcomes.[43] This stronger focus on environmental and social issues by millennial investors compared to older generations appears to be even more emphasised in the US according to

---

[38] Department for Business, Innovation & Skills, Exploring the Intermediated Shareholding Model, BIS Research Paper Number 261 (January 2016).

[39] Ibid., p 16.

[40] Ibid., p 16.

[41] For an analysis of the impact of shareholder-sponsored proposals, see Gantchev and Giannetti (2018).

[42] Greg B. Davies and Centapse, SII Attitudinal and Behavioural Research (2017), https://assets.publi shing.service.gov.uk/government/uploads/system/uploads/attachment_data/file/659060/Social_Impact_ Investment_Attitudinal_and_Behavioural_Research__Centapse.pdf (accessed 3 Oct 2021), p 6.

[43] IFF Research (Ethex), Understanding the positive investor (2017), https://www.ethex.org.uk/under standing-the-positive-investor-2017_1923.html (accessed 3 Oct 2021); Annual Triodos Bank Impact Investing Survey: Socially Responsible Investing market on the cusp of momentous growth, Press Release (5 September 2018), https://www.triodos.co.uk/press-releases/2018/socially-responsible-inves tingmarket-on-cusp-of-momentus-growth (accessed 3 Oct 2021); Barclays, Investor motivations for impact: a behavioural examination (2018), https://www.barclays.co.uk/content/dam/documents/wealt hmanagement/investments/impact-investing-product/investor-motivations-for-impact.pdf (assessed 28 April 2020); AXA Investment Managers UK, Consumer Survey (2018), https://adviser.axa-im.co.uk/a more-responsible-approach-toinvesting?linkid=consumersurvey2018-navigationbanneramoreresponsib leapproachtoinvesting (accessed 3 Oct 2021); Newton Investment Management, Matching Strategies to Investors' Goals (2019), https://www.newtonim.com/uk-institutional/insights/articles/social-investment matching-strategies-to-investors-goals/ (accessed 3 Oct 2021).

recent market and research evidence.[44] It is encouraging that there exists a group of suppliers of sustainable and stewardship active investment products who envisage a robust future for their market, including State Street and Blackrock.[45] Either way, however, today the portion of small end-portfolio investors who prioritise sustainable investment rather than returns is relatively small and does not have the economic power to bring about responsible practices in investee companies.

3.3 Beneficiaries of Workplace and Personal Pensions

Beneficiaries of pension schemes are a significant group of investors. In the UK they make up 90% of the revenues of investment consultants and fiduciary managers.[46] In terms of motivation they mainly focus on financial return and tax benefits. For instance, the Law Commission cites a study carried out by Ignition House for the Financial Conduct Authority (FCA). The respondents to this study report that they interact with pension providers to enquire what their fund is currently worth, to find out whether they could access tax-free cash, and to let the providers know they wanted access to their pension money due to a change in circumstances such as redundancy or health issues.[47]

The purpose of a pension scheme is to accumulate money for retirement, so it is not a surprise that financial value, including employer contribution levels, investment returns and tax allowance, is a dominant factor for beneficiaries. When asked to describe what they were thinking about when they were making retirement plans, the most common unprompted consideration was how much tax-free cash they can have and what the maximum level of income was that they can generate with the rest. Beyond this, respondents needed to be prompted to consider factors such as longevity, health and inflation.[48]

We have seen above that the empirical evidence as to whether sustainable investment enhances the financial performance of funds is mixed.[49] It is therefore no surprise that pension beneficiaries in the UK revert to default investment choices. This default option bias is well-documented across many countries.[50] In addition pension beneficiaries report that they are 'uncertain about their ability to make equity-based investments'.[51] They also felt that

---

[44] Barzuza et al. (2020), p 1289.

[45] See, e.g., Fearless Girl, McCann Worldgroup, https://www.mccannworldgroup.com/work/fearlessgirl (accessed 3 Oct 2021).

[46] Competition & Markets Authority, Investment Consultants Market Investigation, Final Report (2018), https://assets.publishing.service.gov.uk/media/5c0fee5740f0b60c8d6019a6/ICMI_Final_Report.pdf (accessed 3 Oct 2021), p 29 para. 1.14.

[47] Ignition House, Exploring Consumer Decision Making and Behaviour in the At-Retirement Landscape, prepared by Ignition House for the Financial Conduct Authority (FCA) (December 2014), p 40.

[48] Ibid., p 45.

[49] See Section 2.1.

[50] For Singapore see, e.g., Fong (2020).

[51] Ignition House, Exploring Consumer Decision Making and Behaviour in the At-Retirement Landscape, prepared by Ignition House for the Financial Conduct Authority (FCA) (December 2014), p 16.

they received too much narrative information that was difficult to navigate and full of jargon.[52]

The Law Commission observes further that members of pension schemes view pension decisions as 'complex, unpleasant, boring, time consuming and something to be put off indefinitely'.[53] In addition, most pension savers do not appear to know how much of their pension is invested ethically.[54] This suggests that most beneficiaries of pensions are, at the moment, not likely to view their pension investment as a means through which they actively contribute to the common good.

There exists industry-funded empirical research showing that only a small proportion of investors are prepared to sacrifice return with a view to ensuring that their savings support a good cause.[55] Younger respondents (18–24 year olds) express a greater interest in investing responsibly than older individuals.[56] It remains to be seen if this interest translates into decisions that prioritise ESG factors over returns once the members of this group begin to make investment decisions in relation to pension. It is nevertheless encouraging that the investment industry has identified sustainable investment as a market with growth potential.

From the perspective of this paper we need to conclude that the beneficiaries of workplace and personal pensions while collectively very significant are currently unlikely to be a source for demand for sustainable investment. This is a shame because they are the major source for the assets invested through investment consultants and fiduciary managers.

It is worth noting, however, that for this group tax is a critical factor. It will be argued below that through tax relief the government is an investor in its own right.[57] At present the government makes pension tax relief available irrespective of whether ESG factors are taken into account. It will be argued in this paper that a good way of integrating sustainability into financial markets is to design pension tax relief in a way that favours sustainable investment products.

---

[52] Ibid., p 40.

[53] Law Commission, Pension Funds and Social Investment, Law Com No. 374 (2017), paras. 1.41 and 9.7.

[54] Madeleine Dates, 'Savers blind to how pensions are invested', Church Times, 28 September 2018, https://www.churchtimes.co.uk/articles/2018/28-september/news/uk/savers-blind-to-how-pensions-invested (accessed 3 Oct 2021).

[55] Movement Research, 'Identifying new ways to engage with savers in Defined Contribution Pensions', Defined Contribution Investment Forum (2013), https://www.dcif.co.uk/wp-content/uploads/2017/06/identifying-new-ways-toengage-with-savers-in-defined-contribution-pensions-.pdf (accessed 3 Oct 2021).

[56] 'New Good Money Week/YouGov poll results announced', https://www.goodmoneyweek.com/media/press-releases/new-good-money-weekyougov-poll-results-announced (accessed 3 Oct 2021); Madeleine Dates, 'Savers blind to how pensions are invested', Church Times, 28 September 2018, https://www.churchtimes.co.uk/articles/2018/28-september/news/uk/savers-blind-to-how-pensions-invested (accessed 3 Oct 2021); Franklin Templeton and Adoreboard, The Power of Emotions: Responsible Investment as a Motivator for Generation DC, https://www.franklintempleton.co.uk/download/en-gb/common/k03xuf49 (accessed 3 Oct 2021); there also exists experimental evidence that investors value sustainability: Hartzmark and Sussman (2018).

[57] Section 5.2.

4 Investment Service Providers

4.1 Pension Trustees and Members of Independent Governance Committees

Most workplace pension schemes are overseen by trustees.[58] There are also pension schemes which operate on the basis of a contract rather than a trust. The providers of personal pensions are overseen by the FCA, which has imposed a requirement for an independent governance committee. The committee has the duty to scrutinise the value for money of the provider's pension schemes taking into account transaction costs. They must act solely in the interests of the relevant scheme members and independently of the provider.[59]

Both pension trustees and members of governance committees are appointed to ensure that pensions are adequately managed. They have the mandate to protect the interests of beneficiaries. Pension trustees identify the service providers who manage pension assets. They rely on advice from investment consultants in taking these decisions. They also appoint and oversee fiduciary management services.

Pension trustees and committee members are bound by the terms on which they have been appointed. Invariably the core focus of their mandate is the generation of financial return. They have to consider ESG factors when these are financially material.[60] The law is sufficiently flexible to permit pension trustees to make investment decisions that are based on non-financial factors (such as environmental and social concerns) provided that they have a good reason to think that the scheme members share the concern, and that there is no risk of significant financial detriment to the fund.[61] Investment by a default fund therefore should not provide a significantly lower return than one available elsewhere.[62]

In relation to sustainable investment, trustees and committee members are likely to tread carefully.[63] Financial materiality is an over-riding factor and there is no evidence that ESG activity leads to generally better financial returns. Even if pension trustees have good reasons to think that beneficiaries hold values that favour investments with a certain impact, they cannot risk significant financial detriment. Trustees are therefore only able to integrate ESG in their assessment of financial risk. They are likely to be more acutely aware of short-term risk factors. These are easier to identify and require a timely response. Medium- or long-term risk factors

---

[58] Pensions Act 1985, section 16–21; Pensions Act 2004, sections 241–243.

[59] FCA, COBS 19.5.

[60] Law Commission, Pension Funds and Social Investment (2017), Law Com No. 374, p 2, p 5, para. 1.25 and p 130, para. 1.20; Law Commission, Fiduciary Duties of Investment Intermediaries (2014), Law Com No. 350, paras. 6.99–6.102; there exists, for example, empirical evidence that climate risk is a factor that institutional investors including pensions funds incorporate into their decision making (https://ecgi.global/working-paper/importance-climate-risks-institutional-investors (accessed 3 Oct 2021)).

[61] Law Commission, Pension Funds and Social Investment (2017), Law Com No. 374, p 2; Law Commission, Pension Funds and Social Investment (2017), Law Com No. 374, p 5, para. 1.26.

[62] Ibid., p 5, para. 1.26.

[63] Barriers, for instance, are posed by the 'interpretative pluralism' of the concept of fiduciary duties. See Tilba and Reisberg (2019).

are more difficult to integrate into decision making. They are harder to predict. Moreover, it is for the trustees' discretion to evaluate which risks are material and how to take them into account.[64] From the perspective of financial return the most likely strategy may be to avoid exposure to issuers associated with these risks rather than exercising stewardship to mitigate these risks. The Church of England has, for example, recently announced that it will withdraw from investing in carbon intensive industries.[65]

From 1 October 2019, trust-based defined contribution pension schemes have been required to set out in their Statement of Investment Principles (SIP) how they take into account financial material considerations, including those arising from ESG.[66] A survey by the UK Sustainable Investment and Finance Association (UKSIF) finds that two thirds of trustees have not complied with the new requirement to publish their policies by mid-November 2019. Among those who have published their SIPs, policies are mostly vague and they have all given their investment manager full discretion for managing financially material ESG risks. The survey concludes that 'building a market in stewardship will require a step change in trustees' approaches'.[67]

Most recently, the government has put forward the Occupational Pension Schemes (Climate Change, Governance and Reporting) Regulations 2021, coming into force on 1 October 2021.[68] They focus on climate change and require trustees of the UK's largest occupational pension schemes (with £5 billion or more in assets) to put in place new governance and risk management arrangements and to fulfil certain reporting requirements in line with the recommendations by the Task Force on Climate-related Financial Disclosures (TCFD).[69] TCFD-aligned disclosures – part of the broader TCFD roadmap published by the government in 2020 – aim to cause

---

[64] Law Commission, Pension Funds and Social Investment (2017), Law Com No. 374, p 130, para. 1.20.

[65] John Gabbatiss, 'Church of England votes to withdraw funds from companies that contribute to climate change', Independent, 9 July 2018, https://www.independent.co.uk/news/uk/home-news/church-of-england-climate-change-investment-withdraw-paris-agreement-fossil-fuels-a8437781.html (accessed 3 Oct 2021).

[66] See the Occupational Pension Schemes (Investment) Regulations 2005, 2(3)(b)(vi) and 2(3)(c) for financially material ESG considerations and stewardship, respectively. On the relationship between these new rules and the UK Code 2020, see Katelouzou and Micheler (2022).

[67] UK Sustainable Investment and Finance Association (UKSIF), Changing course? How pensions are approaching climate change and ESG issues following recent UK reforms (February 2020), https://www.responsible-investor.com/reports/uksif-or-changing-course-how-pensions-are-approaching-climate-change-and-esg-issues-following-recent-uk-reforms (accessed 3 Oct 2021).

[68] Department for Work & Pensions, The Occupational Pension Schemes (Climate Change Governance and Reporting) Regulations 2021: Consultation outcome (18 June 2021), https://www.gov.uk/government/consultations/taking-action-on-climate-risk-improving-governance-and-reporting-by-occupational-pension-schemes-response-and-consultation-on-regulations/the-occupational-pension-schemes-climate-change-governance-and-reporting-regulations-2021 (accessed 3 Oct 2021).

[69] Occupational Pension Schemes (Climate Change, Governance and Reporting), Regulations 2021, regs 3-6 and Schedule 1.

trustees to integrate the short-, medium- and long-term risks and opportunities associated with rising global temperatures into their decision making.[70]

The Regulations identify climate change as an ESG factor of particular importance. The government points out that they do not intend for trustees to solely focus on climate change and further observes that climate change is linked to wider social factors.[71] They do, however, not undermine the financial materiality requirement. The government expressly states that it does not intend to direct the investment decisions or strategies of trustees of pension schemes. They 'will never exhort or direct private sector schemes to invest in a particular way. Trustees have absolute primacy in this area'.[72] Notwithstanding the work that went into the clarification of the duties of trustees, financial materiality continues to be the over-riding factor.

In addition, there exists a structural problem. The new mandatory climate-related disclosures only apply to the UK's largest occupational pension schemes. The CMA finds that trustees of small schemes and trustees of defined contribution schemes are less engaged.[73] Less engaged trustees do, for example, not set objectives against which the quality of their investment consultants can be judged.[74] This observation that engagement is difficult for small scheme trustees and trustees for defined contribution schemes seems to still exist notwithstanding the 2019 regulatory changes.[75]

Small schemes are likely to suffer from the fact that they do not have sufficient resources. Defined contribution schemes suffer from the limited oversight by their beneficiaries. In defined contribution schemes the beneficiaries are the individual members and we have already seen that they do not take great interest in their pensions. In defined benefit schemes members receive retirement income depending on the years worked and depending on their final salary. The employer thus bears the risk of poor investment outcomes.[76] It is possible that trustees of such schemes benefit from greater engagement by employers. The CMA has made recommendations addressing the lack of engagement by trustees.[77] These however do not modify the mandate of trustees to prioritise in the financial interest of their beneficiaries.

---

[70] https://www.gov.uk/government/publications/uk-joint-regulator-and-government-tcfd-taskforce-inter im-report-and-roadmap (accessed 3 Oct 2021).

[71] Department for Work & Pensions, Government response: taking action on climate change: improving governance and reporting by occupational pension schemes (8 June 2021), Ministerial Foreword, https://www.gov.uk/government/consultations/taking-action-on-climate-risk-improving-governance-and-repor ting-by-occupational-pension-schemes-response-and-consultation-on-regulations (accessed 3 Oct 2021).

[72] Department for Work & Pensions, Clarifying and strengthening trustees' investment duties (September 2018), p 3.

[73] Competition & Markets Authority, Investment Consultants Market Investigation, Final Report (2018), https://assets.publishing.service.gov.uk/media/5c0fee5740f0b60c8d6019a6/ICMI_Final_Report.pdf (accessed 3 Oct 2021), p 13, para. 32.

[74] Ibid., p 11, para. 24 and p 15, para. 48.

[75] Ibid., p 13, para. 32.

[76] Ibid., p 17, paras. 58-59. For an analysis of decisions taken by pension trustees acting for defined benefit schemes, see Cocco and Volpin (2007).

[77] Competition & Markets Authority, Investment Consultants Market Investigation, Final Report (2018), https://assets.publishing.service.gov.uk/media/5c0fee5740f0b60c8d6019a6/ICMI_Final_Report.pdf (accessed 3 Oct 2021), p 7.

From the perspective of this paper, we therefore need to conclude that the financial materiality requirement presents a barrier to the ability of most trustees to make a contribution for the benefit of the public good and prioritise altruism over financial return.

4.2 Investment Consultants and Fiduciary Managers

Investment consultants provide advice in relation to strategic asset allocation, manager selection, fiduciary management. Fiduciary managers make and implement investment decisions including but not limited to the responsibility for asset allocation and fund/manager selection.[78]

These services providers are able to integrate ESG factors into their decisions. But the conclusion of the previous sections has been that they currently receive limited demand from their clients for sustainable investment.[79] Beneficiaries of workplace and personal pensions contribute 90% to the revenue of these providers.[80] But their focus is on financial return and there is no equivocal evidence that responsible investment increases the return of investors. Small portfolio end-investors who care about stewardship are unlikely to use the services of investment consultants or fiduciary managers. They are more likely to put together their own portfolios and hold securities directly or, alternatively, invest in savings accounts or ISAs.[81] There is a hope that the market for sustainable investment will grow in the future when younger individuals, who have expressed an interest in sustainable investment products, come into money. Some large portfolio end-investors care about sustainability but, while their efforts can serve as role models, their market share is too small to bring about a shift towards responsible business practices. On the whole, therefore, the terms on which investment consultants and fiduciary managers are appointed are very likely to focus on the generation of financial return without substantially integrating sustainability factors.

---

[78] Competition & Markets Authority, Investment Consultants Market Investigation, Final Report (2018), https://assets.publishing.service.gov.uk/media/5c0fee5740f0b60c8d6019a6/ICMI_Final_Report.pdf (accessed 3 Oct 2021), p 8, para. 3.

[79] For previous literature highlighting the lack of incentives to engage in stewardship arising from the perspective of the internal governance and business structures of funds, see Barker and Chiu (2017). Davies (2020) and Fisch (2020) also highlight the limited ability of institutional investors and index funds (respectively) to deliver stewardship activity.

[80] Competition & Markets Authority, Investment Consultants Market Investigation, Final Report (2018), https://assets.publishing.service.gov.uk/media/5c0fee5740f0b60c8d6019a6/ICMI_Final_Report.pdf (accessed 3 Oct 2021), p 29, para. 1.14.

[81] See, e.g., IFF Research (Ethex), Understanding the positive investor (2017), https://www.ethex.org.uk/understanding-the-positive-investor-2017_1923.html (assessed 3 Oct 2021) (finding that most of the UK population are most interested in less sophisticated savings and investment products (44% interested in savings accounts, 43% in current accounts and 40% in a positive ISA) as the method of making a positive investment).

5 The Role of the Government

It will be argued in this section that the UK Government falls short of fully appreciating its role in relation to sustainable investment. It commits substantial resources to overseeing the market for sustainable investment but does not give sufficient weight to the fact that it makes a significant financial contribution by subsidising the provision of pensions through the tax system. It will first be shown how the government currently oversees the market and then suggested that the government is an investor in its own right. It should do what it expects of other market participants and insist on sustainable investment.

5.1 The Government as a Facilitator of the Market for Responsible Investment

The approach of the UK Government in relation to the interface between investor capitalism and sustainable investment is nicely illustrated in a video explaining NEST, the workplace pension scheme set up by the UK Government. That scheme was created to support auto-enrolment into workplace pensions. The video is 47 s long and can be found on YouTube.[82] The animated video visualises the following text, which is read out by a narrator:

> Welcome to Nest. We are a workplace pension scheme set up by the government helping millions to earn a better retirement. You can save with Nest by making contributions to your pension pot, that you may receive tax relief on. You will also benefit from employer contributions. We believe in investing all your contributions responsibly, including with companies we encourage to meet high standards of environmental, social and corporate governance, not only because it is the right thing to do, but because it has been shown to give you better returns over time.

The video articulates the mindset the government would like investors to adopt. In the government's analysis, investors play a key role in shaping the behaviour of the companies that they have bought securities in. Investors are encouraged to invest in companies which display 'high standards of environmental, social and corporate governance'. They are encouraged to do this for two reasons. It is 'the right thing to do' and it 'has been shown to give you better returns over time'.

This suggests that ESG investment is associated with better returns. In light of the empirical evidence discussed above, it is not wrong to claim that 'it has been shown' that high ESG standards give better returns over time. There are studies which reach this conclusion. Because there are, however, also studies to contest this conclusion,[83] it would be better to tell investors that, given that it does not appear to make a difference either way, investors should do the 'right thing' and invest responsibly. Admittedly, that message is less attractive.

---

[82] Nestpension, Welcome to Nest, https://www.youtube.com/watch?v=tQA4dBxTt14 (accessed 3 Oct 2021).

[83] Friede et al. (2015), p 226.

Connected to this urging of investors to 'do the right thing', the government then puts in place disclosure requirements for issuers, who are encouraged to generate information that investors can rely on and use to make their respective (responsible) investment decisions. It also sets up reporting requirements for fiduciary managers and other financial service providers encouraging them to support sustainable investment strategies.

The government's overall strategy can be further illustrated by the reference to the recent reforms relating to climate change. We have already seen that pension trustees are now required to implement certain governance measures and report on climate risks and opportunities.[84] To perform this task, pension trustees need information on the assets contained in their portfolios. The government explicitly notes that trustees were concerned that they had to undertake 'analysis and report, whilst other parts of the investment chain on which trustees rely for data were not held to the same regulatory standards'.[85] It has further announced that the disclosure requirements drafted by the Financial Stability Board's Task Force on Climate-related Financial Disclosures (TCFD) will be made mandatory for issuers.[86]

The FCA is also planning on putting in place rules for asset managers and for workplace and personal pension schemes that align with the TCFD rules. Subject to consultation, final rules will be published by the end of 2021 and come into force in early 2022.[87] The aim is to ensure that the 'right information on climate-related risks and opportunities is available across the investment chain—from companies in the real economy to financial services firms, to end investors'.[88]

Indicative of the government's overall strategy in the area of sustainable investment are the UK Corporate Governance Code and the UK Stewardship Code, which are published by the Financial Reporting Council, soon to be transformed into the Audit, Reporting and Governance Authority.

The UK Corporate Governance Code is addressed to premium listed companies, which are required to either adopt certain governance measures or explain why they have decided to implement alternative solutions.[89] In its introduction, the authors of the Code observe that companies do not exist in isolation. 'Successful and sustainable businesses underpin our economy and society by providing employment and

---

[84] Section 4.1.

[85] Department for Work and Pensions, Government response: taking action on climate change: improving governance and reporting by occupational pension schemes (8 June 2021), Ministerial Foreword, para. 8, https://www.gov.uk/government/consultations/taking-action-on-climate-risk-improving-governance-and-reporting-by-occupational-pension-schemes-response-and-consultation-on-regulations (accessed 3 Oct 2021).

[86] HM Treasury, Interim Report of the UK's Joint Government-Regulator TCFD Taskforce (November 2020), https://assets.publishing.service.gov.uk/government/uploads/system/uploads/attachment_data/file/933782/FINAL_TCFD_REPORT.pdf (accessed 3 Oct 2021), pp 4-5.

[87] Ibid., p 16.

[88] Ibid., para. 2.3.

[89] Financial Reporting Council, The UK Corporate Governance Code (July 2018), https://www.frc.org.uk/getattachment/88bd8c45-50ea-4841-95b0-d2f4f48069a2/2018-UK-Corporate-Governance-Code-FINAL.pdf (accessed 3 Oct 2021) (hereinafter: UK Corporate Governance Code 2018); Listing Rules, DTR rules 7.2.2, https://www.handbook.fca.org.uk/handbook/DTR/7.pdf (accessed 3 Oct 2021).

creating prosperity. To succeed in the long-term, directors and the companies they lead need to build and maintain successful relationships with a wide range of stake-holders'.[90] The Code also stresses that the 'value of good corporate governance to long-term sustainable business' is at its 'heart'.[91]

In a complementary fashion, the Stewardship Code aims at encouraging investors to have regard to environmental, social and governance factors when making invest-ment decisions and undertake shareholder stewardship.[92] Stewardship is defined as the 'responsible allocation, management and oversight of capital to create long-term value for clients and beneficiaries leading to sustainable benefits for the economy, the environment and society'.[93] The Code provides 12 principles for asset managers and asset owners and 7 principles for service providers which operate on an apply-or-explain basis.[94] Asset owners and asset managers are asked to integrate 'material' ESG issues, including climate change, while undertaking stewardship.[95] Among others, asset owners are asked to ensure that when they award their mandates they require ESG integration in alignment with the investment horizon of their benefi-ciaries.[96] When they outsource stewardship activities, both asset owners and asset managers need to ensure that their service providers 'have received clear and action-able criteria to support integration of stewardship and investment, including material ESG issues'.[97] Service providers are asked to support clients' stewardship, includ-ing ESG integration.[98] Asset owners, asset managers and other service providers are encouraged to adopt the Code and publish information on how they implement it.[99] These disclosures are designed to supply ultimate investors with the informa-tion they need to make their investment choices. But the degree to which ultimate investors make informed decisions based on these reports and the degree to which these reports are tied to an overarching sustainable strategy on the part of the issuer is questionable.[100]

The UK Government defines its role as facilitating a market for sustainable investment by encouraging investors, issuers and financial services providers to act

---

[90] UK Corporate Governance Code 2018, introduction.

[91] Ibid.

[92] Financial Reporting Council, The UK Stewardship Code 2020, introduction, https://www.frc.org.uk/getattachment/5aae591d-d9d3-4cf4-814a-d14e156a1d87/Stewardship-Code_Final2.pdf (accessed 3 Oct 2021).

[93] Ibid.

[94] Only FCA-authorised asset managers are obliged to sign up to the Code. See FCA Handbook, COBS Conduct of Business Sourcebook, 2.2.3R (06/12/2010).

[95] UK Stewardship Code 2020, Principle 7, https://www.frc.org.uk/getattachment/5aae591d-d9d3-4cf4-814a-d14e156a1d87/Stewardship-Code_Final2.pdf (accessed 3 Oct 2021).

[96] Ibid.

[97] Ibid.

[98] Ibid., Principle 5 for service providers.

[99] The first list of signatories to the UK Stewardship Code 2020 was published in September 2021 and their statements can be found here: https://www.frc.org.uk/investors/uk-stewardship-code/uk-stewardship-code-signatories.

[100] See, e.g., https://www.investmentexecutive.com/inside-track_/shilpa-tiwari/esg-reporting-a-means-to-progressor-a-means-to-an-end/ (accessed 19 Oct 2021).

responsibly. This is supported through disclosure requirements. These are designed to create a process of self-reflection on those responsible for producing reports, stimulate clients to seek more information from their managers and also to ultimately impress end-investors allowing them to invest their savings in a way that can be described as 'responsible'. The government wants to discourage an attitude that solely focuses on short-term economic return without directly intervening with how businesses are run.

The problem with this approach is that it relies on the weakest participant in the investment chain doing the heavy lifting. The approach can only work if ultimate investors decide to do two things: first, become actively involved in their work-related pension savings, and, secondly, decide to take these active investment decisions with a view to enhance environmental, social and governance aims. In light of the observations made earlier this will require a significant shift in the attitudes of pension savers. The next section will show that the government can contribute to this shift. It will be argued that the government itself is part of the problem. It contributes to the reluctance of ultimate investors to engage with investment decisions. The government is a financial contributor to the investment markets and the government's contribution undermines the ability of ultimate investors to actively select investment products.

5.2 The Government as Financial Investor

Since the mid-twentieth century, UK securities markets have undergone a significant structural change. In the 1960s, investors were individuals, who were assisted by brokers at fixed and high rates of commission.[101]

This changed with the advent of occupational pension schemes. By the 1990s, UK insurance companies and pension funds together held about half of UK issued shares.[102] Since then globalisation has encouraged UK equity investors to hold more overseas assets, and many more UK shares are held by foreign institutions. In addition, sovereign wealth funds have become important institutional investors.[103]

We can also note that this structural change in financial services was not driven by spontaneous demand from individual savers. It was rather caused by the government's own policy measures. The design of pension tax relief has had an important impact on the current structure of investor capitalism.

Pension tax relief was introduced by the Finance Act 1921. It was originally made available for contributions made to 'superannuation funds'.[104] From the 1960s the coverage of occupational pension schemes among UK employees was greatly

---

[101] The Kay Review of UK Equity Markets and Long-term Decision Making, Final Report (July 2012), https://assets.publishing.service.gov.uk/government/uploads/system/uploads/attachment_data/file/253454/bis-12-917-kay-review-of-equity-markets-final-report.pdf (accessed 3 Oct 2021) (hereinafter: Kay Review), para. 3.2.

[102] Kay Review, para. 3.3.

[103] Ibid., para. 3.3.

[104] 1921 ch 32 (11 and 12 Geo 5), s 32.

extended.[105] In the late 1970s/early 1980s the tax treatment of institutionalised pension investments was so generous that it had the effect of multiplying investment returns.[106] Auto-enrolment has recently further widened the scope of occupational pensions.[107] The current design of tax relief continues to encourage individuals to save for retirement through funds and other institutional forms of investment.[108] Individuals who decide to opt for a self-invested personal pension, can, for example, invest their pension money in real estate investment trusts, but will not benefit from tax relief if they invest directly in residential real estate.[109]

This tax policy is justified by policy aims. It encourages and helps individuals to save for their retirement. It provides funding to issuers, which benefit from deep capital markets. The way the policy is designed has also subsidised the rise of institutional investors and other financial intermediaries.[110] These businesses would probably not exist if it were not for pension tax relief.[111] They provide employment and also contribute tax to the public purse.

Professor John Kay observes that many 'insurers and pension funds have outsourced their investment to specialist asset managers'.[112] In some cases these are 'spin offs from the sponsoring insurance company or pension fund',[113] which encouraged the 'divested business to seek external customers'.[114] Asset managers are supplemented by a myriad of other service providers. Examples of these are advisors who allocate funds to specialist asset managers, trustees, investment consultants, agents who 'wrap' products, retail platforms, distributors, independent financial advisors, registrars, custodians and proxy advisors.[115]

Unsurprisingly, the replacement of individual investors with investment intermediaries has given rise to a set of problems of its own. The Kay Review observed in 2012 that the current structure of the investment landscape has the effect of turning the long-term interests of savers into short-term signals to issuers. This is because asset managers and other service providers operating in the investment chain report to their respective clients in line with the short-term time frames contained in their

---

[105] Kay Review, para. 3.2.

[106] Cheffins (2008), pp 346-347.

[107] See https://www.gov.uk/workplace-pensions/joining-a-workplace-pension (accessed 22 June 2021).

[108] Tax on your private pension contributions, https://www.gov.uk/tax-on-your-private-pension (accessed 22 June 2021); The Pensions Advisory Service, Tax relief and contributions, https://www.pensionsadvisoryservice.org.uk/about-pensions/saving-into-a-pension/pensions-and-tax/tax-relief-and-contributions (accessed 3 Oct 2021).

[109] The Money Advice Service, Self-invested personal pensions (SIPPS), https://www.moneyadviceservice.org.uk/en/articles/self-invested-personal-pensions (accessed 3 Oct 2021).

[110] Cheffins (2008), pp 346–349.

[111] The CMA concluded that pension schemes contribute 90% to the revenue of investment consultants and fiduciary managers: Competition & Markets Authority, Investment Consultants Market Investigation, Final Report (2018), https://assets.publishing.service.gov.uk/media/5c0fee5740f0b60c8d6019a6/ICMI_Final_Report.pdf (accessed 22 June 2021), p 29, para. 1.14.

[112] Kay Review, para. 3.3.

[113] Ibid., para. 3.3.

[114] Ibid., para. 3.3.

[115] Ibid., para. 3.7.

respective contracts. They pass this pressure on to investee companies. This has the effect of bringing short-term results into sharper focus.[116] The requirement to identify a benchmark against which financial services providers can be assessed has also supported the shareholder-primacy model that has been dominating the corporate governance debate starting from the later twentieth century.[117] A short-term focus on generating value for shareholders can distract issuers from paying attention to the long-term consequences of their business for their ecological and social stakeholders. The analysis above has shown that the obsession with short-term value is currently fading and sustainable investment is gaining traction especially among millennials.

Yet, we are coming full circle. The government's tax contribution not only supports a structure that inadvertently prioritises short-term shareholder return. It also causes beneficiaries to disengage. Pension savers receive return through tax savings. This discourages them from paying close attention to selecting their investment portfolios. This in turn deprives the investment consultancy and fiduciary management industry of oversight. It also means that the hope that investors will step up to the task of exercising demand for responsible investment practices is optimistic.

In so far as the government makes a financial contribution to investments it is entitled to involve itself in how investment decisions for pensions are taken. It also has a responsibility to engage and act as a steward. Like all other beneficiaries of and contributors to the market, the government should act responsibly in relation to its own investment.

Finally, the government is a financial stakeholder as a residual loss bearer. When the financial system collapsed in 2008 the government bore the financial burden of the rescue. The government is likely to feel obliged to intervene if the pension system experiences a shock.

6 The Way Forward

Investor capitalism and sustainable investment are coming closer together with both the demand and the supply sides of the market for sustainable investments expanding exponentially. Yet, there are still loose ends, and the government has a key role to play in tying them up. A well-discussed solution to the problem of self-regulation of the market for sustainable investment is that of the imposition of regulatory duties on financial service providers to integrate stewardship.[118] Such a duty would, however, cover all investments, in particular also those to which the government has not made a financial contribution. For these the government has no right to insist on any particular investment strategy. An indiscriminate regulatory duty also does not resolve the problem that the government is currently distorting the market. This

---

[116] Ibid., paras. xiv–xv.

[117] Lund and Pollman (2021).

[118] See Chiu and Katelouzou (2017) and Chiu and Katelouzou (2018).

paper therefore looks at the role of the government as an investor itself rather than as a regulator.

The view advanced in this paper is that the government's decision to invest, by granting tax relief, its own money into the pension sector without insisting on sustainable investment is a significant barrier preventing a shift to sustainable investment practices. There is no doubt that long-term sustainable investment is more difficult in defined contribution schemes which tend to concentrate on conventional asset classes. Yet, the government should acknowledge that it is an investor in the industry. In that capacity the government has its own responsibilities. It should take these seriously and ensure that its own money is invested responsibly. The proposal advanced in this paper is that pension relief should be attached to conditions that funds invested through these schemes be invested responsibly.[119] Whilst we acknowledge that our proposal falls within the concurrent, but still infant debate of how to best inform appropriate metrics and meaningful standards for sustainable investment,[120] it is out of the scope of this paper to draw the specifics of a sustainability- or ESG-benchmark to justify pension tax relief. What we aim, however, is to direct the future of pension tax relief as a long-standing policy instrument by realigning it as a solution to a new problem.[121]

Originally pension tax relief was introduced to support private pension saving. Today pension tax relief can serve an additional purpose: it can motivate retail investors to pay attention to 'G' as well as 'E' and 'S'. Given that a bias towards sustainable investment does not appear to generate financial harm for investors, it would seem that the government should also 'do the right thing' in its capacity as a financial contributor to the financial markets. Reforming pension tax reliefs is already the subject of intense debate in the UK.[122] But no attention has been given so far to the potential social value of pension tax reliefs.[123] Connecting pension tax reliefs to sustainability criteria will help to promote the sustainability of the financial system and redeem the 'soul' of investor capitalism: the stewardship potential of retail investors.

---

[119] For similar tax proposals in the UK and the US connecting tax reliefs to the mitigation of climate change, see Baker and Murphy (2020); see also the special tax relief available for social investments: https://www.gov.uk/government/consultations/social-investment-tax-relief-call-for-evidence/social-investment-tax-relief-call-for-evidence#contents (accessed 3 Oct 2021).

[120] On the EU debate on ESG benchmarks, see https://ec.europa.eu/info/business-economy-euro/banking-and-finance/sustainable-finance/eu-climate-benchmarks-and-benchmarks-esg-disclosures_en (accessed 20 October 2021).

[121] On the evolution of social investment policy instruments in the UK, see Nicholls and Teasdale (2021).

[122] House of Commons, Reform of pension tax relief (7 February 2020), https://commonslibrary.parliament.uk/research-briefings/cbp-7505/ (accessed 3 Oct 2021).

[123] Note that the social value of tax relief in the UK has already been utilised in relation to community investment and the aim to develop a 'social impact investment market'. See, e.g., Wiggan (2018).

References

Baker A, Murphy R (2020) Modern monetary theory and the changing role of tax in society. Soc Policy Soc 19:454–469

Barker RM, Chiu IHY (2017) Corporate governance and investment management: the promises and limitations of the new financial economy. Edward Elgar Publishing, Cheltenham

Barko T, Renneboog L (2016) Mutual funds: management styles, social responsibility, performance, and efficiency. In: Baker HK, Filbeck G, Kaymaz H (eds) Mutual funds and exchange-traded funds. OUP, Oxford, pp 268–290

Barko T, Cremers M, Renneboog L (2018) Shareholder engagement on environmental, social, and governance performance. https://ssrn.com/abstract=2977219. Accessed 3 Oct 2021

Barzuza M, Curtis Q, Webber DH (2020) Shareholder value(s): index fund ESG activism and the new millennial corporate governance. South Calif Law Rev 93:1242–1321

Berry CP (2015) Take the long road? Pension fund investments and economic stagnation. The International Longevity Centre, UK. https://e-space.mmu.ac.uk/620793/. Accessed 20 Oct 2021

Cheffins B (2008) Corporate ownership and control: British business transformed. OUP, Oxford

Chiu I, Katelouzou D (2017) From shareholder stewardship to shareholder duties: is the time ripe? In: Birkmose HS (ed) Shareholders' duties. Kluwer Law International, The Netherlands

Chiu I, Katelouzou D (2018) Making a case for regulating institutional shareholders' corporate governance roles. J Bus Law 2018(1):67–99

Cocco FK, Volpin PF (2007) Corporate governance of pension plans: the U.K. evidence. Financ Anal J 63:70–83

Davies P (2020) The UK Stewardship Code 2010–2020 from saving the company to saving the planet. ECGI Law Working Paper No 506/2020. https://papers.ssrn.com/sol3/papers.cfm?abstract_id=3553493. Accessed 3 Oct 2021

Denes MR, Karpoff JM, McWilliams V (2017) Thirty years of shareholder activism—a survey of empirical research. J Corp Finan 44:405–424

Dimson E, Karakas O, Li X (2015) Active ownership. Rev Financ Stud 28:3225–3268

Dimson E, Karakas O, Li X (2019) Coordinated engagements. https://ssrn.com/id=3209072. Accessed 3 Oct 2021

Fisch J (2020) The uncertain stewardship potential of index funds. ECGI Law Working Paper No 490/2020. https://papers.ssrn.com/sol3/papers.cfm?abstract_id=3525355. Accessed 3 Oct 2021

Fong JH (2020) Taking control: active investment choice in Singapore's national defined contribution scheme. J Econ Ageing 17:1–11

Friede G, Busch T, Bassen A (2015) ESG and financial performance: aggregated evidence from more than 2000 empirical studies. J Sustain Financ Invest 5:210–233

Gantchev N, Giannetti M (2018) The costs and benefits of shareholder democracy. ECGI Finance Working Paper Series 586/2018

Gibson R, Krueger P (2018) The sustainability footprint of institutional investors. Swiss Finance Institute Research Paper No 17-05. ECGI Finance Working Paper No 571/2018. https://ssrn.com/abstract=2918926. Accessed 3 Oct 2021

Gibson R et al (2019) Responsible institutional investing around the world. Swiss Finance Institute Research Paper No 20-13. https://ssrn.com/abstract=3525530. Accessed 3 Oct 2021

Gilson RJ, Gordon JN (2013) The agency costs of agency capitalism: activist investors and the revaluation of governance rights. Columbia Law Rev 113:863–927

Goodman J (2015) Religious organizations as shareholders: salience and empowerment. In: Maranova M, Ryan LV (eds) Shareholder empowerment. Palgrave, New York, pp 201–222

Hartzmark SM, Sussman AB (2018) Do investors value sustainability? A natural experiment examining raking and fund flows. ECGI Finance Working Paper No 565/2018

Katelouzou D (2018) Reflections on the nature of the public corporation in an era of shareholder activism and shareholder stewardship. In: Barnali C, Petrin M (eds) Understanding the modern corporation. Cambridge University Press, Cambridge

Katelouzou D (2022) The path to enlightened shareholder stewardship. Cambridge University Press, Cambridge

Katelouzou D, Micheler E (2022) The market for stewardship and the role of the government. In: Katelouzou D, Puchniak DW (eds) Global shareholder stewardship: complexities, challenges and possibilities. Cambridge University Press, Cambridge. https://ssrn.com/abstract=3704258 or https://doi.org/10.2139/ssrn.3704258. Accessed 3 Oct 2021

Katelouzou D, Puchniak D (2022) Global shareholder stewardship: complexities, challenges, and possibilities. In: Katelouzou D, Puchniak DW (eds) Global shareholder stewardship: complexities, challenges and possibilities. Cambridge University Press, Cambridge. https://ecgi.global/working-paper/global-shareholder-stewardship-complexities-challenges-and-possibilities. Accessed 3 Oct 2021

Katelouzou D, Siems M (2022) The global diffusion of stewardship codes. In: Katelouzou D, Puchniak DW (eds) Global shareholder stewardship: complexities, challenges and possibilities. Cambridge University Press, Cambridge. https://ecgi.global/working-paper/global-diffusion-stewardship-codes. Accessed 3 Oct 2021

Lund DS, Pollman E (2021) The corporate governance machine. Columbia Law Rev 121. https://papers.ssrn.com/sol3/papers.cfm?abstract_id=3775846. Accessed 3 Oct 2021

Mähönen J, Sjåfjell B, Mee M (2020) Stewardship Norwegian-style: fragmented and state-dominated (but not without potential?). https://papers.ssrn.com/sol3/papers.cfm?abstract_id=3635359. Accessed 3 Oct 2021

Margolis JD, Elfenbein HA, Walsh JP (2009) Does it pay to be good … and does it matter? A meta-analysis of the relationship between corporate social and financial performance. https://ssrn.com/abstract=1866371. Accessed 3 Oct 2021

Nicholls A, Teasdale S (2021) Dynamic persistence in UK policy making: the evolution of social investment ideas and policy instruments. Public Manag Rev 23:802–817

Sandberg J, Juravle C, Hedesström TM et al (2009) The heterogeneity of socially responsible investment. J Bus Ethics 87:519–533

Schanzenbach MM, Sitkoff RH (2020) Reconciling fiduciary duty and social conscience: the law and economics of ESG investing as a trustee. Stanf Law Rev 72:381–454

Talan G, Sharma GD (2019) Doing well by doing good: a systematic review and research agenda for sustainable investment. Sustainability 11:353

Tilba A, Reisberg A (2019) Fiduciary duty under the microscope: stewardship and the spectrum of pension fund engagement. Mod Law Rev 82:456–487

Useem M (1996) Investor capitalism: how money managers are changing the face of corporate America. Basic Books, New York

Wiggan J (2018) Policy boosting the social impact investment market in the UK. J Soc Policy 47:721–738

Publisher's Note Springer Nature remains neutral with regard to jurisdictional claims in published maps and institutional affiliations.

European Business Organization Law Review (2022) 23:241–271
https://doi.org/10.1007/s40804-021-00236-w

ARTICLE

Private Investments, Public Goods: Regulating Markets for Sustainable Development

Celine Tan[1]

Accepted: 13 December 2021 / Published online: 28 February 2022
© The Author(s) 2022

Abstract

In the new ecosystem for financing the sustainable development goals (SDGs), private actors are no longer passive bystanders in the development process, nor engaged merely as clients or contractors but as co-investors and co-producers in development projects and programmes. This 'private turn' in the financing of international development and other global public goods sees the enmeshment of public and private finance that brings aid and other forms of official development finance into sharp contact with regulatory regimes commonly associated with commercial investments, capital markets and corporate activity. The shift away from public resources for financing (e.g., multilateral sovereign loans) to leveraging financial markets for development capital (e.g., equity and portfolio investments) will insert countries into global financial markets and engagements with corporate actors in ways that will change forms of regulation, accountability and transparency of public finance. Zooming in on the creation of markets for sustainable development investments (SDI), this paper explores how this broader 'reengineering of public finance' is establishing new forms of governance that are restructuring the relationship between states and markets and between transnational capital and their host communities. Specifically, the movement towards private investments and financial markets as key drivers of financing for sustainable development has two critical impacts on transnational governance: (a) the use of private markets, in their capital allocation roles, as quasi-regulatory tools for achieving the SDGs and other global public goods; and (b) the deployment of private regulatory regimes (e.g., contracts, codes of conduct, corporate governance codes) as mechanisms to govern the social and environmental externalities of transnational economic activity. These developments have wide-ranging impacts on the domestic legal, political and civic constitution of states that can paradoxically constrain fiscal and policy space for enabling the attainment of the SDGs.

Keywords Aid · Environmental, social and governance · Financial markets · International development · Sustainable development goals · Public finance

---

Extended author information available on the last page of the article

1 Introduction

A significant shift is taking place in the landscape of international development finance. Premised on the notion of public–private partnerships, this latest evolution in global public policy sees the growing involvement of private actors in the mobilisation, disbursement and delivery of financing for sustainable development and other global public goods. In what has been referred to as the 'new ecosystem of investment for sustainable development',[1] private actors are no longer passive bystanders in the development process, nor engaged merely as clients or contractors but as co-investors and co-producers in development projects and programmes.

This strategy of enabling private financing for sustainable development has intensified recently as the global community faces the critical task of pandemic response and recovery. There is an emerging consensus among major international development financiers that constraints on public resources in the foreseeable future mean that reliance cannot be placed on official sector flows to meet the enormous financial challenges faced by countries in the post-pandemic, climate critical world. Accordingly, mobilising private finance is seen as critical to responding to global social, economic and humanitarian needs, especially in developing countries, and tackling global collective action problems, including pandemics and the climate crisis. The private sector, especially private investors, is now viewed as a necessary partner in global efforts to 'rebuild' the global economy in the wake of COVID-19.[2]

An important component of this private turn in international development is the harnessing of national and international capital markets to mobilise investments in SDG and climate-related sectors through the promotion and development of sustainable development investments. Tapping into commercial debt and equity markets via sustainable and socially responsible investing and impact investing is seen as key to generate the leap from 'billions to trillions'[3] in the resources available to attain global public policy objectives, notably the sustainable development goals (SDGs) and climate change mitigation and adaptation.[4]

This paper focuses on the relationship between international development policy and practice and the creation of markets for sustainable development investing (SDI).[5] It considers the active role played by official sector development actors – international financial institutions (IFIs), multilateral and bilateral development agencies and international organisations – in facilitating, incentivising and funding the shift towards financial markets as sources for SDG attainment. The paper

---

[1] Blended Finance Innovators (2016).

[2] Bayliss and Romero (2021); Gabor (2021); UN Economic Commission for Africa (2020).

[3] World Bank (2015).

[4] Gabor (2021); Jafri (2019).

[5] For ease of reference, the paper uses the term 'sustainable development investing/investments' (SDI) to refer to the diverse range of investment strategies and financial products that aim to raise capital and fund a similarly broad range of products, services, operations and programmes that meet global sustainable development objectives, including sectors mapped under the United Nations (UN) Sustainable Development Goals (SDGs), such as health, education, energy, poverty reduction, economic growth, gender equality and climate change mitigation and adaptation, to name a few (GISD, undated).

explores how this broader 'reengineering of public finance'[6] is (1) establishing new forms of governance that are restructuring the relationship between states and markets and between transnational capital and the host communities for transitional capital; and (2) how these emerging governance formations impact on global distribution of resources for public policy goals.

Specifically, the paper argues that the movement towards private investments and financial markets as key drivers of financing for sustainable development has two critical impacts on transnational and domestic governance. First, the shift to financial markets as sources of capital for collective public goods and services is shifting the resource allocation role of states to private actors with attendant question marks over corresponding regulatory oversight of this quasi-public function. Second, the emergence of financial markets as primary sources for financing sustainable development is resulting in the deployment of private regulatory regimes to govern both social and environmental externalities of transnational economic activity as well as the sustainability of financial flows and funding for public goods and services.

The paper argues that these transformations have wide-ranging impacts on the domestic legal, political and civic constitution of states that can paradoxically constrain the fiscal and policy space available for enabling the attainment of the SDGs and other ecological sustainability goals. The movement towards financial markets as key sources for SDG financing is also likely to constrain the civic voice and participation of local communities in resource allocation and to undermine national ownership of social, economic and environmental policymaking while risking access to mechanisms for redress and accountability for harmful financial and operational acts of development projects and programmes.

The concern of this paper is therefore less about the endogenous development of SDI regimes and the general incorporation of sustainability and environmental, social and governance (ESG) considerations into investment decisions or about enacting behavioural change in financial market actors to align with collective global development and public goods targets. Instead, the focus is on the shift away from public finance and publicly allocated capital towards reliance on private financial markets to provide the resources to meet global public goods, and the impact this will have on meeting the SDGs and other sustainability objectives. The paper focuses specifically on the securities markets for sustainable development investing.

The paper proceeds as follows. The next Section provides an overview of the 'private turn' in international development finance and discusses how the SDG financing agenda is creating markets for public goods investments, locating this within the historical and contemporary role of international development policy and practice in restructuring regulatory and governance infrastructure in developing countries. Section 3 explores how these interventions in the modalities of global public goods financing are reorienting the role of the state and civil society in developing countries and discusses the implications for governance and public policy administration in these countries. Section 4 considers the regulatory gaps in the shift towards financial markets as providers of SDG resources and the effect of the enmeshment of public and private finance that brings aid and other forms of official development

---

[6] Kaul and Conceição (2006).

finance into sharp contact with regulatory regimes commonly associated with commercial investments, capital markets and corporate activity. The final section concludes.

2 Private Finance for Sustainable Development

Although the 'private turn' in international development finance has longer histori-cal roots,[7] it has gained significant momentum with the inception of the UN 2030 Agenda for Sustainable Development (Agenda 2030) and the aforementioned SDGs and the Paris Agreement. The impetus to overcome the gaps between the ambitious SDGs and climate change mitigation and adaptation targets and the massive finan-cial investments needed to meet them precipitated calls to mobilise financial capi-tal beyond official sector finance. Private finance is seen as the key to scaling up resources to meet the challenges of these two major global agreements and the role of private finance is recognised and embedded within their implementation blue-prints. For example, the Addis Ababa Action Agenda (AAAA), which sets out the framework for SDG implementation, underscores the importance of private finance in meeting long-term financing needs and commits states to developing regulatory and policy frameworks to enable private investments for sustainable development while encouraging the promotion of public–private partnerships in the financing of SDG needs, such as infrastructure and clean energy.[8]

2.1 Public Incentives for Private Capital

A corollary of the evolving architecture of international development finance is the shifting role of official financing away from direct funding of development and other global public goods towards brokering financial investments in these areas.[9] Opera-tionally, this has meant the channelling of official finance, including concessional finance (also known as official development assistance or ODA), into (1) private investments and public–private partnerships (PPPs), particularly through bilateral or multilateral development finance institutions (DFIs);[10] and (2) technical, policy and regulatory reforms or 'upstream' activities which create 'enabling environments' for private investments in development projects.[11] The mobilisation of private finance has thus evolved into 'a development policy goal in its own right' with official

---

[7] See Bayliss and Van Waeyenberge (2018), Gabor (2021) and Mawdsley (2018) for details on the longer historical relationship between international development and private sector engagement and promotion.

[8] UN (2015), para. 49.

[9] Tan (2021), p 17.

[10] DFIs are bilateral or multilateral institutions controlled or owned by national governments that lend to or invest in private sector entities in developing countries. They are generally funded by governments through their ODA or other development aid budget and also raise capital through banks and financial markets. See, for instance, Romero (2014), p 7.

[11] Romero (2014), p 7; IFC (2021). See also Sect. 2.2 for further discussion.

financiers increasingly viewing private finance mobilisation as a key component of their *raison d'être* and a central part of their operational mandate.[12]

These developments have dovetailed with the exponential growth of the SDI market in recent years with green, social and sustainable bond issuances reaching a cumulative US\$1.7 trillion at the end of 2020, doubling the amount issued in 2019 and expected to rise further in 2021.[13] The resulting architecture has been termed a 'framework for SDG aligned finance' that is premised on the integration of 'double materiality' (financial and non-financial returns) in private finance decision-making and investments.[14] In this emerging landscape, official development agencies and international organisations are being reoriented towards creating the enabling environment at global and national levels to tap into the estimated US30.7 trillion worth of assets under management[15] available to finance sustainable development.[16]

This transformative change in the trajectory of international development policy and practice has been described as the movement from the Washington Consensus model of development to the Wall Street Consensus model of development. Where the Washington Consensus sought to 'escort private capital'[17] into developing countries through the restructuring of policy and regulatory regimes (for example, through deregulation and liberalisation policies of structural and sectoral adjustment conditionalities),[18] the Wall Street Consensus is seeking to do so by providing financial incentives and regulatory interventions that aim to 'de-risk' private investments for public goods.[19] As discussed in the following Section, this is often done at the granular level to foster 'conditions of bankability',[20] creating new or adapting existing financial instruments to facilitate investor appetite in SDG investments while developing or restructuring the regulatory frameworks to constitute these new instruments and markets and to codify investor/creditor rights and mitigate or manage risk to private investments in this new SDG financing ecosystem.[21]

In this manner, the Wall Street Consensus extends the Washington Consensus policy prescriptions and interventions towards the creation of an enabling environment for financialised capital. It reflects the broader shifts in the global economy away from bank/relational-based modalities of debt financing towards market-based finance as a source of financing global economic activity. The SDG financing agenda must be located within the broader context of the 'assemblage of private development finance', the complex and interlocking framework of discourses,

---

[12] Bayliss and Romero (2021), p 6.

[13] Jones (2021).

[14] OECD and UNDP (2020), p 4.

[15] Global Sustainable Investment Alliance (2018), p 8.

[16] UN (2021), p 18; CFLI et al. (2020), p 13.

[17] Gabor (2021), p 433.

[18] See Babb and Kentikelenis (2021) for a discussion on the history of the Washington Consensus and the role played by IFIs, notably the International Monetary Fund (IMF) and the World Bank, in operationalising the policy prescriptions of this 'ideational' infrastructure.

[19] Gabor (2021), p 441; Mawdsley (2018), p 192.

[20] Bigger and Webber (2020), p 40.

[21] Ibid.; Gabor (2021), p 443.

policies, programmes, facilities and practices that seek to rationalise, endorse and embed the prominent participation of private actors in the mobilisation, disbursement and delivery of development finance.[22]

As with the Washington Consensus, law and regulatory regimes are central to the constitution of this new landscape of financialised development, providing the 'legal code'[23] for creating and structuring assets for SDI investments and providing the regulatory framework for constituting and deepening SDI markets[24] in order to 'open up new circuits for financial investment, speculation and extraction'.[25] The role of law and regulation in this context is to render social, economic and ecological sectors in the Global South accessible and investible to global capital through the apportionment, creation and enforcement of legal rights to assets and the establishment of a conducive domestic and transnational environment in which those conditions of bankability are promoted and protected.[26]

2.2 Creating Markets for Public Goods Investments

Financial markets are central to the implementation of the emerging hybrid financing architecture for sustainable development. The movement away from official sector funding, such as grants and sovereign loans and guarantees, towards private commercial and non-profit financing, such as commercial loans, bonds and other securities, and 'blended finance' instruments and PPPs, has resulted in a greater reliance on debt and equity markets for resourcing SDGs and other global public goods. Financial markets are viewed as critical intermediaries between capital and SDG financing needs, serving as important sources of finance for development financiers *and* recipient states and communities. International policymakers have increasingly focused on scaling up access to and deployment of these sources of financing for SDG-related sectors.[27]

Correspondingly, since the acceleration of the 'private turn' in development finance, there has been significant investment of official sector resources – financial and technical – in the construction of sustainable finance markets with the aim of creating a large liquid and credible asset class for SDG investments.[28] Specifically, in recent years, there has been a concerted emphasis on debt securities – corporate and sovereign bonds – as important vehicles for channelling capital to developing countries. International development financiers have engaged in the construction of

---

[22] Tan (2021), pp 6–7.

[23] See Pistor (2019), pp 2–4. Pistor's landmark work on 'the code of capital' expands on previous scholarship exploring the operation of law and regulation in constituting markets for economic activity (see, e.g., De Sousa Santos (2002); Halliday and Carruthers (2009); Picciotto (2011)) by exposing how law encodes 'assets' – material or intellectual – as capital in order to render them, among other things, durable and convertible for the purpose of wealth generation for the asset owner.

[24] See Gabor (2021), p 433; Pistor (2019), pp 2–4; Tan (2021), p 8.

[25] Mawdsley (2018), p 192.

[26] Ibid.; Bigger and Webber (2020), p 40.

[27] Amacker and Donovan (2021), p 36; IPSF (2020), pp 13–20.

[28] UN and UNEP (2019), pp 4–5, 16–17.

SDI markets through: (1) participation in financial markets as issuers of SDI bonds; and (2) financial and regulatory interventions in global and domestic financial markets through their financing and technical assistance operations. The latter includes the development of policy and regulatory tools to create SDG-specific asset classes[29] to incentivise SDI investments and enhance countries' ESG 'readiness'.[30]

First, IFIs, multilateral development banks (MDBs) and bilateral development agencies have started issuing SDG, green and sustainability-related bonds to finance their operations. While most MDBs and regional development banks have traditionally raised funds from international capital markets, their issuance of so-called 'labelled bonds' is relatively new and has accelerated with the development of the sustainable finance frameworks by the International Capital Markets Association (ICMA).[31] The World Bank, for example, has been at the forefront of issuing green bonds since 2008 through its main lending facility, the International Bank for Reconstruction and Development (IBRD), and its private sector arm, the International Finance Corporation (IFC),[32] but has recently issued sustainable development bonds (IBRD) that are consistent with the ICMA's Sustainability Bond Guidelines (SBGs)[33] and social bonds (IFC) that are aligned with the ICMA's Social Bond Principles (SBPs).[34] Regional development banks, such as the Asian Infrastructure Investment Bank (AIIB) and Development Bank of Latin America (CAF), have also similarly issued green, SDG and social bonds respectively.[35]

Additionally, in 2018, the World Bank's concessional financing arm, the International Development Association (IDA), which has traditionally drawn its funds from donor replenishments and IBRD contributions, issued its first benchmark bond, marking its debut foray into the SDI capital market.[36] Bilateral development agencies have also similarly tapped into sustainable finance markets to expand their capital base. France's *Agence française de développement* (AFD), for example, issued a climate bonds framework in 2017 and an SDG bond framework in 2020 to raise capital for onward lending to sovereign and non-sovereign entities for eligible projects ringfenced by the terms of its climate or SDG bond 'use of proceeds'.[37]

Aside from mobilising capital for their own operations, the participation of international development agencies in SDI markets sends important signals to other

---

[29] Asset classes are financial instruments with similar financial characteristics and sharing similar regulatory structures. Development of a new asset class includes 'the adoption by the investment community of metrics, benchmarks and ratings that standardize performance and risk measurement'. See O'Donohoe et al. (2010), pp 8–9.

[30] Boitreaud et al. (2020), p 31.

[31] These frameworks include the development of voluntary guidelines for issuance of green, social and sustainability bonds, notably the Green Bond Principles (GBP), Social Bond Principles (SBPs) and Sustainability Bond Guidelines (SBGs). See ICMA (2020). See also the ICMA website https://www.icmag roup.org/sustainable-finance/ (accessed 9 May 2021).

[32] IBRD (undated); IFC (2020a).

[33] IBRD (2021), p 4.

[34] IFC (2020b).

[35] AIIB (2021); Bruni (2020).

[36] World Bank (2018a).

[37] AFD (2020); Davies et al. (2020).

market participants. Leveraging existing operational and regulatory frameworks for SDG finance, SDG-linked securities issued by multilateral and bilateral development financiers lend credibility to emerging SDI markets and promote confidence in nascent normative frameworks linked to sustainable finance, notably the private regulatory regimes governing SDI markets, such as the ICMA sustainable bond and sustainable loan frameworks and third-party audit mechanisms (see further discussion in Sect. 3). In fact, DFIs, such as the IFC, have been central to the development of these sustainable finance standards, such as the Green Bond Principles (GBP), and are important standard-setters in the industry, building on their pioneering roles in developing sustainable lending frameworks, notably the Equator Principles, the environmental and social risk management framework for project finance.[38]

This market-building function of official development financiers is complemented by their operational policies and practices which have involved the deployment of funds towards the development of *financial* and *regulatory* incentives to mobilise private investments in green, sustainability and other SDG sectors. Driven by the overarching rationale that public finance, including concessional official development assistance (ODA),[39] can act as financial and regulatory lever to 'crowd in' private sector finance for SDGs, policy and operational interventions by major development actors have focused on the use of *financial* and *regulatory* incentives to steer private capital into SDG sectors and to use private regulatory regimes to manage and supervise the engagement of private actors in what were previously state-dominated SDG sectors. This catalytic role of public finance is driven at both the 'systemic, market-level' and the transactional 'deal-level'.[40] Where the former aims to create enabling policy and institutional and market environments for private capital, such as through legal, regulatory and policy reforms, the latter involves the deployment of specific interventions to directly engage 'private actors for individual investment projects'.

A key rationale for capital market interventions by development financiers is to reduce 'investors' informational and operational costs' of participating in SDI markets[41] and improve the risk profile of SDG investments to leverage private finance.[42] As a recent study on green capital found, institutional investors from developed countries searching for green assets 'want EM level yields without accepting EM

---

[38] Le Houérou (2018).

[39] See OECD (2021), p 6. The OECD classifies ODA as resource transfers to developing countries and multilateral institutions from donor countries which are: (1) provided by official agencies, including state and local governments, or by their executive agencies; (2) concessional (i.e., grants and soft loans) and administered with the promotion of the economic development and welfare of developing countries as the main objective. Concessionality of loans is now calculated according to a new system of 'grant equivalents' introduced in 2019. Negotiations remain ongoing on the appropriate measurement of private sector instruments which include some of the forms of blended finance and derisking instruments used to catalyse SDI markets, but most private sector development activities by donor countries can be recorded as ODA if they meet the established criteria.

[40] Caio (2018), p 3.

[41] Park (2018a), p 254.

[42] UN (2021), pp 59–71.

level risk'.[43] Policy, regulatory and financial interventions have therefore been used to: (1) create pipelines of 'investible' projects for SDI markets, including through the securitisation and pooling of SDG debt; utilisation of 'risk-sharing' instruments, such as joint issuances, guarantees and first-loss capital in labelled bonds; and provision of technical assistance and project preparation support; and (2) support the establishment of 'mainstream SDG investment' markets through, *inter alia*, the development of regulatory standards and audit mechanisms at national and international levels, including the development of ESG benchmarks and taxonomies for SDI bond issuances.[44]

Examples of IFI and MDB-backed capital market interventions include the issuance of a social bond by Ecuador in March 2020, backed by a partial credit guarantee from the Inter-American Bank (IDB), with proceeds to be allocated to addressing the country's housing deficit,[45] and a privately placed blue bond issued by the Seychelles to finance sustainable marine and fisheries projects that is partially guaranteed by the IBRD and supported by a concessional loan from the Global Environmental Facility (GEF) that covers part of the interest payments for the bond.[46]

The IFC has also actively supported the development of local capital markets through collaborative financing mechanisms, such as the Amundi Planet Emerging One (EGO) green bond fund that combines risk-adjusted green bond investments with capacity and market- building activities funded by the Green Bond Technical Assistance Programme (GB-TAP).[47] The latter is a donor-funded initiative aimed at providing technical assistance and capacity-building initiatives to develop green bond markets, including developing ESG 'indicators and tools for emerging market issuers of bonds and other products'.[48] In Ghana, the GB-TAP is supporting the Securities and Exchange Commission (SEC) in the development of guidelines for issuers and investors of green bonds in Ghana.[49]

As discussed in Sect. 2.1, at the heart of these initiatives is the creation and establishment of markets for sustainable development and other public interest investments. This is leading to the transformation of official development agencies from *funders* of social and economic development and ecological sustainability to *brokers* of financing for these global public goods and services. IFIs, MDBs and other donors have increasingly conditioned public financing on 'regulatory, policy and governance-related reforms in the context of private sector engagement'.[50] This approach to development policy is encapsulated in the World Bank's 'Maximising Finance for Development' or 'Cascade' approach which sees the Bank stepping in to provide public loans or guarantees for development projects only as a last resort

---

[43] Amacker and Donovan (2021), p 19.

[44] Ibid.; UN and UNEP (2019), p 10.

[45] Environmental Finance (2020).

[46] World Bank (2018b).

[47] IFC (undated).

[48] Ibid.

[49] IFC (2021).

[50] UNCTAD (2019a), p 75.

after regulatory and policy reforms and the deployment of financial incentives have not leveraged the necessary commercial finance for these projects.[51]

Additionally, non-financial development agencies are also progressively reorienting their roles away from direct development operations towards facilitating private finance in SDG sectors. For, example in 2021, the UN Development Programme (UNDP), in collaboration with the UN-sponsored Global Investors for Sustainable Development (GISD) Alliance, launched the SDG Investor Platform as a means of providing private investors with country-level information to scale up sustainable development investments. UNDP country offices will be utilised to 'lead research and preparation of market intelligence for private sector investors to translate country level SDG gaps and priorities into private sector investment opportunities' and to convene '[p]ublic–private policy dialogues [...] to identify recommendations to improve the enabling environment for SDG aligned investments'.[52]

3 Governing Markets for Sustainable Development

The reliance of low and middle-income countries on external finance renders them vulnerable to shifts in global economic conditions but also to changes in the international law and policy governing the global economy, including law and policy relating to the distribution and allocation of global capital and financial resources. International development policy, practice and governance have long been influential in shaping the economic development trajectories and social and political organisations of developing countries in the Global South,[53] with attendant law reform and regulatory interventions that accompany countries' receipt of external finance and participation in cross-border economic activity acting as significant drivers in reconstituting domestic regulatory regimes and countries' engagement with the exterior.[54]

Cumulatively, the reorientation towards private financing for sustainable development represents a progressive privatisation of international development finance that can lead to what Karwowski has called the 'financialization of the state'.[55] Defined broadly, the process of privatisation involves the transfer of assets or functions, in whole or in part, from the public or official sector to the private or non-state sector, involving 'the increased reliance on private actors and market forces to pursue social goals'.[56] Meanwhile, state financialisation can be described as 'the increasing influence of financial logics, instruments, markets and accumulation strategies in state activities', including in the design of fiscal and monetary policies.[57] These twin processes of privatisation and financialisation can reconstitute, and have reconstituted, the modalities and governance at the market, state and transnational levels, with

---

[51] Alexander (2017); World Bank (2017), p 2.

[52] UNDP (2021), p 3.

[53] Craig and Porter (2006); Pahuja (2011); Tan (2011).

[54] Ibid. See also Anghie (1999) and Swablowski (2007).

[55] Karwowski (2019), p 1001.

[56] Feigenbaum and Henig (1994), pp 185–186.

[57] Karwowski (2019), p 1002.

significant implications for public accountability and scrutiny and for the legal and regulatory oversight of government and private entities involved in the mobilisation, disbursement and delivery of sustainable development finance.

3.1 Displaced Engagement and Ownership

First, the movement away from public resources for financing to leveraging financial markets for development finance is changing the role and function of the state in developing countries, particularly in its revenue-generation and resource-distribution roles. There are concerns that many under-resourced and capacity-constrained developing countries will struggle with the legal and regulatory transition to these new private modalities of finance with adequate public interest safeguards.

Moreover, as financial markets constitute an ever-increasing share of resources available for essential services, social provision and environmental sustainability, they will also increasingly serve as quasi-regulatory tools for access to and use of such global public goods, structuring the terms and conditions on which resources are allocated and utilised. These terms, as Davis has observed in relation to development finance more generally, are important in determining the impact of development finance as they 'define the balance that has been struck between the potentially conflicting interests of the various actors implicated in the transaction, namely, financiers, intermediaries, ultimate recipients of funds and other residents of developing countries'.[58]

Scholars of privatisation and financialisation of public services have long cautioned that shifting the responsibilities from the government to the market for the financing and provision of public goods and services fundamentally alters the process and outcomes of distributive contests within states and communities as well as the underlying regulatory and administrative architecture governing fiscal and monetary policy and the provision of domestic and global public goods and services. As Karwowski argues, 'how public revenue is raised directly impacts on how public expenditure is shaped and welfare policies designed', resulting in a 'democratic deficit' that undermines oversight and scrutiny over decisions taken in relation to the mobilisation and deployment of public finance and relatedly, in the context of financial markets, potential contracting of sovereign debt or other contingent liabilities on the state.[59]

The turn to financial markets for sustainable development finance can and does displace national ownership of and participation in social and economic policymaking, including SDG sectors. Decisions on which sectors to prioritise in fiscal decision-making will increasingly be determined not by public institutions or elected representatives or communities but by institutional investors, asset managers and, increasingly, index providers, credit rating agencies, and financial actors and private investors based in advanced economies. As scholars and observers have noted, debt-based financing for sustainability and social provision is a double-edged sword.

---

[58] Davis (2009), p 172.

[59] Karwowski (2019), p 1014.

While it can offer financial, legal and regulatory tools to influence corporate and sovereign conduct vis-à-vis meeting SDG and other global public objectives, it can also constrain the exercise of state authority over external finance and limit public and community engagement in the prioritisation of public finance and design of social, economic and environmental policies and programmes.[60] These new modalities of finance not only 'transfer resources from public to private investors', they also 'remove social provision from democratic decisions and scrutiny into the realm of financial markets'.[61]

The United Nations Conference on Trade and Development (UNCTAD) has warned that the SDG financing agenda as oriented towards private investments can subordinate countries' 'ownership of development policy' to the interests and priorities of private actors, particularly those based in OECD countries that have been heavily influential in reshaping the aid architecture and prioritising private finance for development.[62] It argues that the more SDG investments are channelled through private actors, the more these investment projects and programmes are 'disconnected from country development plans' as DFIs, the main intermediaries between private finance and SDG investments on the ground, often bypass state agencies to contract directly with the private sector in the host state.[63]

At the same time, the segmentation and earmarking of income derived through SDI arising from the contractual provisions of labelled bonds, notably the use of proceeds and project evaluation, selection requirements and attendant reporting criteria,[64] can place constraints on governments' ability to manage public finance as well as to respond to domestic financing needs and meet community demands for investment in specific SDG sectors that may not necessarily fall into earmarked funds from labelled bond issuances. In addition to donor-driven policy and regulatory reforms, private governance regimes regulating sustainable finance markets can also exercise significant leverage over developing country governments and can undermine rather than complement or strengthen domestic SDG-related policymaking.

Most of the policy and regulatory guidance for the establishment of SDI markets has emerged from public and private commercial or non-profit entities based in OECD and other major capital-exporting states. Labelled bond markets and the market for impact investments are governed primarily by 'a constellation of quasi-regulatory standards, procedures, and institutions' that are loosely based on private corporate social responsibility (CSR) regimes and ESG frameworks developed by

---

[60] Karwowski (2020); Park (2018a); Park SK (2019); Roy et al. (2018); Tan (2019); Tan (2021).

[61] Roy et al. (2018).

[62] UNCTAD (2019a), pp 65–78.

[63] Ibid., pp 86–87.

[64] Use of proceeds and project evaluation and selection criteria are deployed by the issuer of labelled bonds to disclose where and how funds raised would be deployed, and they must conform with the overall criteria or taxonomies established by standard-setting bodies such as the ICMA, while reporting criteria require issuers to report regularly on the use of these funds. See Mathew (2018); Park (2018b), pp 12–14. A robust earmarking exercise would involve 'integration of the solicitation of financing, the sale of the financial instrument, the selection of the project, and the allocation of funds into a sub-account or a sub-portfolio prior to disbursement'. See Park (2018b), p 12.

public and private entities in advanced market economies.[65] This can lead to what Soederberg has termed the 'new conditionality' or the ways in which market indices and non-financial benchmarking that are used to guide socially responsible investing can reproduce or exacerbate the dynamics of power inherent in traditional donor-recipient relationships.[66]

The rapidly growing interest in sustainable and socially responsible investing has led to a proliferation of ESG data and service providers that remain, for the most part, dominated by private providers or industry associations and unregulated by the public sphere.[67] The benchmarks, indicators and taxonomies used to develop SDG sectors into asset classes for sustainable development investments (see Sect. 2.2) act not only as 'market-building' devices[68] but also as market-screening or gatekeeping tools that can paradoxically exclude and constrain access of countries and communities to external capital.[69]

Indicators and benchmarks can therefore act as technologies of governance and regulation[70] in the SDI market, changing decision-making processes 'by altering the forms of knowledge that are relied upon by decision-makers'.[71] Indicators can serve as 'norm-vessels that transport social and environmental "value" into commercial investing' and 'creating new forms of knowledge' to inform investors' decision-making about what is an 'investible' social or environmental product.[72] Accordingly, private bodies and industry associations active in the construction of SDI markets, such as the ICMA, the Sustainable Accounting Standards Board (SASB), Impact Reporting and Investment Standards (IRIS), and the Global Impact Investing Rating System (GIIRS), can and do exert enormous influence over where capital is deployed and into which sectors in developing countries.

Private regulatory authority in the SDI market is also exercised by financial indices that track the performance of green, social and sustainability bonds, a form of 'informational regulation' that relies on corporate and sovereign issuers responding to signals produced by the aforementioned ESG rankings or ratings and adapting corporate or sovereign behaviour accordingly.[73] Like ESG data providers, there has also been a proliferation of ESG-titled indices, including from major index providers such as MSCI, S&P and FTSE Russell.[74] Indices as gatekeepers to capital 'are reputational intermediaries' between issuers and investors and their 'prescriptive

---

[65] Park (2018b), p 17; see also Dadush (2015), pp 172–184; Gabor (2021), pp 12–18; Tan (2021), pp 12–15.

[66] Soederberg (2007a, b).

[67] Boitreaud et al. (2020), p 21.

[68] Dadush (2012), p 394.

[69] Ibid.; Dadush (2015); Tan (2021).

[70] For examples of the extensive literature on this, see Broome and Quirk (2015); Davis et al. (2012). For a detailed discussion on their application in the SDI market and other forms of private finance for development, see Tan (2021).

[71] Dadush (2012), p 425.

[72] Ibid.

[73] Park (2018b), p 26.

[74] Boitreaud et al. (2020), p 18; ICMA (2018).

authority' is based on the threat of removal of non-compliant securities from an index.[75] These indices have become increasingly influential in global capital allocation in the movement from active to passive funds as decision-making about where to invest in the latter is delegated to indices that can 'de facto steer capital' through inclusion or exclusion of firms and countries that can cause large quasi-automatic capital inflows or outflows from countries.[76]

The displacement of government decision-making and oversight in public revenue raising and public expenditure management resulting from the shift from official to private sector financing, including the diversion of ODA and other official development finance towards leveraging private finance instead of direct funding of SDG needs, is contrary to long-standing commitments underpinning international development cooperation. National ownership of and inclusive participation in social and economic development policymaking have been key principles underpinning international development cooperation and enshrined in numerous agreements, including the Paris Declaration on Aid Effectiveness, the Accra Agenda for Action and the Addis Ababa Action Agenda.[77] It is difficult to see how a dispersed framework for financing sustainable development that is primarily dominated by the interests of OECD and other major 'donor' states and operationalised chiefly through private governance regimes outside the oversight of financier and recipient governments meets the development cooperation commitments established by the international community.

3.2 Outsourced Oversight and Accountability

A key feature in the shift towards private finance in sustainable development is the proliferation of private commercial and non-profit actors in the arenas where international development cooperation is negotiated, implemented and regulated. Private entities, including investors, corporate firms, non-profit organisations and industry associations, are becoming central to this hybrid development finance landscape, playing critical roles as financiers, service providers, regulators and decision-makers. This rapid diversification of actors in the sphere of development finance (see Fig. 1 for an example) and the fragmentation of financial sources, facilities and institutions are complicating domestic and international oversight and accountability of development finance and raises significant questions about the capacity of current legal and regulatory frameworks to govern this new regime and new non-state actors in development finance policy and practice.

The privatisation and financialisation of development finance exacerbate the already highly fragmented regulatory architecture of international development cooperation that is characterised by a diversity rather than unity of substantive and

---

[75] Ibid.

[76] Petry et al. (2021), p 154.

[77] See UN (2015), para. 127. See also UN (2015), para. 58; OECD (2005); OECD (2008). The AAAA specifically recognises 'the importance of national ownership of the post-2015 development agenda' and commits to aligning 'activities with national priorities' and 'reducing fragmentation' as well as promoting 'country ownership' in international development finance cooperation and policymaking.

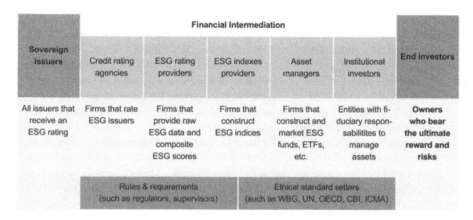

Fig. 1 The structure of the ESG financial ecosphere. Source: Boitreaud et al. (2020)

procedural rules and procedures and overlapping jurisdiction, parallel competences and differing levels of enforceability of rights and obligations.[78] This not only creates significant operational burdens in recipient countries, particularly countries with weak administrative capacities (see Sect. 3.1), but also disperses attempts at securing accountability for the practice and outcomes of development finance, including monitoring of decision-making processes, transparency over financial disbursements and procurement of goods and services, and oversight over the implementation of development policies and projects.

Several concerns arise here vis-à-vis accountability of SDG finance delivered through financial markets. First, this reorientation has not been matched by robust measures to map, track and account for financial flows to countries in support of SDG and other global public goods. While there remain weaknesses in the current system of aid accounting, civil society pressure over the past few decades has ensured that there is now greater transparency of official resource flows to developing countries and the terms and conditions accompanying such flows with some measure of harmonisation across different official financiers, especially IFIs and MDBs. Major MDBs, such as the World Bank and regional development banks, have access to information policies that make most information on projects and programmes funded through loans and grants publicly available.[79] OECD member states also provide relatively robust annual reporting of ODA and other official flows (OOF) to the OECD Development Assistance Committee (DAC).

In many cases, disclosure of information by external development financiers constitutes an important part of domestic accountability in developing countries, enabling access to financial and economic policymaking that will not otherwise have been made available through domestic channels. Thus, there is a concern that the dispersal of financing will disperse information about financial flows and dilute access to information and therefore oversight of executive fiscal decision-making

---

[78] Tan (2019), pp 311–322.

[79] See, for example, Asian Development Bank (2018); IBRD and IDA (2015).

within countries due to a combination of weak capacity and, occasionally, deliberate obfuscation. In recent years, there have been concerns about the transparency of private sovereign debt contracts and the impact of so-called 'hidden debts' on the debt sustainability of countries, particularly low-income and highly indebted states. For example, Mozambique remains embroiled in a series of litigation over previously undisclosed US$2 billion worth of private bank loans and bonds contracted by state-owned companies without the approval of the Mozambique parliament and backed by hidden government guarantees.[80]

Transparency concerns also arise because private sector investments, even when routed through official development finance institutions such as DFIs and public–private facilities or multi-stakeholder partnerships (MSPs), are subjected to weaker transparency and information disclosure regimes than their counterparts.[81] Most DFIs, which on-lend proceeds from SDI bond issuances or injection of capital from governments to the private sector, are not subjected to the same standards of public disclosures and are 'not obliged to share information with local authorities'.[82] The IFC's Access to Information Policy, for example, excludes the release of 'commercially sensitive and confidential information' which includes 'financial, business, proprietary or other non-public information about its clients, its member countries or third parties'.[83] The IFC argues that as a financial service provider to the private sector, it will be 'contrary to the legitimate expectations' of their private sector clients to disclose such information for 'fear of compromising their projects or other proprietary information in a highly competitive marketplace'.[84]

Lack of disclosure also makes it difficult for communities affected by development projects and programmes financed by DFIs and their intermediaries to obtain accurate information about ESG risks and options for recourse to mitigate or remedy harms arising from these projects. A study by development finance watchdog Publish What You Fund found that while most DFIs have broadly transparent and well-developed ESG disclosure policies, there were significant shortcomings in policy implementation, particularly in the disclosure of ESG risks to affected communities.[85] In other words, even where DFIs have relatively good disclosure policies at the global level (for example, through websites and institutional mechanisms), there is limited evidence that this information reaches project-affected communities, which can hamper access to local accountability.[86]

Current operational practice of DFIs demonstrates the problems with the use of '[d]isclosure-based mechanisms', such as the aforementioned 'reporting frameworks, labeling, and ranking/awards' as a means of 'informational regulation' of SDI markets.[87] Aside from the lack of standardisation in ESG frameworks, leading

---

[80] Spotlight on Corruption (undated).

[81] Romero (2014); Vervynckt (2015).

[82] UNCTAD (2019a), p 93.

[83] IFC (2012), para. 11(a).

[84] Ibid.

[85] Publish What You Fund (2021), p 3.

[86] Ibid., p 34.

[87] Park (2018b), p 26.

to what has been called the '"alphabet soup" of acronym-heavy measurement and reporting standards',[88] there is a question mark over the efficacy of such standards and codes in preventing 'greenwashing' or 'SDG-washing' in financial market lending as investors have little legal recourse for non-compliance with use of proceeds or management of proceeds provisions. Unlike sustainability-linked loans from banks, there is no contractual provision to penalise issuers for failure to comply with green or social obligations. For example, the provision to apply green bond proceeds to green projects 'is not generally a contractual obligation' unlike green loan obligations, so investors of green bonds have limited options if green bond issuances do not meet declared investment objectives.[89]

There are also deeper systemic problems with the current disclosure regime. SDI markets are currently primarily regulated by industry-led private governance regimes, which significantly increases the risk of regulatory capture by private interest groups.[90] Stakeholders, including governments and communities, remain 'passive beneficiaries' of the standards and audit regimes established by investors and other market actors.[91] Specifically, the labelling of public and collective social and sustainability services as 'market opportunities' leads to a 'boundary shift' that 'profoundly alters the character of a service' and transforms communities and the environment into commodities.[92] Thus, accompanying the 'inevitably complex contract arrangements' of these new innovative financialised schemes for sustainable development is the transformation of policy accountability frameworks, 'with governance and reporting systems geared toward the needs of private funders rather than elected officials'.[93]

For many developing countries, this form of privatisation and exercise of private authority over public policymaking and service delivery exacerbates the loss of policy autonomy discussed in Sect. 3.1. For individuals and communities, this shift 'potentially alters the institutional framework through which citizens normally articulate, mediate, and promote their individual and shared interests', with the impact of this 'institutional restructuring' falling differentially across different constituencies.[94] In these countries, the provision of services is often the main process in which citizens and residents encounter the state, and the removal of the state from the financing and delivery of public services can have detrimental effects on the democratic and participatory policymaking that also constitute important commitments under the UN SDGs, AAA and other international agreements on development cooperation.

The primary focus of the private regime governing SDI markets has been on disclosure, reporting, certification and ratings and rankings, mainly to meet the financial and regulatory due diligence requirements of investors. What has been

---

[88] Murray (2021).

[89] Mathew (2018), pp 312–313.

[90] Park (2018b), pp 30–32; Gabor (2021), pp 15–17.

[91] Park (2018a), pp 250–251.

[92] Roy et al. (2018).

[93] Ibid.

[94] Feigenbaum and Henig (1994), p 186.

overlooked is the responsibility of investors for harms caused by projects and programmes funded by their investments. A 'remedy gap'[95] already exists within the traditional financial services sector where banks and other financial institutions may sit one step removed from project operations that may lead to displacement, social or environmental harms to local communities. This gap has been increasingly closing over the years, driven mainly by MDBs and DFIs promoting and operationalising ex ante ESG assessments as well as ex post accountability processes, including the promotion and establishment of institutional and project-level grievance mechanisms and independent accountability mechanisms (IAMs).[96]

While not without their limitations, the accountability mechanisms of MDBs and DFIs have become standard bearers in the financial industry, providing an important normative and procedural framework governing the financing of development projects and programmes and enabling a regime through which grievances against development actors can be evaluated and investigated and some form of redress can be obtained.[97] Once again, here, the World Bank Group has been at the forefront of developing environmental and social safeguards and establishing mechanisms, such as the Grievance Redress Service (GRS) and Inspection Panel at the IBRD and IDA and the Compliance Advisor Ombudsman (CAO) at the IFC,[98] which have been adopted by other MDBs and DFIs. However, the movement away from bank-based finance towards diversified and dispersed SDI market-based finance extends the chain of responsibility for harms, and fragments potential avenues of remedy for communities harmed by a project or programme ostensibly financed through a green, social and sustainability bond.

SDI securities mostly mimic 'plain vanilla' securities (see Sect. 4.1) and there is no recourse to the investor if individuals or communities are harmed in a project or programme funded through such means. Additionally, while external 'impact' measurement and third-party assurance providers can capture some negative externalities in their review of an SDI bond issuance framework which can lead to loss of investor confidence or interest in the bond, there is little redress for communities that have been harmed to seek mitigation or remedies for social and environmental harm and little recourse to the investors despite such securities being designated specifically as sustainable development investments. Accordingly, aside from screening or divesture, SDI bondholders have limited leverage over operational ESG practices of funded entities.

Meanwhile, the overwhelming focus of development agencies on SDI market-building and de-risking private capital has paradoxically marginalised concerns about ESG risks of funded projects to communities. This regulatory architecture addresses less the 'risk-to-people' than it does the 'risk-to-corporation'[99] while

---

[95] Kovick (2018).

[96] Ibid.; Park S (2019).

[97] Bradlow (2010); Park S (2019).

[98] See the GRS website: https://www.worldbank.org/en/projects-operations/products-and-services/grievance-redress-service; the Inspection Panel website: https://www.inspectionpanel.org/ and the CAO website: http://www.cao-ombudsman.org/ (all accessed 27 May 2021).

[99] Shamir and Weiss (2012), p 129.

decentring communities from the processes of social investment and economic transformations that are purportedly aimed at improving their lives. The expectation that ESG risks in securities markets will be mitigated and addressed through traditional CSR practices, such as social audit regimes, has not been borne out by past experience. Studies of CSR audit regimes have found that while such frameworks may lead to incremental advances in addressing CSR concerns, such as labour, health and safety standards, in supply chains, the audit regime is designed more to minimise reputational risks to investors and enhance corporate legitimacy than to intervene in or resolve harmful practices.[100] Further, there are concerns that audit regimes can actually harm communities by failing to carry out accurate and responsible audits, leading to the continuation or exacerbation of social (and environmental) externalities of corporate behaviour.[101]

4 Regulatory Gaps and Market Failures

The shift to financial markets as an alternative to official sector funding for sustainable development must be located within a broader framework of the international financial architecture and the legal and regulatory framework which governs it. The privatisation and financialisation of development finance deepen countries' exposure to international capital markets, increasing their porousness to shifting global financial conditions and the policy and regulatory responses to such developments by systematically important countries and international financial actors and networks. This has the potential of generating financial and regulatory risks not only for domestic financial sectors but also for the international financial system more generally, and can impede the resolution of financial and sovereign debt crises if and when they occur.

4.1 Transmission Nodes for Financial Instability

The development and use of novel financial instruments to create and develop SDI markets can create new transmission channels for financial instability that can have adverse consequences both for the sustainability of individual financial interventions and for the broader financial and economic health of states in receipt of such financing. Despite the role played by the unregulated growth of innovative financial engineering, including derivatives and complex securitisation structures, in the build-up to the global financial crisis of 2007–08,[102] there remains an under-appreciation of the financial risks posed by reliance on and proliferation of such financial instruments. This is especially pronounced when accompanied by the liberalisation and deregulation of domestic financial sectors that has been either a feature of structural and sectoral conditionalities attached to development finance or a result of

---

[100] LeBaron et al. (2017).

[101] De Lacey (2021).

[102] UNCTAD (2019b), p 75.

commitments under the World Trade Organisation's (WTO) General Agreement on Trade in Services (GATS) or under bilateral or regional free trade agreements (FTAs) or investment treaties.[103]

Developing countries are particularly vulnerable to the volatility in international financial markets due their relatively weak structural positions in the global economy as well as their lack of control over the fiscal and monetary policies in advanced economies and the marginalisation from the sites of decision-making in the international financial architecture.[104] Even before the onset of the global COVID-19 pandemic, developing counties, especially emerging markets, witnessed heightened instability in cross-border capital transactions concomitant with their increased integration into global financial markets. Portfolio flows, cross-border bank loans and other debt instruments were and have remained particularly volatile for developing countries due their ease of cross-border entry and exit facilitated by the aforementioned liberalisation of capital account and foreign investment regimes in developing countries.[105]

The vulnerability of developing countries to the volatility of capital flows was demonstrated by the massive and sudden outflows of capital from developing and emerging economies (DEEs) at the start of the global pandemic in the first half of 2020 when almost US\$103 billion was withdrawn from DEEs between mid-January and mid-May 2020.[106] At the same time, the costs of servicing foreign-currency denominated debt have increased significantly as the cost of borrowing has soared for DEEs and investors look to shelter from the crisis in the 'safe asset' markets and higher yields of advanced economies.[107] Developing countries' experience with the behaviour of financial markets during the COVID-19 crisis mirrors past experience with financial crises and exemplifies the hierarchical and asymmetrical nature of the international financial architecture and the procyclicality of financial markets.[108]

Additionally, in efforts to create an enabling environment for private investments in developing countries, official sector financiers can and do accelerate their loss of policy and regulatory autonomy. The development of novel financial innovations, such as securitisation, which are increasing the availability of credit by 'converting non-tradeable financial assets into tradeable securities, transforming liability risks into financial instruments and diversifying individual creditor risks' to create SDI markets can lead to short-term speculation and domination of foreign financial actors in domestic markets that render countries 'more vulnerable to the vagaries of international financial markets' and subservient to private financial entities than ever before.[109] This is leading to 'a profound loss of control by developing country

---

[103] Akyüz (2018), p 85.

[104] UNCTAD (2019b), p 35.

[105] Akyüz (2018); UN (2021), p 132.

[106] OECD (2020).

[107] Patricio Ferreira Lima (2020).

[108] Ibid.

[109] UNCTAD (2019b), pp 75–76.

governments over the pace and direction of credit creation in their own economies' and accentuating their exposure to volatile and unpredictable short-term capital.[110]

There is no evidence that the private ordering regimes governing the SDI market can or will overcome these structural deficits within the international financial system. Instead, the drive towards greater integration of developing countries into international capital markets, in terms of both contracting foreign currency debt by sovereign and corporate labelled bond issuances in external financial markets and the liberalisation of domestic capital markets to foreign investors, will continue to render countries vulnerable to global financial instability. Consequently, there are significant concerns that the exponential rise in the interest in and issuance of labelled bonds and other SDI securities is leading to an 'ESG bubble'[111] that can have significant financial and regulatory ramifications as well as harmful consequences for communities reliant on these instruments to fund social, economic and environmental goods and services.

The regulatory design of SDI markets which mimics conventional capital market regulation, discussed in Sect. 3.2, is unlikely to insulate developing countries from this vulnerability as these frameworks are designed to protect the interests of investors rather than those of the host states of SDI markets and 'investment-affected' communities, considered as 'distant secondary beneficiaries'.[112] Regulation of SDI markets is 'primarily shaped by the very same market participants that sell, buy, trade or assess these financial instruments',[113] which has consequently resulted in the phenomenon known as 'blueprinting' whereby new markets – such as SDI markets – are 'created based on a template that is set by an already-existing market, such as conventional finance'.[114] While this 'systemic mimicry' is often understood as a deliberate exercise to incentivise investment 'through the strategic use of language, institutions, and metrics that are familiar to investors', there is a danger in converting tools made to measure and market conventional finance and apply them to social and sustainable finance.[115]

Aside from the potential for greenwashing and SDG-washing discussed in Sect. 3.2, 'blueprinting' conventional securities regulation for the SDI market can transfer the same regulatory deficits of these regimes to the SDI market, including oversight of third-party ESG assurance providers or labelled bond verifiers that are playing key roles in the allocation of ESG capital. Concerns have been raised about the governance and supervision of such ESG service providers that mirror the operations of credit rating agencies (CRAs), the failings of which have been widely attributed as contributing to the global financial crisis in 2007–08.[116] Like CRAs, ESG data providers exert enormous influence over financial markets as their ratings provide investors with qualitative information to guide investment decisions, but

---

[110] Ibid., p 76.

[111] Dillain (2020).

[112] Dadush (2015), pp 191–192.

[113] Park (2018a, b), p 6.

[114] Dadush (2015), p 173; Park (2018a), pp 240–241.

[115] Dadush (2015), pp 173–178.

[116] Banahan (2019), pp 849–850; Rose (2019).

unlike CRAs, ESG data providers are not publicly regulated.[117] This lack of regulatory oversight can lead to poor quality certifications and inflated ratings of the kind that contributed towards the previous financial crises.[118]

Moreover, while SDG-labelled securities, such as green, social or sustainability bonds, are targeted at financing specific SDG or ESG sovereign or corporate expenditure, there is no provision which prevents investors from divesture due to financial considerations, even if such divestiture, particularly for large institutional investors, would mean ramifications for the beneficiary communities. Conversely, due to the regulatory expectations of asset managers and institutional investors and the role of credit ratings and financial indices in downgrading the investment ratings of sovereign and corporate debt in DEEs during times of crisis, divesture is often a measure that is imposed on investors by the regulatory authorities of their home jurisdiction. This short-term focus of financial market investors and the absence of contractual or regulatory mechanisms to mitigate these structural deficits and the cyclical nature of portfolio flows in the SDI markets are why the rush to replace direct, official sector financing of sustainable development with private capital may result in financial contagion that can jeopardise the attainment of SDGs themselves.

4.2 Private Finance, Public Debt

Reliance on financial markets as a source of sustainable development finance can lead, and has led, to an accumulation of unsustainable debt in developing countries, exacerbating the systemic vulnerabilities of developing countries in the global economy. While having the potential to scale up resources, experience has demonstrated that private finance also has the potential for ratcheting up the external debt burdens of developing countries and complicating arrangements for sovereign debt crisis management and resolution. Private sector debt held by developing countries as a share of total sovereign debt had already almost doubled between 2000 and 2019 with corresponding rising debt servicing costs,[119] and the turn to SDI markets will only contribute to this increased risk profile.

First, bond finance has been considered the 'most volatile component' of public debt due to the 'strong speculative features of international financial markets' as well as the terms of such financing which are more onerous than official sector finance with shorter maturities, higher and more variable interest rates and easier exit terms.[120] As labelled SDI bonds follow structures and investment trajectories similar to those of traditional securities, they are likely to follow a similar profile, enabling such bonds to be traded with ease on primary and secondary markets.

Second, while the turn to private finance can shift debt off government balance sheets and the creation of domestic financial markets can reduce countries' exposure to foreign currency-denominated debt, high levels of private debt can be of

---

[117] Boitreaud et al. (2020), p 21.

[118] Banahan (2019), pp 849–850; Rose (2019), pp 75–76.

[119] UNCTAD (2020), pp 114–115.

[120] Ibid.; Akyüz (2018); Gelpern (2018).

significant concern as 'they represent a large contingent liability on public sector finance'.[121] These contingent liabilities can be *express*, such as government guarantees, or *implicit* when widespread private sector indebtedness in a financial crisis is socialised or converted into sovereign liabilities as occurred in previous sovereign debt crises.[122] This means that the financial and regulatory incentives discussed in Sect. 3.2 that are promoted by international development agencies as levers to catalyse SDG resources from the private sector may in turn generate additional liabilities and risk of debt build-up for developing countries in the longer term.

Third, the diversification of the creditor base will compound the international process for intervening in and resolving financial and sovereign debt crises that currently relies on the loose coordination of informal and voluntary negotiations between the sovereign debtor and its creditors.[123] In the absence of a formal sovereign insolvency process, the introduction of new creditors and new debt instruments into a sovereign debt landscape is likely to complicate efforts to restructure sovereign debt. Unlike official sector debt, which is easier to restructure through channels such as the Paris Club, the introduction of a broad base of private creditors can lead to more disorderly debt restructuring in the event of a sovereign debt crisis, prolonging debt distress in affected countries and undermining social provision and jeopardising climate transitions.[124] Thus, transitioning developing countries from official financing to commercial markets can impose significantly new and more onerous legal obligations on already struggling governments, as noted in Sect. 3.1.

Negotiations with private creditors, particularly bondholders, in the event of a sovereign debt crisis have historically been challenging and fraught given the absence of a standardised procedure to deal with such debt. As discussed, aside from provisions relating to the use of proceeds and meeting key performance indicators and monitoring requirements in market guidance such as the GBP or SBP, there are no specific contractual provisions that distinguish labelled bonds from ordinary sovereign or corporate bonds. SDI securities will therefore be subjected to the same treatment as other securities in a solvency crisis. Most notably, despite the importance of the sectors they purport to finance, including essential services such as health, education, water and energy infrastructure, there are no provisions to ensure that investors must enter into negotiations to restructure such debt in situations of unsustainable debt burdens in host states.

Once again, the COVID-19 pandemic has starkly demonstrated the perils of the shift from official financing to commercial financing for many low and middle-income countries. International organisations have warned of an impending global sovereign debt crisis as rising financing costs and erratic growth threaten already fragile debt positions of many DEEs, with many emerging economies servicing considerably higher interest rates than advanced economies, despite less borrowing on international financial markets.[125] Many countries have also headed off immediate

---

[121] UNCTAD (2020), p 113.

[122] Ibid.; Akyüz (2018), pp 12–15; Gelpern (2018), pp 329–330.

[123] Gelpern (2018).

[124] Ibid.

[125] Wheatley (2021).

debt crises by borrowing heavily from official financiers, notably the International Monetary Fund (IMF), and accessed concessional debt relief facilities, such as the IMF's Catastrophe Containment Relief Fund (CCRT) which writes off eligible IMF debt service for eligible countries.[126]

However, private creditors have so far failed to participate in multilaterally agreed debt relief measures and continued to profit from debt repayments, including from highly indebted states that are spending more in debt service repayments than on pandemic intervention and mitigation.[127] At time of writing, none of the private creditors of the 73 eligible countries have participated in the G20 Debt Service Suspension Initiative (DSSI) – which provides for a temporary moratorium on eligible debt service payments – or the G20 Common Framework for Debt Treatments – which provides for restructuring of eligible debt.[128] Many countries have also been reluctant to seek private sector debt relief due to the impact this would have on their credit ratings and subsequently on their future capacity to borrow on international capital markets, once again raising concerns about the operations of CRAs and other private regimes governing international financial markets.[129]

In response to the lack of private sector participation in pandemic debt relief measures, the Institute for International Finance (IIF) has reiterated calls for 'improving the sovereign debt restructuring process' through, *inter alia*, greater 'public–private sector dialogue' and more 'debt transparency' as well as the promotion of industry codes of conduct such as the G20 and OECD-endorsed Principles for Stable Capital Flows and Fair Debt Restructuring.[130] Importantly, despite not addressing concerns raised about the contribution of private finance to debt sustainability in developing countries, the IIF emphasises the salience of ESG investing as a source of 'sustainable capital flows' to these countries.[131] It highlights current efforts to 'build a blueprint for scaling global sustainable capital markets across asset classes', including labelled bonds, 'money market products, derivatives and insurance solutions' as well as 'SDFG-linked and sustainability-linked instruments' such as the novel 'nature performance bonds' that build on the so-called 'debt-for-nature' swap instruments and link sovereign debt relief with commitments to protect biodiversity in DEEs.[132]

While these new initiatives hold out promises to scale up financing for sustainable finance capital, like the other capital market instruments discussed in this paper, the broader concerns about the short and long-term impacts of these instruments within the broader framework of the global financial architecture and massive regulatory gaps which still exist will exacerbate rather than alleviate the financial and debt burdens of DEEs. The IIF proposals continue to rely on private governance regimes and the development of the aforementioned informational regulatory tools

---

[126] IMF (2021).

[127] Munevar (2021), p 4.

[128] Ibid.

[129] Ibid.

[130] Institute of International Finance (2021).

[131] Ibid.

[132] Ibid.; see further Finance for Biodiversity Initiative (2021).

to supervise the operations of the new actors and new markets for sustainable development investing while placing considerable responsibility for managing debt on the debtor state and official sector agencies.

5 Conclusion

Financial markets are being heralded as the panacea to the challenges faced by developing countries in securing resources for meeting the SDGs and other global public goods and sustainability targets. This turn to private finance in international development policy and practice has occurred in tandem with the increasing mainstreaming of ESG investing as financial markets are subjected to growing investor demand, policy and regulatory pressures, particularly in advanced economies, to pivot capital towards socially responsible and sustainable investments. Official sector financing has been routed away from direct funding of development projects and programmes towards brokering private capital for meeting sustainable development expenditure.

However, the development of SDI markets has not been matched by a corresponding development of regulatory mechanisms at domestic and international levels to mitigate the consequences of market failures in these sectors. The rapid integration of developing countries into global financial markets via SDI markets and international development policies encouraging them does not account for the specific vulnerabilities of these countries within the international financial system that remain unresolved despite several cycles of sovereign debt and financial crises over the past two decades. Instead, operating with pre-existing regulatory gaps in financial markets and relying on private governance regimes designed and dominated by advanced economies to govern these new forms of development finance can reinforce existing economic and geopolitical asymmetries between countries.

Moreover, the enmeshment of public and private finance will insert countries into global financial markets and engagements with commercial investors in a way that will bring public institutions into sharp contact with regulatory regimes commonly associated with commercial investments, capital markets and corporate activity. Entry into new financial markets will inevitably have implications for developing countries' broader international legal obligations in the longer term, concerns that are not ameliorated by current gaps in the architecture governing international financial markets and sovereign financing.

Instead, the privatisation of development finance is leading to greater privatisation of regulation where economic sectors, traditionally regulated by the state, will slowly be transferred to private governance regimes with knock-on impacts on civic accountability and transparency of public action. The 'creation of new legal regimes and practices and the expansion and renovation of some older forms' as a consequence of this shift to SDI markets can 'have the effect of replacing public regulation and law with private mechanisms, sometimes bypassing national legal systems'.[133] Further, as Picciotto has argued, the move towards 'private institutional

---

[133] Sassen (1999), p 412.

legal forms' under this new re-engineered landscape of states and markets in public finance and elsewhere has been shown to be 'ill-suited to managing the wider social responsibilities which decentred regulation requires them to accept'.[134]

Failure to account for these regulatory gaps will not only impact on the efficacy of SDI markets to deliver sustainable development objectives, but will paradoxically undermine efforts to do so, including by reinforcing pre-existing economic and geopolitical asymmetries between developing countries and industrialised economies and creating more platforms for wealth accumulation by northern-based private investors at the expense of global redistribution and collective financing of global public goods.

Acknowledgements This paper was originally presented at the International Conference on Sustainable Finance and Capital Markets, National University of Singapore (NUS), 16 April 2021. It is based on research that has been supported by the Institute for Global Sustainable Development (IGSD), University of Warwick, under the auspices of the New Frontiers in International Development Finance (NeF DeF) project. The author wishes to thank Iris Chiu, Lin, the anonymous reviewer and the participants at the conference for their comments and feedback on the paper. She would also like to thank Ivan Tan and Suzanne Habraken for editorial assistance. All errors and omissions remain her own.

References

Agence française de développement (AFD) (2020) Sustainable finance: success of AFD's first SDG bond issue for a total of 2 billion euros, 21 October 2020. https://www.afd.fr/en/actualites/communique-de-presse/sustainable-finance-success-afds-first-sdg-bond-issue-total-2-billion-euros. Accessed 9 May 2021

Akyüz Y (2018) Playing with fire: deepened financial integration and changing vulnerabilities of the Global South. Oxford University Press, Oxford

Alexander N (2017) The G20, the World Bank's 'cascade', and Trump: going to any length to 'crowd in' the private sector? 23 May 2017. Just Governance. https://www.Justgovernance.Boellblog.Org/2017/05/23/Beware-The-Cascade-World-Banck-To-The-Future. Accessed 1 May 2021

Amacker J, Donovan C (2021) Marathon or sprint? The race for green capital in emerging markets. Report by the Centre for Climate Finance and Investment, Imperial College Business School. https://www.imperialcollegelondon.app.box.com/s/ge9thj52rcehma4bwxyt0fchi3q2niv5. Accessed 9 May 2021

Anghie A (1999) Time present and time past: globalization, international financial institutions, and the Third World. N Y Univ J Int Law Polit 32(2):243–290

Asian Development Bank (ADB) (2018) Access to information policy. Institutional Document, September 2018, Manila

---

[134] Picciotto (2017), p 685.

Asian Infrastructure Investment Bank (AIIB) (2021) Sustainable Development Bond Framework, April 2021. https://www.aiib.org/en/news-events/news/2021/AIIB-Launches-Sustainable-Development-Bond-Framework.html. Accessed 15 May 2021

Babb S, Kentikelenis A (2021) Markets everywhere: the Washington consensus and the sociology of global institutional change. Annu Rev Sociol 47:521–541

Banahan CM (2019) The bond villains of green investment: why an unregulated securities market needs government to lay down the law. Vermont Law Rev 43(4):841–870

Bayliss K, Romero MJ (2021) 'Rebuilding better', but better for whom? A review of the WBG response to the Covid-19 crisis. Briefing Paper. European Network on Debt and Development (Eurodad). https://www.eurodad.org/rebuilding_better. Accessed 30 Apr 2021

Bayliss K, Van Waeyenberge E (2018) Unpacking the public private partnership revival. J Dev Stud 54(8):577–593

Bigger P, Webber S (2020) Green structural adjustment in the World Bank's resilient city. Annals Am Assoc Geograph 111(1):36–51

Blended Finance Innovators (2016) Improving impact: increasing blended finance to achieve the Sustainable Development Goals. Discussion draft. https://www.meda.org/investment-publications/286-improving-impact-increasing-blended-finance-to-achieve-the-sustainable-development-goals/file. Accessed 1 May 2021

Boitreaud S, Gratcheva EM, Gurhy B, Paladines C, Skarnulis A (2020) Riding the wave: navigating the ESG landscape for sovereign debt managers. Equitable growth, finance and institutions insight. World Bank, Washington, DC

Bradlow D (2010) International law and the operations of the international financial institutions. In: Bradlow D, Hunter D (eds) International financial institutions and international law. Kluwer Law International, Alphen aan den Rijn

Broome A, Quirk J (2015) Governing the world at a distance: the practice of global benchmarking. Rev Int Stud 41(5):819–841

Bruni J (2020) 'CAF sells first social bonds in euros', LatinFinance, 28 May 2020. https://www.latinfinance.com/daily-briefs/2020/5/28/caf-sells-first-social-bonds-in-euros. Accessed 15 May 2020

Caio C (2018) The enabling environment for private sector development: donor spending and links to other catalytic uses of aid. Development Initiatives, Discussion Paper. https://devinit.org/resources/enabling-environment-private-sector-development/. Accessed 8 Nov 2021

Climate Finance Leadership Initiative (CFLI) European Development Finance Institutions (EDFI) and Global Infrastructure Facility (GIF) (2020) Attracting private climate finance to merging markets. Consultation paper on private sector considerations for policymakers. https://www.edfi.eu/news/edfi-and-cfli/. Accessed 1 May 2021

Craig D, Porter D (2006) Development beyond neoliberalism? Governance, poverty reduction and political economy. Routledge, Abingdon and New York

Dadush S (2012) Impact investment indicators: a critical assessment. In: Davis K, Fisher A, Kingsbury B, Merry SE (eds) Governance by indicators: global power through quantification and rankings. Oxford University Press, Oxford

Dadush S (2015) Regulating social finance: can social stock exchanges meet the challenge? Univ Pa J Int Law 37(1):139–230

Davies PA et al. (2020) French Development Agency unveils new SDG bond framework. Latham and Watkins LLP. https://www.globalelr.com/2020/10/french-development-agency-unveils-new-sdg-bond-framework/. Accessed 9 May 2021

Davis K (2009) Financing development as a field of practice, study and innovation. Acta Juridica 2009:168–184

Davis K, Kingsbury B, Merry SE (2012) Indicators as a technology of global governance. Law Soc Rev 46(1):71–104

De Lacey C (2021) Who audits the auditor? Shaping legal accountability strategies to redress social audit failing. https://www.business-humanrights.org/en/blog/who-audits-the-auditor-shaping-legal-accountability-strategies-to-redress-social-audit-failings/. Accessed 27 May 2021

De Sousa Santos B (2002) Toward a new legal common sense: law, globalization, and emancipation. Cambridge University Press, Cambridge

Dillain J (2020) ESG investing looks like just another stock bubble. Bloomberg. https://www.bloomberg.com/opinion/articles/2020-10-05/esg-investing-looks-like-just-another-stock-bubble. Accessed 29 May 2021

Environmental Finance (2020) Social bond of the year, sovereign, and Award for innovation—bond structure (social): Republic of Ecuador. https://www.environmental-finance.com/content/awards/green-social-and-sustainability-bond-awards-2020/winners/social-bond-of-the-year-sovereign-and-award-for-innovation-bond-structure-(social)-republic-of-ecuador.html. Accessed 8 Nov 2021

Feigenbaum H, Henig J (1994) The political underpinnings of privatization: a typology. World Polit 46(2):185–208

Finance for Biodiversity Initiative (2021) Greening sovereign debt: building a nature and climate sovereign bond facility. https://www.f4b-initiative.net/publications-1/greening-sovereign-debt%3A-new-paper%3A-building-a-nature-and-climate-sovereign-bond-facility. Accessed 8 November

Gabor D (2021) The Wall Street Consensus, development and change. Early view. https://doi.org/10.1111/dech.12645. Accessed 8 Nov 2021

Gelpern A (2018) About government debt … Who knows? Cap Mark Law J 13(3):321–355

Global Investors for Sustainable Development (GISD) Alliance (undated) Definition of Sustainable Development Investing. https://www.gisdalliance.org/our-work/create-impact/sustainable-development-investing-sdi. Accessed 17 May 2021

Global Sustainable Investment Alliance (2018) 2018 Global sustainable investment review. http://www.gsi-alliance.org/wp-content/uploads/2019/06/GSIR_Review2018F.pdf. Accessed 22 June 2021

Halliday TC, Carruthers BG (2009) Bankrupt: global lawmaking and systemic financial crisis. Stanford University Press, Stanford

IBRD (2021) World Bank Sustainable Development Bond Framework. https://www.thedocs.worldbank.org/en/doc/43b360bfda1e6e5b8a094ef2ce4dff2a-0340012021/original/World-Bank-IBRD-Sustainable-Development-Bond-Framework.pdf. Accessed 9 May 2021

IBRD (undated) The World Bank Green Bond Process Implementation Guidelines. http://pubdocs.worldbank.org/en/217301525116707964/Green-Bond-Implementation-Guidelines.pdf. Accessed 9 May 2021

IBRD and IDA (2015) Bank policy: access to information. 1 July 2015. World Bank Group, Washington, DC. https://policies.worldbank.org/en/policies/all/ppfdetail/3693. Accessed 8 Nov 2021

ICMA (2018) GBP SBP Databases and Indices Working Group: Summary of green—social—sustainable fixed income indices providers. https://www.icmagroup.org/sustainable-finance/resource-centre. Accessed 9 May 2021

ICMA (2020) Guidance handbook. https://www.icmagroup.org/sustainable-finance/the-principles-guidelines-and-handbooks. Accessed 9 May 2021

IFC (2012) Access to information policy. https://www.ifc.org/wps/wcm/connect/topics_ext_content/ifc_external_corporate_site/sustainability-at-ifc/publications/publications_policy_aip. Accessed 24 May 2021

IFC (2018) IFC, Amundi successfully close world's largest green bond fund. https://pressroom.ifc.org/all/pages/PressDetail.aspx?ID=25980. Accessed 15 May 2021

IFC (2020a) Green Bond Factsheet. https://www.ifc.org/wps/wcm/connect/5520688c-c2e6-4198-bd4b-0d0cc5ec9d16/1_IFC_Factsheet_Green+Bonds_FY21_final.pdf?MOD=AJPERES&CVID=nvKCSv6. Accessed 9 May 2021

IFC (2020b) Social Factsheet. https://www.ifc.org/wps/wcm/connect/64504841-7171-4cac-a443-04e8895a79f4/2_IFC_Factsheet_Social+Bonds_FY21_final.pdf?MOD=AJPERES&CVID=nvKCTjQ. Accessed 9 May 2021

IFC (2021) 'IFC and Ghana's Securities and Exchange Commission to develop green bonds market', 5 May 2021. https://pressroom.ifc.org/all/pages/PressDetail.aspx?ID=26337. Accessed 16 May 2021

IFC (undated) Green Bond Technical Assistance Program: Global Public Goods. https://www.ifc.org/wps/wcm/connect/Industry_EXT_Content/IFC_External_Corporate_Site/Financial+Institutions/Priorities/Climate_Finance_SA/GB-TAP/. Accessed 15 May 2021

Institute of International Finance (2021) IIF Letter to the G20 on common framework, debt transparency. ESG considerations. https://www.iif.com/Publications/ID/4371/IIF-Letter-to-the-G20-on-Common-Framework-Debt-Transparency-ESG-Considerations. Accessed 31 May 2021

International Monetary Fund (IMF) (2021) Catastrophe Containment and Relief Trust, IMF Factsheet. https://www.imf.org/en/About/Factsheets/Sheets/2016/08/01/16/49/Catastrophe-Containment-and-Relief-Trust. Accessed 31 May 2021

International Platform on Sustainable Finance (IPSF) (2020) Annual Report of the International Platform on Sustainable Finance. https://ec.europa.eu/info/files/international-platform-sustainable-finance-annual-report-2020_en. Accessed 9 May 2021

Jafri J (2019) When billions meet trillions: impact investing and shadow banking in Pakistan. Rev Int Polit Econ 26(3):520–544

Jones L (2021) Record $700bn of Green, Social and Sustainability (GSS) Issuance in 2020: Global State of the Market Report. https://www.climatebonds.net/2021/04/record-700bn-green-social-sustainabi lity-gss-issuance-2020-global-state-market-report. Accessed 2 June 2021

Karwowski E (2019) Towards (de-)financialization: the role of the state. Camb J Econ 43(4):1001–1027

Karwowski E (2020) Commercial finance for development: a back door for financialization. Rev Afr Polit Econ. https://doi.org/10.1080/03056244.2021.1912722. Accessed 8 Nov 2021

Kaul I, Conceição P (2006) Why revisit public finance today? What the book is about. In: Kaul I, Conceição P (eds) The new public finance: responding to global challenges. UNDP and Oxford University Press, New York and Oxford

Kovick D (2018) The remedy gap. https://shiftproject.org/rethinking-remedy-and-responsibility-in-the-financial-sector/. Accessed 27 May 2021

LeBaron G, Lister J, Dauvergne P (2017) Governing global supply chain sustainability through the ethical audit regime. Globalizations 14(6):958–975

Le Houérou P (2018) Opinion: the Equator Principles just turned 15, we should celebrate their impact. Devex. https://www.devex.com/news/opinion-the-equator-principles-just-turned-15-we-should-celebrate-their-impact-93435. Accessed 15 May 2021

Mathew J (2018) Shades of green in financing: a discussion on green bonds and green loans. Butterworths J Int Bank Financ Law 33(5):311–313

Mawdsley E (2018) From billions to trillions: financing the SDGs in a world beyond aid. Dialogues Hum Geogr 8(2):191–195

Munevar D (2021) Sleep now in the fire: sovereign bonds and the Covid-19 debt crisis. Eurodad. https://www.eurodad.org/sovereign_bonds_covid19. Accessed 31 May 2021

Murray S (2021) 'Measuring what matters: the scramble to set standards for sustainable business', Financial Times, 14 May 2021

O'Donohoe N, Leijonhufvud C, Saltuk Y, Bugg-Levine A, Brandenburg M (2010) Impact investments: an emerging asset class. JP Morgan Global Research Paper. https://thegiin.org/research/publication/impact-investments-an-emerging-asset-class. Accessed 22 May 2021

OECD (2005) Paris Declaration on Aid Effectiveness. OECD, Paris

OECD (2008) Accra Agenda for Action. OECD, Paris. https://www.oecd.org/dac/effectiveness/45827 311.pdf. Accessed 12 Nov 2021

OECD (2020) COVID-19 and global capital flows. OECD policy responses to coronavirus (COVID-19). https://www.oecd.org/coronavirus/policy-responses/covid-19-and-global-capital-flows-2dc69002/. Accessed 29 May 2021

OECD (2021) Official Development Assistance (ODA). https://www.oecd.org/dac/financing-sustainable-development/development-finance-standards/What-is-ODA.pdf. Accessed 15 May 2021

OECD and UNDP (2020) Framework for SDG aligned finance. OECD and UNDP. http://www.oecd.org/development/financing-sustainable-development/Framework-for-SDG-Aligned-Finance-OECD-UNDP.pdf. Accessed 1 May 2021

Pahuja S (2011) Decolonising international law: development. Economic growth and the politics of universality. Cambridge University Press, Cambridge

Park S (2019) Holding new forms of development finance to account: an action plan for multilateral development banks. Global Economic Governance Programme Policy Brief https://www.geg.ox.ac.uk/sites/geg.bsg.ox.ac.uk/files/2019-02/Park%20Policy%20Brief%20GEG%20-%20February%202019.pdf. Accessed 8 Nov 2021

Park SK (2018a) Social bonds for sustainable development: a human rights perspective on impact investing. Bus Hum Rights J 3(2):233–255

Park SK (2018b) Investors as regulators: green bonds and the governance challenges of the sustainable finance revolution. Stanf J Int Law 54(1):1–48

Park SK (2019) Green bonds and beyond: debt financing as a sustainability diver. In: Sjåfjell B, Bruner CM (eds) The Cambridge handbook of corporate law, corporate governance and sustainability. Cambridge University Press, Cambridge

Patricio Ferreira Lima K (2020) Another lost decade? Phenomenal World. https://phenomenalworld.org/analysis/crisis-in-the-periphery. Accessed 29 May 2021

Petry J, Fichtner J, Heemskerk E (2021) Steering capital: the growing private authority of index providers in the age of passive asset management. Rev Int Polit Econ 28(1):152–176

Picciotto S (2011) Regulating global corporate capitalism. Cambridge University Press, Cambridge

Picciotto S (2017) Regulation: managing the antinomies of economic vice and virtue. Soc Legal Stud 26(6):676–699

Pistor K (2019) The code of capital: how law creates wealth and inequality. Princeton University Press, Princeton and Oxford

Publish What You Fund (2021) ESG and accountability to communities. Workstream 3 Working Paper, DFI Transparency Initiative. https://www.publishwhatyoufund.org/projects/dfi-transparency-initiative/3-esg-accountability-to-communities/. Accessed 25 May 2021

Romero MJ (2014) A private affair: shining a light on the shadowy institutions giving public support to private companies and taking over the development agenda. Eurodad. https://www.eurodad.org/aprivateaffair. Accessed 8 Nov 2021

Rose P (2019) Certifying the 'climate' in climate bonds. Cap Mark Law J 14(11):59–77

Roy J, McHugh N, Sinclair S (2018) A critical reflection on social impact bonds. Stanford Social and Innovation Review. https://ssir.org/articles/entry/a_critical_reflection_on_social_impact_bonds. Accessed 21 May 2021

Sassen S (1999) Making the global economy run: the role of national states and private agents. Int Soc Sci J 51(161):409–416

Shamir R, Weiss D (2012) Semiotics of indicators: the case of corporate human rights responsibility. In: Davis K, Fisher A, Kingsbury B, Merry SE (eds) Governance by indicators: global power through quantification and rankings. Oxford University Press, Oxford

Soederberg S (2007a) Socially responsible investment and the development agenda: peering behind the progressive veil of non-financial benchmarking. Third World Q 28(7):1219–1237

Soederberg S (2007b) The 'new conditionality' of socially responsible investing strategies: the politics of equity financing in emerging markets. New Polit Econ 12(4):477–497

Spotlight on Corruption (undated) Mozambique and the 'Tuna Bond' scandal. https://www.spotlightcorruption.org/mozambique-and-the-tuna-bond-scandal/. Accessed 8 Nov 2021

Swablowski D (2007) Transnational law and local struggles: mining, communities and the World Bank. Hart Publishing, Oxford and Portland

Tan C (2011) Governance through development: poverty reduction strategies, international law and the disciplining of Third World states. Routledge, Abingdon and New York

Tan C (2019) Creative cocktails or toxic brews? Blended finance and the regulatory framework for sustainable development. In: Gammage C, Novitz T (eds) Sustainable trade, investment and finance. Toward responsible and coherent regulatory frameworks. Edward Elgar, Cheltenham

Tan C (2021) Audit as accountability: technical authority and expertise in the governance of private financing for development. Soc Leg Stud. https://doi.org/10.1177/0964663921992100. Accessed 8 Nov 2021

UN (2015) Addis Ababa Action Agenda of the Third International Conference on Financing for Development. UN General Assembly Resolution 69/313. A/RES/69/313 https://www.google.com/url?sa=t&rct=j&q=&esrc=s&source=web&cd=&ved=2ahUKEwismp_p0Ij0AhXJTcAKHS7pACAQFnoECAwQAQ&url=https%3A%2F%2Fwww.un.org%2Fen%2Fdevelopment%2Fdesa%2Fpopulation%2Fmigration%2Fgeneralassembly%2Fdocs%2Fglobalcompact%2FA_RES_69_313.pdf&usg=AOvVaw0NjazAkrFCfDlVGUPcHXTX. Accessed 8 Nov 2021

UN (2021) Financing for Sustainable Development Report 2021: Report of the Inter-Agency Task Force on Financing for Development. UN, New York. https://developmentfinance.un.org/fsdr2021 Accessed 8 Nov 2021

UN and UNEP (2019) SDG bonds: leveraging capital markets for the SDGs, prepared by the UN Global Compact on Financial Innovation for the SDGs, UN Global Compact and UN Environment Programme (UNEP). https://www.unglobalcompact.org/library/5713. Accessed 8 Nov 2021

UN Conference on Trade and Development (UNCTAD) (2019a) The Least Developed Countries Report 2019. The present and future of external development finance: old dependence, new challenges. UNCTAD, New York. https://unctad.org/webflyer/least-developed-countries-report-2019. Accessed 8 Nov 2021

UNCTAD (2019b) Trade and Development Report 2019: Financing a Global Green New Deal. UNCTAD, New York. https://unctad.org/webflyer/trade-and-development-report-2019. Accessed 8 Nov 2021

UNCTAD (2020) SDG Pulse 2020: UNCTAD takes the pulse of the SDGs. UNCTAD, Geneva. https://sdgpulse.unctad.org/introduction/. Accessed 8 Nov 2021

UN Development Programme (UNDP) (2021) SDG Impact: catalysing private sector capital for the SDGs. Q2 2019 updates. https://sdgimpact.undp.org/SDG-Impact.pdf. Accessed 8 Nov 2021

UN Economic Commission for Africa (UNECA) (2020) Building forward together: financing a sustainable recovery for the future of all. https://repository.uneca.org/handle/10855/43829. Accessed 8 Nov 2021

Vervynckt M (2015) An assessment of transparency and accountability mechanisms at the European Investment Bank and the International Finance Corporation. 30 September 2015. Eurodad. https://www.eurodad.org/an_assessment_of_transparency_and_accountability_mechanisms_at_the_europ ean_investment_bank_and_the_international_finance_corporation. Accessed 8 Nov 2021

Wheatley J (2021) Feeble growth and chunky debt piles hold back emerging economies. Financial Times, 14 March 2021

World Bank (2015) From billions to trillions: transforming development finance post-2015 financing for development: multilateral development finance. Development Committee Discussion Note DC2015-0002.   https://pubdocs.worldbank.org/en/622841485963735448/DC2015-0002-E-Finan cingforDevelopment.pdf. Accessed 8 Nov 2021

World Bank (2017) Maximising finance for development: leveraging the private sector for growth and sustainable development. Development Committee Discussion Note DC2017-0009. https://www.worldbank.org/en/about/partners/maximizing-finance-for-development. Accessed 8 Nov 2021

World Bank (2018a) IDA makes historic capital market debut with inaugural US$1.5 billion benchmark bond.   https://www.worldbank.org/en/news/press-release/2018/04/17/ida-makes-historic-capital-market-debut-with-inaugural-usd-1-5-billion-benchmark-bond. Accessed 9 May 2021

World Bank (2018b) Seychelles launches world's first sovereign blue bond. https://www.worldbank.org/en/news/press-release/2018/10/29/seychelles-launches-worlds-first-sovereign-blue-bond. Accessed 15 May 2021

Publisher's Note Springer Nature remains neutral with regard to jurisdictional claims in published maps and institutional affiliations.

Authors and Affiliations

Celine Tan[1]

✉ Celine Tan
   Celine.Tan@warwick.ac.uk

[1] Reader in Law, School of Law, University of Warwick, Coventry, UK

European Business Organization Law Review (2022) 23:273–312
https://doi.org/10.1007/s40804-021-00235-x

ARTICLE

Sustainability, Justice and Corporate Law: Redistributing Corporate Rights and Duties to Meet the Challenge of Sustainability

Benedict Sheehy[1]

Accepted: 13 December 2021 / Published online: 21 February 2022
© T.M.C. Asser Press 2022

Abstract

Sustainability is the main challenge for humanity. The current climate crisis and growing inequality are both the direct consequence of human choices and activities, particularly through the corporation. Addressing these challenges requires clarity on what we mean by sustainability and justice and precisely how the corporation contributes to the situation. Both sustainability and justice have geographic and time dimensions. Law, however, is limited because it is largely jurisdictionally based and corporate law is heavily short-term orientated. This set of circumstances creates an imperative to consider how the issue can be resolved including changes to the long-standing institutions of corporate law. This paper considers the sustainability challenges and places them in the context of justice. It argues for corporate reforms of board and shareholder structures such that rights and duties are redistributed to parties with greater interests in sustainability and justice. It then explores how that could be done and the corporation re-normed to better serve society.

Keywords Corporate law · Climate justice · Law reform · Shareholder primacy norm · Institutional reform · Stakeholder rights

1 Introduction

Humanity's destruction of the natural environment at a global scale is set to have dire, irreversible consequences. Those impacts will be experienced by people too young to take decisions to protect themselves and their interests, as well as the billions of people yet to be born.[1] The issue is fundamentally a justice issue at a

---

[1] Green (1977). See further development in Barry (1997).

✉ Benedict Sheehy
benedict.sheehy@canberra.edu.au

[1] Professor of Law, Canberra Law School, University of Canberra, Bruce, ACT, Australia

🦋 Springer 🟢 ASSER PRESS

structural level. If justice is addressed properly, the environmental remedies will ensue. While there are several levels to the problem, from the individual level of cognition,[2] motivation and ideology,[3] to the institutional level of markets, and finally to the top level of governmental regulatory solutions such as the EU's efforts in sustainable finance,[4] there needs to be fresh thinking and reconsideration of institutionalised norms more broadly. Indeed, in terms of legal institutions, the courts have recently become active in the area of sustainability. For example, a recent German Constitutional Court ruling in a challenge to provisions of the Federal Climate Change Act of 12 December 2019 (*Bundes-Klimaschutzgesetz*—KSG) held that the Act's provisions 'governing national climate targets and the annual emission amounts allowed until 2030 are incompatible with fundamental rights insofar as they lack sufficient specifications for further emission reductions from 2031 onwards'.[5] This holding illustrates the main issue of this paper: the concept of justice in ecological matters extends over a time period beyond the interests of the current generation.

As will be argued, law, and corporate law in particular, is not well designed to deal with issues of broad public interest globally or intergenerationally. Rather, its limited jurisdictional focus and the private, anti-social character of corporate law all exacerbate issues of global, intergenerational justice arising from the global climate change crisis and economic inequality.[6] In this environment of crisis, maintaining current institutional norms such as corporate law is wholly inappropriate. This article proposes significant structural changes and new institutional norms to address the issues. It proposes dividing directors' rights and duties and redistributing them across two newly created boards impressed with climate and social decision-making responsibilities. Similarly, it proposes dividing shareholders' rights and redistributing them between existing shareholders and a newly minted stakeholder organ. These changes, however, must be seen within the larger considerations of justice.

Justice is an innate value to our species. It is not only a value driving the legal system, but a human value that expresses our basic psychology.[7] It allows people to participate in societies of all types, whether hunter-gatherer, animistic or polyvalent, multicultural ones.[8] A stable, secure society requires a healthy environment—governments unable to address environmental issues risk political instability.[9] Plato argued over two thousand years ago that the foundation of a stable society is an acceptable degree of justice.[10] Although justice is often considered at an individual level, it has usually included a significant element of public interest as well, and

---

[2] Rouch (2020).

[3] Micheler (2021).

[4] Chiu (2021).

[5] Federal Constitutional Court (2021).

[6] Sjåfjell and Bruner (2020).

[7] Arfken and Yen (2014).

[8] Steensma and Vermunt (2013), Vermunt and Steensma (1991).

[9] https://www.abc.net.au/news/2020-10-23/china-climate-change-security-water-renewables-carbon-neutrality/12772034?utm_source=abc_news_web&utm_medium=content_shared&utm_content=mail&utm_campaign=abc_news_web (accessed 9 December 2021).

[10] See, for example, the dialogue in Plato (360 BCE), Bk 1.

today given rise to a broad social justice movement. Concepts of justice and the breaches of justice feed much of the daily news headlines around the world. Justice is intimately tied to issues of sustainability. As the American naturalist James Audubon observed several generations ago: 'We do not inherit the earth from our ancestors; we borrow it from our children.'[11] Yet, sustainability only became a broad area of government concern in recent decades.

Early discussions of sustainability focused on government action, and it was expected that such action would be aligned with international conventions. The basic challenge was one of balancing conflicting interests between current exploitation advocates and future-oriented conservationists. This conflict is expressed as a choice between a depletion policy focused on meeting the demands of the current generation with less regard for the environment, and a conservation policy which emphasises the need to preserve sufficient environmental integrity for future generations to sustain themselves. The earlier environmental dialogue, however, changed. As Gomez-Baggethun and Naredo note there has been 'a shift in focus from direct public regulation to market-based instruments'.[12] This shift places the legal corporation at the intersection of public interests in conservation and private wealth through exploitation. It is the legal actor making decisions, buying and selling in markets and responding to various regulatory landscapes. It is the critical actor in the contest for ecological and social sustainability.

In this contest, as Sjåfjell argues, the greatest obstacle to sustainability is the shareholder primacy corporation.[13] So normed, it is an actor lacking social embeddedness,[14] narrowly focused on financial wealth objectives. This financially focused actor has tipped the balance not only in the natural environment, but also in society more broadly, in favour of one value, namely financial wealth, for the benefit of a small elite. And significantly, a much larger proportion of the population around the planet, both present and future, bears the increasing injustice of a depleted environment and high levels of economic inequality. Perhaps at no time prior to the present has this issue of justice induced by the legal corporation been such an issue of broad-based, global importance.

The corporation, though an ancient invention, came to the fore in the nineteenth century. In that period, it became the preferred legal vehicle for the plethora of businesses spawned by the Industrial Revolution. Industrialisation, in turn, has relied on burning of fossil fuels and extraction of natural inputs leading to vast amounts of greenhouse gas emissions.[15] Further, present day corporations own the great majority of the world's fossil fuel reserves.[16] They determine consumption and use of fossil fuels through product and service development as well as mass marketing.[17]

---

[11] Quoted in Berry (1971).

[12] Gómez-Baggethun and Naredo (2015), p 385.

[13] Sjåfjell et al. (2015).

[14] Sheehy (2017a).

[15] Heede (2014).

[16] Vitali et al. (2011).

[17] Heede (2014).

They control production and distribution,[18] and through their economic and political power have considerable influence over political processes and resulting legal frameworks. With their power, corporations to a very significant degree dictate the policy choices among major countries and influence public discourse[19] on the vital issue of greenhouse gases.[20]

Recognising the critical role reform of corporate law must play if social goals such as sustainability are to be achieved, Kent Greenfield, argued:

> There is reason to think hard about the possibility of using corporate law as a regulatory tool. Indeed, there are major public policy problems that otherwise seem intractable, and reforms in corporate governance may prove to be powerful and efficient mechanisms to address them.[21]

This article adopts Greenfield's perspective and particularises them through the proposal of new boards and stakeholders and a correlative redistribution of corporate rights to address the issues of justice and institutional reform.

The article begins with a consideration of the idea of sustainability. It then turns to consider justice, distributions and the dimensions of justice in terms of time and geography. It then discusses the nature of the corporation and justice in that context. The subsequent section proposes corporate reform that integrates sustainability and broader justice concerns into the corporation by way of disaggregating and redistributing corporate rights and duties. It does so by proposing a tripartite board—a strategic board, an environmental board and a social board—along with the creation of a stakeholder organ which exercises voting rights currently held by shareholders. It is critical to note at the outset that there are vast literatures on the main themes of sustainability, justice and climate change.[22] Accordingly, a very selective approach has been taken to these issues and related literature to address the matter at hand.

2 Sustainability: Depletion Versus Conservation in Ecology, Economics and Time

Sustainability dialogue and policy have been built to a considerable degree on work initiated by Boulding in the 1960s[23] and carried forward in a subsequent landmark work by Meadows et al. who wrote:

> It is the predicament of [hu]mankind that … [humankind] can perceive the problematique [of limited planetary resources], yet, despite … considerable knowledge and skills, … does not understand the origins, significance, and

---

[18] Griffin (2017).

[19] Fuchs (2007), Sapinski (2016).

[20] Consider, for example, Chevron and Exxon-Mobil's concerted disinformation campaign supporting the climate change denial industry, Dunlap and McCright (2011).

[21] Greenfield (2005), p 39.

[22] See, for example, Eckersley (1992).

[23] Boulding (1966).

interrelationships of its many components and thus is unable to devise effective responses.[24]

Thus, while on the one hand natural scientists engaged in the study of the ecology express alarm at the demise of several aspects of the ecology, on the other hand, orthodox economists not only do not acknowledge a problem, but may deny that the planet has limits, or believe that there is an infinite, commensurable way of satisfying human wants.[25] These profoundly conflicting views of prominent public disciplines provide insight into the misunderstanding Meadows et al. note. This failure of understanding results from assumptions and poorly articulated values at play in the conceptual foundations of the sustainability dialogue.

Sustainability is a matter of social institutions and value systems over time. The social institutions concern the organisation of society and related quality of life we expect for humanity as a whole. The value question is a political question about what is worth preserving—ranging anywhere from the quality of life for the current generation in a single nation or the global ecology for the indefinite future. The timelines involved are: the short timeline of corporate profits, the medium timeline of individual human lives and the longer timeline of the survival of the human species.[26] In respect of climate change, there is a broad consensus that the preservation of the natural environment, in particular a climate conducive to human survival, is an ultimate value worth pursuing.

Contemporary discussion of sustainability conflates two distinct approaches: an ethical approach and a technological approach which sees sustainability as a problem in search of a technological solution.[27] The ethical approach identifies values such as ecology and economics, present and future generations and aims to balance them fairly.[28] The technological approach is focused on human impacts, primarily carbon release, and what specific methods are required to address those impacts.[29]

As Bañon Gomis et al. argue, however: 'What gives sustainability its importance is not as an engineering, environmental, or management concept, but as an ethical concept that can and should guide conduct.'[30] Following this logic, their definition is useful:

> Sustainability refers to a moral way of acting, and ideally habitual, in which the person or group intends to avoid deleterious effects on the environmen-

---

[24] Meadows et al. (1972).

[25] Norton and Toman (1997), p 555, Daly and Cobb Jr. (1989). Ecological and other heterodox economists make an important contribution. See Røpke (2005). Barry explains the rationale sharply in Barry (1997), pp 51-4. McAfee (2019) offers an optimistic case and method for reconciling aspects of this discourse.

[26] Lozano et al. (2015).

[27] See discussion in Bañon Gomis et al. (2011).

[28] Barry (1997), p 54.

[29] Bañon Gomis et al. (2011).

[30] See discussion in Bañon Gomis et al. (2011).

tal, social, and economic domains, and which is consistent with a harmonious relationship with those domains that is conducive to a flourishing life.[31]

In the context of business, Sjåfjell and Richardson describe sustainability as

business and finance creating value in a manner that is environmentally sustainable, in that it ensures the long-term stability and resilience of the ecosystems that support human life; socially sustainable, in that it facilitates the achievement of human rights and other basic social rights, as well as good governance; and economically sustainable, in that it satisfies the economics needs necessary for stable and resilient societies.[32]

This paper adopts the idea of sustainability as an ethical guide for decision-making and in considering reforms focuses on the spheres identified by Sjåfjel and Bruner.

This understanding of sustainability as an ethical guide to decision-making provides a framework for evaluating and choosing between the two alternative policies under consideration and the proposed corporate law reforms. The policy alternatives in the sustainability debate are depletion versus conservation. These alternatives represent a choice between two conflicting interests—the interests of the present generation as opposed to the interests of future generations. The determination of the alternatives is an equation requiring calculation of future scarcity and harm (depletion) with current sacrifice and harm (conservation).[33] The calculation is a justice equation which Caney explains as follows:

To ask by how much current generations should lower emissions requires one to assess their interests with the legitimate interests of future people and so the question of whether a discount rate should be applied to future generations is crucial.[34]

As a justice issue, one must be able to justify to the losing side of the policy decision why that decision was considered just. If a depletion policy is favoured, one must be able to justify to future generations why they have been deprived of a healthy ecology in favour of current generations.[35] If one favours a conservation policy, one must be able to justify to the current generation, the party harmed by the prohibition from exploiting resources, why s/he should be harmed or deprived of that right in favour of a person located elsewhere in time or space.

When applying this to the corporate person, it should be stated that the corporation itself is limited to pecuniary interests, has no non-pecuniary interest in the

---

[31] Bañon Gomis et al. (2011), p 176.

[32] Sjåfjell and Bruner (2020), p 11.

[33] Barry (1997), p 44.

[34] Caney (2009), p 164.

[35] For justification, I am using Scanlon's contractarian test. Contractarianism describes as just those actions and policies which are justifiable to another person on grounds to which the latter could not reasonably object. It places two criteria for justice: first, a person must be harmed by an action or policy, and second, the complaint about the harm must be unanswerable. Scanlon (1998).

ecology or in future generations, but does have distinct interests in the present. It is particularly interested in property rights permitting it unlimited exploitation of the natural environment in pursuit of profits.[36] The only interest a corporation has in future generations and locations is only insofar as these impact present revenues or costs. This interest is appropriately reflected in accounting practices which include a net present value calculation discounting future values, representing the view that the present value of money is greater than the value of money in the future.[37] Accordingly, both the corporation's time and approach to sustainability resonate with depletion policies and are in direct opposition to conservation policies.

3 Theories of Justice

As a human concept (as opposed to supernatural dictum), justice is important because as John Rawls, echoing Locke, famously observed, '[justice] is the first virtue of social institutions'.[38] In other words, no social institution, and hence no society, will survive for long without justice. No society is sustainable without justice. Once societies realised that the existing social order was not the handiwork of the gods or nature, an interest in justice took on a dramatic intensity and great unrest followed as different parties contended over policy choices and related laws.[39] The following Section explores some of the dimensions of justice, particularly in the contexts of sustainability and the corporation.

3.1 Justice and Distributions

The concept of justice reflects a diverse range of values. Justice can be understood pragmatically[40] as the appropriate application of a society's norms. For example, a monarch retaining all the land of a nation may be considered just if the monarch is understood to be the representative of the divine. If a person other than the monarch were to hold such land, it would be considered unjust. Another example of justice as the application of social norms is punishing someone who takes something to which he or she is not entitled. In this case, punishment is considered a just desert for the injustice act of taking in a society that values property rights, breaching society's norms around private property. These examples are not at all obvious: a similar scenario in another society may have a very different outcome where that society values strategy and tricky behaviour and decides to reward the taker for exercising that strength. What is evident from the above examples is that justice has a fundamental focus on distributions,[41] and further, as the appropriate distribution as between

---

[36] Sheehy (2004a).

[37] Weisbach and Sunstein (2008).

[38] Rawls (1999), p 3.

[39] Lamont and Favor (2017).

[40] As opposed to 'universally' which has been the quest of philosophers over the millennia.

[41] Initially identified in Aristotle, Book V, paras. 3:1131a-4:1132b. See Lamont (1941).

parties based on the respective values embedded in the cultures and value systems which those parties inhabit.[42] In the context of sustainability, clearly, the issue is the distribution of the costs and benefits of the ecology between the current generation and the generations to come.

There is little consensus on what values provide an ethical foundation for justice in distributions. In some regions of the world virtue-based theories are supported, others prefer religion-based theories, while yet others resort to cultural, economic and time-based theories.[43] This is not to say that there are no common value justifications. The common categories for justifying distributions are needs, desert and moral value. That is, distribution decisions are said to be just when they are based on meeting people's needs, or that people deserve them, or that there is some special moral value which requires recognition through an allocation or particular distribution. The disagreement lies in the basis on which they are to be allocated or applied. Perhaps the two most widely accepted frameworks for advocating and evaluating distributions are: utilitarianism and egalitarianism. While neither of these frameworks speaks directly to the problem at hand, they provide a background for arguing the particular issues of sustainability and corporations in the contexts of justice over time and place.

Utilitarian reasoning leads to the suggestion that 'the greatest good for the greatest number of people' test, as applied to ecological sustainability, could include people of all future generations located all over the globe. Conversely, utilitarianism could be used to argue that the greatest good for the greatest number currently alive requires despoiling the planet for the needs of the present generation, and that subsequent generations will adjust to the circumstances they inherit, limiting their own numbers to maximise what they determine to be their own greatest good.[44] Applying utilitarianism to corporations, it may be argued that to the extent that the corporation concentrates wealth among a few and decimates the environment for that purpose, it is unjust. By way of contrast, where a corporation provides public good as through the efficient production of goods and services and increased choice, it can be argued to be just. Accordingly, utilitarianism provides little guidance for determining whether depletion or conservation policies are more or less just. As Rawls noted some decades ago, 'the fundamental idea in the concept of justice is fairness; … [and] it is this aspect of justice for which utilitarianism, in its classical form, is unable to account, but which is expressed, even if misleadingly, by the idea of the social contract.'[45] Accordingly, the paper turns next to consider egalitarianism using social contract-type arguments.

Egalitarian reasoning on sustainability leads to the view that no person, regardless of when or where born, has a lesser right to enjoy the earth's fruits than any other. Where applied to the corporation, egalitarianism diverges from law. While law sees the corporation as a person, egalitarianism as a philosophical approach sees

---

[42] Scanlon (1998).

[43] Rokeach (1973).

[44] Page (1999).

[45] Rawls (1958).

 Springer   ASSER PRESS

it as a non-human device, without innate rights, serving human interests. Accordingly, where the corporation creates new, or exacerbates existing, inequalities or otherwise restricts access to or destroys the earth's natural resources favouring one person or group over another without appropriate human-based ethical justification, it is unjust. Where the corporation is busy engaged in such injustices, it is breaching social contract norms and ought not to be excluded from that contract.[46] Extrapolating from Rousseau's ideas of the social contract, all members of a society should have a say not only in a society's organisation but also in its distributions.[47]

Among egalitarian theorists, two distinct camps arise:[48] the 'cosmopolitans' who believe that egalitarianism must extend around the globe, and the 'statists' who maintain that egalitarianism is a domestic concern. Addressing the matter at hand, global sustainability, it is clear that the statist position is inadequate in dealing with value judgements beyond the state and the cosmopolitan position is well suited to address the issue. Taking egalitarian thinking forward then requires further consideration of the dimensions of justice in terms of time and space.

3.2 Dimensions of Justice

Justice is not unidimensional. It is affected by context: justice is affected by location and time, as well as the parties and interests being considered. With respect to sustainability, time and location are two very significant dimensions of justice. Time and place present two large separations or distances. The first is the separation in time between those who benefit from depletion of the natural environment and those who bear depletion's costs. People today will benefit from exploitation policies while those of future generations will bear the cost. And if choosing a conservation policy, vice versa: current generations will bear the cost while future generations will reap the benefits. The second separation is the geographic distance that often separates those benefiting from policies and those bearing the costs. While all people will ultimately feel the effect of climate change, those with unequal economic power are insulated from those bearing the brunt of climate change resulting from the unsustainable habits of those with power. These two separations, discussed in some detail in the next Section, lead to profound injustices.[49]

While egalitarians argue that the context ultimately makes no difference in sustainability justifications—as Barry puts it: '[T]he core idea of universalism—that place and time do not provide a morally relevant basis on which to differentiate

---

[46] Sheehy (2004a, b-5).

[47] Contractarianism has its roots in Hobbes, whose account is based on mutual self-interest, whereas Rousseau saw contractualism as being based on egalitarianism.

[48] An emerging third camp, in which differentiated application is justified depending on the nature of the issue under examination, appears to be underway. This paper does not need to address it given the clear global nature of the problem.

[49] Eckersley (2016), p 358, Meyer and Roser (2006).

the weight to be given to the interest of different people—has an immense rational appeal'[50]—nevertheless, time and place must be addressed. They are the two generally accepted justifications for unequal distributions and thus the paper next turns to examine these dimensions of justice in some detail.

3.2.1 Geographic Dimension: Global Justice

In terms of the geographic dimension, the concept of global justice is not a new concern, for as the eighteenth-century philosopher Kant noted: 'The peoples of the earth have ... entered in varying degrees into a universal community, and it has developed to the point where a violation of rights in one part of the world is felt everywhere.'[51] The idea of global justice really took hold as a result of a broader global justice movement that started in the 1970s[52]—roughly the same time as concerns about the global environment were emerging. While prior conceptions of legal and political philosophers considered justice as a matter limited to the borders of the nation-state, given the intensity and extent of globalisation, that unit of analysis is no longer sufficient, and the principles of justice must be extended to address the larger point of reference.[53] The basic question at this level of analysis is: 'What principles should guide international action?'[54]

The global justice dialogue draws from developments in the international legal system. The international system, with instruments such as conventions on the natural environment and human rights, provides these instruments as significant points of normative reference. In terms of justice, it is important to note that the international legal system explicitly rejects the justification for unequal distributions on the basis of origin. Rather, international legal instruments provide universal standards regardless of locale. They provide an explicit statement of the things that human society as a whole values, what should be sustained and the basis for distributions. People living on any part of the globe deserve the same rights and respect as anyone, anywhere else.

These basic rights are not contingent or distributed upon the basis of needs, desert and moral value. Rather, they are possessed by people by virtue of their membership in the human species. Similarly, the international instruments place an equal and strong emphasis on the preservation of the natural environment regardless of where it is located. No single location is more valued because of jurisdictional locale.

One example drawing these different instruments and concerns together on the topic, the Sustainable Development Goals, provides evidence of the global value placed on the natural environment, regardless of where that environment is located. Significantly, contrary to the above-mentioned effort of corporations to exploit differences in location, these same Goals include an obligation on businesses to

---

[50] Barry (1997), p 49.

[51] Kant (1983), p 119.

[52] Della Porta et al. (2015), pp 6-7.

[53] Valentini (2011), p 2.

[54] Brock (2017).

contribute to sustainability globally and sustainable development specifically in jurisdictions lacking resources of their own to do so.[55] Thus, the Goals specify sustainability as a global value and obligation, and they include in that broad obligation a specific obligation on business to contribute to sustainability.

In contrast to international soft law, international agreements and conventions applicable globally, the nation-state's hard law with its actionable rights and duties is largely limited by national jurisdiction via the doctrine of extraterritoriality. As a result, it is evident that hard law is as poorly suited to addressing issues of global justice as international law is weak in the face of governments pressured by corporations.

The corporate response to the weakness of law as a means to address justice's global geographic dimension is a strategic decision to exploit that weakness. Multinational corporations actively seek low cost, low regulatory environments[56]— whether for occupational health and safety, securities, tax, human rights or environmental law—to reduce operating and compliance costs. That is, rather than engaging in positive distributive justice on a global basis, corporations generally do the opposite, seeking out jurisdictions which facilitate regulatory arbitrage favouring the privatisation of wealth while leaving the costs to the public. The legal right and economic ability of the legal corporation to ignore the geographic dimension of justice and, in fact, to actively and strategically exploit that element for its own advantage are grounds for arguing for serious corporate reform. As will be argued below, a disaggregation of directors' and shareholders' rights and their reassignment will be critical to infusing corporations with new justice norms that take account of the geographic dimension.

In sum, the geographic dimension does not justify unequal distributions in matters of sustainability. Further, neither national, hard law nor soft law at the international level offer much of substance to sustainability on the geographic dimension. Finally, corporations see the geographic dimension as an opportunity to be exploited rather than a matter of justice to be remedied. The paper next turns to consider the time dimension of justice.

3.2.2 Time Dimension: Intergenerational Justice

The second dimension of distributive justice in the context of sustainability is the time dimension, termed 'intergenerational justice'. The issue in this dimension is determining how resources should be distributed across time. In his consideration of justice and anthropogenic climate change some fifty years ago, the ethicist Robert Green echoed what was already a widely shared view of the world's scientists.[57] He stated that environmental degradation and resource depletion 'threaten a massive evil for generations yet unborn, … [creating for us] moral responsibility to future

---

[55] Understanding the differences between these concepts of sustainability and sustainable development is important, Sheehy and Farneti (2021).

[56] Chiu and Donovan (2017).

[57] Green (1977). See further development in Barry (1997).

generations'.[58] This 'evil', unsustainability or negative value, presents a challenge for societies that adopt egalitarian approaches toward the young and the unborn.

To address this intergenerational problem, Green posited three ethical axioms of intergenerational justice. These axioms are:

> [1] We are bound by ties of justice to real future persons .... [2] The lives of future persons ought ideally to be 'better' than our own and certainly no worse, and .... [3] Sacrifices on behalf of the future must be distributed equitably in the present, with special regard for those presently least advantaged.[59]

These axioms face the same challenge as does the geographic dimension, namely, creating a benefit for one group while imposing the cost on another. Green noted this challenge at the time of writing, for he observed that 'although we are responsible to the future, our efforts to improve the future quality of life must not become an excuse for neglecting our responsibilities to our neighbours in the present'.[60] While there is an immediate justice imperative in dealing with our neighbours of today, it can be less clear what that imperative may be for the future. Indeed, there are some who argue that depletion today will induce future generations to act in ways that will have been adapted to the conditions they inherit and that their preferences may well be different from and satisfied differently from those preferences of current generations, and accordingly, to constrain current generations' consumption to meet the needs of hypothetical people whose needs and preferences are unknown, is an unreasonable injustice.[61]

Nevertheless, egalitarian reasoning in the context of intergenerational justice leads to non-depletion as the preferred policy choice —conservation by the present generation in favour of the next. As Page explains it:

> [E]xisting generations owe it to their distant successors not to despoil the natural environment in general, and the climate system in particular, ... [and] proposes that each generation should hand down to the next a no less abundant share of resources than that which it inherited from previous generations.[62]

Thus, chronologic justice is a matter of distributive justice—a question of distribution between present and future generations.

Unlike geographic justice, which law addresses through strictly limited jurisdictional boundaries, when it comes to time, law works differently. Law extends its rule through time generously both forward into the future and backward judging past events. Indeed, as an institution, law is curious in that it looks both forward and backward simultaneously. Its forward, future-looking orientation is based on largely stable rules and guided by looking backward at precedents representing long established social norms and institutions.

---

[58] Green (1977).
[59] Ibid.
[60] Ibid.
[61] Page (1999).
[62] Ibid., p 55.

As with other problems and issues, law takes two approaches to dealing with time. Firstly, law does so by *restricting rights*. It places limits on the current generation's ability to interfere with future generations. It does so, for example, by limiting 'the dead hand of the past'—the mortmain principles of property law. In terms of addressing the future, at the individual level, law provides declining levels of control as the future arrives. So, while it facilitates extensive control in the present and for a limited time period thereafter, by way of contract, as it shifts to transfers affecting the next generation, the limitations increase. For example, no discussion of wills and estates is complete without a discussion of limitations on future interests. As far back as the sixteenth century, and traceable at least to the fourteenth century, the Rule in Shelley's Case placed a limitation on interference with subsequent generations' property rights.[63] A related rule, the Rule Against Perpetuities, derived from the Duke of Norfolk,[64] is based on the related principle that future generations need to be able to deal with property free from the 'perpetual clogs' or constraints imposed by prior generations. Both of these cases limit the impact or harm that one generation can visit upon succeeding generations.

What is particularly interesting for this discussion of the chronological dimension of distributive justice in these cases (and the general rules dealing with future interests) is their justifications. The Rule in Shelley's Case was based on an understanding of the capriciousness of the future and justified restrictions on rights on the egalitarian basis of avoiding future generations' ability to address their future circumstances. In the Duke of Norfolk case, the judge noted the utilitarian problem of 'clogging up title' restricting further alienation but also the egalitarian concern of allowing future generations the ability to deal with property as they may see fit.

These historical cases are not generally read in this light; however, as we face a markedly uncertain future and the cases represent an effort within the legal system to allow future generations to address their contexts, they merit a reconsideration. Interestingly, the Duke of Norfolk case is the result of a long struggle between conservatives seeking to retain power in the status quo and newer merchants pursuing new agendas.[65] This same struggle appears today between those conservative, entrenched powers benefiting from the corporation with distributions of rights that facilitate exploitation of the natural environment using economic utilitarian justifications and those looking to reform corporate rights using egalitarian justifications to conserve the natural environment in the interests of future generations.

Law's second approach to time aims to secure the future by *creating duties*. These duties are found, for example, in rules of equity such as the doctrine of *in loco parentis,* a private law doctrine for the protection of minors. Public law struggles to secure the future because the ruling party generally seeks to continue its rule more

---

[63] Shelley's Case 1579-81 1 Co. Rep. 88b, 76 ER 199. For scholarly treatment, see Smith (2009).

[64] Duke of Norfolk's Case 1682 3 Ch Cas 1; 22 ER 931. For scholarly treatment, see Haskins (1977) and, of course, the classic tome Gray (2003), originally published in 1915.

[65] Writing on the Duke's case, Haskins stated: '[The] case marked the climax of a long struggle between the conveyancers, who wanted more freedom for the landed classes to control their estates, and the royal judges who had stood firm against those efforts for centuries. The conclusion seems inescapable that the conveyancers and their clients, not the judges, were the ultimate victors', Haskins (1977), p 21.

than anything else, including securing the interests of future generations. After all, the voters that count are those alive today and able to cast a vote. Thus, although there are bodies of law aimed at securing the future, for the most part, contemporary law makers struggle to create rules that extend beyond the mandate of the government of the day. These pressures on legislators make efforts at intergenerational justice addressing distributive justice's time dimension highly problematic. The problem can be seen, for example, in environmental law.

When initially enacted at the federal level in the USA in response to environmental disasters and related alarm, for example, the powerful Environmental Protection Agency was actively engaged in protecting the environment and, in consequence, restricting business exploitation of the natural environment and placing duties of conservation. Subsequently elected governments, however, subject to business interests, systematically reduced environmental protection objectives, granting greater rights to exploit the natural environment accompanied by decreased obligations to conserve the natural environment for future generations. Subsequent governments reduced power by reducing funding to the Agency and repealing certain legal powers.

Broadly speaking, law has addressed the time dimension of the natural environment between current and future generations through the development of a special area of law, namely, environmental law and its distribution of rights and duties. There are three generally accepted environmental law duties or norms: the polluter pays principle, the principle of prevention and the precautionary principle.[66] Briefly, the polluter pays principle allows current exploitation of the natural environment on economic principles but creates a duty to pay for the costs—presumably to the benefit of future generations. The basic assumption is that economic capital is commensurate with any other type of capital including 'natural capital', and there is no particular value associated with the natural environment other than its transactional or consumption value. Thus, Barry's 'X' value as sustainability, in economists' eyes, is no more than want satisfaction. As Barry holds the view that

> if plastic trees are as satisfying as real ones, there is no reason for worrying about the destruction of the world's tress so long as the resources exist to enable plastic replacement to be manufactured in sufficient numbers.[67]

This principle embodies the financial incentive driving natural exploitation, a utilitarian principle embodied in the corporation. Such exploitation further creates unjust distributions, it can be argued, as the exploitation is in all likelihood done by a corporation that privatises wealth while imposing social costs on the public at large. Thus, the polluter pays principle is a potential source of injustice at least in terms of the time dimension.

The second environmental law principle, prevention, is a clear duty. This duty aims to conserve the environment to address the needs of future generations. It

---

[66] de Sadeleer (2002), Gaines (1991). See also Larson (2005).

[67] Barry (1997), p 51.

requires parties to avoid, prevent or remedy harms to the environment.[68] As de Sadeleer has it, the duty of prevention arises when damages are 'likely to be irreversible or too insidious or diffuse to be effectively dealt with through civil liability or when reparation would be extremely expensive'.[69] This law distributes the costs and the benefits across the time dimension, between the generations. The current generation has the responsibility to do what it can to care for the environment as it reaps the benefits. It is a duty to preserve more than plastic trees for the next generation. It is a recognition that the environment has an incommensurate value and deserves to be protected as an inheritance for future generations. Further, this conservation is based on an implicit egalitarian justification of weighing equally present generations' needs and those of future generations.

Finally, the third principle, the precautionary principle, is a restriction on property rights. It recognises the inherent danger posed by the combination of ability to inflict harm and lack of clear understanding of the implications—Meadow et al.'s 'problematique'.[70] De Sadeleer describes the precautionary principle as the third evolutionary phase of environmental law. It is a curious development in that it wholly reverses a foundational, long-standing principle of liberalism. Rather than law facilitating maximum liberty and related use of rights and only requiring remedy after a harm has been inflicted, the precautionary principle works in the opposite manner. It operates on the assumption that we humans are dealing with 'unknown harms, perhaps unquantifiable harms, even [where] ... the underlying evidence or knowledge is accepted to be less than certain'[71] in certain environmental matters. As a result, maximum liberty is a poor approach, inimical to sustainability, and so limitations on human activity are appropriate as our ability to rectify harms is unknown. Again, this principle is founded upon implicit egalitarian distributive principles: the future generation has the same right to enjoy nature's gifts as the current generation.

These three principles of environmental law attempt to provide a balance between depletion policy for present needs and conservation for future generations. These principles of environmental law are at odds with the institutions of corporate law and related economic ideology.[72] While environmental laws distribute the opportunity to exploit the environment between the current and future population by placing constraints on current populations in favour of preservation for future populations, corporate law, as discussed in the next Section, places no constraint on exploitation or depletion, nor does it place a non-monetary interest in generations to come.

In terms of law constraining corporate exploitation, such activity occurs not from within corporate law but in areas of law external to corporate law. The main legal tool has been for activists to bring lawsuits against corporations to protect the rights of future generations. Indeed, to date, over 1400 climate change cases have been litigated by persons pursuing climate justice. Some of these cases have achieved

---

[68] Sheehy (2019), p 275.

[69] de Sadeleer (2002), p 61.

[70] Meadows et al. (1972).

[71] Sheehy (2019), p 276.

[72] Easterbrook and Fischel (1991).

remarkable successes. In May 2021, for example, a panel of three judges in a Dutch court case against Royal Dutch Shell required the company and its subsidiaries worldwide to reduce carbon emissions as a matter of human rights for future generations—enlivening the international soft law of the UN Climate Change Convention Article 2 in hard law.[73] A similar ruling was issued in the recent German Constitutional Court's judgement referred to in the Introduction: '[C]urrent measures "violate the freedoms of the complainants, some of whom are still very young" because they delay too much of the action needed to reach the Paris targets until after 2030.'[74]

Nevertheless, this case-by-case approach is inadequate to the challenge of climate change. While these cases are not insubstantial in number, from economic, procedural and systemic perspectives they lack the overall power to substantially shift the global balance of justice away from current generations to future generations. Procedurally, they require activists to litigate against each and every corporate body in order to achieve future-oriented justice. Too often, they fail the time dimension in that they are efforts to achieve post facto justice, seeking remedies for injuries from environmental exploitation in the past rather than conserving and preserving the environment for future generations. Institutionally, they are inadequate. They are a much less efficient solution based on individual initiative and resources to a problem that is systemic in nature—a matter for law reform rather than utilisation of existing laws. In sum, they are economically costly, procedurally time and resource-intensive affairs incapable of achieving the radical systemic changes needed for egalitarian justice in its time dimension to prevail in sustainability matters.[75]

Thus, while it is obvious that law attempts to balance depletion of the natural environment for current needs and conservation for the future, it is out of balance as the climate crisis and social inequality—the time and geographic dimensions—make clear.

Further, the underlying justifications from utilitarian and egalitarian approaches are not clearly articulated, delineated and developed. As courts consider the distribution of costs and benefits of depletion across generations, it is clear that current approaches, whether territorially limited national laws, international soft law or specific cases, are inadequate institutionally to make the required systemic changes. Accordingly, revisiting the ancient institution of the corporation and considering its potential reform is imperative and it is to that matter that the article turns next.

Before doing so, however, it is worth considering the rationale for the existing state of affairs. There is certainly the argument to be made that these issues of climate change and inequality are not the appropriate province of corporate law which should be focused on internal matters. In this view, corporate law should be left to wealth generation, and environmental law and various tax and transfer policies left to address these extra-corporate affairs.

---

[73] *Milieudefensie v Royal Dutch Shell RDS*, 25 May 2021, The Hague, at para. 2.4.2. ECLI:NL:RBDHA: 2021:5339.

[74] Translated by the BBC.

[75] Amelang et al. (2021).

Environmental law at best has operated as a partial restraint and offered limited post facto remedies on a case-by-case basis. The precautionary principle, the third phase of environmental law, while enlivened in certain legislated procedures such as environmental assessments and approvals, is readily avoided by companies and politicians whose priorities are wealth and personal advancement. As a result, environmental law has proven to be inadequate to the task of implementing the constraints required to preserve the ecology for future generations, as the climate crisis demonstrates.

Other scholars prefer to leave inequality outside of corporate law and rely on tax and transfer policies. The issue with this approach is that the increased inequality in societies is a consequence of increased corporate power and corporate lobbying, the power of the elite, capturing political agendas, precluding tax amendments and locking in inefficient, ineffective trickle-down economic policies which have demonstrably failed.[76] Finally, carbon tax and carbon trading systems have been tried with varying degrees of success.[77] These too fail to address more comprehensively the issues of sustainability. As Greenfield has argued, there are a number of public policy problems that have proven intractable without including the corporation as a key actor in the resolution. Accordingly, considering the corporation and how it might be used in these ways is justified and addressed next.

4 The Legal Framing of the Corporation

The corporation is unique. It is an intangible body, a creature, existing exclusively in the legal system. As a creature, it has been described as humanity's greatest invention[78] as well as its monster.[79] Within the legal system, it is a robust if neutral bundle of rights and duties.[80] Although for much of the last 900 years, the corporation was a body serving public, non-profit and charitable purposes,[81] a widely accepted view today is that the main role of the corporation is as a pool of capital, creating limited liability for members, shielding directors acting within the scope of their powers and existing in perpetuity providing continuity for business operations despite changes in personnel and investors.[82]

From a functional perspective, corporate law has two roles: it creates the corporation as an actor within the legal system and provides a set of rules organising parties and procedures. It constitutes the organs, the members and directors, and provides for the name, creating categories, rights, duties and tests. So considered, the corporation is a value-neutral vehicle. To understand this, one may think of the

---

[76] Kanbur (2019).
[77] McAfee (2019).
[78] Maitland (1893).
[79] Wormser (1931).
[80] A better view is the real person theory. Micheler (2021).
[81] Horwitz (1977), Ireland (2001).
[82] Stout et al. (2016).

corporation as one does of an automobile. An automobile may be used as an ambulance or criminal's get-away car and so too is an inherently value-neutral vehicle. In its traditional function, the corporation has provided a collective identity, suited to collective objects, and facilitated the contribution of limited amounts of personal property to such objects and their continued existence.[83] Further, procedurally, it functions as a deliberative body in which members and directors are expected to consider and vote on different options.[84] These important features developed over time in answer to the social challenges over the centuries and are worth preserving through any corporate reform.

4.1 Corporate Law and Internal Justice

Positive corporate law, like all law, is focused on categories, rights, duties and tests. Corporate law creates the following four main categories: (1) members, (2) directors, (3) corporate identity name, and (4) assets (see Fig. 1).[85] It further creates the rights and duties which apply within and between those categories, and the tests for entering and exiting them. Corporate law thus sets up the internal governance framework as a set of default rules and can be analysed as a collection of property, contract and fiduciary rights and duties.

Justice within the framework of corporate law is a matter of economic desert—corporate rights are granted in return for or as a desert for payment. It is a very narrowly based justice in that it is limited exclusively to those parties internal to the corporation and, as an economically based desert, it precludes other justifications for distributions. It relies exclusively on formal rights, exercised in a commercial context. Given that the exercise of rights is very costly, justice comes only to those with the resources to pursue it—a very clear instance of the old epithet 'you'll have as much justice as you can afford!'

Fig. 1 Traditional corporation

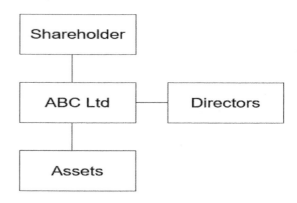

---

[83] Sheehy (2017a).

[84] Bottomley (2007), chapter 5.

[85] Set out in Sheehy (2016).

As is evident from the foregoing, justice in the context of corporate law is markedly different from justice in other contexts discussed above. This situation prevails for two main reasons. First, corporate justice diverges because the focus of corporate law is not on the interaction between the corporation and wider society—parties external to the corporate body. Justice in corporate law is focused internally, primarily on obligations and relations within the legal body itself. Second, corporate justice diverges because the corporation has no moral interest in human society, nor necessary reliance on the natural environment. It is to this corporate-society relationship that this article turns next.

4.2 Corporate Law and Justice in Society

In considering the question of justice at the interface between corporate law and society, there are two competing narratives. The first narrative argues that corporate law is just on utilitarian bases.[86] Using economic norms, it can be argued that the greatest good for the most people has been secured by the corporate form, for as a market institution, corporations have facilitated pooling of capital which in turn has spurred on industrialisation and lifted the quality of life for hundreds of millions around the globe. As such, corporations create the goods and services individuals want and it follows that, in terms of satisfying individual wants, the corporation is a superior form of organising production and distribution. Further, it does so in a way that provides an efficient allocation of capital, an argument advanced by shareholder primacy theorists.[87] Broadly speaking, beyond the foregoing analysis, justice in the relationship between the corporate form and the rest of society has relied on well-established areas of law associated with harms, namely, tort and criminal law.[88]

As is evident from the foregoing analysis, justice in the context of corporate law has been argued using utilitarian lenses in the applied context of economics. This approach has led to the rise of shareholder primacy. Over the course of the 20th century, the scholarship in corporate law, business and economics, as well as related practice, has been reshaped by shareholder primacy—a normative agenda which prioritises shareholder (private) wealth over all other social objectives[89]—identified in a recent EU study as the driver of short-termism in corporate governance and unsustainability.[90] Starting with the Berle and Dodd debate, in which the core question of director responsibility and control was posed, a question later picked up by Henry Manne and subsequently by law and economics scholar Fischel, the normative foundations of company law shifted from being value neutral to advocating economic norms of efficiency and (private) wealth creation. In corporate law, the shift was

---

[86] Hansmann and Kraakman (2004). See argument in Cary (1974).
[87] Jones and Felps (2013).
[88] Sheehy (2017a).
[89] Ireland (2005), Smith (1997).
[90] See Abstract in Directorate-General for Justice and Consumers (European Commission) (2020), p i.

marked by a change in modelling from corporate concession and person theories to mere nexus of contracts.[91]

Corporate law scholarship, government policy, and the practice of corporate law have all supported shareholder primacy. In neo-classical economic orthodoxy and neo-liberal political theory, the corporation is best suited to creating wealth while matters of distribution, such as distribution of environmental contamination and distribution of wealth leading to social inequality sufficient to harm society,[92] were best left to other institutions and other areas of law. The scholarship and practice have increased the corporation's focus on privatising or internalising benefits and externalising costs (i.e., social costs).[93] In practice, this shareholder-centric vision of the corporation has led to greater distributive injustice, increased environmental contamination and social inequality across both geographic and chronological dimensions.

The problem with the first argument supporting the status quo as a just ordering at the corporate-society interface and so underpinning shareholder primacy is that it ignores precisely the critical issue at hand. The corporate creature of shareholder primacy stands in opposition to social justice in all dimensions. It rejects socially just distributions in both geographic and time dimensions. Further, although purportedly facilitating the efficient satisfaction of individual wants, as Nobel laureate Kenneth Arrow demonstrated, aggregation of individual wants does not equate to an appropriate policy for public good, in this case sustainability and justice.[94]

The second narrative argues that corporate law is unjust on several bases.[95] It argues that current legal orderings of tort, crime, certain economic and environmental laws and regulations are fatally flawed as the current climate crisis and growing inequality make clear. It points to ongoing law reforms affecting corporations, such as taxation, wages and the environment, which continue to further privilege private corporations to the detriment of the rest of the population.[96]

Parties subscribing to this narrative argue that the current legal order is flawed for a variety of reasons: in a nutshell, the formal administration of justice does not address the growing inequalities in society nor the general depredation of the natural environment by the corporation. Further, as corporate law does not provide rights to parties who receive no benefit from the corporation's social costs—i.e., outsiders—few parties have rights to challenge corporate decision-making affecting these issues. In addition, the costs of litigating against corporate bodies are prohibitive for all but a few that pool resources to challenge corporate decisions.[97] Furthermore, when it comes to matters of compliance, as Ostas and others have argued, corporations often take an economic approach as opposed to a citizenship approach.[98] That

---

[91] Bratton (1989), Bratton and Wachter (2008).

[92] Piketty (2014).

[93] Sheehy (2004a).

[94] Arrow (1963).

[95] Greenwood (2005).

[96] Hilling and Ostas (2017).

[97] See, for example, Sheehy et al. (2021).

[98] Laufer (2006), Ostas (2004).

means that compliance with law is only desirable to the extent that it costs less than the alternative. They follow the letter of the law only insofar as it is cheaper than breach and do so without regard for social costs.[99] Finally, the corporation with its massive economic clout wields inordinate political power denied to all but the wealthiest of society.[100] In sum, the post facto nature of remedies and the strategic approaches taken to ex ante compliance undermine the effective, proactive approach needed to avoid harms. Further, even if this currently institutionalised approach were suitable, corporations would not be equal contestants on a level playing field. Rather, they are privileged actors with greater professional nous, greater financial resources, greater experience as repeat litigators,[101] and often capable of creating and exploiting regulatory capture.[102]

To gain some conception of the degree of social injustice facilitated through the corporate form, consider the following situation. The two leading beneficiaries of corporate law, Elon Musk and Jeff Bezos, have a combined net worth greater than the GDP of the *12th most populous country on earth*. That country, Ethiopia, hosts a population of 117,000,000—a population larger than the largest European country. Indeed, Musk and Bezos' combined net worth places them at the 51st spot among the 213 *countries* on earth.

Such contrasting of corporate profits and countries' economics is not vain academic speculation. A recent Dutch court noted this precise issue in the context of greenhouse gases. Concerning the relative responsibilities of companies and countries, the judgement stated the following:

> The court is of the opinion that much may be expected of RDS [Royal Dutch Shell, Defendant]. RDS heads the Shell group, which consists of about 1,100 companies, and operates in 160 countries all over the world. It has a policy-setting position [and] ... is a major player on the worldwide market of fossil fuels and is responsible for significant CO_2 emissions, which exceed the emissions of many states and which contributes towards global warming and a dangerous climate change.[103]

Corporations can no longer be analysed solely in terms of private interests, particularly where sustainability issues are at stake. The extensive environmental damage of the planet today is the handiwork of large industrial organisations, mostly organised as corporations.[104] As a result, law is taking account of the large public footprint of these corporations and imposing a greater public orientation on them.

---

[99] See discussion in Hilling and Ostas (2017).

[100] There exists a whole literature on the topic and this empowerment of the corporation as a political actor has been to a large degree the work of the courts attributing the rights developed for human citizens to corporate citizens.

[101] Galanter (1974).

[102] Carpenter and Moss (2013).

[103] *Milieudefensie v Royal Dutch Shell RDS*, 25 May 2021, The Hague, at para. 2.4.2. ECLI:NL:RBDHA: 2021:5339., para. 4.4.16

[104] Heede (2014), Vitali et al. (2011), Sheehy (2017b).

The result of this corporate injustice is a significant discontent and push back against corporate power and despoilment across society. Indeed, a global, anti-corporate narrative and activism has arisen in response to the corporate injustice just described.[105] The demand for social and environmental justice, as evidenced in actions taken largely by corporate outsiders, in actions ranging from consumer boy-cotts and extensive legal challenges, to such things as outright, physical attacks on corporate assets like mine sites, oil wells and corporate headquarters, demonstrates the breadth and depth of discontent with current distributions.[106]

From a strictly legal point of view, as noted earlier, corporate law is focused on insiders, facilitating the ordering of their affairs, particularly by reducing the risks of being visited by liability for the actions taken by the collective.[107] As a result, the corporation can engage legally in activities which are risky and anti-social but prof-itable, for the benefit of the insiders—shareholders, directors and executives. The negative consequences remain in the public realm while the positive consequences are concentrated to the benefit of the insiders. Thus, the corporate structure encour-ages the production of 'social costs'[108]—something simply considered as the natu-ral state of affairs.[109] Accordingly, implementing shareholder primacy, it should be expected that corporations exploit the natural and social capital of the planet without regard for other interests or values. It is expected that the creation of such social costs increases private profits and is part of the legal design of the corporation.[110] In a sense, the corporation is the perfect economic actor exploiting and destroying ecological and social systems in order to generate financial wealth. As Paddy Ire-land describes it: '[What] we are now experiencing is corporate capitalism operating according to its normal, financialized, and inherently unethical logic.'[111] Ireland's point is sharp: ethics is a matter of social justice and concern and not a matter of corporate law. Again, the corporation itself can be described as a neutral vehicle; however, when put to use as it is currently for the exploitation of today's social and environmental resources without regard for any other persons or social institutions, present or future, it creates a serious problem. This problem of 'social costs' cannot be left to other institutions as, for a variety of reasons, doing so has triggered the crises we face.

This configuration of law at the corporate-society interface poses a direct chal-lenge to the social contract—a metaphorical contract between the governing and the governed on the basis of mutual benefit.[112] In the case of the corporation, the social contract is challenged by an actor that has neither moral sense nor personal incen-tive to engage in social relations. The corporation lacks human social characteristics.

---

[105] Mac Sheoin (2014).

[106] Soule (2009).

[107] This view opposes the economic explanation of the corporation as being the natural and logical out-come of efficient allocation of risk and reward. Ireland (2017).

[108] Sheehy (2004a).

[109] Eckersley (2016), p 346.

[110] Sheehy (2004a).

[111] Ireland (2018).

[112] Sheehy (2004–2005).

It is on this ground that it is correctly identified as a 'Frankenstein'[113] and 'psychopath'[114] as such persons, like corporations, do not share social norms generally and lack motivation for sustainability and justice.[115] This phenomenon has been explained in the literature as the corporation's lack of social embeddedness in society[116] and as a matter resolved in part through corporate social responsibility.[117]

The foregoing analysis of the current state of affairs of the corporate-society interface can be summarised as follows: the shareholder primacy corporation is best described as a powerful economic and political actor, socially parasitical, pursuing short-term financial interests[118] inimical to sustainability and distributive justice in its geographic and time dimensions. The status quo is inadequate for the task of addressing sustainability and distributive justice.

In sum, the corporation's internal focus and lack of interest in matters external invite reconceptualising the corporation to address the critical issue of sustainability—a value placed by society on the natural environment—and the potential for reform. Accordingly, the article now turns to consider what reforms of corporate law might be suitable to address the issues.

5 Corporate Rights and Duties Redistributed for Sustainability

As noted above, Greenfield has argued that 'there are major public policy problems that otherwise seem intractable, and reforms in corporate governance may prove to be powerful and efficient mechanisms to address them'.[119] The geographic and time dimensions of justice are precisely such major public policy problems that cannot be addressed without discussing the corporation.

Currently, corporate decision-makers—directors and shareholders—exercise their corporate rights as they choose. Corporations are subject to the law only and are not encumbered by moral obligations or sentiments:[120] their institutional design is neutral. Despite their ostensibly deliberative, democratic decision-making procedures, decision-makers tend to follow interests narrowly defined by management.[121] In sum, the corporation, by virtue of its legal architecture, shareholder primacy norms, unlimited geographic reach and unlimited chronological life, is indifferent if not inimical to the time and geographic concerns of justice and the social and ecological values of sustainability—those things of 'value which should be maintained … into the indefinite future'.[122]

---

[113] Wormser (1931).
[114] Bakan (2004).
[115] Barry (1997), p 64.
[116] Polanyi (1944, 2001).
[117] Amstutz (2011).
[118] Sheehy (2017b).
[119] Greenfield (2005), p 39.
[120] Sheehy (2004–2005).
[121] Bottomley (2007).
[122] Barry (1997), p 50.

This state of affairs is failing in terms of justice and sustainability as argued above and, accordingly, the solution must be to reform corporate law. The basic principles underpinning all such reforms have been argued elegantly by Kent Greenfield. The five Principles he has identified are:

1. The ultimate purpose of corporations should be to serve the interests of society as a whole;
2. Corporations are distinctively able to contribute to the society good by creating financial prosperity;
3. Corporate law should further Principles 1 and 2;
4. A corporation's wealth should be shared fairly among those who contribute to its creation; and
5. Participatory, democratic corporate governance is the best way to ensure the sustainable creation and equitable distribution of corporate wealth.[123]

Tying these Principles to the argument, it is clear that the sustainability of society is dependent in part on distributive justice (the other part being ecological). Further, distributive justice can be achieved in corporate law by implementing Principle 1, ensuring the corporation serves the interests of society as a whole (across time and geographic dimensions), and Principle 4, fair distributions of wealth across the same dimensions. Greenfield's Principle 5 is a principle for procedural as well as structural reform of the corporation. Implementation of these Principles calls for reform at two levels: an internal, corporate level and an external, societal level. The article turns next to consider what reforms would be required at these levels to achieve sustainability and distributive justice across time and geography.

5.1 Redistributions: Internal Reforms to the Corporation

Internal to corporate law, a reform of categories, rights, duties and tests is required. Again, Greenfield states the problem comprehensively:

> Instead of creating a governance system that would help internalize the concerns of customers, employees, or society in general, the system of corporate governance … sets up shareholder interests as supreme and centralizes decision making so that those interests are served. Other stakeholders are left to depend on mechanisms outside corporate law, primarily in the form of express contracts or government regulation, both seriously imperfect, to protect their interests.[124]

Applying Greenfield's broad critique requires a proposed reform to be aimed at internalising social concerns and demands, among other things, a re-ordering of

---

[123] Greenfield (2005).

[124] Ibid., p 17.

corporate norms so as to displace the shareholder primacy norm and a redistribution of decision-making power necessary to ensure a reallocation of costs and benefits. For a reform to integrate the interests of future and distant peoples, it must identify the interests of those people, analyse existing rights and duties, and consider how a grant of legal rights and imposition of duties could provide for those interests. There are currently two active policy agendas investigating such reform: the EU's recent Study of Directors' Duties[125] and the UK's 2018 Corporate Governance Review. Taking these insights, the article turns next to consider further specifics of the categories and associated rights and duties of directors, followed by a consideration of shareholders.

5.1.1 Directors Duties and Tripartite Board

The innovative empirical work of the EU Directorate-General for Justice and Consumers, the Study on Directors' Duties and Sustainable Corporate Governance, investigates drivers of short-termism, given that it is this time dimension which is a main driver of unsustainable practices.[126] Specifically, the Study declares that the EU should adopt as a specific objective 'promoting corporate governance practices that contribute to company sustainability' and that such an objective justifies an

> EU intervention [to] … address corporate governance practices that favour short-termism and hinder the integration of sustainability into company decision-making (e.g. in the area of corporate reporting, board remuneration, board composition, stakeholder involvement).[127]

The Study specifically recommends a reform 'requiring corporate boards to establish mechanisms for engaging with and involving internal and external stakeholders in identifying, preventing and mitigating sustainability risks and impacts as part of their business strategy.' A comprehensive framework for assessing recommendations was developed which took into account impacts on regulatory frameworks, companies, fundamental rights, broader economic, social, and environmental impacts, and public administrations, in terms of effectiveness, efficiency, coherence and proportionality.[128] The outcome of the assessment demonstrates that such a reform could have a strongly positive impact on sustainability.[129]

The UK's Financial Reporting Council has a similar idea and provides the following directive:

> The board should understand the views of the company's other key stakeholders and describe in the annual report how their interests and the matters set out in section 172 of the Companies Act 2006 have been considered in board

---

[125] Directorate-General for Justice and Consumers (European Commission) (2020).

[126] Ibid., p 40, along with market pressures and the shareholder primacy norm.

[127] Ibid., p 47, at 4.3.1 General and specific policy objectives.

[128] Ibid., p 61, at 5 Assessment of options.

[129] Ibid., p 142, at 5.6.4 Assessment of option C6, which entails the proposal made by the Commission.

discussions and decision making. The board should keep engagement mechanisms under review so that they remain effective.

For engagement with the workforce, one or a combination of the following methods should be used: a director appointed from the workforce; a formal workforce advisory panel; a designated non-executive director. If the board has not chosen one or more of these methods, it should explain what alternative arrangements are in place and why it considers that they are effective.[130]

The issue, as presaged by the UK proposal, is how such a reform might best be executed. There is no a priori reason for the EU proposal to leave it to existing 'corporate boards to establish mechanisms for engaging with and involving internal and external stakeholders in identifying, preventing and mitigating sustainability risks and impacts'. In fact, there is good reason to believe that existing institutions will persist and that structural change may be the preferred method.[131] Similarly, the UK's proposal of a workforce appointed director, workforce advisory panel or non-executive director does not adequately empower non-short-term views and priorities. Accordingly, a proposal to reform decision-making structures may be more appropriate.

Thus, rather than leaving decisions, whether economic, social or environmental, to people whose traditional focus is primarily on finance, disaggregating these decision-making rights and duties is more likely to deliver on sustainability goals—by involving parties whose view of compliance is not merely an economic calculus. This disaggregation of director rights and reform could be accomplished by taking the German co-determination model one step further, from a two-board structure to a three-board structure—a proposal that has been an area of progressive corporate law scholarship for decades.[132] Such disaggregation provides a clear, direct way to implement the proposal.

The proposal would see companies of a certain size be mandatorily structured with three boards. The three-board structure includes a redistribution of decision-making power among directors, such that each board is charged with decisions affecting its area of distinct competence, providing for a greater possibility of just and sustainable outcomes. The three boards would be the following: a strategic board focused on business strategy, operations and finance, as are current boards; a second board, focused on the ecological sustainability of operations, perhaps making decisions on the spend of carbon budgets; finally, a third social board, taking account not only of present employee concerns, but also of current community and future generations' concerns. This third board would contribute to decision-making in areas with particular attention to social and intergenerational justice concerns. An introduction of new boards would be a structural reform sufficient to re-norm the corporation away from shareholder primacy toward ecological and social sustainability. As Greenfield has put it in his 5th Principle, 'participatory, democratic

---

[130] Financial Reporting Council (2018), p 5, at Board Leadership and Company Purpose, Provision 5. Sheehy (2004b).

[131] See, for examples, Pierson (2000a, 2000b), Schneiberg (2007), Schneiberg and Bartley (2008).

[132] See Greenfield (2005), p 158.

Fig. 2 Three-tiered board

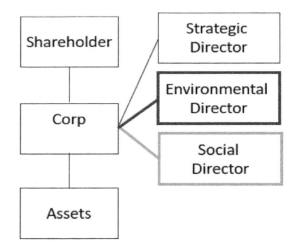

corporate governance is the best way to ensure the sustainable creation and equitable distribution of corporate wealth'.[133]

This proposal is illustrated graphically above in Fig. 2.

For such a proposal to be effective, each one of the boards and their members need to be granted rights and duties. Such rights might be distributed as follows: where a proposal of the strategic board has a negative impact on the natural environment, whether through consumption or emission of greater than 1% of existing operations, for example, the environmental board has the right to block the company from taking the decision. It further could have a right to put forward an alternative method for achieving the proposed increase.

Taking the example and applying it to the social board, if the same proposal were to benefit society, whether present or future generations, by a sufficient amount or in a significant way, or create a positive significant impact on the immediate community, the social board could support the strategic board. Alternatively, it could decide that the environmental board was correct or that the negative social impact was sufficient to block the strategic board. In the same way as the environmental board, the social board could have the right to block the company from taking a strategic decision. And further, it could have a right to put forward an alternative method for achieving the proposed increase. Charging and empowering these different boards with decision-making rights and duties to pursue sustainability and justice goals along with financial success would be a significant step toward achieving all three goals.

Although a tripartite board may be structurally novel and, some may argue, lead to irresolvable disagreements among directors and boards, such disagreements are not novel at all. All directors come to decisions with their own idiosyncratic ways of looking at things, their own concerns and areas of responsibility and competence. In the corporate context, directors' duties properly discharged require directors to come

---

[133] Greenfield (2005).

together to deliberate and negotiate compromises.[134] These compromises allow them to set a course for and monitor the company. Using a tripartite board structure to make these critical sustainability and justice goals and conflicts clear and requiring explicitly addressing them through a negotiated process is a way to achieve those critical goals.

Membership in the boards would need to come about through nominating committees in ways that do not follow conventional norms where management proposes and boards adopt nominees. Rather, the boards would need to be populated by parties external to current C-suite candidates. These board members would need to be drawn from among suitably qualified experts in the respective fields of environmental sciences and relevant social concerns who could be nominated for election by appropriately assembled constituents, whether community groups, labour or environmental groups. Their professional commitments could act as a proxy for identifying parties interested in compliance with legal obligations rather than the limited economic calculus of directors. Restructuring the direction of corporations so that environmentally focused parties and stakeholders pursuing broader society's sustainability objectives are empowered by rights provides a clear way of achieving goals of sustainability and justice.

Along with these decision-making rights there must be duties. Accordingly, directors' duties of care, diligence and good faith[135] should be applied to all three of the boards. Further, as the corporation is operating a for-profit enterprise, all boards would need to consider profitability or at least wealth broadly defined to include natural and social capital.

Having discussed the board of directors as a decision-making body appropriate for reform, we turn next to consider the other decision-making body of the corporation, the shareholders.

5.1.2 Shareholders and Stakeholders

Commonly, shareholders' rights are of two types: economic and political.[136] Shareholders have rights to dividends, the right to sell their shares and rights to vote on various matters. There is no question whether shareholders value the economic rights: rights to a share of profits and capital gains are the fundamental rights for which they pay. As to justice-based arguments for redistribution of shareholder economic rights—the broader social sustainability concern—that is a matter of economic systems and well beyond the scope of mere corporate law reform.[137]

The situation is different, however, with respect to shareholders' political rights. Shareholders in public companies, whose choices are described as 'exit or voice',

---

[134] Bottomley (2007).

[135] Velasco (2009), see consideration in Reyes (2018), p 155.

[136] Sheehy (2006).

[137] The justice argument against investment in shares arises in political philosophy, most influentially put by Marx.

are for the most part uninterested in their voting rights (at least where sufficient liquidity exists).[138] As Adam Smith put it nearly 250 years ago,

> the greater part of those … [shareholders] seldom pretend to understand any thing of the business of the company; and … give themselves no trouble about it, but receive contentedly such half yearly or yearly dividend, as the directors think proper to make to them.[139]

For all but the largest shareholders, exit is the economically rational, preferred choice. There is little to be gained in today's managerial corporation from exercising rights to voice—at least if not done strategically in a concerted manner.[140] Accordingly, redistributing shareholder votes to parties interested in exercising these political powers is eminently justified and practical.

Where decision rights have been granted to shareholders, corporate law could be reformed by redistributing such rights. Corporate law could create a mandatory new category of denominated 'stakeholders'. That category would form a new corporate organ in addition to the existing organs of shareholders and the board of directors. The stakeholder organ would exercise the voting rights currently granted to shareholders, including personal rights, on issues of stakeholder concern, namely sustainability issues—things of 'value that should be maintained … into the indefinite future'.[141]

This new corporate organ would make a significant contribution to deliberative corporate decision-making because its focus, unlike the wealth focus of shareholders, would be on concerns associated with sustainability where those decision-making rights currently reside within the decision-making domain of shareholders. This proposed reform is significant because in the status quo, sustainability concerns that currently fall within the domain of shareholders' rights are difficult to exercise. Shareholders' rights are generally restricted to avoid encroachment on directors' discretion and breach of the separation of powers doctrine in company law.[142] Accordingly, courts seek to preserve directors' decision-making domain and, in some jurisdictions, suppress ESG shareholder activist voices.[143] The notable, recent successes by activist shareholders in forcing Exxon and Chevron[144] to take action on climate change[145] and are newsworthy because they are exceptional instances proving the general rule that shareholders struggle when seeking to exercise their rights.

---

[138] Coffee (1991), McCahery et al. (2016).

[139] Smith (2007), p 574. See Anderson and Tollison (1982).

[140] Sheehy et al. (2021).

[141] Barry (1997), p 50.

[142] Sheehy et al. (2021).

[143] Sheehy et al. (forthcoming).

[144] Yahoo!Finance (2021).

[145] Crowley and Deveau (2021).

It may even be desirable to grant this organ some directors' rights. It is hard to see why the UK would recognise that boards of directors are failing to deal adequately with stakeholders—'The board should understand the views of the company's other key stakeholders and describe in the annual report how their interests and the matters set out in section 172 of the Companies Act 2006 have been considered'[146]—yet continue to support directors wielding decision-making powers. Directors do have the discretion to consider stakeholder concerns: the issue is their failure to do so and use them for stakeholder ends.[147]

Creating a stakeholder organ and empowering it with a grant of decision-making rights would be a very significant reform. A common criticism of stakeholderism and corporate social responsibility generally is that without rights, these non-shareholder, non-director parties will never have power to influence decision-making and corporate operational decisions.[148] The consequence of such lack of legal rights is that issues of unsustainability and injustice continue as institutionalised within the discretionary scope of directors' decision-making.[149]

The proposed reform would put powerful rights into the hands of stakeholder parties—parties concerned with corporate social responsibility and strong form sustainability.[150] Stakeholders, contemplated to extend beyond employees and creditors,[151] could include parties with particular interests and expertise in social and environmental matters, much the same as the proposed directors of the tripartite environmental and social boards and nominated in the same way. The stakeholder organ would provide an effective counter-balancing corporate organ with rights sufficient to restrain or displace the shareholder primacy norm. Again, this proposal aligns with Greenfield's fifth Principle of participatory, democratic governance. The new

Fig. 3 New stakeholder organ

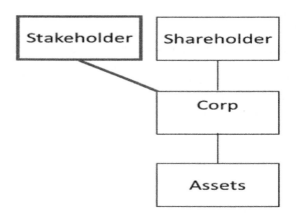

[146] Financial Reporting Council (2018), p 5, at Board Leadership and Company Purpose, Provision 5. Sheehy (2004b).
[147] Sheehy and Feaver (2014).
[148] Welling (2009).
[149] Sheehy (2012).
[150] Sheehy (2015), Sheehy and Farneti (2021), Sjåfjell and Bruner (2020).
[151] See discussion in Reyes (2018), pp 165-6.

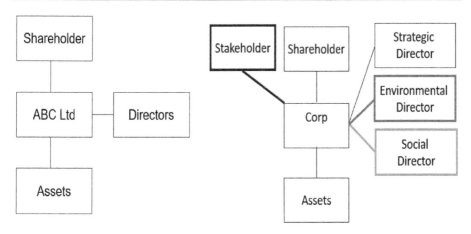

Fig. 4 Traditional and reformed corporations

corporate organ, the stakeholder category, can be represented in diagrammatic form (see Fig. 3 above).

Implemented together, the additional boards and new stakeholder organ would create a significantly reformed corporation. The corporation would be a different creation in terms of both structure and operating norms. That overall difference can be illustrated. In Fig. 4 above, the traditional model corporation is on the left and can be contrasted with the proposed reformed corporation on the right.

This reformed corporation re-embeds the corporation in society, creating clear, direct social connections and environmental norms in what is otherwise an exclusively self-interested, profit-driven legal actor.

5.2 Redistribution: Corporate Relationship with Society

Turning next to consider the corporation's relationship with society, the corporate-society interface,[152] a reconsideration of the egalitarian principles of the social contract, and as argued in this article, sustainability as well as the geographic and time dimensions of justice is required.[153] As noted, currently, the corporate-society relationship is regulated by tort and criminal law along with a range of economic and environmental laws and regulations, and further, as argued above, it is failing critically. The corporate actor in the corporate-society relationship has no innate regard for non-corporate impacts on present or future generations or people located elsewhere,[154] and has no object beyond financial self-interest.[155] If the corporation is to

---

[152] Sheehy (2017a, 2017b).

[153] I have argued elsewhere that these social contract principles include corporations. See Sheehy (2004–2005).

[154] Bakan (2004).

[155] Gatti and Ondersma (2020).

take account of social concerns, it cannot be expected to do so merely responsively to external law; rather, some internal reform is necessary.

To orient a reform of norms for the corporate relationship with society, it is useful to return to Greenfield's Principles. His first Principle provides an appropriate normative foundation: 'The ultimate purpose of corporations should be to serve the interests of society as a whole.'[156] Applying this Principle in the broader context of this article provides a startling insight. There is no reason to limit the 'interests of society as a whole' to the populace of a particular jurisdiction at a specific moment in time. In other words, the corporate-society relationship must begin with principles of ecological and social sustainability and justice.

Greenfield continues with his second Principle: 'Corporations are distinctively able to contribute to the society's good by creating financial prosperity.'[157] They are able to do so by facilitating the division of labour that allows the efficient production of a vast array of goods and services. Greenfield goes on to offer his third Principle: 'Corporate law should further Principles 1 and 2.' Thus, while the corporation is useful to society as a means of pooling wealth and putting it to productive purposes, it cannot be used for this purpose alone and turn a blind eye to unsustainable operating procedures and unjust distributions. Accordingly, from a normative perspective, the ultimate test for corporations should be their overall contribution to society and while basic efficiency and profit norms should remain, they cannot be the ultimate or exclusive norms determining corporate law reform. Efficiency in use of capital, natural resources and social resources are a contribution to sustainability. Efficiency helps preserve resources not immediately needed for consumption in the production process. Profitability too is critical in private enterprise or the enterprise will fail. Ignoring the other impacts, however, is a fatal error. His fourth Principle, dealing with wealth distributions, could be extended to include compensation for social costs. Finally, his fifth Principle, 'Participatory, democratic corporate governance is the best way to ensure the sustainable creation and equitable distribution of corporate wealth',[158] provides a normative foundation for the proposed tripartite board and stakeholder body.

Returning more broadly to the issue, the question is raised: how can the corporate-society interface be reformed to address sustainability and justice? The relationship needs to be reconceptualised as a question of distributive norms and public actors rather than a private right to wealth acquisition. Distributions from the currently configured corporations cannot be justified on utilitarian or egalitarian grounds. These inequitable distributions are an obvious breach of the utilitarian norm of the greatest happiness for the greatest number of people. By the same token, this distribution is out of alignment with any egalitarian justification. Further, such a distribution cannot be justified on the specifically distributive norms of needs, desert or moral value. These distributions are simply the result of strategic use of corporate

---

[156] Greenfield (2005).

[157] Ibid.

[158] Ibid.

law representing the political choices which have shaped contemporary corporate law and governance.[159]

Accordingly, four new norms need to be introduced to reform the corporate-society relationship. First, a new norm of fairness needs to be created. This norm, expanding Greenfield's focus on those who have contributed to wealth creation, should include fairness in distribution of costs and benefits as between present and future generations, and around the globe—that is to say, in both time and geographic dimensions. Thus, as a sustainability argument, fairness requires distribution of wages and dividends, public goods, and social costs.

A second and related norm needs to be introduced. This norm should be aimed at displacing the shareholder primacy norm with its externalising effect. It would focus instead on internalisation of social costs and take a direct step away from neo-classical economic theory of social costs.[160] It acknowledges the very real limitations of the Coase theorem,[161] such as the problems of incomplete markets and information asymmetries—i.e., the failures of markets that require regulatory solutions.[162] Imaginary ideal worlds where transaction costs are zero and information is timely and complete are a policy for the sustainability disaster unfolding around the world and rampant inequality. The new norm would provide a new rationale and theory for the corporation[163] and provide a major impetus for exploring and reconfiguring the society-corporation interface.[164]

This new internalising norm would be readily implemented in law via a shift of risk. The burden currently in the form of public environmental law norms, namely, polluter pays, prevention and precautionary principle, would need to be shifted from the public to the private realm. That is, the private corporation would have internal obligations, associated with the proposed environmental tier of the board of directors, stiffened by an associated directors' duty and encumbrance of assets or shares. Such a shift would address chronological injustice. Whereas the current justice model requires ex post corrective justice, the changed model is a shift to distributive justice ex ante. Costs must be paid in real time, rather than left to people remote in geography or time.

The third new norm should focus on a greater externalising of benefits. As the corporation's greatest public benefit is the creation of wealth, so too must the distribution of this benefit be a leading reform. This externalising, or redistribution as a form of justice, could be implemented not only by limiting executive pay to a multiple of employee wages, but also by limiting share dividends to a benchmark, for example, a proportion of national GDP growth. In other words, privatisation of wealth is restrained by commensurate public wealth growth. In terms of justice,

---

[159] Roe (2006).

[160] Coase (1960).

[161] Ibid.

[162] Cooter (1982), Fischel (1992), Medema (2008).

[163] As, for example, Blair and Stout's teamwork theory in Blair and Stout (2001) or Greenwood's democratically informed vision in Greenwood (2005).

[164] Sheehy (2017a).

this redistribution would be readily justified on egalitarian grounds. It would implement the justification for much neo-classical economic inspired neo-liberal policy reform—'a rising tide lifts all boats'—which, while a widely accepted justification, has failed to deliver much for any group other than the top 0.1% according to a 30-year study.[165] If the latter is to be the policy objective as well as its justification, it is hard to imagine a more effective means of doing so.

A fourth, final and critical new norm needs to be created to address current decisions by corporate executives with respect to compliance. Laws represent a society's bargain, its social contract with the corporation—a type of lateral social contract as between fellow citizens.[166] As compliance is indicative of a corporation's membership in society, its 'citizenship'[167]—a reform and re-embedding of the corporation in that society through a revision of corporate compliance practice is critical. The present practice ignores all social obligations and moral impetus and views compliance merely through an economic lens. It does not consider a legal obligation using a political citizenship lens.[168] In the economic lens, compliance and non-compliance are merely prices on various types of activity, a cost of doing business around the globe.

Creating a new norm and approach to compliance, argues Ostas, requires reconsideration of the difference between legal compliance and legal cooperation. The distinction, he argues,

> becomes critical whenever the law has ambiguities, has loopholes, or is underenforced. One cooperates by interpreting legal ambiguities in the light of the public good, by resisting temptations to exploit unintended loopholes, and by complying with the letter of the law even when the law is underenforced.[169]

As he has written elsewhere, 'the letter of the law may have loopholes, but the spirit of the law does not'.[170] Taking Ostas' thinking further, the new compliance norm would expect corporations to seek to fulfil the public good, to comply with the spirit of the law as the default rather than the opposite approach, a norm of searching for loopholes and one of economic calculus without consideration of citizenship obligations.

Combined, the creative redistribution by internal reforms by way of tripartite boards and stakeholder bodies proposed in this article would be expected to deliver a re-embedding of the current socially disembedded actor. These reforms, if implemented, would radically alter the global trajectory of sustainability and justice both over time and geographically in a world still dominated by corporations.

---

[165] Kwon and Salcido (2019). See also Throsby (2017).
[166] Sheehy (2004–2005).
[167] Crane and Matten (2016), Edward and Willmott (2008), Matten and Crane (2005), Néron (2016).
[168] Sheehy (2015).
[169] Ostas (2004), p 594.
[170] Hilling and Ostas (2017), p 20.

🍃 Springer   ⚫ ASSER PRESS

6 Conclusion

As Kent Greenfield observes, 'corporate law, just like every other area of common and statutory law, is predicated upon our collective political decisions about what we want our society to look like'.[171] This article has argued that society is looking for sustainability—the preservation of the ecology and social well-being such that the generations into the indefinite future are able to live fulfilling lives. For this to occur, there needs to be significant change in social institutions, and particularly the legal form of the corporation, the preferred organisation used for the production and distribution of goods and services.

Corporate law in its current form is contributing to the climate crisis and social inequality in the present and will continue to do so into the foreseeable future. It lacks social embeddedness, has no duty to consider impacts of environmental destruction or social inequality beyond those found in the laws of tort, property, environment and economics.

The need for corporate law reform is evident. Building on the principles advanced by Greenfield, this article has argued that sustainability and justice cannot be achieved without significant attention to corporate law. Canvassing utilitarian and egalitarian ideas of justice and distributive justice with its chronological and geographic dimensions, the article has investigated the implications of those issues for corporate reform. Having proposed structural reforms to the board of directors as well as to shareholders' rights, the article proposes new norms. The intention is to provide directions for future dialogue and debate about how one of humanity's more useful inventions may be reformed for continued use in the challenging and changing times we are facing as a species.

References

Amelang S, Appunn K, Nijhuis C, Wettengel J (2021) 'Top court rules German climate law falls short, in "historic" victory for youth' 30 Apr 2021. https://www.climatechangenews.com/2021/04/30/top-court-rules-german-climate-law-falls-short-historic-victory-youth/. Accessed 15 May 2021

Amstutz M (2011) The double movement in global law: the case of European corporate social responsibility. In: Joerges C, Falke J (eds) Karl Polanyi, globalisation and the potential of law in transnational markets. Hart Publishing, London

Anderson GM, Tollison RD (1982) Adam Smith's analysis of joint-stock companies. J Polit Econ 90(6):1237–1256. http://www.jstor.org/stable/1830946. Accessed 2 Jun 2021

Arfken M, Yen J (2014) Psychology and social justice: theoretical and philosophical engagements. J Theor Philos Psychol 13(1):1–13

Aristotle (2009) The Nicomachean ethics. In: Brown L, Ross D (eds) Oxford World's Classics. OUP, Oxford

Arrow K (1963) Social choice and individual values, 2nd edn. John Wiley & Sons Inc, New York

Bakan J (2004) The corporation: the pathological pursuit of profit and power. Simon and Schuster, New York

Bañon Gomis AJ, Guillén Parra M, Hoffman WM, McNulty RE (2011) Rethinking the concept of sustainability. Bus Soc Rev 116(2):171–191

---

[171] Greenfield (2005), p 37.

Barry B (1997) Sustainability and intergenerational justice. Theoria 44(89):43–64

BBC (2021) 'German climate change law violates rights, court rules', BBC News, 1 May 2021. https://www.bbc.com/news/world-europe-56927010. Accessed 5 May 2021

Berry W (1971) The unforeseen wilderness: an essay on Kentucky's Red River Gorge. The University Press of Kentucky, Lexington

Blair M, Stout L (2001) A team production theory of corporate law. Va Law Rev 85:247–328

Bottomley S (2007) Constitutional corporation: rethinking corporate governance. Ashgate Publishing Limited, Aldershot

Boulding K (1966) The economics of the coming spaceship earth. In: Jarrett H (ed) Environmental quality in a growing economy. Johns Hopkins University Press, Baltimore, pp 3–14

Bratton W (1989) The new economic theory of the firm: critical perspectives from history. Stanf Law Rev 41:1471–1527

Bratton WW, Wachter ML (2008) Shareholder primacy's corporatist origins: Adolf Berle and 'the modern corporation'. J Corp Law 34:99–152

Brock G (2017) Global justice. In: Zalta EN (ed) The Stanford Encyclopedia of Philosophy (Spring 2017 edn)

Caney S (2009) Climate change and the future: discounting for time, wealth, and risk. J Soc Philos 40(2):163–186

Carpenter D, Moss DA (2013) Preventing regulatory capture: special interest influence and how to limit it. Cambridge University Press

Cary WL (1974) Federalism and corporate law: reflections upon Delaware. Yale Law J 83(4):663–705

Chiu IHY (2021) The EU sustainable finance agenda—developing governance for double materiality in sustainability metrics. European Business Organization Law Review, this volume

Chiu IHY, Donovan A (2017) A new milestone in corporate regulation: procedural legalisation, standards of transnational corporate behaviour and lessons from financial regulation and anti-bribery regulation. J Corp Law Stud 17(2):427–467. https://doi.org/10.1080/14735970.2017.1312061

Coase R (1960) The problem of social cost. J Law Econ 3(1):1–44

Coffee JC (1991) Liquidity versus control: the institutional investor as corporate monitor. Columbia Law Rev 91(6):1277–1368

Cooter R (1982) The cost of Coase. J Leg Stud 11(1):1–33

Crane A, Matten D (2016) Business ethics: managing corporate citizenship and sustainability in the age of globalization. Oxford University Press

Crowley K, Deveau S (2021) 'Exxon CEO is dealt stinging setback at hands of new activist', Bloomberg Green, 27 May 2021. https://www.bloomberg.com/news/articles/2021-05-26/tiny-exxon-investor-notches-climate-win-with-two-board-seats. Accessed 5 Jun 2021

Daly H, Cobb J Jr (1989) For the common good: redirecting the economy toward community, the environment, and a sustainable future. Beacon Press, Boston

de Sadeleer N (2002) Environmental principles: from political slogans to legal rules (S. Leubusher, Trans). Oxford University Press, Oxford

Della Porta D, Andretta M, Calle A, Combes H, Eggert N, Giugni MG, Hadden JJ, M, Marchetti, R, (2015) Global justice movement: cross-national and transnational perspectives. Routledge, London

Directorate-General for Justice and Consumers (European Commission) (2020) Study on directors' duties and sustainable corporate governance. https://op.europa.eu/en/publication-detail/-/publication/e47928a2-d20b-11ea-adf7-01aa75ed71a1/language-en#document-info. Accessed 6 May 2021

Dunlap RE, McCright AM (2011) Organized climate change denial. Oxf Handb Clim Chang Soc 1:144–160

Easterbrook F, Fischel D (1991) The economic structure of corporate law. Harvard Univ Press, Cambridge

Eckersley R (1992) Environmentalism and political theory: toward an ecocentric approach. Suny Press, Albany

Eckersley R (2016) Responsibility for climate change as a structural injustice. In: Gabrielson T, Hall C, Meyer JM, Schlosberg D (eds) The Oxford handbook of environmental political theory. OUP, pp 346-361

Edward P, Willmott H (2008) Corporate citizenship: rise or demise of a myth? Acad Manag Rev 33:771–775

Federal Constitutional Court. (2021) 'Constitutional complaints against the Federal Climate Change Act partially successful' [Press release]. https://www.bundesverfassungsgericht.de/SharedDocs/Pressemitteilungen/EN/2021/bvg21-031.html. Accessed 21 Jun 2021

Financial Reporting Council (2018) The UK Corporate Governance Code. https://www.frc.org.uk/getat
tachment/88bd8c45-50ea-4841-95b0-d2f4f48069a2/2018-UK-Corporate-Governance-Code-
FINAL.PDF. Accessed 5 Jun 2021

Fischel DR (1992) Review: Dr. Pangloss meets the Coase theorem. The economic structure of corporate
law by Frank H. Easterbrook. Harvard Law Rev 105(6):1408–1413

Fuchs DA (2007) Business power in global governance. Lynne Rienner, Boulder

Gaines SE (1991) The polluter-pays principle: from economic equity to environmental ethos. Tex Int'l LJ
26:463–496

Galanter M (1974) Why the 'haves' come out ahead: speculations on the limits of legal change. Law Soc
Rev 9(1):95–160

Gatti M, Ondersma CD (2020) Can a broader corporate purpose redress inequality? The stakeholder
approach chimera. 46 J Corp L 1 (2020)

Gómez-Baggethun E, Naredo JM (2015) In search of lost time: the rise and fall of limits to growth
in international sustainability policy. Sustain Sci 10(3):385–395. https://doi.org/10.1007/
s11625-015-0308-6

Gray JC (2003) The rule against perpetuities. The Lawbook Exchange, Ltd.

Green RM (1977) Intergenerational distributive justice and environmental responsibility. Bioscience
27(4):260–265

Greenfield K (2005) The failure of corporate law: fundamental flaws and progressive possibilities. University of Chicago Press, Chicago

Greenwood DJ (2005) Markets and democracy: the illegitimacy of corporate law. UMKC l. Rev.
74:41–104

Griffin P (2017) The Carbon Majors Database: CDP Carbon Majors Report 2017. https://b8f65cb373
b1b7b15feb-c70d8ead6ced550b4d987d7c03fcdd1d.ssl.cf3.rackcdn.com/cms/reports/documents/
000/002/327/original/Carbon-Majors-Report-2017.pdf?1499691240. Accessed 12 Apr 2019

Hansmann H, Kraakman R (2004) What is corporate law? Yale Law & Economics Research Paper No.
300

Haskins GL (1977) Extending the grasp of the dead hand: reflections on the origins of the rule against
perpetuities. Univ Pa Law Rev 126:19–46

Heede R (2014) Tracing anthropogenic carbon dioxide and methane emissions to fossil fuel and
cement producers, 1854–2010. Clim Change 122(1–2):229–241. https://doi.org/10.1007/
s10584-013-0986-y

Hilling A, Ostas DT (2017) Corporate taxation and social responsibility. Wolters Kluwer Sverige AB,
Stockholm

Horwitz MJ (1977) The transformation of American law, 1780–1860. Harvard University Press,
Cambridge

Ireland P (2001) Defending the rentier: corporate theory and the reprivatization of the public company.
In: Parkinson J, Gamble A, Kelly G (eds) The political economy of the company. Hart, Oxford

Ireland P (2005) Shareholder primacy and the distribution of wealth. Mod Law Rev 68(1):49–81

Ireland P (2017) Finance and the origins of modern company law. In: Baars G, Spicer A (eds) The corporation: a critical, multi-disciplinary handbook. Cambridge University Press, Cambridge

Ireland P (2018) From Lonrho to BHS: the changing character of corporate governance in contemporary
capitalism. King's Law J 29:3–35

Jones TM, Felps W (2013) Shareholder wealth maximization and social welfare: a utilitarian critique.
Bus Ethics Q 23(2):207–238

Kanbur R (2019) Inequality in a global perspective. Oxf Rev Econ Policy 35(3):431–444. https://doi.org/
10.1093/oxrep/grz010

Kant I (1983) Perpetual peace and other essays. Hackett Publishing

Katelouzou D, Micheler E (2021) Investor capitalism, sustainable business and the role of tax relief.
European Business Organization Law Review, this volume

Kwon R, Salcido B (2019) Does a rising tide lift all boats? Liberalization and real incomes in advanced
industrial societies. Soc Sci Res 79:127–140. https://doi.org/10.1016/j.ssresearch.2019.01.006

Lamont W (1941) Justice: distributive and corrective. Philosophy 16(61):3–18

Lamont J, Favor C (2017) Distributive justice. In: Zalta EN (ed) The Stanford Encyclopedia of Philosophy (Winter 2017 edn)

Larson ET (2005) Why environmental liability regimes in the United States, the European Community,
and Japan have grown synonymous with the polluter pays principle. Vanderbilt J Transnatl Law
38:541–575

Laufer WS (2006) Corporate bodies and guilty minds: the failure of corporate criminal liability. The University of Chicago Press, Chicago

Lozano R, Carpenter A, Huisingh D (2015) A review of 'theories of the firm' and their contributions to corporate sustainability. J Clean Prod 106:430–442. https://doi.org/10.1016/j.jclepro.2014.05.007

Mac Sheoin T (2014) Transnational anti-corporate campaigns: fail often, fail better. Soc Just 41(1/2 (135-136)):198–226. http://www.jstor.org/stable/24361598. Accessed 2 Aug 2019

Maitland F (1893) The corporation aggregate: the history of a legal idea. Cambridge

Matten D, Crane A (2005) Corporate citizenship: toward an extended theoretical conceptualization. Acad Manag Rev 30(1):166–179. http://www.jstor.org/stable/20159101. Accessed 9 Sept 2016

McAfee A (2019) More from less. Simon & Schuster, New York

McCahery JA, Sautner Z, Starks LT (2016) Behind the scenes: the corporate governance preferences of institutional investors. J Financ 71(6):2905–2932

Meadows DH, Meadows DH, Randers J, Behrens III WW (1972) The limits to growth. https://donellameadows.org/wp-content/userfiles/Limits-to-Growth-digital-scan-version.pdf. Accessed 4 May 2021

Medema S (2008) Ronald Coase as a dissenting economist. Studi e Note Di Economia 13:427–448

Meyer LH, Roser D (2006) Distributive justice and climate change. The allocation of emission rights. Analyse & Kritik 28(2):223–249

Micheler E (2021) Company law—a real entity theory, 14 April 2021. https://ssrn.com/abstract=3783696 or https://doi.org/10.2139/ssrn.3783696. Accessed 9 Dec 2021

Néron P-Y (2016) Rethinking the ethics of corporate political activities in a post-citizens united era: political equality, corporate citizenship, and market failures. J Bus Ethics 136(4):715–728. https://doi.org/10.1007/s10551-015-2867-y

Norton BG, Toman MA (1997) Sustainability: ecological and economic perspectives. Land Econ 73(4):553–568

Ostas DT (2004) Cooperate, comply, or evade? A corporate executive's social responsibilities with regard to law. Am Bus Law J 41(4):559–594. https://doi.org/10.1111/j.1744-1714.2004.04104004.x

Page E (1999) Intergenerational justice and climate change. Polit Stud 47(1):53–66

Pierson P (2000a) The limits of design: explaining institutional origins and change. Gov Lnt J Policy Adm 13(4):475–499

Pierson P (2000b) Path dependence, increasing returns, and the study of politics. Am Polit Sci Rev 94(2):251–267

Piketty T (2014) Capital in the twenty-first century. Belknap Press, Cambridge, MA

Plato (1894) (360 BCE) The Republic (B. Jowett, Trans.). (1894 edn). Oxford Clarendon Press

Polanyi K (1944) The great transformation. Beacon Press, Boston

Rawls J (1958) Justice as fairness. Philos Rev 67(2):164–194

Rawls J (1999) A theory of justice, revised. The Belknap Press of Harvard University Press, Cambridge

Reyes J (2018) Reframing corporate governance: company law beyond law and economics. Edward Elgar Publishing, Cheltenham

Roe MJ (2006) Political determinants of corporate governance: political context, corporate impact. Oxford University Press on Demand

Rokeach M (1973) The nature of human values. The Free Press, New York

Røpke I (2005) Trends in the development of ecological economics from the late 1980s to the early 2000s. Ecol Econ 55(2):262–290

Rouch D (2020) The social licence for financial markets: reaching for the end and why it counts. Palgrave Macmillan

Sapinski JP (2016) Constructing climate capitalism: corporate power and the global climate policy-planning network. Glob Netw 16(1):89–111

Scanlon T (1998) What we owe to each other. Harvard University Press

Schneiberg M (2007) What's on the path? Path dependence, organizational diversity and the problem of institutional change in the US economy, 1900–1950. Soc Econ Rev 5(1):47–80. https://doi.org/10.1093/ser/mwl006

Schneiberg M, Bartley T (2008) Organizations, regulation, and economic behavior: regulatory dynamics and forms from the nineteenth to twenty-first century. Ann Rev Law Soc Sci 4:31–61

Sheehy B (2004a) Corporations and social control: the Wal-Mart case study. J Law Commer 24:1–55

Sheehy B (2004b) The importance of corporate models: economic and jurisprudential values and the future of corporate law. DePaul Bus Commer Law J 2(3):463–513

Sheehy B (2004–2005) Corporation and the lateral obligations of the social contract. Newctle Law Rev 8(2):29-42

Sheehy B (2006) Shareholders, unicorns and stilts: an analysis of shareholder property rights. J Corp Law Stud 6(1):165–212

Sheehy B (2012) Understanding CSR: an empirical study of private self-regulation. Monash Univ Law Rev 38(2):103–127

Sheehy B (2015) Defining CSR: problems and solutions. J Bus Ethics 131(3):625–648. https://doi.org/10.1007/s10551-014-2281-x

Sheehy B (2016) Explaining the corporation to non-specialists: a graphic approach. Univ West Aust 40(2):69–84

Sheehy B (2017a) Conceptual and institutional interfaces among CSR, corporate law and the problem of social costs. Va Law Bus J 12(1):95–145

Sheehy B (2017b) Private and public corporate regulatory systems: does CSR provide a systemic alternative to public law? Univ Calif Davis Bus Law J 17:1–55

Sheehy B (2019) CSR and environmental law: concepts, intersections, and limitations. In: McWilliams A, Rupp DE, Siegel DS, Stahl GK, Waldman DA (eds) The Oxford handbook of corporate social responsibility, 2nd edn. OUP, Oxford, pp 261–282

Sheehy B, Farneti F (2021) Corporate social responsibility, sustainability, sustainable development and corporate sustainability: what is the difference, and does it matter? Sustainability 13(11):5965. https://www.mdpi.com/2071-1050/13/11/5965. Accessed 7 Jun 2021

Sheehy B, Feaver DP (2014) Anglo-American directors' legal duties and CSR: prohibited, permitted or prescribed? Dalhousie Law J 37(1):347–395

Sheehy B, Pender H, Diaz-Granados J (forthcoming) Restraint of shareholder voice in Australia: corporate governance, corporate law and politics. Aust J Corp Law

Sheehy B, Pender H, Jacobson B (2021) Corporate social responsibility/ESG shareholder activism in Australia: a case study of the Australasian Centre for Corporate Responsibility (ACCR). Australian Journal of Corporate Law 36(2):156–177

Sjåfjell B, Bruner CM (2020) Corporations and sustainability. In: Sjåfjell B, Bruner CM (eds) The Cambridge handbook of corporate law, corporate governance and sustainability. Cambridge University Press, Cambridge, pp 1–12

Sjåfjell B, Johnston A, Anker-Sørensen L, Millon D (2015) Shareholder primacy: the main barrier to sustainable companies. In: Sjåfjell B, Richardson BJ (eds) Company law and sustainability. Cambridge University Press, Cambridge, pp 79–147

Smith A (2007) An inquiry into the nature and causes of the wealth of nations (Soares SM, ed). Metalibri Digital Library, Amsterdam, Lausanne, Melbourne, Milan, New York, São Paulo

Smith DA (2009) Was there a rule in Shelley's Case? J Legal Hist 30(1):53–70

Smith DG (1997) The shareholder primacy norm. J CorP l 23:277–322

Soule S (2009) Contention and corporate social responsibility. Cambridge University Press, Cambridge

Steensma H, Vermunt R (2013) Social justice in human relations. Volume 2: societal and psychological consequences of justice and injustice. Springer Science & Business Media

Stout LA, Robé J-P, Ireland P, Deakin SF, Greenfield K, Johnston A, Schepel H, Blair MM, Talbot LE, Dignam AJ, Dine J, Millon DK, Sjåfjell B, Villiers CL, Williams CA, Koutsias M, Pendleton A, Davis GF, Galanis M, Chandler D, Keay AR, Moore MT, Du Plessis J, Bather AJ, Lefler BL, Bradshaw C, Bruner CM, Joo TW, Greenwood DJH, Clarke T, Johnson L, Mulazzi F, Lipton M, Liao C, Johnson R, Alon-Beck A, Markel G, Currie W, Partnoy F, Peklar LF, Di Miceli da Silveira A, Sitbon O, González-Cantón C, Chanteau J-P, Franco Donaggio AR, Esser I-M, North G, Gramitto Ricci SA, Tomasic RA, Pillay RG, O'Kelly C, Keating C, Willmott HC, Veldman J, Morrow P (2016) The modern corporation statement on company law. https://ssrn.com/abstract=2848833 or https://doi.org/10.2139/ssrn.2848833. Accessed 8 Dec 2021

Throsby D (2017) A rising tide raises all boats. In: Frey BS, Iselin D (eds) Economic ideas you should forget. Springer, pp 149–150

Valentini L (2011) Justice in a globalized world: a normative framework. Oxford University Press

Velasco J (2009) How many fiduciary duties are there in corporate law? S Cal l Rev 83:1231–1318

Vermunt R, Steensma H (eds) (1991) Social justice in human relations. Societal and psychological origins of justice, vol 1

Vitali S, Glattfelder JB, Battiston S (2011) The network of global corporate control. PLoS ONE 6(10):e25995. https://doi.org/10.1371/journal.pone.0025995

Weisbach D, Sunstein CR (2008) Climate change and discounting the future: a guide for the perplexed. Yale L Pol'y Rev 27:433–457

Welling B (2009) Corporate social responsibility—a well-meaning but unworkable concept. Corporate Governance eJournal. http://epublications.bond.edu.au/cgej/15. Accessed 25 Mar 2019

Wormser I (1931) Frankenstein, incorporated. McGraw-Hill Book Company Inc, New York

Yahoo!Finance (2021) 'UPDATE 2-Chevron investors back proposal for more emissions cuts'. https://finance.yahoo.com/news/1-chevron-shareholders-approve-proposal-171654107.html?guccounter=1&guce_referrer=aHR0cHM6Ly93d3cuYmluZy5jb20v&guce_referrer_sig=AQAAABFySP H6KSNkaB6iIjPrb1UP9Qy7jLp6BiSoWkmLZgiDB_mD40ier55-Kzmi5Ky7Z4hhYExb8_5sLsg w36jkzJG_0KqWN4Gipwf0jApjzPJCJd3LR5NTFx32YKN_EnHupIUEEMTNAfgkB227UYm6R Lrh6l6A-Y8jq45hNizzmJDV. Accessed 1 Jun 2021

Publisher's Note Springer Nature remains neutral with regard to jurisdictional claims in published maps and institutional affiliations.